AF148806

The Undiscovered C. S. Lewis

Essays in Memory of
Christopher W. Mitchell

Copyright © 2021 Bruce R. Johnson

Winged Lion Press
Hamden, CT

All rights reserved. Except in the case of quotations embodied
in critical articles or reviews, no part of this book may be
reproduced or transmitted in any form or by any means, electronic
or mechanical, including photocopying, recording, or by any
information storage or retrieval system, without written permission
of the publisher. Winged Lion Press www.WingedLionPress.com

Cover photo of The Marian E. Wade Center courtesy of Will Vaus

WINGED LION PRESS

ISBN 13   978-1-935688-13-6

To
Christopher W. Mitchell
(1951-2014)

"But I will sit and hearken, and be glad
that through you great beauty
has been awakened into song."
from
Ainulindalë
J. R. R. Tolkien

ACKNOWLEDGEMENTS

Photos of C. S. Lewis as a British Army cadet in 1917 are courtesy of Bridgeman Images. Used by permission.

Minutes of the Oxford English Literature Discussion Group by Nevill Coghill reproduced with permission of Curtis Brown Ltd, London, on behalf of the Estate of Nevill Coghill. © Nevill Coghill 1923.

Minutes of the Oxford English Literature Discussion Group from 1923 by C. S. Lewis, © C. S. Lewis Pte. Ltd. Used by permission.

The essay "The Figure of Merlin in *That Hideous Strength*" by David C. Downing appeared in an earlier form as "The Discarded Mage: Lewis the Scholar-Novelist on Merlin's Moral Taint" in *Christian Scholars Review*, 27:4 (Summer 1998), 406-15. Used by permission.

The essay "The Shorter Planetary Fiction of C. S. Lewis" by Bruce R. Johnson appeared in an earlier form as "Enchanting Luna and Militant Mars: The Shorter Planetary Fiction of C. S. Lewis" in *Sehnsucht: The C. S. Lewis Journal*, 4 (2010), 111-24. Used by permission.

TABLE OF CONTENTS

FOREWORD

Vale Christopher

I am not much of a scholar, nor much of a writer, nor indeed much of anything, and in that I have the advantage over most if not all of those whom you will meet in the pages of this book, for I knew Chris Mitchell from no scholarly viewpoint, nor from any academic specialty nor from any disadvantageous denominational tunnel vision. I asked nothing of Chris in the way of instruction, nor of ministry and little in the way of education. And yet he unstintingly gave me all of those things and a great deal more besides; he gave me his friendship.

Although I have known Chris for a good many years now, and look forward to the next time we meet, we saw each other only at intervals of years, either when I would journey to The Wade Center in Wheaton, or some venue where he would also be attending, or he would be on our side of the planet and visit us at our home. As with all real friendships, we merely took up where we had left off the last time we had been together. The next voyage I make to be with Chris will be a great deal further but take much less time and the meeting will be eternal.

When we got together, we talked of every conceivable topic that came to mind, we talked of our own salad days when we had, still green as grass, first forayed out into the world and of the mess we had so often made of things. We talked (and this most of all) of Jesus, how we met Him and came to serve and follow Him and His teachings and helped each other to misunderstand a little less completely how we might serve Him better. And to this day I have no idea of what faction or denomination of Christianity Chris adhered to, or even if he adhered to any.

Chris and I walked the docks and the street-market of Marsaxlokk together and I introduced him to my stall-holder friends whom he greeted with his customary and evident good will and friendship. We drove through the erratic traffic of the island upon which I live, in my tiny hyper-performance car and Chris never batted an eyelid but enjoyed (or at least seemed to) the ride from one end of the island to the other. We looked at and into the ancient and in many cases crumbling fortresses that still dot the surface of Malta and sorrowed over their decay.

It is very hard to describe the kind of man that Chris was and is, he was a scholar surely, but he was also an adventurer at heart. He was a man who gladly strode the paths that Jesus had laid before him and seemed to shoulder aside the fiery darts of temptation that the enemy cast at him.

I have sat at our little kitchen table with Chris, podding Broad Beans (AKA Fava Beans and many other names) and talking of all things under the sun, while Merrie blanched the beans and prepared them for freezing. It was a task that Chris seemed to relish, and he took part with evident glee. We found a chameleon out in the garden and brought him in to meet Chris who promptly placed the little creature on his sleeve and waited patiently while the chameleon did their usual party trick of slowly changing color.

It is my permanent regret that when Chris was last at our home, and this time with Julie his wife, I was away on some foreign errand and missed them.

His career took him on to the Torrey Honors Institute at Biola University, a place for which I have considerable affection having spoken there over the years, and I was looking forward to seeing Chris there on one of my periodic business trips to Los Angeles. Alas that cannot happen now.

Chris will always be in my memory. The most dangerous thing one can do in this world is to love, and Chris was a man who had learned how to love with the love of Jesus. It showed clearly in his joyous approach to life. In Yiddish, Chris would be called a "Mensch" and he was all of that and more. In Australia there is a word we use to describe a mensch who is a friend and more than a friend, and that word is "a mate." Chris was one of my mateS. I miss him, not in the sense that he hasn't visited for a while, but that I know he will not visit again. He has gone on ahead of us and I hope he will put in a good word for me to the Boss. And next time, it will be once again my turn to go and visit him and as I said, it's a long trip that takes very little time and then we will again have some real conversations.

Doug Gresham
Malta

ESSAYS IN MEMORY OF CHRISTOPHER W. MITCHELL

THE UNDISCOVERED C. S. LEWIS

PREFACE

Of all things, the recording equipment failed. That is the short answer as to how this project began. In June 2008, popular interest in C. S. Lewis was surging due to the release of the first two large-budget movies based on his series of children's stories. "The Chronicles of Narnia: The Exhibition" was a traveling museum display filled with more than 150 props from these films assembled with some authentic furniture and personal belongings of Lewis himself. The Marion E. Wade Center in Wheaton, Illinois had loaned most of these personal artifacts. Since the world premiere of the exhibition was to open at the Arizona Science Center in Phoenix, Dr. Christopher W. Mitchell, Director of the Wade Center from 1994-2013, was coming into town. He offered to give a public lecture to the members of the Arizona C. S. Lewis Society on the eve of the opening, and it fell upon me, as Society president, to make the arrangements. Scottsdale Presbyterian Church seemed the logical choice for a lecture venue because our sound system was newly refurbished, and I, as pastor, could offer use of the sanctuary free of charge.

The future of academic work related to C. S. Lewis was less clear. The monumental third and final volume of *The Collected Letters of C. S. Lewis* was at last in print.[1] However, the worn dichotomy of either scorn for Lewis or hagiography, intellectual famine or over-indulgence, loomed large in the minds of many scholars. With the publications of the tribute volume of essays *Light on C. S. Lewis*, edited by Jocelyn Gibbs,[2] and the *Letters of C. S. Lewis*, edited by his brother Warren Hamilton Lewis,[3] one could say that the first generation of scholarship on Lewis began during his own lifetime and concluded shortly after his death in 1963. The second generation of Lewis scholarship encompassed the next forty years during which time more than two dozen posthumous collections of Lewis's essays and short stories appeared in print and major biographies were completed by

---

[1] C. S. Lewis, *The Collected Letters of C. S. Lewis*, ed. by Walter Hooper, 3 vols. (San Francisco: HarperCollins, 2004-7).

[2] Jocelyn Gibbs, ed. *Light on C. S. Lewis* (London: Geoffrey Bles, 1965).

[3] C. S. Lewis, *Letters of C. S. Lewis*, ed. by W. H. Lewis (London: Geoffrey Bles, 1966).

Green and Hooper,[4] Carpenter,[5] Sayer,[6] and Wilson.[7]

As a third generation of Lewis scholars began to emerge, it could legitimately be asked, "What more work is there to be done on Lewis?" In reply to this important question, Chris Mitchell decided to speak in Arizona on what he called the "unexplored" or "undiscovered" C. S. Lewis. He had a vision for where Lewis studies needed to go in the future, where a more nuanced approach or a further reassessment could yield light. So, in 2008, he laid out six broad categories in which significant academic work on Lewis should occur in the coming decades. These were (1) historical studies that set Lewis in his own time, since he is no longer a contemporary writer, (2) reassessments that clarify previous misreading of his work or misunderstandings of his biography (such as his 1948 debate with Elizabeth Anscombe), (3) comparative studies of Lewis and other thinkers and writers of his own day or earlier, (4) assessments of what Lewis wrote and thought in light of current writers and current trends (particularly post-modern and post-Christian thought), (5) explorations of his lesser known material, and (6) previously unpublished material by Lewis (such as his Elizabethan play "Lewis the Bald"). Along with these categories, Mitchell also cautioned that future scholars must be introduced to and build upon the good academic work on Lewis that has already been done. We must look back and remember even as we forge ahead. It was a brilliant analysis filled with many specific examples worthy of pursuit. And on that evening, our church's new recording equipment failed.

Chris still had the manuscript of his talk, of course, and he was approached numerous times in the years that followed with an open invitation to print his address within the pages of our society's academic publication, *Sehnsucht: The C. S. Lewis Journal*. Each time, he responded that his text still needed a bit more work: another reference to track down, one more loose thread to be tied up. Other responsibilities and academic projects necessarily took precedence over our small request. Life moved on—until the day it no longer did.

---

[4] Roger Lancelyn Green and Walter Hooper, *C. S. Lewis: A Biography* (London: Collins, 1974).

[5] Humphrey Carpenter, *The Inklings: C. S. Lewis, J. R. R. Tolkien, Charles Williams, and Their Friends* (London: Allen and Uwin, 1978).

[6] George Sayer, *Jack: C. S. Lewis and His Times* (San Francisco: Harper and Row, 1986).

[7] A. N. Wilson, *C. S. Lewis: A Biography* (London: Collins, 1990).

Chris passed away suddenly, and unexpectedly, on July 10, 2014.

Very soon afterwards, Jerry Root and I began discussing the seeds of an idea which eventually became the collection before you. Specific scholars were asked to contribute chapters either in the field of C. S. Lewis scholarship or on topics related to one of the six other British authors whose work is the focus of the Wade Center. Several chapters intentionally glance back towards or are examples of past Lewis scholarship. All six of Mitchell's original categories of emerging trajectories are represented here: historical studies, reassessments, comparative studies with past writers, interactions with current thought and current writers, explorations of his more obscure work, and new Lewis material. Individual chapters examine aspects of Lewis and his writings from a variety of disciplines: history, literary studies and criticism, philosophy, theology, apologetics, biography, imagination, mythology, ethics, Christian spirituality, cultural studies, and rhetoric. One essay each focuses on three related authors (George MacDonald, Dorothy Sayers, and J. R. R. Tolkien) providing additional historical and literary context. Together, they chart a course for the future of Lewis studies.

In a collaborative effort such as this, the number of people to be thanked is legion. First, I am grateful to Jerry Root for his wisdom and counsel as this project was initially being considered. Second, I remain indebted to Marjorie Lamp Mead for granting the Wade Center's blessing on our common effort. Grayson Carter and Will Gentrup were particularly helpful as the work began to take shape, saving me hours of time through their frank and insightful suggestions. Moreover, Will Gentrup's tireless help in proofreading the completed manuscript was a kindness I shall long remember. The various contributors whose words fill these pages have each earned my gratitude, not only for their scholarship but for their enduring good humor as various revisions were requested. Maxie B. Burch, Mark Neal, Arend Smilde, and Richard C. West served as academic readers and improved the quality of a great many chapters. Several proposed chapters had to be dropped due to space limitations, and the writers of those essays have received my apologies already. Special thanks to Douglas Gresham, surviving stepson of C. S. Lewis, for his foreword introducing the collection. The entire Editorial Body of *Sehnsucht* offered their moral support and Assistant Editors Jennifer Frasier and Megan Novello aided by copy-editing various chapters. Gregory Lippiatt, Andy Reyes, and Simon Horobin all helped prepare the late

Walter Hooper's essay for publication. Amy Baldwin used her own expertise to enhance old photographs. Generous patrons provided financial support at precisely the right moment: Steven Beebe, Guy and Jean Duerbeck, Will Gentrup, Jim Hankins, Jonnie Novello, Martin, and Cynthia O'Malley, the Arizona Center for Christian Studies, and Christ Presbyterian Church in Goodyear, Arizona. My lovely wife Laurie provided a listening ear to my editorial musing on far more occasions than any rational husband could reasonably expect his wife to endure, yet still she loves me. Thank you. Finally, to the man whose insights gave the form and shape to this volume and to whom all of these contributors feel a continuing debt, to the memory of Chris Mitchell this work is humbly dedicated. I hope it makes amends for that failed recording.

Bruce R. Johnson
Scottsdale, Arizona

I.

HISTORICAL STUDIES

Chapter 1

"GUNS AND GOOD COMPANY"
C. S. LEWIS AND THE FIRST WORLD WAR

Grayson Carter

Although the life and writings of C. S. Lewis have been extensively examined, his military service—including the war's influence on his spiritual development and on his literary, critical, and apologetic endeavors—has only recently begun to attract scholarly attention.[1] Several possible reasons for this neglect can be identified. In part, it may have been due to the long-standing embargo on British Army records from the First World War. It may have been due to the nature of Lewis's war record itself, which, when it was finally made available in 1998, revealed relatively little of interest or importance.[2] Another reason may have been the scarcity of primary source material. This last point has been remedied in part by the republication of Lewis's early poetry, *Spirits in Bondage* (1984), by the appearance of the first volume of his *Collected Letters* (2000), and by the publication of several reminiscences of Lewis's life.[3] These writings have deepened

---

[1] For example, Colin Duriez, "Lewis and Military Service: War and Remembrance (1917-1918)," in *C. S. Lewis: Life, Works, and Legacy*, ed. by Bruce L. Edwards, 4 vols. (Westport, CN: Praeger, 2007), 1:79-101; K. J. Gilchrist, "2nd Lieutenant Lewis," in *VII: An Anglo-American Literary Review*, 17 (2000), 61-78 and *A Morning After War: C. S. Lewis and WWI* (New York: Peter Lang, 2005); Joseph Loconte, *A Hobbit, a Wardrobe, and a Great War: How J. R. R. Tolkien and C. S. Lewis Rediscovered Faith, Friendship, and Heroism in the Cataclysm of 1914-1918* (Colorado Springs, Colorado: Thomas Nelson, 2015); Brian Melton, "Into the Trenches of Narnia: C. S. Lewis the Soldier and the Narnian Way of War" in *The Lamp-Post of the Southern California C. S. Lewis Society*, 31.4 (Winter 2010), 3-23; Richard Van Emden and Victor Piuk, *Famous: 1914-1918* (Barnsley, England: Pen and Sword, 2010); Chris Baker, "The army history of author Clive Staples Lewis (C. S. Lewis)," 2016. https://www.longlongtrail.co.uk/army-history-author-clive-staples-lewis-c-s-lewis/

[2] Although around 60% of British service records from the war were destroyed by German bombing in 1940, Lewis's survived and are preserved at the National Archives. See WO 339/105408, National Archives, Kew.

[3] Ann Bonsor, "Beyond Personality: Recollections of C. S. Lewis from Former Colleagues, Pupils, and Friends," *BBC Radio Four*, 14

our comprehension of Lewis's war experience and stimulated further examination into a neglected area of scholarship. In the final analysis, however, the principal cause of this negligence may have been Lewis himself, or, more specifically, his economical and often dispassionate account of his military service in *Surprised by Joy.* Here, details of his time on the Western Front, wartime reading and writing, army friendships and their influence, and battle injuries and convalescence are all covered in a single brief chapter.[4]

Lewis's retrospective treatment of the war is complex, though in some respects not unusual. Men who fought in the war were reluctant to speak about their experience, and, when they did, it was often in muted terms and typically only with other veterans. Of course, numerous accounts of the war have been published, though collectively they represent the experiences of only a small percentage of those who actually fought in it. In addition to Lewis's autobiographical treatment, details of the war can also be found in his poetry and correspondence and, indirectly, in his imaginative fiction. As helpful as these are in filling in the blank spaces on the historical canvas, they do not compensate for the type of full and candid treatment of a person's military experience that would naturally appear in a book of this nature. Lewis's single chapter on the war, in fact, is not only surprisingly economical but also potentially misleading. In particular, readers could be forgiven for taking at face value Lewis's description of the war as little more than "a ghastly interruption" preceding the commencement of his "rational life" at Oxford.[5] His war experience was much more significant than that, however, for it came to influence numerous aspects of his subsequent life and outlook. Unfortunately, however, he has left us with too few details, little sense of the human sacrifice involved, and only a vague perception that British society and Lewis's life itself had been permanently transformed by

---

December 1988; Grayson Carter, ed., "Beyond Personality: Recollections of C. S. Lewis," in *Sehnsucht: The C. S. Lewis Journal,* 2 (2008), 47-68; James Como, ed., *Remembering C. S. Lewis: Recollections of Those Who Knew Him,* 3rd ed. (San Francisco: Ignatius, 2005); Laurence Harwood, *C. S. Lewis, My Godfather* (Downers Grove, IL: InterVarsity Press, 2007); Michael Travers, ed., *C. S. Lewis: Views from Wake Forest* (Hamden, CT: Winged Lion Press, 2008).

[4] C. S. Lewis, *Surprised by Joy* (London: Geoffrey Bles, 1956). See a portion of chapter XII and the initial section of the following chapter.

[5] Lewis, *Surprised by Joy,* 188.

these historic events. Likewise, there are relatively few references to Lewis's emotional response to the war—his anguish and suffering, for example, his profound grief over the loss of friends and colleagues, or even his own feelings of guilt for surviving. In producing such an account, Lewis transmitted to posterity, unintentionally or otherwise, an image of himself as less than entirely forthcoming, at times insensitive to the sufferings of others, and as holding jejune views of human nature and relationships.

Suffice it to say, additional investigations into Lewis's military service are long overdue, not merely to identify a number of outstanding biographical details but also because the war occurred at an important stage in his intellectual, emotional, and spiritual development, lodged between the completion of his studies under W. T. Kirkpatrick and the commencement of his work at Oxford. For these reasons, future attempts to understand fully Lewis's life, to chart the course of his spiritual development, and to understand the nature of his poetry and poetic ambitions, criticism, apologetic works, and imaginative fiction, must take into account his experiences during the First World War.

This chapter will provide a brief, contextualized description of Lewis's military service followed by commentary on the influence the war had on his life and writings with the aim of identifying areas in which future studies of Lewis may profitably concentrate.

OXFORD, O.T.C., AND O.C.U.

While the assassination of Archduke Franz Ferdinand in Sarajevo in June 1914 sent shock waves throughout Europe, it had little direct effect on Lewis, who was then completing his final term at Malvern College.[6] Of greater concern were the tensions in Ulster surrounding Home Rule and the widespread indifference in England to Irish affairs.[7] In mid-September, Lewis began his studies under Kirkpatrick. Though rumors of war had been circulating for some time, conscription had not yet been enacted or (at least at that time)

---

[6] C. S. Lewis, *The Collected Letters of C. S. Lewis*, ed. by Walter Hooper, 3 vols. (San Francisco: HarperCollins, 2004-7), 1:64-7.

[7] Lewis, *Collected Letters*, 1:52. The Easter Rising of April 1916 made little impression on Lewis, however. He was visiting Ireland at the time but wrote nothing about it until July 1917, when he briefly equated the rebels with the dark principles found in modern poetry. Lewis, *Collected Letters*, 1:326-7.

seriously considered. In any case, Lewis was unlikely to be directly affected by the war for the foreseeable future, since he was only fifteen when hostilities broke out and thus ineligible for military service for at least three years.[8] Like many young men, he hoped that the war would be over before he reached the age of service. Furthermore, despite being educated in England, Lewis remained an Irish resident and thus technically not subject to conscription.[9] Consequently, it appeared to him and his family––at least initially––that he would remain safe from the events then unfolding across the Channel.

Lewis, however, was not inclined to avoid personal responsibility. Despite several generations of Irish residence, his family's ties to Britain remained strong. His maternal grandfather, the Revd. Thomas Robert Hamilton, had served in the British military,[10] and his brother, Warnie, would soon pass out of Sandhurst to serve on the Western Front.[11] Consequently, by May 1915, with no armistice in sight, Lewis began to reconsider his future.[12] Conscription was now a distinct, though unattractive, possibility.[13] Despite being technically exempted from conscription, Lewis was instead inclined to volunteer for the army.[14] As he wrote to his father, "I sincerely hope that one of two things may happen. Either that the war may be over before

---

[8] Lewis, *Collected Letters*, 1:171, 178. Legally, Lewis became eligible for military service a month after his eighteenth birthday, on 29 December 1916.

[9] Over 200,000 Irishmen volunteered to serve in the British Army during the war, of whom around 30,000 died. When the government threatened to impose conscription on Ireland in 1918, a broad popular coalition of nationalists and the Roman Catholic Church combined to resist it. See S. J. Connolly, ed. *The Oxford Companion to Irish History* (Oxford, Oxford University Press, 1998), 195-6.

[10] Duriez, "Lewis and Military Service," 29. As Chaplain in the Royal Navy from 1854 to 1870, he later became Rector at St Mark's, Dundela, where Lewis was baptized and confirmed.

[11] Lewis, *Collected Letters*, 1:73, 1012. Warren Lewis was rushed through an accelerated officers' training course at Sandhurst before being commissioned a 2nd Lieutenant in the Army Service Corps in October 1914. Four weeks later, he was deployed to France with the British Expeditionary Force.

[12] Lewis, *Collected Letters*, 1:125, 130, 198-9.

[13] After raising over 2,000,000 men by voluntary enlistment, only in early 1916 was conscription finally enacted. See Wavell, "Armed Forces and the Art of War," 262.

[14] Lewis, *Collected Letters*, 1:159, 204-5.

I am eighteen, or that conscription may not come into force before I have volunteered. I shouldn't fancy," he continued (perhaps betraying a sense of class consciousness) "going out to meet the others—as a conscript."[15] When the Military Service Act finally came into effect in February 1916, the question of Irish conscription remained unresolved. Lewis then consulted a solicitor in an attempt to clarify his status, who advised him to speak to the local chief recruiting officer. When he did, Lewis was informed, paradoxically, that he would be exempt from conscription if he registered immediately for it. This he did.[16] His future now began to come into focus. Earlier, Kirkpatrick had advised Lewis's father, "You may make a writer or a scholar of him, but you'll not make anything else."[17] Lewis and his father thought the same. Lewis therefore made, as he put it, "a treaty with reality" in which he would volunteer for military service but only after completing his studies and taking the Oxford scholarship exam.[18] As Albert Lewis wrote to Kirkpatrick in May 1916, "Clive has decided to serve, but he also wishes to try his fortune at Oxford."[19]

After applying for a place at New College, Lewis sat for the scholarship exam in December 1916.[20] Despite years of close reading and rigorous preparation, he concluded that he had performed poorly on the exam.[21] His despair was short lived, however. On 13 December, he received word that he had been elected a Scholar of University College, having been passed over by New College.[22] He was of course elated, but he now faced another challenge: what to do between December and the following October, which marked the commencement of a new academic year at Oxford. Lewis wrote seeking advice from the Master of University College, who advised him to volunteer for military service.[23] Despite his earlier "treaty with reality," Lewis remained unconvinced of this course of action. Kirkpatrick suggested that Lewis spend the intervening period preparing for

---

[15] Lewis, *Collected Letters*, 1:125.

[16] Lewis, *Collected Letters*, 1:261.

[17] Lewis, *Surprised by Joy*, 183.

[18] Lewis, *Surprised by Joy*, 158, 183.

[19] Lewis, *Collected Letters*, 1:179.

[20] Lewis, *Collected Letters*, 1:198-9, 208, 247, 262.

[21] Lewis, *Surprised by Joy*, 185.

[22] *The Times*, 14 December 1916.

[23] Lewis, *Collected Letters*, 1:264.

Responsions (or "Smalls"), the three-part University examination admitted students were required to pass in order to matriculate.[24] In January, the College agreed that if he passed Responsions he could come into residence in the spring, when he could join the University O.T.C. (Officers' Training Corps).[25] This, at last, provided a way forward. As Lewis commented: "How glad I am that my fate is once for all settled for good or bad."[26]

Lewis failed Responsions, algebra proving his undoing. Nevertheless, the college allowed him to come into residence in April in order to enter the O.T.C.[27] as his "most promising route into the army" and to prepare for another attempt at Responsions.[28] Shortly after he began officers' training, Lewis had a physical examination. He weighed 13 stone (182 pounds) and was 5 feet 10¾ inches tall. His chest was 34 ½ inches expanded and 32 inches at rest. His vision was good. Under the category of "Special Remarks," the commanding officer noted that Lewis was "likely to make a useful officer but will not have had sufficient training for admission to an O.C.U. [Officer Cadet Unit] before end of June."[29]

Overall, Lewis seems to have enjoyed his time in the O.T.C. His colleagues proved congenial, and his superiors, though eccentric, placed few unreasonable demands on his time or talents. As he remarked to his childhood friend, Arthur Greeves, "It is on the whole a very pleasant life," adding (a week later), "The O.T.C. gets more interesting as we go on . . . our C.O., a certain Colonel Stanning, is quite cracked."[30]

On 7 June, Lewis's comfortable routine came to a predictable conclusion. He was now ordered to join an O.C.U. — an event that marked his official entry into the British Army in anticipation of

---

[24] The exam consisted of three parts, covering Latin, ancient Greek, and mathematics. Though widely used, it was not required of all applicants until 1926.

[25] Lewis, *Collected Letters*, 1:266, 267, 291.

[26] Lewis, *Collected Letters*, 1:287.

[27] Lewis had been a member of the O.T.C. while attending Malvern College in 1913 and 1914. See Baker, "The army history."

[28] Lewis, *Surprised by Joy*, 186; *Collected Letters*, 1:294. Lewis was eventually spared from passing Responsions by a blanket exemption granted to those who had served in the war. Lewis, *Surprised by Joy*, 187.

[29] Lewis, *Collected Letters*, 1:294.

[30] Lewis, *Collected Letters*, 1:299-314.

receiving a commission at the end of his training.[31] Fortunately, he was allowed to remain temporarily at Oxford.[32] "It is a great change," he wrote, "to leave my own snug room at Univ for a carpetless room, with beds without sheets or pillows, kept miserably tidy & shared with another cadet at Keble." He was more sanguine over other demands. Though the work "is very hard & not very interesting, I am by now quite reconciled to my lot. It is doing me a lot of good (days of trench digging and route marching under a blazing sun . . .) and I have made a number of excellent friends." The "advantages of being in Oxford," he added, "are very great, as I can get weekend leave (from 1 o'clock Saturday till 11 o'clock p.m. Sunday) and go to Univ where I enjoy the rare luxury of sheets & a long sleep."[33] Years later, Lewis commented on the nature of his fellow recruits, remarking, "I think some of the best friends I would have made were those soldiers I trained with."[34]

"E" Company, the OTC Battalion of C. S. Lewis,
at Keble College, Oxford, 1917.
Copyright © Bridgeman Images. Reprinted with permission

---

[31] On his application to join the O.C.U., Lewis indicated a preference to serve in the infantry, especially with the King's Own Scottish Borderers, the Royal Fusiliers, or with a horse transport unit of the Army Service Corps. As he was under 21, his application had to be signed by his father. References were supplied by Kirkpatrick and Arthur Allen, Lewis's former schoolmaster at Malvern. See Baker, "The army history."

[32] Lewis, *Surprised by Joy*, 187; *Collected Letters*, 1:315-6.

[33] Lewis, *Collected Letters*, 1:317, 319.

[34] Joseph Loconte, "Preserving the Legacy of C. S. Lewis," in *The Wall Street Journal*, 20 November 2020.

C. S. Lewis in his OTC Uniform
at Keble College, Oxford, 1917.
Copyright © Bridgeman Images. Reprinted with permission.

Lewis's most important friends from his unit were Martin Ashworth Somerville, Laurence Bertrand Johnson, and Edward "Paddy" Moore. Somerville was subsequently commissioned into the Rifle Brigade but perished in Palestine in September 1918. Johnson, who was commissioned into the same regiment as Lewis, perished in April 1918. Of the three, it is Moore whose connection with Lewis is the most significant. This is perhaps ironic given Lewis's initial coolness toward Moore, whom he described as "quite a good fellow too, tho' a little too childish and virtuous for 'common nature's daily food.'"[35] The two were soon brought closer, however, through the efforts of Moore's mother, Janie, who, along with her daughter, Maureen, had recently relocated to Oxford.[36] Lewis's personal entanglement with Janie would intensify as his

---

[35] Lewis, *Collected Letters*, 1:317, 322.

[36] Since the separation of Moore and her husband in 1907, Janie had resided in Bristol with Paddy and Maureen, and close to her brother, Dr. Robert Askins, a local medical officer. Though the daughter of a clergyman, she was now opposed to Christianity.

departure for France drew nearer and continue in various forms until her death in 1951. Though this relationship has been extensively explored elsewhere, a brief mention of its origins might be helpful. As we have seen, Lewis reported to his father that he was relatively happy during this time. Maureen, however, saw matters differently. As she later recalled, Lewis was "not at all happy" in the O.C.U., which prompted Janie to incorporate him into their close-knit family life.[37] Remarkably, within months Lewis was referring to Janie, along with Greeves, as one of "the two people who matter most to me in the world."[38] Under circumstances that have never been entirely clear, it appears that Lewis and Paddy made a mutual promise, overheard by Maureen, that if either man perished in the war, the survivor would care for the deceased's parent.[39] Moore, who was commissioned a 2nd Lieutenant in the 5th Battalion of the Rifle Brigade (later transferred to the 2nd Battalion), died at the battle of Pargny on 24 March 1918.[40] This event, and Lewis's earlier promise, would profoundly influence the course of Lewis's remaining life.

On 26 September 1917, Lewis received a temporary commission as a 2nd Lieutenant and was given a month's leave.[41] On 16 October, while on vacation in Belfast, he was gazetted into the 1st Battalion of the Somerset Light Infantry, the old XIIIth Foot. He left Belfast two days later and joined his regiment at Crownhill, in south Devon.[42] Lewis's battalion was under the command of the 11th Infantry Brigade in the 4th Division—one of the most highly regarded divisions in the army, which had been among the British Expeditionary Force that had seen action in France early in the war. At the time of Lewis's commissioning, the division was undergoing a period of reorganization after suffering terrific loses at the Battle of Passchendaele.[43] On 16 November, Lewis telegraphed home from

---

37 Bonsor, "Beyond Personality."

38 Lewis, *Collected Letters*, 1:348.

39 Lewis, *Collected Letters*, 1:337, 987.

40 T. R. Eastwood, and H. G. Parkyn, *List of Officers and Other Ranks of the Rifle Brigade Awarded Decorations, or Mentioned in Dispatches, for Services During the Great War* (London: Rifle Brigade Club, 1936), 64-5. Moore was awarded the Military Cross for "conspicuous gallantry and initiative," the third highest military decoration in Britain.

41 Lewis, *Collected Letters*, 1:336, 424.

42 Lewis, *Collected Letters*, 1:338.

43 Baker, "The army history."

Bristol: "Orders France. Reporting Southampton 4 p.m. on Saty."[44] He arrived at the Western Front thirteen days later, on his nineteenth birthday. No amount of training could have prepared him for what he encountered there: constant noise, putrid smells, extreme discomfort, inclement weather, deep mud, continuous exhaustion, and extensive human carnage.

FRANCE: BATTLEFIELDS, INJURY, AND CONVALESCENCE

Before and during Lewis's time in France, his father attempted to have him transferred from the infantry to the artillery, which he considered a safer option. Lewis opposed the idea. "As to the artillery," he wrote to his father, "only those who have 'some special knowledge of mathematics' will be recommended."[45] A few days later, with a growing sense of frustration, he pleaded that Albert "give up that idea," pointing out his own mathematical ineptitude. Moreover, he added, "every one else puts up with the infantry, and I think we ought to do so too."[46] Albert, however, continued to press the matter. In July 1917, Lewis wrote in even stronger terms, mentioning again his mathematical ineptitude and objecting in moral terms to his father securing his transfer to the artillery through influence.[47] Albert remained unconvinced, however, and the "artillery debate" rumbled on. Finally, after his arrival in France, Lewis changed tactics. He now reported that he had "become very much attached" to his regiment and to several friends in particular and that he was just beginning to understand the work. Perhaps more convincingly, he argued that the artillery should not be regarded as a safe option, given its frequent exposure to German bombardment. Finally, a transfer from the Infantry would require the support of his Commanding Officer, which would be unlikely to occur.[48] Albert then judiciously dropped the matter.

The details of Lewis's movements in France during 1917 and 1918 can be pieced together by consulting the War Diary

---

44 Lewis, *Collected Letters*, 1:346.

45 Lewis, *Collected Letters*, 1:316.

46 Lewis, *Collected Letters*, 1:322.

47 Lewis, *Collected Letters*, 1:328.

48 Lewis, *Collected Letters*, 1:347-8, 351.

of the Somerset Light Infantry,[49] with additional details and perspective being provided by the diary of Henry Cook.[50] After his commissioning, Lewis spent about fifteen months on active duty, six of those at various locations at, or close to, the Western Front.[51] After deploying from Southampton through Le Havre, his battalion was first billeted at a staging area near the town of Arras, where, Lewis reported, the work was "hard and (which is worse) irregular."[52] On his first day at the front, he discovered that his Captain had been a master at one of his old schools, which, to Lewis's disappointment, the man was reluctant to acknowledge.[53] By early January 1918, Lewis was enrolled in a bombing course, which he described to his father in mostly glowing terms, apparently anxious to spare him from worry.[54] The course proved short-lived, however. Within a month, Lewis developed pyrexia (or "trench fever") and was evacuated to a British Red Cross hospital in the coastal town of Le Tréport.[55] Again, Lewis was anxious to reassure his father, dismissing his symptoms as little more than "a high temperature arising from the general irregularity of life at the front.[56] Indeed, during his hospitalization, Lewis had a "wholly delightful" time, reading, walking, and exploring the area. While taking no notice of the historic passage of women's suffrage in England during this time,[57] he did make time for reflection and

---

[49] This has been thoroughly examined by Gilchrist in *Morning After War*, 53-127.

[50] Arthur Henry Cook, "Diary," 1914-1918. Somerset Heritage Centre, MS DD/SLI/17/1/39. Later published as *A Soldier's War* (Taunton, England: Goodman and Son, 1958). Cook served on the Western Front for over four years—and survived. Both men participated in the battle in which Lewis was wounded. Cook's previously unexamined diary thus provides a valuable first-hand description of the events surrounding Lewis's injuries.

[51] He was commissioned a Second Lieutenant on 26 September 1917; arrived in France on ca. 18 November 1917; Western Front on 29 November; returned to England 22 May 1918; discharged 24 December 1918.

[52] Lewis, *Collected Letters*, 1:348.

[53] Lewis, *Surprised by Joy*, 194.

[54] Lewis, *Collected Letters*, 1:351-2.

[55] Lewis, *Collected Letters*, 1:352.

[56] Lewis, *Collected Letters*, 1:356.

[57] It was enacted into English law on 6 February 1918.

letter writing.[58] Most importantly, he was now out of harm's way. "As an alternative to the trenches," he later wrote, "a bed and a book were 'very heaven.'"[59] Hospital life, however, was not without its colorful moments. During his first week, his roommate conducted an intense affair with one of the night nurses. His place was soon occupied by, as Lewis described him, "a musical misogynist from Yorkshire," whose presence was equally trying.[60] As his condition continued to improve, however, Lewis began to lament the prospect of returning to the chaos unfolding at the Western Front.[61]

Lewis rejoined his battalion on 28 February[62] and was soon thrown back into the thick of it,[63] his company experiencing heavy shelling and numerous casualties. During the next four days he had "about as many hours sleep,"[64] with weariness and flooded trenches being his chief enemies. As he commented, "I have gone to sleep marching and woken again and found myself marching still. One walked in the trenches in thigh gum boots with water above the knee; one remembers the icy stream welling up inside the boot when you punctured it on concealed barbed wire." The sight of lifeless soldiers confirmed that view of corpses formed the moment he had seen his dead mother. Such experiences helped him "to know and pity and reverence the ordinary man," especially his own Sergeant.[65] The shelling was part of the so-called Spring Offensive—a final attempt by the Germans (incorporating their troops from the now quiet Eastern Front) to defeat the Allies before the arrival of fresh American divisions. It involved four separate German advances, the first of which began on 21 March. Employing storm troopers, it aimed to break quickly through the Allied lines, outflank the British positions, and force the surrender or destruction of the British Army. The French would then be compelled to seek an armistice. The offensive enjoyed considerable early success, producing intense

---

[58] Lewis, *Collected Letters*, 1:355.

[59] Lewis, *Surprised by Joy*, 189.

[60] Lewis, *Surprised by Joy*, 189-90.

[61] Lewis, *Collected Letters*, 1:358.

[62] Gilchrist, *Morning After War*, 96.

[63] Accounts of this period differ. See Lewis, *Collected Letters*, 1:363; Gilchrist, *Morning After War*, 100, 102.

[64] Lewis, *Collected Letters*, 1:363.

[65] Lewis, *Surprised by Joy*, 195-6.

commotion and retreat in the Allied ranks. The Germans, however, were unable to supply their rapidly advancing troops, and, by 5 April, their advance was halted. The second advance, further north (in which Lewis was involved) was launched on 9 April. The Germans quickly broke through the Allied lines, forcing them to retreat several miles and leaving the Channel Ports vulnerable to capture. The situation soon became so desperate that, on 11 April, Field Marshall Haig issued his famous Special Order to all British forces in France:

> With our backs to the wall and believing in the justice of our cause each one of us must fight on to the end. The safety of our homes and the freedom of mankind alike depend upon the conduct of each one of us at this critical moment.[66]

Haig's order achieved the desired results. A combination of stiff British resistance and continued supply problems halted the German advance, which was finally abandoned on 29 April. Around 110,000 Allied troops had been wounded or killed, however, together with an equal number of Germans, or well over 5,000 men per day.[67]

Lewis's battalion spent most of the period between 19 March and 7 April at or near the front, where they experienced heavy shelling and some direct combat with German troops, followed by several days of "general clean up" near Arras.[68] On 12 April, they were transported to forward positions along the La Bassée Canal, north of Mont-Bernanchon, where the situation was "all confusion."[69] The following day was relatively quiet, with numerous refugees moving back and forth through the lines in search of something to eat or salvage. At 6:30, on the evening of the 14th, several companies, including Lewis's, were ordered to advance toward the village of Riez du Vinage, supported from behind by a British artillery barrage.[70] German resistance proved stiff, however. After his company took up forward positions, Lewis was surprised when a group of about sixty

---

[66] Vera Brittain, *Testament of Youth* (London: Victor Gollancz, 1933), XVII.14.

[67] Martin Marix Evans, *1918: The Year of Victories* (London: Sirius, 2002), 81.

[68] Cook, "Diary," 225.

[69] Cook, "Diary," 226.

[70] Lewis, *Collected Letters*, 1:364. British 18-pounders, with a range of between approximately 6,000 and 10,000 meters (depending on the version).

"field-grey figures . . . suddenly appeared out of nowhere, all had their hands up" —an event he later described, characteristically, as "not worth telling, save as a joke,"[71] Given the intensity of the fighting that day and the next, however, and given the advance's importance to German military strategy, the surrender of such a large group of soldiers was, in fact, highly significant. Further advances by Lewis's company were then attempted, but to little avail. Cook's first-hand description of the fighting on the morning of the 15th provides a unique window into the chaotic battlefield conditions that confronted Lewis.[72] On the same day, Lewis was severely wounded by an exploding artillery shell.

The details surrounding this event are not entirely clear. What is known is that on 15 April, while Lewis was standing near Sergeant Ayres and Laurence Johnson, a shell exploded nearby. The origin of the shell remains uncertain, but it was likely British (so-called "friendly-fire"), given the intense artillery barrage that accompanied the battalion's advance on the 14th and 15th. Ayres and Johnson were both killed by the explosion, with shell fragments penetrating the left side of Lewis's chest (and breaking one of his ribs), the back of his left hand, and his left leg just above and behind the knee.[73] Despite the severity of his injuries, Lewis remained conscious long enough to consider his circumstances. "Just after I had been hit," he later wrote, "I found (or thought I found) that I was not breathing and concluded that this was death. I felt no fear and certainly no courage. It did not seem to be an occasion for either. The proposition 'Here is a man dying' stood before my mind as dry, as factual, as unemotional as something in a textbook. It was not even interesting."[74]

After crawling away from the scene of the explosion, Lewis was picked up by a stretcher-bearer and evacuated to the Number 6 British Red Cross (or Liverpool Merchants Mobile) Hospital at the port town of Étaples, a distance of some fifty miles over rough roads[75]. Étaples, the site of a large Allied transit camp and five base hospitals, had a troubled history. Just months before Lewis's arrival, it had experienced an outbreak of rioting among soldiers, the so-called Étaples Mutiny,

---

[71] Lewis, *Surprised by Joy*, 197.

[72] Cook, "Diary," 230.

[73] Lewis, *Collected Letters*, 1:366-8.

[74] Lewis, *Surprised by Joy*, 197-8; *Collected Letters*, 1:356.

[75] Lewis, *Collected Letters*, 1:366.

while recent epidemiological theories have traced the outbreak of the 1918 Spanish Flu Epidemic to an earlier appearance at Étaples. In her acclaimed autobiographical account of the war, *Testament of Youth*, Vera Brittain, who served as a VAD nurse at No 24 General Hospital (only a few steps from where Lewis was being treated and at precisely the same time), memorialized the intense horror and threat posed by the Spring Offensive, as well as the atrocious and putrefying atmosphere at Étaples during March and April 1918:

> I shall never forget the crushing tension of those extreme days. Nothing had ever quite equaled them before—not the Somme, not Arras, not Passchendaele—for into our minds had crept for the first time the secret, incredible fear that we might lose the War. Each convoy of men that we took in—to be dispatched, a few hours later, to England after a hasty wash and change of dressing, or to the cemetery after a laying-out too hurried to be reverent—gave way to a discouragement that none of us had met with in a great battle before . . .. Gradually we became conscious that we were in the midst of what a War historian afterwards called 'the most formidable offensive in the history of the world.' . . . This horror . . . monstrous, undreamed of, incredible . . . this was defeat. For nearly a month the camp resembled a Gustave Doré illustration to Dante's *Inferno*.[76]

Characteristically, Lewis was rather dismissive of having been wounded. On the day after his arrival at Étaples, for example, he dictated a brief note to his father stating that he had been "slightly wounded and am now in Hospital." On the following day he wrote again but without providing much detail.[77] Given what must have been Lewis's state of mind, one can easily overlook the economical nature of his correspondence. The brief account of his being wounded that appeared in his autobiography, however, produced much later, cannot so easily be dismissed: "Nor does it concern the reader to know how I got a sound 'Blighty' from an English shell," he wrote.[78] In fact, the event is of considerable concern for a number of reasons. First,

---

[76] Brittain, *Testament of Youth*, XVII.13. Additional details of Lewis's time at Étaples, and his wartime experience more generally, may be gained from a close reading of Brittan's *Testament of Youth* and from her unpublished novel "The Pawn of Fate" (or "Folly's Vineyard"), which was drawn from her experiences at Étaples during the Spring of 1918.

[77] Lewis, *Collected Letters*, 1:366.

[78] Lewis, *Surprised by Joy*, 197.

Lewis had not been "slightly wounded" but had come very close to dying; the explosion left permanent scarring on his body and may have inflicted long-term and serious damage to his emotional well-being (discussed below). So serious, in fact, were Lewis's injuries that he was not included among those who were quickly dispatched back to England, but he remained at Étaples for over a month, despite an acute shortage of beds. Second, the death of Ayres and Johnson must have left Lewis with feelings of grief and remorse and possibly with a sense of guilt over having survived. Perhaps most significantly, Lewis's injuries resulted in him being removed from the fighting for the remainder of the war. Given the high loss of life in his regiment during the weeks and months following 15 April, it is entirely possible that the injuries Lewis received on that day actually saved his life.[79]

Eventually, Albert received a telegram from the War Office informing him that his son had been "wounded April fifteenth," but providing no details. As an experienced lawyer, however, he understood that there was more to the story. On 24 April, Warnie, now stationed near the village of Behucourt, near Doullens, received word from his father that Jack had been "severely wounded" and was hospitalized in Étaples. He immediately borrowed a motorbike and rode the fifty miles to Étaples. From the surviving records, it is difficult to assess what he discovered there. When he returned to camp later that night, he wrote reassuringly (but perhaps misleadingly) to his father that Jack's condition was not serious and that he "is not much the worse, and is in better spirits than I have seen him for a long time."[80] Ten days later, Lewis wrote to his father in a similar vein, assuring him that he was "getting on excellently" and expressing concern over missing letters.[81] Nothing was mentioned about his state of mind —a matter about which Lewis himself may not have been particularly aware. A further ten days passed before Lewis wrote again, this time claiming to be "exceedingly well," though also admitting that his injuries had been more serious than he had previously reported, and that the two shell fragments would remain lodged in his chest for the rest of his life.[82] By this time also, Lewis had received word that Paddy Moore had been

---

[79] Lewis, *Collected Letters*, 1:388.

[80] Lewis, *Collected Letters*, 1:366.

[81] Lewis, *Collected Letters*, 1:367.

[82] Lewis, *Collected Letters*, 1:368. The fragments were finally removed in August 1944.

missing in action for over a month and was almost certainly dead.[83] Though his condition was improving, Lewis was still experiencing restriction of movement, shortness of breath, fatigue, headaches, and emotional difficulties.[84]

Lewis's convalescence, which occurred between April and December of 1918, not only provided time for his physical and emotional recuperation, it also proved influential upon his intellectual and spiritual development. He remained at Étaples until 22 May, when he was well enough to be evacuated to England.[85] Three days later, he telegraphed his father informing him that he was now resident at the Endsleigh Palace Hospital, 25 Gordon Street, London—a 100-bed facility that occupied the former Endsleigh Palace Hotel.[86] Lewis was promptly visited in London by Janie and Maureen Moore, but not— significantly—by his father. As Maureen recalled, though common perception was that Lewis would soon be redeployed to France, a wound on his left wrist proved difficult to heal "and that really saved him being sent back again."[87] Lewis was soon recounting to Arthur Greeves the comforts of London, including its gardens and bookshops, as well as the pleasures afforded him by Janie Moore's visits.[88] By this stage of the war, Endsleigh (like many hospitals) was seriously understaffed, the supervision of patients relatively relaxed. By mid-June, Lewis was well enough to visit the bookshops on Charing Cross Road, and (with Janie) to call on Kirkpatrick at Great Bookham.[89]

---

[83] Lewis, *Collected Letters*, 1:369. As we have seen, Moore had, in fact, died almost two months earlier.

[84] Lewis, *Collected Letters*, 1:417-18.

[85] War Office, Armed Forces. "British Army Military Record" National Archives. TNA (PRO) WO339/105408.

[86] Lewis, *Collected Letters*, 1:373. The hospital is now the University College London Union (or UCLU).

[87] Lady Maureen Dunbar, (Maureen Moore Blake), Oral History Interview, 9 August 1984, OH / SR-8 and OH / VR-6, Marion E. Wade Center, Wheaton, Illinois. Used by permission from the Marion E. Wade Center.

[88] Lewis, *Collected Letters*, 1:373-4.

[89] Lewis, *Collected Letters*, 1:380, 384-5.

Ashton Court, Bristol, c. 1918

Hospital Ward in the Large
(downstairs) Patient Room, Ashton Court, Bristol

On 25 June, Lewis was moved to Ashton Court Red Cross Hospital for Officers outside Bristol, a large country house set in beautiful gardens. Lewis disliked Ashton Court, however, dismissing it as a "stucco work of the worst Victorian period (à la Norwood Towers)". [90] Such a view may have been influenced by the harsh regime

---

[90] Though he also admitted that there were "one or two fine paintings and a ghost," and that the park was "very pleasant and stocked with deer."

enforced by the nursing staff. As a contemporary wrote, upon arrival the patients were received "by a fierce little matron in scarlet uniform," who "recites the regulations to us almost like a litany which ended with a peremptory demand for a fee for use of certain amenities." Any attempt to introduce informality, games, or forms of recreation was strictly resisted, and the 9.00 p.m. curfew was rigorously enforced.[91] Much of Lewis's time at Ashton Court was spent revising his poems and organizing them to be sent out for publication.[92]

Lewis remained at Ashton Court until 4 October, when he was sent to Down Camp in east Wiltshire, a venue for toughening up recent convalescents in preparation for their return to their unit.[93] Given the camp's close proximity to the trench-mortar range, however, it provided little respite, especially for those recovering from shell shock. Rat hunting with entrenching tools became a common distraction.[94] Finally, in mid-November, after the armistice had been signed and in anticipation of a general demobilization, Lewis was sent to the Officers' Command Depot at Eastbourne, East Sussex, a convalescent camp on the south coast.[95] Billeted in a local house, he remained uncertain as to when, or if, he might be discharged, or even allowed leave. Unexpectedly, on 24 December, almost six weeks after the armistice had been signed, he was discharged from the hospital and demobilized.[96] Three days later, he arrived in Belfast, an event marked triumphantly by Warnie in his diary.[97]

Lewis remained in Belfast for several weeks. On the 18th of January, he wrote to the War Office inquiring about a pension or gratuity. Two weeks later, he received a reply stating that, despite the

---

See *Collected Letters*, 1:387-8.

[91] Harold Essex-Lewis, "Recollections of Lt Col Essex-Lewis of Ashton Court as a Red Cross Hospital," Bristol Record Office, MS 41648/P 2/13; 41648/P 1/59.

[92] Lewis, *Collected Letters*, 1:389-90.

[93] Lewis, *Collected Letters*, 1:403.

[94] T. S. Crawford, *Wiltshire and the Great War* (Ramsbury, England: Crowood, 2012), 221.

[95] Lewis, *Collected Letters*, 1:416.

[96] Lewis, *Collected Letters*, 1:423. Lewis was promoted to the rank of First Lieutenant on 26 March 1919. See War Office, Armed Forces. "British Army Military Record" National Archives. TNA (PRO) WO339/105408, 22; Lewis, *Collected Letters*, 1:513.

[97] Lewis, *Collected Letters*, 1:423.

severity of his injuries, he was not entitled to any form of compensation. On 5 March, his father wrote a strong appeal on the matter to the War Office, but nothing seems to have come of it.[98] By this time, Lewis had returned to Oxford to commence his undergraduate studies, where he would remain for the remainder of his life.

WARTIME READING

Lewis's wartime reading formed an important, but often overlooked, component of his emotional, intellectual, and spiritual development. Thankfully, documentation of much of this activity has been preserved in his correspondence, especially in his letters to his father, brother, and Greeves. As has often been observed, wartime, despite its intensity, also provides occasional periods of inactivity and even boredom. For the literary-minded, such moments present opportunities for reading, though regrettably, as Lewis noted, only "in small mouthfuls."[99] Lewis had been an industrious reader prior to the war. His mother was a voracious reader of fiction while his father loved Trollope's political novels, various types of humorous writing, and poetry.[100] While preparing for the Oxford scholarship examination, Lewis devoured enormous quantities of literature and poetry, drama and history, biography and philosophy, either in translation or in their original languages.[101] As Kirkpatrick remarked, "He has read more classics than any boy I ever had—or indeed I might add than any boy I have ever heard of."[102] During his military training at Oxford and even after his deployment to France, Lewis continued to read at a prodigious rate.[103] The latter may appear improbable given the demands on his time, his frequent movements, and the relative difficulty in securing (and moving) books in wartime France; however, as the record indicates, the nature of his reading appears to have changed very little during this time. His letters are punctuated with references to and often criticism of various volumes, and with requests for more books. He seems to have discovered new books

---

[98] Baker, "The army history."

[99] Lewis, *Collected Letters*, 1:348.

[100] Lewis, *Surprised by Joy*, 4.

[101] Lewis, *Surprised by Joy*, 132-48.

[102] Lewis, *Collected Letters*, 1:178.

[103] The nature and scope of his reading is revealed in various letters. See Lewis, *Collected Letters*, 1:300-34.

wherever he went, bought or borrowed books whenever possible, and had numerous volumes sent to him by his Aunt Lily, his father, Greeves, and his Belfast and London booksellers. Happily, his army salary, not wasted on the normal distractions of military life, proved adequate to supply him with a long list of new books throughout his deployment.[104]

Lewis's wartime reading was as intense as it was diverse. He read literature, philosophy, history (both classical and modern), biography, and poetry. He wrote enthusiastically about many of the works he encountered: *Adam Bede* he "liked immensely," while *The Mill on the Floss* was "even better". *Middlemarch* and indeed all of George Elliot were reviewed positively, as was Boswell's *Life of Johnson*. Though equally "delighted" by Trollope's *Barchester Chronicles* (despite Greeves' disapproval) and Gissing's *The Private Papers of Henry Ryecroft*, Tennyson, Scott, and Blackwood all failed to make much of an impression.[105]

Even during his convalescence, Lewis's appetite for reading material seemed insatiable; while still in his sick-bed, he read Hume's *A Treatise of Human Nature*, unidentified volumes of Maeterlinck (presumably in French) and Swinburne,[106] Burton's *Anatomy of Melancholy*, Mais' *A Schoolmaster's Diary*, and "a good deal" of Wordsworth.[107] He also read Belloc's *The Four Men*, selections from Emerson, and the poems of Bottomley and Abercrombie.[108] Having earlier been enchanted by George MacDonald's *Phantastes*, he now encountered his *The Princess and the Goblin*, noting "few things have pleased me more."[109] At one point, he seems to have been engaged with Locke's *Essay Concerning Human Understanding*, which deepened his thinking about materialism, beauty, and the spiritual world.[110] Two additional works, produced by the French philosopher, Henri Bergson, *L'Évolution créatrice* and *L'Énergie Spirituelle*, "had a revolutionary effect on my emotional outlook . . .. From him I first learned to relish energy, fertility, and urgency; the resource, the triumphs, and even the

---

104 Lewis, *Collected Letters*, 1:350, 370.

105 Lewis, *Collected Letters*, 1:348-80.

106 Lewis, *Collected Letters*, 1:380.

107 Lewis, *Collected Letters*, 1:393.

108 Lewis, *Collected Letters*, 1:398.

109 Lewis, *Collected Letters*, 1:393.

110 Lewis, *Collected Letters*, 1:371, 372.

insolence, of things that grow."[111] Many of these works, in expanding Lewis's imagination while challenging his materialistic assumptions (discussed below), were to prove influential on the development of his emotional, intellectual, and spiritual life.

WARTIME POETRY

Lewis's wartime poetry has recently begun to attract considerable scholarly attention,[112] and so only a brief summary of its context and significance is required here. Lewis became fond of poetry as a child and wrote his first verse at age ten. As we have seen, his father was also fond of poetry and composed verses himself. Beginning at age sixteen, his "one single ambition" in life was to become a poet;[113] for various reasons this ambition was later set aside, though he continued to write and enjoy poetry for the rest of his life.[114] During the early years of the war, between Easter 1915 and Easter 1917, Lewis composed fifty-two poems,[115] while a number of others were written during his initial residence at Oxford in the Spring and Summer of 1917. Lewis intended to submit a collection of his poetry for publication before leaving for France, but time intervened and the task was put off.[116] He continued to write poetry while serving at the front, entrusting his

---

[111] Lewis, *Surprised by Joy*, 198, 204-5.

[112] For example, John Bremer, *C. S. Lewis, Poetry and the Great War 1914-1918* (Lanham, MD: Lexington Books, 2012); Gilchrist, "2nd Lieutenant Lewis," *Morning After War*; Don W. King, *C. S. Lewis, Poet: The Legacy of His Poetic Impulse.* (Kent, OH: Kent State University Press, 2001), "Columns of Light: The Preconversion Narrative Poetry of C. S. Lewis," and "Early Lyric Poetry: *Spirits in Bondage* (1919) and 'Joy' (1924)," in *C. S. Lewis: Life, Works, and Legacy,* ed. by Bruce L. Edwards, 4 vols. (Westport, CN: Praeger, 2007), 2:209-32; C. S. Lewis, *The Collected Poems of C. S. Lewis: A Critical Edition,* ed. by Don W. King (Kent, OH: Kent State University Press, 2015), and "Making the Poor Best of Dull Things: C. S. Lewis as Poet" in *VII, An Anglo-American Literary Review,* 12 (1995), 79-92; George Musacchio, "War Poet," in *The Lamp-Post of the Southern California C. S. Lewis Society,* 2.4 (October 1978), 8; and Chad Walsh, "The Almost Poet" in *The Literary Legacy of C. S. Lewis* (New York: Harcourt Brace, 1979), 35-58.

[113] Lewis, *Collected Letters,* 1:925.

[114] See Walter Hooper, "The Failure of 'Dymer,'" in *C. S. Lewis Companion and Guide* (San Francisco: HarperSanFrancisco, 1996), 154-5, 172-4.

[115] Hooper, "C. S. Lewis: *A Companion and Guide,* 139.

[116] Lewis, *Collected Letters,* 1:321.

verses to a small pocket book he carried with him.[117] In the summer of 1918, he submitted a carefully revised collection of poems to Macmillan, but it was rejected. Heinneman proved more receptive, however, and the volume, *Spirits in Bondage: A Cycle of Lyrics*, was published in March 1919 under the pseudonym Clive Hamilton. It attracted little attention.[118] In 1926, Lewis published a long narrative poem, *Dymer*, under the same pseudonym—a work he had begun in 1918 but which was not taken up again until 1922.[119] It, too, attracted little attention.

Should each of the poems in *Spirits in Bondage* be regarded as wartime poetry? While each was composed *during* the war, only a portion *concern* the war or wartime activities. That is, only some of the poems in the volume reflect narrower, traditional themes often associated with wartime, combat, or the field of battle. It could be argued that each of Lewis's early poems should be regarded as war poetry, for they all draw from Lewis's first-hand experience in the war, while also reflecting those experiences he had in anticipation of—and recovering from—the war. In this light, wartime seems to provide a common denominator within each of Lewis's early poems. If, on the other hand, a narrower and often overlooked context is applied to the question, then a different perspective begins to emerge. That narrower context concerns the intellectual, emotional, and spiritual conflict that Lewis experienced during 1917. As he later described it:

> The two hemispheres of my mind were in the sharpest contrast. On the one side a many-islanded sea of poetry and myth; on the other a glib and shallow 'rationalism.' Nearly all that I loved I believed to be imaginary; nearly all that I believed to be real I thought grim and meaningless.[120]

Though the intensity of this conflict diminished after the war, it took several years for it fully to resolve. It is, however, within the context of this narrower, personal, and principally intellectual, emotional, and spiritual conflict, and not from Lewis's anticipation of (and recovery from) the war, that the majority of poems in *Spirits in Bondage* might

---

[117] Lewis, *Collected Letters*, 1:396.

[118] Hooper, *Companion and Guide*, 144.

[119] Lewis, *Collected Letters*, 1:277, 699; *All My Road Before Me: The Diary of C. S. Lewis, 1922-1927*, ed. by Walter Hooper (London: HarperCollins, 1991), 23-4 (2 April 1922).

[120] Lewis, *Surprised by Joy*, 161.

justifiably be placed. A smaller number found in the volume may strictly be regarded as wartime poetry, for they were composed during Lewis's time in France and reflect more traditional wartime themes, such as death and the horrors associated with life on the Western Front.

Lewis's second work, *Dymer*, appears, at first glance, quite different in nature. Composed principally after the war, it is the story of a young man's rebellion against society and his seeking of the spirit behind *Sehnsucht*—the melancholy and acute longing for something (or someone) else that Lewis himself experienced. While the wartime nature of the poem is obvious, so too is its similarity to various themes found in Lewis's earlier poetry, which reflect the protagonist's struggle to come to terms with various intellectual, emotional, and spiritual conflicts. Though, of course, contemporary readers will easily recognize the outcome of this conflict—Lewis's search for Joy—which culminated in his conversion to Christianity about a decade later, *Dymer* provides a glimpse into Lewis's unsettled state of mind in the immediate aftermath of the war. As such, it sheds helpful retrospective light on the principal issues Lewis had to face—and overcome—as he was being drawn closer and closer to Joy.

The publication of Lewis's poetry raised a certain practical problem: his atheism. Worried that his father would be unsettled by this revelation, Lewis wrote to him, claiming, rather disingenuously, that all references to atheism in his poems should not be taken at face value: "You know who the God I blaspheme is and that it is not the God that you and I worship, or any other Christian."[121] Warnie also weighed in on the matter (equally disingenuously), claiming that his brother's atheism was "purely academic" in nature, and that no "useful purpose" could possibly be "served by [him] endeavouring to advertise oneself as an Atheist."[122] Albert took a more insouciant view of the matter, however, belying his sons' opinion that he was lacking in sound judgment: "He is young and he will learn in time that a man has not absolutely solved the riddle of the heavens above and the earth beneath and the waters under the earth at twenty."[123] In a moment of prophetic insight, he added: "I do think that if Oxford does not spoil him . . . he may write something that men would not willingly let

---

[121] Lewis, *Collected Letters*, 1:443.

[122] Lewis, *Collected Letters*, 1:443, n.44.

[123] Lewis, *Collected Letters*, 1:443.

die."[124]

EFFECTS OF WAR ON LEWIS'S LIFE, WRITING, AND RELIGIOUS VIEWS

Although Lewis's imaginative writings have been subject to extensive study and commentary, the influence of his military experience during the First World War on the nature of that literature has, with few exceptions, been largely overlooked.[125] Of course, war-related themes and activities can be found throughout The Chronicles of Narnia, the first of which, *The Lion, the Witch and the Wardrobe*, is set in the context of English schoolchildren being evacuated from London during the early days of the Second World War. Other imaginative works by Lewis, such as *The Screwtape Letters*, also have a wartime feel about them. All of which raise a number of mostly unanswered questions. To what extent did Lewis's experiences during the First World War influence the writing of these volumes? More specifically, were Lewis's depictions of warfare in Narnia or of human nature in *Screwtape*, inspired by his experience during the war? What about Lewis's depictions of good and evil: were these drawn from his wartime experience, or elsewhere? Did Lewis believe children should be brought up to recognize such evil and be willing to confront it through warfare? Would a number of Lewis's imaginative works even have been written in their present form *sans* his wartime experience? Perhaps more interestingly, did Lewis romanticize war in his imaginative literature, creating scenes resplendent in their medieval pageantry and heroics, while suggesting that the formation of a child's identity occurs through participation in armed combat? Or, should Lewis's depictions of war be regarded as more realistic in nature, discouraging a romantic (or heroic) interpretation of warfare, and pointing children to a deeper sense of personal identity? Interestingly, Douglas Gresham recalls his stepfather reproving him for speaking "words of admiration" about combat, adding that "no matter what people or newspapers or politicians try to tell you, there is no glory in war."[126] As the narrative in the Narnia stories and elsewhere in Lewis's imaginative literature seem to paint a different picture, further

---

[124] Hooper, *Companion and Guide*, 142.

[125] Melton, "Into the Trenches of Narnia," 3-23.

[126] Douglas Gresham, *Jack's Life: The Life Story of C. S. Lewis* (Nashville, TN: Broadman & Holman, 2005), 44-5.

investigation into this issue would be of considerable interest.

What, then, were the principal effects of the First World War on Lewis's life and writings? Admittedly, this is not easy to answer. As we have seen, the principal difficulty arises from Lewis's own treatment of the war in his autobiography and correspondence, which requires judicious and careful evaluation. Elsewhere, especially in the historical details of Lewis's life as well as in his writings, further evidence of the effects of the war can also be discerned, though again this must be weighed with considerable care. Given these limitations, it might be helpful to set out the principal effects of the war on Lewis's life and writings in a series of diverse, but not altogether divergent, levels.

At its most immediate level, the war postponed the commencement of Lewis's undergraduate studies at Oxford and removed him temporarily from friends, family, and familiar surroundings. At a slightly deeper level, the war provided Lewis with time for personal reflection and conversation, for encountering new views and opinions, for reading books drawn from a remarkably wide range of authors and subjects, and for writing poetry. It provided a salary that enabled him to buy books; it forced him to endure hardships and sacrifices previously unknown and unimagined; moreover, it gave him a chance to mature and, by his own admission, jettison much of his youthful naiveté. At a deeper level still, the war took Lewis out of himself and his rather narrow public-school, middle-class, and parochial Ulster upbringing. It exposed him to a variety of men and women drawn from a wide range of backgrounds, nationalities, and outlooks, and required him to serve alongside—and under the authority of—men in his battalion of the sort he rarely, if ever, encountered at home, at school, or at Oxford. The benefits of this exposure are revealed in striking fashion by contrasting Lewis's initial impressions of the officers in his regiment with those of his later reflections. In October 1917, shortly after arriving at the regimental camp at Crownhill, Lewis made the following observations on his fellow officers:

> I should say the gentlemen are about 65 percent of the whole crowd of officers, which is quite as large a majority as one has a right to expect now-a-days. One or two of them I think I shall like, though of course it is hard to say at present. It must be admitted that most of them are hardly after my style: the subjects of conversation are shop . . . sport and theatrical news recurring with a rather dull regularity—that is in the few

moments of conversation which interrupt the serious business of bridge and snooker. However, they are for the most part well bred and quite nice to me.[127]

Some years later, Lewis's reflections on the men he encountered in his battalion illustrate the extent to which his thinking had matured, especially in his appreciation for those drawn from the lower orders of society:

> Ours was a very nice battalion . . .. You could get as good talk there as anywhere. Perhaps the best of us all was our butt, Wallie. Wallie was a farmer, a Roman Catholic, a passionate soldier . . .. The technique was to criticize the Yeomanry. Poor Wallie knew that it was the bravest, the most efficient, the hardest and cleanest corps that ever sat on horses. He knew all that inside, having learned it from an uncle in the Yeomanry when he was a child. But he could not get it out. He stammered and contradicted himself and always came at last to his trump card: 'I wish my Uncle Ben was here to talk to you. Uncle Ben'd talk to you. He'd tell you.'[128]

Lewis, however, was more influenced by Wallie than the other way around. "I doubt," he added, "whether any man fought in France who was more likely to go straight to Heaven if he were killed. I would have been better employed cleaning his boots than laughing at him."[129] When Lewis arrived at the front for the first time, the inadequacy of his experience and military training was quickly revealed. Like virtually every young subaltern thrown directly into combat, he was highly dependent on his sergeant, Harry Charles Ayres, to instruct him on how to lead soldiers—and remain alive—in trench warfare.[130] When, for example, Lewis suggested 'pooping' a rifle grenade into a nearby German post, Ayres quickly put him right. "'Just as 'ee like, sir'. . . scratching his head, 'but once 'ee start doing that kind of thing, 'ee'll get zummit back, zee?'"[131] Not long afterwards, when Lewis

---

[127] Lewis, *Collected Letters*, 1:338.

[128] Lewis, *Surprised by Joy*, 193.

[129] Lewis, *Surprised by Joy*, 193.

[130] Harry Charles Ayres (1885-1918) was the son of Albert and Rhoda Ayres of Frome, Somerset. His father was a painter by trade. He was baptized at Christ Church, Frome, on 27 December 1885. In the 1911 Census, he was listed as living as a boarder at 24 Box Lane, Ipswich, and working as a brewer's engineer laborer.

[131] Lewis, *Surprised by Joy*, 194.

received the surrender of sixty German soldiers, Ayres suggested that he should at least remove his service revolver from its holster.[132] "I was a futile officer," Lewis admitted, "(they gave commissions too easily then), a puppet moved about by him [Ayres], and he turned this ridiculous and painful relation into something beautiful, became to me almost a father."[133] Tragically, Ayers did not survive the shell that wounded Lewis. Standing where he was, Ayres may in fact have saved Lewis's life, having borne the major force of the explosion. Lewis's emotional response to Ayres' death has not been recorded, though he could hardly have been forgotten.

At a still deeper level, the war left Lewis not only physically but emotionally scarred, exposing him to death, suffering, and personal loss on a scale that, for most people, is simply unimaginable. Over 4,700 soldiers from his regiment died in the war, with the average life expectancy on the Western Front being around six weeks, even less for stretcher-bearers and junior officers, like Lewis.[134] Of the six friends in the O.T.C. at Oxford, all but Lewis and Denis Howard de Pass were killed in action (de Pass was taken prisoner)[135]. Besides the death of Ayres, there was the death of Lewis's friend, Laurence Johnson. Lewis may also have killed a number of Germans during the war, and he certainly witnessed the death of many more. These collective experiences engaged Lewis's emotions at a profound level. Gilchrist has, in fact, argued that Lewis suffered the devastating effects of Post-Traumatic Stress Disorder (PTSD) or "shell shock" as it was then known. This was covered up by Lewis and Warnie after the war, and kept from their closest friends, despite the existence of a number of tell-tale signs, such as depression found throughout his life and writings[136]—a point that has gained some acceptance in recent Lewis scholarship. A few brief examples help illustrate this point. What, for instance, can possibly be made of the existential comment Lewis proffered to Arthur Greeves in August 1918: "Oh don't you

---

[132] Harold Ivan Smith, *Borrowed Narratives: Using Biographical and Historical Grief Narratives With the Bereaving* (New York: Routledge, 2012), 214.

[133] Lewis, *Surprised by Joy*, 96.

[134] John Lewis-Stempel, *Six Weeks: The Short and Gallant Life of the British Officer in the First World War* (London: Orion, 2010), 5.

[135] Lewis, *Collected Letters*, 1:317, 402.

[136] Gilchrist, *Morning After War*, 153-73.

sometimes feel that everything is dead?"[137] Three months later, he was complaining to his father of constant "nightmares—or rather the same nightmare over and over again."[138] Almost four years later, Lewis continued to suffer from what appears to have been depression, which he attributed to the pressure of the Oxford exam system, but which may well have been the result of more long-term influences:

> I woke up late this morning in such a state of misery and depression as I never remember to have had. There was no apparent reason. Really rather ridiculous—found myself in tears, for the first time in many a long day, while dressing. I concealed this as well as I could and it passed off after breakfast. I suppose it is some form of pathological reaction by which I pay for not having had conscious wind up or exhaustion during schools.[139]

Later still, as the dark clouds of conflict began gathering once again over Europe, a friend wrote asking if Lewis had joined the Territorials. He was too old, Lewis replied, before adding this revealing comment:

It wd. be hypocrisy to say that I regret this. My memories of the last war haunted my dreams for years . . .. I think death wd. be much better than to live through another war. Thank God, He has not allowed my *faith* to be greatly tempted by the present horrors.[140] Such comments speak to the long-term emotional hardships experienced by Lewis brought about by the First World War and thus to the importance of understanding its continued influence on his life and writings.

Finally, at perhaps its most profound level, the war influenced the nature of Lewis's spiritual life. Though he remained an atheist throughout the war (there was no "foxhole conversion") and would remain so for another decade, a series of friendships and experiences that occurred during the war set in motion a long and important process in which, as Lewis described it, his rationalism was "assailed" and eventually overcome in favor of belief in the existence of God and later in Christianity itself.[141]

---

[137] Lewis, *Collected Letters*, 1:395.

[138] Lewis, *Collected Letters*, 1:417.

[139] Lewis, *All My Road*, 51 (18 June 1922).

[140] Lewis, *Collected Letters*, 2:258.

[141] Lewis, *Surprised by Joy*, 191.

EFFECTS OF FRIENDSHIPS AND READING
ON LEWIS'S ATHEISM IN THE WAR YEARS

The first installment in this was Lewis's friendship with John Edwards, whom he met at University College in the spring of 1917.[142] As Lewis wrote to Greeves, "what interests me is that he [Edwards] was an atheist until lately, and is now engaged in becoming a Catholic, or is very near it. He came into my rooms last night, and we sat until about 12. We had a long talk about religion."[143] Years later, Edwards described Lewis as able to "join in any discussion on any subject and talk fluently and knowledgably; he was particularly interested in those early days in religion."[144] There was also Lewis's close friendship with Martin Somerville, a scholar of Eton and, later, an Exhibitioner (scholarship awardee) of King's College, Cambridge.[145] The two met while serving in the O.T.C. during the spring of 1917, with Somerville quickly becoming Lewis's "chief friend." Lewis described Somerville affectionately as "a very quiet sort of person, but very booky and interesting."[146] Elsewhere, we find that Somerville, though "a strict Anglo-Catholic," was not above "scoffing at religion."[147] It appears that the two friends lost contact when they joined different regiments. After the war, Somerville planned to be ordained in the Church of England, though this was prevented by his early death.[148] Among his few effects at the time of his death were a Prayer Book and a Rosary.[149]

---

[142] John Robert Edwards (1897-1992) graduated from Manchester Grammar School and then read Greats at University College, Oxford. He was medically unfit for duty, however, and so remained in Oxford for the duration of the war. Subsequently, he had a successful career as a teacher and headmaster.

[143] Lewis, *Collected Letters*, 1:307.

[144] Lewis, *Collected Letters*, 1:350.

[145] Martin Ashworth Somerville (1898-1918) was born in December 1898 in Eton, Berkshire, the son of Annesley Ashworth and Ethel Somerville. His father was a Housemaster at Eton who, between 1922 and 1942, served as Conservative MP for Windsor, and was knighted in the 1939 Honours List.

[146] Lewis, *Collected Letters*, 1:317.

[147] Lewis, *All My Road*, 45 (4 June 1922).

[148] "In Memoriam. Martin Ashworth Somerville," *The Eton College Chronicle*, 3 October 1918. https://archives.etoncollege.com/Authenticated/Maintenance/AddArticle.aspx?RecID=7781&Mode=View&TableName=ta_chronicles_articles

[149] Gilchrist, *Morning After War*, 117.

Admittedly, from the extant material it is difficult to determine the degree of influence Somerville had on Lewis's spiritual development, though at the very least he was remembered fondly by Lewis as a respected friend who held serious intellectual and religious views, as well as a vocation to the priesthood. That Lewis was quickly drawn to such a man at this time of life is itself revealing.

Second, Lewis's rationality was assailed during the war in practical ways. No doubt, for the majority of men serving on the Western Front, atheism remained a luxury beyond their reach. Death, whether their own or that of their neighbor, remained a constant threat. Despite the extended nature of the war, and despite the horrors of modern warfare with its highly mechanized, impersonalized, and senseless forms of killing, the majority of British people (including those in the military) still maintained a certain religious outlook, and not a few accepted the patriotic (if not propagandist) notion that the Allies were doing God's work in opposing German militarism, expansion, and aggression. This raises the interesting question—though one that lies beyond the scope of this investigation—of Lewis's wartime patriotism and how it may have influenced his outlook. There is little or no evidence to suggest that he was sympathetic toward, or even interested in, the notion that opposition to German aggression should be based on religious idealism. Nor is there evidence that such claims by way of reaction intensified Lewis's opposition to religion. At the same time, the constant threat of death or being wounded and the insistent pleas of those around him for divine protection and mercy, combined with the presence of numerous chaplains and religious services,[150] would have constantly assailed Lewis's adherence to atheism.

Lewis's rationality was also assailed through his encounter with various Christian authors. After falling under the spell of George MacDonald in March 1916 and again two years later, Lewis now encountered another author who would come to exert almost as much influence upon his views: G. K. Chesterton. When Lewis began to read a volume of essays while convalescing at La Tréport he had not heard of the author and knew nothing of what he stood for. In Chesterton, however, Lewis was to meet one of the most insightful and appealing

---

[150] At the outbreak of the war, there were 117 chaplains in the British Army; by its conclusion that number had increased to 3,475. See Alan Wilkinson, *The Church of England and the First World War* (London: SPCK, 1978), 124.

writers of his generation. He quickly made an "immediate conquest" of Lewis. Especially appealing were Chesterton's sense of humor and his sense of goodness. As Lewis later reflected, "in reading Chesterton, as in reading MacDonald, I did not know what I was letting myself in for. A young man who wishes to remain a sound Atheist cannot be too careful of his reading."[151] Given that Chesterton appealed to Lewis principally as a humorist and moralist, his direct influence on Lewis's spiritual life is difficult to assess. Like a number of other writings and experiences of Lewis's during this time, however, Chesterton's arguments presented a striking—and appealing—alternative to the stark rationalism and dark pessimism of Kirkpatrick—views then largely shared by Lewis. This influence was acknowledged by Lewis in 1962 in reply to a request to identify the writings that have most shaped his vocational attitude and philosophy of life. MacDonald's *Phantastes* topped the list, followed by Chesterton's *The Everlasting Man*.[152] Although it is difficult to identify direct lines of causation, it does seem clear that Chesterton along with MacDonald and other Christian authors came to play an important role in shaping Lewis's outlook on life, which may well have extended to the further development of his historical and spiritual views.

Finally, Lewis's rationalism was assailed through the influence of several close friends during the war, including Laurence Johnson.[153] It seems likely, as Lewis predicted, that the two would have remained friends after the war. After all, Johnson was bookish, highly intelligent, and deeply invested in literature, poetry, ideas, and the pursuit of truth. He held his own against Lewis in debate, while retaining an acute sense of humor. Even the passage of time did not diminish Lewis's admiration for Johnson's special qualities, as the following passage makes clear:

> In him I found dialectical sharpness such as I had hitherto known only in Kirk, but coupled with youth and whim and

---

[151] Lewis, *Surprised by Joy*, 190-1.

[152] C. S. Lewis, "Ex Libris" or "Booklist submitted in response to this department's query: 'What books did most to shape your Philosophy of life?'" in *The Christian Century*, 79.23 (6 June 1962), 719.

[153] Laurence Bertrand Johnson (1898-1918), the son of Bertrand and Emma Johnson, had been elected a Scholar of The Queen's College, Oxford. Emma's father was a wealthy ship owner who left a substantial fortune when he died in 1908. The family then relocated to fashionable Lyndhurst Road in Hampstead.

poetry. He was moving towards Theism and we had endless arguments on that and every other topic . . .. The important thing was that he was a man of conscience. I had hardly now encountered principles in anyone so nearly my own age and my own sort. The alarming thing is that he took them for granted. It crossed my mind for the first time since my apostasy that the severer virtues might have some relevance to one's own life . . . it had not seriously occurred to me that people like . . . Johnson and me who wanted to know whether beauty was objective . . . should be attempting strict veracity, chastity, or devotion to duty. I had taken it that they were not our subjects . . .. I accepted his principles at once, made no attempt internally to defend my own 'unexamined life.'[154]

This passage is both significant and revealing. Curiously, among Johnson's few personal effects at the time of his death were his crucifix and chain,[155] which suggests that his spiritual life was more developed than Lewis may have realized or cared to admit. In any case, Lewis's spiritual development could hardly have remained unaffected by his discussions with Johnson, given his respect and affection for his friend. That Lewis had experienced a change in outlook at this time (however modest) was hinted at in a letter to Arthur Greeves in May 1918. As Lewis wrote: "The conviction is gaining ground on me that after all Spirit does exist . . .. I fancy that there is Something right outside time & place, which did not create matter, as the Christians say, but is matter's great enemy."[156] Moreover, the death of Johnson among so many others must have produced in Lewis a number of powerful emotions, including thoughts on the death of his own mother and on immortality itself. Mourning mixed with guilt, the experience of killing and that of surviving, now assailed Lewis's rationalistic conception of life at a profound level. As he confessed to his father, he found the death of Johnson particularly difficult to accept.[157]

Given the cumulative effects of these various assaults on Lewis's rationality during and after the war, prior characterizations of his early spiritual views, which have often been set out in rather fixed terms, should perhaps be reconsidered. That is, Lewis was probably less of a Christian during his childhood, and probably less of an atheist during

---

[154] Lewis, *Surprised by Joy*, 191-3.

[155] Gilchrist, *Morning After War*, 125.

[156] Lewis, *Collected Letters*, 1:374.

[157] Lewis, *Collected Letters*, 1:388.

and after the war, than many accounts have previously assumed. Such a view is supported (rather than countered) by the rather *outré* manner in which Lewis referred to his atheistic views during this period, as revealed in some of his early poems and in everyday conversations. On one occasion, for example, when he was asked by his undergraduate friend, Leo Baker, if he had experienced fear during the war, Lewis responded (with great emphasis) "all the time, but I never sank so low as to pray." Such comments lend weight to the suggestion that Lewis was more of "an abundantly posturing atheist" at this time than an atheist by conviction.[158]

Lewis was fortunate to have survived the war, as he himself acknowledged. "Never a day passes," he wrote toward the end of 1918, "but I thankfully realize my great good fortune in getting wounded when I did and thus being spared the very deadly months that followed."[159] Like many other survivors, Lewis agonized over the necessity and moral significance of the war: "One cannot help wondering why," he later asked, such things must occur. Like many of his contemporaries, he was left without an answer. As he simply concluded, "Let us be silent and thankful."[160]

In Lewis's autobiography, written between 1948 and 1955, he refused to dwell on the grief and suffering experienced during the war, or even on the depravity associated with modern forms of killing. Instead, he took a more philosophical and irenic approach, recalling, for example, his delight in the two Canadian officers who kindly took charge of him on his first night at the front and his emotional reaction to the first time a bullet passed nearby.[161] Despite its limitations as an account of his wartime experiences, *Surprised by Joy* richly documents Lewis's encounter with men of different outlooks and backgrounds, which in turn exposed him to many of the realities and hardships often experienced by ordinary people.

In light of that, it is perhaps surprising that the death of Lewis's mother combined with his wartime experience did not result in Lewis developing, at an earlier age, a more emotionally holistic view of suffering and grief. While his robust—and often-quoted—description of pain, published some twenty years after the war, as

---

[158] Como, *Remembering C. S. Lewis*, 13, 69.

[159] Lewis, *Collected Letters*, 1:398-9.

[160] Lewis, *Collected Letters*, 1:416-17.

[161] Lewis, *Surprised by Joy*, 188-9, 196,

God's "megaphone to rouse a deaf world"[162] appealed to some, it seemed far too rational and impersonal to others. Years later, after the death of his wife, an important transformation in outlook can be located in *A Grief Observed*, which documents a greater degree of emotional honesty, insight, and empathy than that found in any of his earlier writings. Why this change took so long to occur remains difficult to answer. Perhaps Lewis was so damaged by the death of his mother, the loss of childhood innocence and wider family connections, the horrible nature of his school experiences, that it stunted his emotional growth. Perhaps it was the result of Lewis's rigid social conditioning, where boys of his background and generation were taught not to express emotion and vulnerability, or to complain. Or, perhaps it was the direct consequence of the emotional damage he experienced as a result of his wartime experience. It is difficult to know. What is more certain is that the First World War represented more than a mere "interruption" of Lewis's rational life, for in numerous ways it influenced his character and outlook, and set in motion important spiritual impulses that would finally come to maturity a decade later. Perhaps most significantly, the war left a distinct imprint on the nature of many of Lewis's apologetic, poetic, and imaginative writings. Future accounts of C. S. Lewis cannot overlook the important influence of the First World War on his life and writings.

---

[162] C. S. Lewis, *The Problem of Pain* (London: Centenary Press, 1940). 93.

Chapter 2

SOLVE FOR X:
C. S. LEWIS, CHARLES LAMB,
AND THE ALGEBRA OF FRIENDSHIP

Diana Pavlac Glyer

In *The Four Loves*, Lewis discusses maternal love, brotherly love, romantic love, and God's *agape* love. *The Four Loves* is a mature work, written late in Lewis's life, and it exemplifies one of the most important features of Lewis's writings: a rare ability to combine personal warmth with creative vision and intellectual vitality. One passage in *The Four Loves* is particularly evocative and serves as the starting point for this essay. Lewis recalls a comment made by Charles Lamb about the nature of brotherly love or friendship. Here's what Lewis says:

> Lamb says somewhere that if, of three friends (A, B, and C), A should die, then B loses not only A but "A's part in C," while C loses not only A but "A's part in B." In each of my friends, there is something that only some other friend can fully bring out. By myself, I am not large enough to call the whole man into activity; I want other lights than my own to show all his facets.[1]

The human personality, the Self, Lewis tells us, is like a jewel made of many facets. What is the light that brings forth each one? Or, as Lewis puts it, what is needed in order to "call the whole man into activity"? Undoubtedly many things play a part, but Lewis emphasizes the important role of friendship. "By myself, I am not large enough," he says. "I want other lights than my own to show all his facets."

In order to explain his point, Lewis continues the discussion by offering a specific example. He tells us that when Charles Williams died, Lewis felt the loss keenly. But when he writes about this loss, he emphasizes that he has not only lost Williams, but he has also lost the way that Williams brought forth various aspects of his other friends. Lewis laments, "Now that Charles is dead, I shall never again see

---

[1] C. S. Lewis, *The Four Loves* (San Diego: Harvest-Harcourt, 1988), 61.

[Tolkien's] reaction to a particularly Caroline joke."[2] He continues, "Instead of having more of [Tolkien], having him 'to myself' now that Charles is away, *I have less*."[3]

Lewis tells us that we are diminished when we are alone; we are somehow greater when we gather together. That is because friends—old friends and new friends, the friends who sit at table, gather at our workplace, and live in our neighborhoods—call forth different aspects of our selves. Community enriches our lives, and it also shapes our personality. When we make time to gather together, to connect with different people from various backgrounds, those connections do more than warm our heart or enhance our experience: those connections affect who we are and make a lasting difference. Various facets of our nature are called forth and shine brighter as we engage with one another.

Here is Lewis again:

> . . . true friendship is the least jealous of loves. Two friends delight to be joined by a third, and three by a fourth . . .. They can then say, as the blessed souls say in Dante, "Here comes one who will augment our loves." For in this love "to divide is not to take away."[4]

Two are joined by x or y, and the end result multiplies; it does not divide. This idea is at the heart of what Lewis believes about friendship. In order to clarify the concept, he makes reference to a passage from Canto Five of Dante's *Paradiso*.[5] There, in Heaven, Dante the Pilgrim sees a thousand blessed souls, and each one recognizes that their ability to love God is augmented, that is, amplified, magnified, and improved, by the addition of other souls who also love God. To divide their attention and share what they have does not take away from their experience of each other: it adds more.

In Dante's account, these souls dance as each new soul arrives—they are so alive with joy as they welcome and greet one another. They rush to gather around each newcomer and say, in essence, "Welcome! I can hardly wait to grow and change as a result of knowing you. I can hardly wait to see what I will discover now that you are here at last."

---

[2] Lewis, *The Four Loves*, 61.

[3] Lewis, *The Four Loves*, 61, emphasis added.

[4] Lewis, *The Four Loves*, 61.

[5] Dante Alighieri, *The Divine Comedy* (*The Inferno, The Purgatorio, and The Paradiso*), trans. by John Ciardi (New York, NAL Trade: 2003).

Now we may not be inclined to do a little dance as we are introduced to one another, but the nature of friendship is clear: to extend welcome to one another, to rejoice over one another with great joy, to stand on tiptoe in eager expectation, to delight in what God is doing in each of us that all of us might shine a little brighter as we enjoy the gift of one another.

CHARLES LAMB

Both Dante and Lewis assume that there are regions of the human soul that lie dormant until contact with another person calls them forth. Researchers have labeled this "dyadic psychology," placing particular emphasis on the way that face-to-face encounters with infants and young children give shape to their psyche. The loving light of a caregiver's eyes "calls forth" new neurological pathways in the brain.

That passage from Charles Lamb, the one that Lewis roughly paraphrases in *The Four Loves*, expresses this concept using mathematical terms, emphasizing the impact of subtraction:

> The going away of friends does not make the remainder more precious. It takes so much from them [because] there was a common link. A, B, and C, make a party. When A dies, B not only loses A, but all A's part in C, and so the alphabet sickens by subtraction of interchangeables.[6]

The loss of a friend means the loss of that person's part in every other person. Each of us has the unique power to draw out certain aspects of others, and when we lose someone, we lose them and we also lose their part in everyone else.

This principle suggests an important mathematical corollary: if the alphabet sickens by the subtraction of interchangeables, as Charles Lamb says that it does, then the alphabet is made healthy and whole by addition. This subtracting, adding, dividing, and multiplying is the principle I call The Algebra of Friendship. In this essay, I am focusing on the "addition" aspect of these equations: Each of us is born with many facets, much potential, but without someone to shine their own particular kind of light on those facets, they may remain dark and hidden. Perhaps they even remain entirely dormant and never really

---

[6] Letter of 20 March 1822 from Charles Lamb to William Wordsworth, in E. V. Lucas, ed. *The Works of Charles and Mary Lamb*, 6 vols. (London: Methuen, 1912), 7:563.

develop at all.

A simple example may serve here. When my daughter Sierra Grace was six years old, her kindergarten teacher was passionate about science. So when they got together, they talked nonstop about evaporation and condensation and precipitation. I'm an English teacher, and I would have to say that those are not exactly household words where I live. But when Sierra was with her teacher, it was the science side of her that would really shine.

My daughter also really loves music, though, I promise you, I am no musician. But you should see what Sierra is like when she is with her Auntie Lynn—Lynn will play the piano and sing, and Sierra will sing right along at the top of her voice, and then they dance around the living room. It's amazing to watch what comes forth when the two of them are together.

Here's the point: When Lynn comes over to our house and the two of them spend the evening making music together, I do not have less of Sierra. I have more. Because suddenly I have a whole side of her that I would not have otherwise. It is true for all of us, to a greater or lesser extent. We grow so much greater in response to the company we keep.

C. S. LEWIS

It is instructive to look at Lewis's life with The Algebra of Friendship in mind. There has been a tendency to think of C. S. Lewis as a sort of brooding, isolated, secluded, lonely intellectual. I think it comes from some stereotype that many people have about writers, or maybe it's just the way people think about college professors. You may remember the movie *Shadowlands* and the rather stiff and stuffy way Lewis was portrayed by Anthony Hopkins.[7]

There are a number of accuracy problems with the film *Shadowlands*, though, in general, I have to admit that I like it very much. But the portrayal of Lewis as an angry introvert is one thing that really irritates me.

So let me do what I can to set the record straight. Lewis wrote such compelling things about friendship because his life was rich in relationships. And he was a greater man as a result of important friendships throughout his life. They marked his life experience, and

---

[7] William Nicholson, *Shadowlands*, dir. by Richard Attenborough (Los Angeles: Price Entertainment. 1993).

they changed him. Lewis was a man with friends.

With that in mind, I have been studying Lewis's letters to see if I could discover specific ways that Lewis's most significant relationships affected the unfolding of his personality. In other words, rather than looking at Lewis's personality as some sort of static entity, I have been interested in seeing if there are aspects of his nature that were called forth or augmented—if there are facets that shine in some particular way—because of particular people in his life. How does Lewis's life reflect The Algebra of Friendship? It seems likely that Lewis became the kind of man he was at least in part as a result of the people he knew. Tracing that influence helps us understand Lewis and also gain insight into the larger question of how relationships with others shape who we are.

The first person I want to consider is Lewis's older brother, Warren Hamilton Lewis.

WARREN HAMILTON LEWIS: Collaboration

C. S. Lewis was born in 1898; his brother Warren was three years old at the time. The two boys were very close, and as they grew up, their playtime blossomed into shared creativity. Warren created an imaginary world he called India. He was particularly interested in the mechanics of it: roads, maps, boats, and trains, that sort of thing.

Lewis also invented an imaginary world, and he called it Animal-land. It was like something out of Beatrix Potter; however, instead of representing common country folk like Peter Rabbit, Squirrel Nutkin, or Jemima Puddleduck, his animals were largely political figures, kings and generals and barons and field marshals. You could say that Animal-land was much like a typical British city. Except that in Animal-land, the king was a rabbit, the general was a goldfish, and the field marshal was a frog.

Over time, Warren Lewis's India and Jack Lewis's Animal-land were joined together under the same parliament, and they called this new world Boxen. The boys produced watercolor illustrations, organized trade routes, wrote stories and plays. They even published a Boxonian newspaper.[8]

This creative work lasted for many years; Lewis was 13 or 14 years old when they abandoned it. This one imaginary sub-created

---

[8] C. S. Lewis and W. H. Lewis, *Boxen: Childhood Chronicles Before Narnia* (San Francisco: HarperChildrens, 2008).

world occupied a significant part of Lewis's life. And one of the most important things he learned from the experience was the give and take of working collaboratively.

Here it is worth noting that the two brothers had very different personalities. By his own admission, Lewis tended to be impatient, arrogant, and a little contentious. By contrast, Warren Lewis was warm, amiable, easy-going, and comfortable. Jill Freud, one of the children evacuated to the Kilns at wartime, knew him well. She observed that Major Lewis was "comfy to be with all the time."[9]

As Warren and Jack worked together, they learned to share creative ideas, to critique and to cooperate, to create whole new worlds together with someone whose temperament and creative vision were really very different from their own. This habit of creative collaboration with those who are different is a pattern that lasted all of Lewis's life.

Keep that in mind as we consider another influential friend, a neighbor whose name was Arthur Greeves.

ARTHUR GREEVES: Charity

The story of how Lewis met his great friend Arthur Greeves has been told many times. The Lewis family lived at 76 Circular Road in Strandtown, Belfast, in a house named "Little Lea."[10] Arthur lived across the street, and in 1914, Lewis was told that his neighbor was ill and would welcome a visit. As Lewis tells it, when he arrived at the house, he found Arthur sitting up in bed, and on the table beside him was a book of Norse Mythology. Lewis noticed the book right away:

"Do you like that?" said I.

"Do you like that?" said he. Next moment the book was in our hands, our heads were very close together, we were pointing, quoting, talking—soon almost shouting—discovering in a torrent of questions that we liked not only the same thing, but the same parts of it and in the same way.[11]

---

[9] Jill Flewett Freud, "Part B: With Girls at Home" in Stephen Schofield, ed., *In Search of C. S. Lewis* (South Plainfield, NJ: Bridge, 1983), 57.

[10] Sandy Smith, "Surprised by Belfast: Significant Sites in the Land and Life of C. S. Lewis, Part 1, Little Lea," in *Knowing and Doing: C. S. Lewis Institute: A Teaching Quarterly for Discipleship of Heart and Mind*, (Spring 2016), 1.

[11] C. S. Lewis, *Surprised by Joy: The Shape of My Early Life* (New York:

Lewis was surprised by friendship, surprised to find someone who was in fact very much like himself. Lewis's description of this moment is really very striking. This is what he says about making this strong and immediate connection with Arthur:

> I had been so far from thinking [that] such a friend was possible that I had never even longed for one; no more than I longed to be King of England . . .. Nothing, I suspect, is more astonishing in any man's life than the discovery that there do exist people very, very like himself.[12]

It is an intoxicating sensation to suddenly find another person who loves the same books that you do or someone who has seen the same movie that you have and can quote and recite the same unforgettable lines. Within minutes, you feel understood and connected. Lewis calls Greeves a type of the "First Friend":

> The First [Friend] is the alter ego, the man who first reveals to you that you are not alone in the world by turning out (beyond hope) to share all your most secret delights. There is nothing to be overcome in making him your friend; he and you join like raindrops on a window.[13]

Although Lewis was very close to his brother Warren, the two were of very different temperaments and fundamentally different interests. For example, Warren and Jack attended many of the exact same boarding schools. Warren liked them just fine. Jack, on the other hand, compared them to concentration camps.

So suddenly, here, as a teenager, Lewis at last found someone who liked the same books, shared the same views, and in many ways, spoke the same language. Lewis writes, "He is, after my brother, my oldest and most intimate friend."[14] Greeves and Lewis remained good friends until the end of Lewis's life. Their letters span nearly fifty years and comprise "the largest collection of letters Lewis ever wrote to anyone"; 296 letters from Lewis to Greeves have been collected and published.[15]

Harcourt, 1955), 130.

[12] Lewis, *Surprised by Joy*, 131.

[13] Lewis, *Surprised by Joy*, 199.

[14] C. S. Lewis, *They Stand Together: The Letters of C. S. Lewis to Arthur Greeves (1914-1963)*, ed. by Walter Hooper (London: Macmillan, 1979), 18.

[15] Lewis, *They Stand Together*, 12; 41.

What sort of man was Arthur Greeves? Warren Lewis and Jack Lewis have both written biographies of him, collected in Vol. III of *The Lewis Family Papers.* Diagnosed with a weak heart as a child and home schooled by a doting mother, Greeves remained housebound as a child, and he lived there most of his life; he never had to work to earn a living.

Greeves had considerable talent in music and in art; he was a member of the Royal Hibernian Academy and won some recognition as a landscape painter. Moreover, he had the gift of enjoying the arts. Warren Lewis writes, "He has a genuine appreciation for what is good in music and literature, and a sense of beauty, a love of the country and of country things, a kindliness, and a generosity which make him an attractive person."[16]

Another glimpse can be found in the poems that Lewis wrote: three of his published poems are dedicated to Greeves. "Ballade of a Winter's Morning" is an invitation to "Draw up beside me, friend by friend / A snugly cushioned easy chair— / A merry morning we will spend."[17] In "Couplets," the narrator invites his companion to "walk and talk upon the hills of Down" and, in the process, to roam "The unknown garden of another's heart."[18] In another poem called "Decadence," the narrator addresses Greeves directly, using his nickname "Oh Galahad!"[19] The poem expresses difficulty and discouragement: "The world is old and very sad, / The world is old and gray with pain." It then suggests that when Arthur wakes (Arthur Greeves? King Arthur? Or both?), he will go forth to offer a needed remedy. All three poems are early in Lewis's life; all three show a deep connection between the two men and celebrate the close bond of friendship they shared.

In fifty years of friendship, what did Lewis learn from his friend? That he wasn't alone in the world, that he wasn't alone in understanding and treasuring certain things. And because they were so much alike, he learned the ease of being completely candid, of opening up and

---

[16] Warren Hamilton Lewis, ed. *The Lewis Family Papers or Memoirs of the Lewis Family (1850-1930),* 11 vols., Unpublished [Leeborough Press], 1933-5, Marion E. Wade Center, Wheaton College, Wheaton, IL., 4:183. Used by permission from the Marion E. Wade Center.

[17] C. S. Lewis, *The Collected Poems of C. S. Lewis: A Critical Edition,* ed. by Don W. King (Kent, Ohio: Kent State University Press, 2015), 52.

[18] Lewis, *Collected Poems,* 67.

[19] Lewis, *Collected Poems,* 68.

sharing all his thoughts and dreams. As I re-read their letters to each other, I am struck by how honest they are with each other. Like the Book of Psalms in the Bible, these letters run the entire range of human emotion: anger, pity, glory, rage, spite, sin, guilt, repentance, forgiveness, joy, exaltation, worry, and fear. It seems that there is nothing these two don't discuss: the excesses and temptations of adolescence; their discoveries, challenges, and achievements; favorite books and beautiful artwork; the inevitable losses that come with old age. And the whole time, through all of it, there they are, as alike as two raindrops on the windowpane.

So finding a friend, someone whose interests were very like his own, who saw things the way he did, is one important thing that Lewis gained from all of this. But there is another dimension of this particular friendship worth mentioning. Lewis says that the most important thing that he learned from Arthur was to appreciate the everyday beauty of ordinary things. "What kinds of things?" Listen to these images. Lewis says that without Arthur, he would not have developed the capacity to notice and appreciate homely and exquisitely ordinary things. He writes,

> But for him I should never have known the beauty of the ordinary vegetables that we destine to the pot. "Drills," he used to say. "Just ordinary drills of cabbages--what can be better?" And he was right. Often he recalled my eyes from the horizon just to look through a hole in a hedge, to see nothing more than a farmyard in its mid-morning solitude, and perhaps a grey cat squeezing its way under a barn door, or a bent old woman with a wrinkled, motherly face coming back with an empty bucket from the pigstye.[20]

Lewis elaborates this whole idea in one of my favorite quotations. It is a statement worth our best attention: I think this is Lewis at his most candid and sincere. Lewis says that Arthur

> ... was not a clever boy, he was even a dull boy; I was a scholar. He had no 'ideas'. I bubbled over with them. It might seem that I had much to give him, and that he had nothing to give me. But this is not the truth. I could give concepts, logic, facts, arguments, but he had feelings to offer, feelings which most mysteriously—for he was always very inarticulate—he taught me to share. Hence, in our commerce, I dealt in superficies, but

---

[20] Lewis, *Surprised by Joy*, 157-8.

he in solids. I learned charity from him and failed, for all my efforts, to teach him arrogance in return.[21]

It is a candid and compelling confession, and I have every reason to believe that it is absolutely true.

As we have seen, Lewis discovered creativity, collaboration, and cooperation along with his brother Warren. And Lewis learned charity, sensitivity, appreciation, awareness, and companionship from Arthur. First a brother, then a neighbor, and now a third: a teacher. William T. Kirkpatrick was the spark that kindled Lewis's intellectual accomplishments.

WILLIAM KIRKPATRICK: Logic

In *Surprised by Joy*, Lewis offers this account of the day he first saw William T. Kirkpatrick:

> He was over six feet tall, very shabbily dressed (like a gardener, I thought), lean as a rake, and immensely muscular. His wrinkled face seemed to consist entirely of muscles, so far as it was visible; for he wore a mustache and side whiskers with a clean-shaven chin like the Emperor Franz Joseph.[22]

I think that the influence of this strong and shabby man has been underestimated. People may know that Kirkpatrick tutored C. S. Lewis as a residential pupil for nearly two years. But he impacted the whole Lewis family: he also tutored Lewis's brother, Warren Lewis, and their father, Albert Lewis, had been his student 1877-1879 when Kirkpatrick served as headmaster at Lurgan College in Northern Ireland.[23] Their entire household bore the stamp of this great intellectual and teacher.

Prior to Kirkpatrick, Lewis had had horrible experiences in horrible boarding schools. They weren't attractive or comfortable places, but that wasn't the real problem. The fact is that Lewis was a serious, bookish student, and the schools he was sent to just didn't challenge him much. He was intellectually hungry, and these schools failed to feed his mind.

---

[21] C. S. Lewis, *The Collected Letters of C. S. Lewis*, ed. by Walter Hooper, 3 vols. (San Francisco: HarperCollins, 2004-7), 1:995.

[22] Lewis, *Surprised by Joy*, 133.

[23] Walter Hooper, *C. S. Lewis: A Companion and Guide* (New York, HarperCollins: 1996), 685.

In 1914, when Lewis was sent from Northern Ireland to England to be tutored by William Kirkpatrick, he was ready. Kirkpatrick was a genius with a large and extravagant personality. The Lewis family referred to him as The Great Knock, and Lewis said that lessons with him were like "red meat and strong beer."[24] Another of Kirkpatrick's students described him as "a man of unusual mental power" and says that he had a level of "intellectual honesty and vigour before which pretence and make believe were dissipated like smoke before a strong wind."[25]

Kirkpatrick was trained in ethics, oriental languages, biblical criticism, ecclesiastical history, and rhetoric, some of the same subjects that were to define much of Lewis's own sphere of interests. What else did Lewis learn from his teacher Kirkpatrick? His clarity of thought, his passion for argument and debate, his grasp on logic, perhaps even his notoriously shabby way of dressing—all were gifts of his two years living and studying with The Great Knock. In *Surprised by Joy*, Lewis devotes an entire chapter to his teacher, concluding with this: "My debt to him is very great, my reverence to this day undiminished."[26]

That is vast, unqualified praise. But perhaps an even better summary of Kirkpatrick's influence is captured in the following excerpt. It comes from a letter written by Lewis to his father upon hearing the news that Kirkpatrick has died:

> Poor old Kirk! What shall one say of Him? It would be a poor compliment to that memory to be sentimental: indeed, if it were possible, he would himself return to chide the absurdity. It is however no sentiment but the plainest fact to say that I at least owe to him in the intellectual sphere as much as one human being can owe another. That he enabled me to win a Scholarship is the least that he did for me. It was an atmosphere of unrelenting clearness and rigid honesty of thought that one breathed from living with him—and this I shall be the better for as long as I live.[27]

---

[24] Lewis, *Surprised by Joy*, 136.

[25] Robert M. Jones, *Royal Belfast Academical Institutions: Centenary Volume 1810-1910* (Belfast: M'Caw, Stevenson and Orr, 1913), 122.

[26] Lewis, *Surprised by Joy*, 148.

[27] Lewis, *Collected Letters*, 1:535.

CONCLUSION

Using a passage from *The Four Loves* and observations from Charles Lamb as our starting point, I have argued that C. S. Lewis was changed in significant ways by time spent with others. I have called this kind of influence "The Algebra of Friendship." There are unexpected factors and puzzling combinations. There are complex variables that change through a very simple process of subtraction, addition, multiplication, and division. When you change one letter or alter one number, it has lasting implications to other parts of the equation, up and down the line.

The Algebra of Friendship. I believe it is a useful concept. It helps us to factor the building blocks of our days, our lives, our friends, and our influences. It helps us understand something of C. S. Lewis, what sort of man he was, what sort of life he had. It gives us a greater sense of the context within which his gifts and talents were cultivated and his weaknesses were overcome.

As a young boy, he was drawn into collaboration with his older brother Warren, a creative companion, a fellow artist and a comrade in adventures, the one who taught him to connect with someone very different, to allow iron to sharpen iron, and to see how profound difference can be the spark to brand new ideas.

In his teens, he connected with Arthur Greeves. Arthur was his first friend, who taught him to closely connect with another much like himself, to share the whole contents of his heart, and also see and appreciate everyday beauty in ordinary things. Arthur taught him charity.

When he was sent away to England to study, he met William Kirkpatrick, and the intellectual life opened before him, his old ways of thinking dissipated like smoke before a strong wind, and his intellect grew clear and sharp and strong.

And if we had more time, we could examine other great influencers who shaped his personality and changed the trajectory of his life. Lewis learned much from other great friends, people like J. R. R. Tolkien, Owen Barfield, Charles Williams, Dorothy L. Sayers, Ruth Pitter, Joy Davidman, and so many more.

Looking at Lewis through this lens helps us understand the effect of others on his life. And it may also help us in our own journey of self-discovery as we think about the human personality less in terms that are static and individual and more in terms that are dynamic and transactional. Lewis was certainly one of the most influential thinkers of the twentieth century, and he continues to influence readers around the world through his books. Lewis has that kind of influence on others because of the ways that others influenced him.

Another implication of this way of thinking comes to mind: who are we influencing? How are we making a difference in the people around us? Each of us has the power to call forth and bless the gifts we see in the people around us, gifts that might not be awakened unless someone is there to recognize them, encourage them, bless them, even challenge and develop them.

In "The Weight of Glory," Lewis declares "There are no ordinary people."[28] You are not ordinary. The siblings you grew up with and that neighbor you have known since grade school are not ordinary. That spouse whom you have shared a thousand cups of coffee with is not ordinary. The stranger sitting across the way from you right now is not ordinary. Lewis says that all day long, every day, we are urging each other in one direction or another, toward either heavenly things or hellish ones. All of us, all day long, helping one another in what we are becoming.

The Algebra of Friendship. It is kind of exponential magic, a synergy that brings forth something greater. It is evident in Lewis's life and in our own. And there are hints of the concept in the roots of the words themselves. "Algebra" is a late Middle English word, derived from the Arabic word "al-jabr" which means "the reunion of broken parts." Its original sense is the "treatment of fractures" or "the setting of broken bones."[29] The mathematical sense of the word comes from the *Hisab al-Jabr w' al-Muqabala* written by the mathematician al-Khwarizmi. *Hisab al-Jabr w' al-Muqabala* means "the science of restoring what is missing."[30]

This perhaps recalls the words of the Apostle Paul, who refers to Christ as "the head, from whom the whole body, nourished and held together by its ligaments and sinews, grows with a growth that is from God" (Colossians 2:19). Here, the word translated "held together" is

---

[28] C. S. Lewis, "The Weight of Glory" in *The Weight of Glory and Other Essays* (New York: HarperCollins, 1976), 46.

[29] "Algebra." *Oxford Dictionaries: Language Matters.* http://www.oxforddictionaries.com/us/definition/american_english/algebra.

[30] Alan Pimm-Smith, "From Ar'a bic to Eng'lish."*Aramcoworld: Arab and Islamic Cultures and Connections.* http://archive.aramcoworld.com/issue/200702/from.arabic.to.english.htm.

the word that describes a physician setting a broken bone or restoring a limb out of joint.

Bringing together. Repairing what is broken. Treating fractures. Bringing restoration. Calling forth what is strong and noble in one another. Making us whole. It seems to me to be a fitting description of the expansive and healing function of friendship, in Lewis's personality and our own.[31]

---

[31] I would like to thank Brian Eck, who read the very first draft of this essay and responded with encouragement and generous advice; Linda Spitser, my mentor, editor, and friend; Doug Jackson, Hannah Thomas, and Bethany Wagner for feedback on an early draft; and Stan Mattson, Gayne Anaker, and the rest of the staff of the C. S. Lewis Foundation for hosting Oxbridge 2008, where a version of this essay was first presented.

Chapter 3

C. S. LEWIS IN AMERICA, 1933-1943

Mark A. Noll

The July/August 2012 number of *Touchstone: A Journal of Mere Christianity* provided full but inadvertent evidence for the comprehensive popularity that C. S. Lewis has gained in American Christian circles. None of the issue's articles, reviews, or editorials featured Lewis as such, but, besides the evocation of his work in the journal's subtitle, he was nonetheless cited at least twenty-two separate times throughout the magazine.[1]

These references linked Lewis with Charles Colson, Thomas Howard, Michael Ward, Wendell Berry, and St. John Chrysostom. Mention of specific works included *Mere Christianity*, the Narnia tales, *An Experiment in Criticism*, and *The Abolition of Man*. The many citations, in keeping with the goal of *Touchstone* to advance "mere Christianity," came from Roman Catholic, Anglican, generic evangelical, and unspecified contexts. As suggested by this example, the nearly universal recognition and strongly pan-denominational appeal of C. S. Lewis goes on and on and on as a remarkable fact of recent Christian history throughout the English-speaking world and beyond. But it was not always so.

On October 29, 1944, Lewis penned a long letter to Charles Brady, chair of the English department at Canisius College in Buffalo. Brady was not the first American with whom Lewis had corresponded, but there were not many others before him. The letter is important, for in it Lewis claimed that a two-part article that Brady had recently published qualified the American as "the first of my critics so far who has really read and understood *all* of my books and 'made up' the subject in a way that makes you an authority."[2] Earlier there had been some notice of Lewis and his writing, with an unprecedented burst of American interest only the year before in 1943, but, again, nothing

---

[1] *Touchstone: A Journal of Mere Christianity*, 25.4 (July/August 2012): 3, 4 (3 references), 5, 7, 8 (two references), 14, 22, 23, 24, 35, 37, 39 (2 references), 42, 52, 53, 58, 59.

[2] C. S. Lewis, *The Collected Letters of C. S. Lewis*, ed. by Walter Hooper, 3 vols. (San Francisco: HarperCollins, 2004-7), 1:629.

like the all-points attention that has obtained in the last few decades.

As a telling indication concerning Lewis's early American readers, Charles Brady was a forthright Catholic layman who had already published stories for children and historical novels with Catholic themes; shortly after corresponding with Lewis he edited an anthology of modern Catholic writing.[3] His essays on Lewis had appeared in *America*, a journal sponsored by the U.S. Jesuit community.[4] Brady's articles were the high point of what had already become a sustained Catholic engagement—highly appreciative, but not uncritical—of Lewis's published oeuvre. Besides this early Catholic interest, the other prime sources of attention to the Oxford don were the high-brow national press and mainline Protestants. By contrast, through the mid-1940s Lewis had received only passing attention from confessional, evangelical, or fundamentalist Protestants; moreover, early notice of Lewis from those quarters was not only spotty, but also ambiguous about how Lewis and his writing should be evaluated. In other words, by 1943 the broad Christian approval of Lewis lay still in the future.

Although early twentieth-century American critical attention is one of the few topics concerning C. S. Lewis that has not received focused study, it is nonetheless a useful subject. Documentation of Lewis's early reception in America, which will take up the bulk of this chapter, may help clarify the picture of what first made Lewis attractive, and for whom. The ending date for this investigation is 1943, by which time he had established a secure American presence. Four years later he would be featured on the cover of *Time* magazine, with universal appeal coming even later after the publication of *The Lion, the Witch, and the Wardrobe* and the revision of his "Broadcast Talks" under the title *Mere Christianity*. Yet earlier American Lewis criticism may also do more insofar as attention to that criticism

---

[3] Charles Brady, *Cat Royal* (New York: Sheed & Ward, 1947); *Stage of Fools* [fictionalizing Thomas More] (New York: Dutton, 1953); ed., *A Catholic Reader* (Buffalo: Desmond & Stapleton, 1947), which begins with Brady explaining that, while "an embattled Church Militant" has needed to publish polemical writing "since that far-off day when Martin Luther nailed his theses to the church door at Wittenberg," he wanted to show that Catholics could write noteworthy literature, exposition, poetry, anecdote, etc. that did not major in controversy (ix).

[4] Charles Brady, "Introduction to Lewis," in *America*, 71 (27 May 1944), 213-14; "C. S. Lewis II," in *America*, 71 (10 June 1944), 269-70

suggests a good deal about the general state of Christianity in the United States during the 1930s and 1940s, a subject that is treated briefly at the close of this chapter.

The first decade of Lewis's reception in America divides naturally into two distinct periods. From 1933 and the U.K. publication of *Pilgrim's Regress* by Dent to February 16, 1943, when Macmillan brought out an American edition of *The Screwtape Letters*, there existed an intriguing but small literary and religious response. Then the year 1943 became an *annus mirabilis*, with a broad range of literary and religious treatments of the several Lewis books that appeared in the U.S. that year. Thereafter began the Lewis Wave where both scholars and journalists devoted increasing attention to works that were published earlier as well as to the books that made their first American appearance in those years, including his space trilogy, more Broadcast Talks, *The Great Divorce*, *Miracles*, and *The Abolition of Man*.[5]

Lewis's first serious American reader seems to have been Paul Elmer More, a scholar, journalist, and eccentric Christian apologist whom Lewis met in Oxford in 1933.[6] More was a student of Sanskrit, literary critic, friend of Irving Babbitt, author of books on Greek philosophy, and supporter of Babbitt's "new humanism" with whom Lewis seems to have hit it off immediately. They exchanged complementary letters about each other's writings—Lewis on More's *The Skeptical Approach to Religion*, which defended Christianity against its modernist interpreters, and More on Lewis's essay that first attacked E. M. Tillyard for "The Personal Heresy."[7] Although they disagreed on important matters—Lewis defended Greek philosophical idealism as a possible way to the God of Christianity, which More disparaged, and More valued T. S. Eliot's work, which Lewis did not—, Lewis obviously found More's defense of Christian faith appealing as More set out that defense in a complex relationship to the main traditions of classical western philosophy. More, however, passed away in 1937, only shortly after Lewis's books began to come out in America.

---

[5] All information on the publication of Lewis's books is from Walter Hooper, *C. S. Lewis: A Complete Guide to His Life and Works* (New York: HarperSanFrancisco, 1996), esp. 801-5 for dates of publication in both the U.K. and U.S. through 1947.

[6] Biographical details are supplied in Bruce C. Lambert, "The Regrettable Silence of Paul Elmer More," in *Modern Age* 41 (Winter 1999), 47-54, with 52-53 on More and Lewis.

[7] Lewis, *Collected Letters*, 1:145-6, 156-8, 163-5.

Published American interest came in response to two kinds of writing. For literary scholars, Oxford University Press made books available in the U.S. that appeared from its London and Oxford offices: *The Allegory of Love* (1936), *Rehabilitations and Other Essays* (1938), *The Personal Heresy* (1939), and *A Preface to Paradise Lost* (1942). For the public at large, the firm of Frank Sheed and Maisie Ward, which was noteworthy for promoting books by serious lay Catholics, sparked considerable interest when in 1935 it made *The Pilgrim's Regress* the first of Lewis's books to be readily available in America.

Of the literary titles, *The Allegory of Love* was praised by a reviewer in the *American Historical Review* for its insights into medieval history but shredded by another critic in *Speculum* for misreading crucial Chaucerian texts.[8] Two scholars read more deeply to catch the theological implications of Lewis's literary argument. In an article in *The Journal of Modern History*, Roland Bainton, more than a decade before he won lasting renown for his biography of Martin Luther, grasped that Lewis was praising Edmund Spenser as "the pioneer in uniting the courtly tradition of the romance of unwedded love with the Christian standard of monogamy."[9] Then in an article on Chaucer's "Troilus and Criseyde," Karl Young of the Yale University English department, with whom Lewis enjoyed a warm personal and epistolary relationship, understood that Lewis in writing about Chaucer intended to counteract the literary exaltation of extra-marital romance.[10] Lewis's book, *The Personal Heresy*, in which he argued for the preeminence of a poem's object, rather than the personality of the poet, as the most important thing in poetry, also elicited learned American reaction, including from Arthur O. Lovejoy in a discussion of poetic criticism.[11]

---

[8] Gray C. Boyce, Review of *The Allegory of Love*, by C. S. Lewis, in *American Historical Review*, 43 (October 1937), 103-4; Howard R. Patch, Review of *The Allegory of Love*, by C. S. Lewis, in *Speculum*, 12 (Apr. 1937), 272-4.

[9] Roland Bainton, "Changing Ideas and Ideals in the Sixteenth Century," in *Journal of Modern History*, 8 (Dec. 1936), 438.

[10] Karl Young, "Chaucer's 'Troilus and Criseyde' as Romance," in *PMLA*, 53 (March 1938), 40-1, 46. See also Lewis to Young, 7 Apr. 1943; and the consoling letter to Young's widow, 6 Apr. 1944. Lewis, *Collected Letters*, 1:567-8, 611.

[11] Arthur O. Lovejoy, "Reflections on the History of Ideas," In *Journal of the History of Ideas*, 1 (January 1940), 10. Lovejoy's essay appeared as the first article in this first issue of *Journal of the History of Ideas*, which

But far and away the most intriguing of all the American responses to Lewis's early literary work was a substantial review of *The Personal Heresy* by Thomas Merton that appeared in the *New York Times*. This review was published in July 1939, less than a year after Merton had sought Catholic baptism and eighteen months before he entered the Cistercian Abbey of Our Lord of Gethsemani in Kentucky. Perhaps more clearly than Lewis himself had stated this matter in the book, Merton summarized its argument like this: Lewis has shown the weakness of modern views, which take for granted that poems exist for contemplation by a higher order of humanity in order to exhibit the poet's personality; Lewis, by contrast, wanted all people of whatever rank to read poems as referring primarily to the poems' objects. To Merton, "Mr. Lewis is using the term 'heresy' not ironically but in the technical Catholic sense."[12] Whether or not Lewis intended to be that specific, it is noteworthy that this Catholic convert recognized the theological message in Lewis's literary work that few readers then, and not too many since, have been able to spell out so clearly. It is the message that human insights, achievements, and breakthroughs are best understood as reflecting an external reality rather than the genius of the human author.

Manifest theological assessment, by contrast, was front and center in American responses to *The Pilgrim's Regress*. For the larger meaning of the survey in this chapter, it is significant that there was confusion among readers, along with consternation from the author, when Sheed & Ward's publicity for the book implied that it documented Lewis's rejection of Ulster Protestantism ("Puritania") for Roman Catholicism ("Mother Kirk"). The first American appearance of the book seems to have been a Sheed & Ward advertisement in the *New York Times* in November 1935 that promoted Lewis's book alongside Evelyn Waugh's biography of the Catholic martyr Edmund Campion as well as new works by G. K. Chesterton and Christopher Dawson— in other words, an all-star lineup of famous Catholic authors.[13] The positive review that appeared in the *Times* only two weeks later praised Lewis's literary skill as an allegorist and for his prose: "plain,

---

went on to become a distinguished academic publication.

[12] Thomas Merton, Review of *The Personal Heresy*, by C. S. Lewis and E. N. W. Tillyard, in *New York Times*, 9 July 1939, 16-17.

[13] Sheed & Ward, Advertisement for *The Pilgrim's Regress*, in *New York Times Book Review*, 24 November 1935, 22.

straightforward and leanly significant." But it also offered a general endorsement of the book's substance: "To those not convincingly materialistic in their outlook it will give new viewpoints. To many it will seem like a fresh wind blowing across arid wastes."[14]

Shortly thereafter followed two enthusiastic Catholic reviews. A Jesuit writing in *America* pointed to the crucial significance of the baptism undergone by the allegory's protagonist before lauding the book's "telling but not bitter satire, skilful diagnosis of philosophical pathology, together with the art of religiotherapy, the ability to personify concretely the aery vagaries of paranoiac geniuses, and the cartoonist's grasp of what is characteristic."[15] In *The Catholic World*, a Paulist father offered even warmer words of praise: "This brilliantly written volume is a caustic, devastating critique of modern philosophy, religion, politics and art; a clear-cut, logical and effective apologia of reason and the Christian faith . . .. We have rarely read a book we so thoroughly enjoyed."[16]

The book's appearance from Sheed and Ward and its allegorical depiction of "Mother Kirk"—combined with these strong Catholic encomia—created a misunderstanding for one evangelical Protestant in the most interesting early American review of *The Pilgrim's Regress*. That review appeared in the June 22, 1936, number of *The Presbyterian Guardian*, a magazine devoted to the interests of conservatives who were in the process of leaving the main body of northern Presbyterians to form a denomination that would soon be called the Orthodox Presbyterian Church. The author was Henry Welbon, a minister who would himself experience a church lock-out, legal tussles, and much local controversy when he tried to take his congregation into the new church body.[17] The review appeared on a page that also listed the names of commissioners to the first general assembly of the new denomination, a roll that included J. Oliver Buswell, Jr.,

---

[14] Jane Spencer Southron, Review of *The Pilgrim's Regress*, by C. S. Lewis, in *New York Times Book Review*, 8 December 1935, 7.

[15] Stewart Dollard, Review of *The Pilgrim's Regress*, by C. S. Lewis, in *America*, 54 (4 Jan. 1936), 305.

[16] Bertrand L. Conway, CSP (as B. L. C.), Review of *The Pilgrim's Regress*, by C. S. Lewis, in *The Catholic World*, 143 (May 1936), 239-40.

[17] Henry G. Welbon, Review of *The Pilgrim's Regress*, by C. S. Lewis, in *Presbyterian Guardian*, 2 (22 June 1936), 117, 141. The lock-out occurred shortly after the review appeared. See http://www.thisday.pcahistory.org/2013/08/august-3/.

Franklin Dyrness, Robert Graham, Edwin Rian, and Gordon Clark. Appended to that roll were the names of several ministers who had attended this first general assembly with the intention of joining the new denomination, including the Rev. Cornelius Van Til and the Rev. Robert Marsden. The issue opened by reprinting an address that J. Gresham Machen, the driving force behind the establishment of this new church, had delivered to the first General Assembly, which had finished its work only days before the appearance of this issue, "A True Presbyterian Church at Last;" the issue closed with several news reports of local congregations trying to withdraw from the northern Presbyterian denomination, including one with the headline "Philadelphia Presbytery Adopts Hitler Methods."[18]

This arcane denominational history is relevant for Henry Welbon's review of Lewis's book, first, because of where the review appeared. In an ecclesiastical landscape where almost all early attention to Lewis came from Catholics, mainline Protestants, literary critics, and the mainstream media, the one conservative Protestant commentary that took any notice of Lewis was the confessional Presbyterians associated with the Orthodox Presbyterian Church. But, second, reaction from that source was striking for the way in which it combined startled approval with serious reservations. The Rev. Welbon identified Lewis as "an Englishman who is a Roman Catholic," but praised the book for exposing "the fallacies of various philosophies throughout the world today" with "lucid arguments in simple direct sentences." At a time when most fundamentalist, evangelical, and confessional American Protestants still regarded Catholicism with abhorrence, this one small group of conservative Presbyterians was a partial exception, in large part because of what J. Gresham Machen had written in his much-publicized book from 1923, *Christianity and Liberalism*. The burden of that work was a forthright indictment of all forms of Protestant modernism as anti-Christian, but along the way Machen paused to assert the unconventional opinion that confessional Protestants shared much more with traditional Catholics than they did with liberal Protestants.[19] That argument was opening enough for Welbon to

---

[18] *Presbyterian Guardian*, 2 (22 June 1936), 110 [Machen], 142 [Hitler].

[19] J. Gresham Machen, *Christianity and Liberalism* (New York: Macmillan, 1923), 52.

conclude his review with these words: "Although we do not agree with the author's theology, nevertheless there is much that we have in common with the message of his book. We greatly appreciated this unusual style of exposing the fallacies of unbelief."[20]

A most interesting sequel followed the publication of this review. Apparently Welbon sent it to Lewis with a request for more information about the author. Lewis's reply of September 18, 1936 immediately set Welbon straight on the facts: Lewis was "born in Belfast" (and so only ambiguously English) and was "an Anglican Layman" (and so not a Roman Catholic). But Lewis also took responsibility for "the mistake which led you, and has led others, to make me a Papist" due to his allegorical depiction of "Mother Kirk." With friends, Lewis was blunter in blaming Sheed & Ward for this mix-up.[21] But in replying to the American Welbon, Lewis set out in 1936 what would eventually become the gist of "Mere Christianity." After telling how his own journey to faith had been guided by an Anthroposophist (Owen Barfield, whom he did not name,), the Presbyterian George MacDonald, the Catholic Dante, and another unnamed Catholic (J. R. R. Tolkien), he then explained why he was "at home" with this ecclesiastical mish-mash: "they are all alike 'evangelical' in the Pauline sense, all concerned with the 'new creature,' and also because they are all genuine *supernaturalists*."[22] In sum, however, the really interesting thing about the Welbon review was that it represented the sole early notice of Lewis from the broadly evangelical part of the American religious landscape. The next such notice would not appear until seven

---

[20] Welbon, Review of *The Pilgrim's Regress*, 141.

[21] Lewis to Arthur Greeves, 7 Dec. 1935 in Lewis, *Collected Letters*, 1:170. "My other bit of literary news is that Sheed and Ward have bought the *Regress* from Dent. I didn't much like having a book of mine, and specially a religious book, brought out by a Papist publisher: but as they seemed to think they could sell it, and Dents clearly couldn't, I gave in. I have been well punished: for Sheed, without any authority from me, has put a blurb on the inside of the jacket which says 'This story begins in Puritania (Mr. Lewis was brought up in Ulster)'—thus implying that the book is an attack on my own country and my own religion. If you ever come across any one who might be interested, explain as loudly as you can that I was not consulted & that the blurb is a damnable lie told to try and make Dublin riff-raff buy the book."

[22] C. S. Lewis, Letter to Henry Welbon, 18 Sept. 1936, C. S. Lewis Letter Collection, Marion E. Wade Center, Wheaton College, Wheaton, Illinois.

more years had passed.

Significantly, American attention to Lewis in the years before the publication of *The Screwtape Letters* set a pattern that would continue into the late 1940s: positive and even sometimes enthusiastic attention from a range of upscale media and mainstream Protestants, deeper and more explicitly theological engagement from Roman Catholics, considerably less notice from sectarian or conservative Protestants.

The American love affair with C. S. Lewis began in 1943 with a burst of positive responses to *The Screwtape Letters* but then followed rapidly by wide and deep engagement with an ever-expanding corpus of his writing. The bean counters at Macmillan, which replaced Sheed & Ward as Lewis's American publisher and would continue as such through the Narnia books, knew they had a hot commodity on their hands as soon as their edition of *The Screwtape Letters* appeared on February 16, 1943. The *New York Times* reported in early July that the book had already gone into its sixth printing.[23] In an effort to exploit that enthusiastic response, Macmillan mobilized quickly to publish *The Case for Christianity* on September 7 (earlier brought out as *Broadcast Talks* in the U.K.), *Out of the Silent Planet* on September 28 (which had appeared five years earlier in Britain), and *The Problem of Pain* on October 26 (three years after its British publication).

Before the end of the year, North American writers, working rapidly, published a wealth of reviews and other miscellaneous notices.[24] Besides a few reviews of *The Problem of Pain*, one of *Perelandra* (that came out before the American edition was published), and several discussions of Lewis in general articles, there were at least eight reviews of *The Case for Christianity*, thirteen for *Out of the Silent Planet*, and an extraordinary twenty-one for *The Screwtape Letters*. In this cornucopia of attention, the same patterns prevailed as in the previous period, with the one major addition being somewhat more notice from the Protestant mainstream.

---

[23] "Books-Authors" (advertisement for *The Screwtape Letters*), in *New York Times*, 8 July 1943, 17.

[24] Included as "North American" are several positive reviews from the *Queen's Quarterly* (Kingston, Ontario), which reviewed a British edition of *The Screwtape Letters* in December 1942: N. M., review, in *Queen's Quarterly*, 49 (1942), 285-6, as part of a longer essay-review that included also Dorothy L. Sayers' *The Mind of the Maker*, 286-7.

For Americans throughout 1943, Lewis as the Oxford literary scholar receded far into the background.[25] Instead, once Macmillan published *The Screwtape Letters* it was C. S. Lewis as allegorist, Christian apologist, and science fiction author who emerged as an instant sensation—except, it appears, among conservative Protestants.

From the standpoint of simply being noticed, the most remarkable thing about American Lewis-attention in 1943 was his enthusiastic reception in the mainstream public media. While deep engagement was rare, enthusiasm for Lewis ran high. The reviewer of *Screwtape* for the *Atlanta Constitution* was Louie Newton, who at the time was serving as vice-president of the Baptist World Alliance. In his delight, Newton was only slightly more ecstatic than others in the mainstream press: "*The Screwtape Letters* . . . is the most intriguing book I have read this year. These brilliant challenging letters . . . are vital restatements of religious truth—a profound, hard-hitting, yet truly reverent book."[26] Significantly, reviews in the *New York Times*, the *Saturday Review*, and the *Los Angeles Times* highlighted the message of *Screwtape* as an antidote to Nazism. In the words of Paul Jordan-Smith of the *L.A. Times*, who would go on to write many positive notices of Lewis's books, "At an hour when Hitler and his anti-Christianity are so closely identified this book comes as a humorous and brilliant antidote to certain forms of German propaganda."[27]

After Macmillan rushed *Out of the Silent Planet* into print, the response was almost as positive. Praise cascaded in from *Time* ("as pitted with morality as *Pilgrim's Progress*'")[28] and the *New York Herald Tribune* ("a delightful fantasy . . . excellent escape fiction as well as . . . criticism of modern life").[29] It also came from the *Chicago Daily Tribune*,

---

[25] Literary criticism seems to have been limited to brief favorable references to *A Preface to Paradise Lost* in the *New York Times* Book Review (review by Edward Wagenknecht [23 May 1943], 17) and the theological-literary quarterly from Queen's University, Ontario, entitled the *Queen's Quarterly* (50 [1943], 103); and another reference to Lewis's account of "the personal heresy," also in the *New York Times* Book Review (by H. W. Horwill, "News and Views of Literary London," [24 Jan. 1943], 16.

[26] Louise Newton, Review of *The Screwtape Letters*, by C. S. Lewis, in *Atlanta Constitution*, 3 March 1943, 7.

[27] Paul Jordan-Smith, Review of *The Screwtape Letters*, by C. S. Lewis, in *Los Angeles Times*, 7 March 1943.

[28] Review of *Out of the Silent Planet*, by C. S. Lewis, in *Time* (11 October 1943), 102.

[29] Charles Nieder, Review of *Out of the Silent Planet*, by C. S. Lewis,

the *Chicago Sun*, *Library Journal*, *The Nation*, *Saturday Review*, and the *Springfield Republican*. Only from the *New York Times* did a balancing word of criticism appear. After Horace Reynolds, an English professor at Brown and Harvard, had likened the book favorably to *Gulliver's Travels* and works by H. G. Wells and John Milton, he opined that the conclusion was disappointing for leaving readers with little sense of how "the wise ruler of Malacandra," Oyarsa, along with "Mr. Lewis," would provide deliverance "from evil."[30]

Attention to other Lewis books from the mainstream media in 1943 was not as extensive as to *Screwtape* and *Out of the Silent Planet*. But the *Christian Science Monitor* obtained a copy of *Perelandra* for favorable notice while the book was still awaiting American publication.[31] Early reviews of books that would be treated more thoroughly in years to come were mixed. Writing in the *New York Herald*, John Haynes Holmes, an indefatigable Unitarian reformer who helped to found both the NAACP and the ACLU, praised *The Case for Christianity* for its clear depiction of the natural law but then scored the second half of Lewis's presentation for "an almost incredibly naïve statement of Christian theology."[32] Only six weeks later and in the same newspaper, George Shuster was unreservedly positive about *The Problem of Pain*. To Shuster, a Catholic who had already served many years as editor of *Commonweal* before becoming president of Hunter College, Lewis "succeeded in making all these points [about the place of pain in the general scheme of things] in terms of orthodox Christianity with unusual effectiveness." Shuster compared Lewis favorably with Baron von Hügel, the first Catholic to receive an honorary doctorate from Oxford since the Reformation, and said that Lewis displayed commendable awareness of "the great sources from which the English spiritual tradition is derived," specifying Aristotle, Aquinas, and Augustine.[33]

---

in *New York Herald Tribune Book Review*, 3 Oct. 1943, 12, 14.

[30] Horace Reynolds, Review of *Out of the Silent Planet*, by C. S. Lewis, in *New York Times Book Review*, 3 October 1943, 16,

[31] Harold Hobson, Review of *Perelandra*, in *Christian Science Monitor*, 5 June 1943, 11.

[32] John Haynes Holmes, Review of *The Case for Christianity*, by C. S. Lewis, in *New York Herald Book Review*, 14 November 1943, 42.

[33] George N. Shuster, Review of *The Problem of Pain*, by C. S. Lewis, in *New York Herald Book Review*, 26 December 1943, 6.

Alongside the Catholic George Shuster's positive evaluation in a mainstream newspaper, opinion from Catholic periodicals was just as positive. A Jesuit, in fact, seems to have published the first review of *Screwtape* in the United States, which appeared one month before Macmillan released the book: "The analysis of diabolical temptation is keen, shrewd and helpful, and appears faultless from the viewpoint of Catholic doctrine."[34] *Screwtape* was also praised by one of the few reviewers who did not like *Out of the Silent Planet*. In December, this reviewer in *The Catholic World* complained about the novel's weak plot, before concluding that it lacked "that suave, sometimes profound commentary on life to be found in the author's *Screwtape Letters*."[35] Yet only shortly before, a brief notice in *Commonweal* had come to the opposite critical judgment: "there is just enough ethics and not too much; just enough story and not too much. He has moved onto one of the most honored and exclusive shelves of literary achievement, and done it with equal humor and wisdom."[36]

Especially prominent from American Catholics in 1943 was appreciation for Lewis's exposition of universal natural law, or the Tao, that he developed in the first part of *The Case for Christianity*. The reviewer in *America* wrote approvingly about how Lewis "with irresistible logic leads us to the universal Natural Law, our fallen condition and the existence of the supernatural. In the second series [of talks] he shows Christianity as the most satisfying answer to our human dilemmas."[37] In *The Catholic World* a Paulist philosopher described the work as "this gem of apologetics" and praised Lewis for his attention to "the basic natural law," particularly in a day of "barbarism and inhumanity" resulting from "the revolt from the Church, the rejection of Christ, the loss or the neglect of God." This same reviewer went out of his way to tell readers that a Catholic priest had vetted the proofs of this book, before the reviewer offered a judgment that summarized general Catholic approbation: "If this is not the book that a Catholic would have written, it says very many

---

[34] John F. Dwyer, S.J., Review of *The Screwtape Letters*, by C. S. Lewis, in *Thought* 18 (January 1943), 364.

[35] N. E. Monroe, Review of *Out of the Silent Planet*, by C. S. Lewis, in *The Catholic World*, 158 (December 1943), 314.

[36] Christopher Morley, Review of *Out of the Silent Planet*, by C. S. Lewis, in *Commonweal*, (29 October 1943), 45-6.

[37] Charles Keenan, Review of *The Case for Christianity*, by C. S. Lewis, in *America* (18 September 1943), 664.

things that desperately need to be said. Armies of men are groping their way back to the religion of Christ; this book will facilitate greatly that sacred journey."[38]

By comparison with Catholic reaction, the opinion of most mainline Protestants was just as enthusiastic, although this corner of the American ecclesiastical world also offered the frankest criticism to appear in that notable year. Notices of Lewis books in *The Christian Herald* were very brief but uniformly positive. This monthly was edited by Daniel Poling, a strong advocate of prohibition, champion of Christian Endeavor, and a preacher designated by the Federal Council of Churches for early radio broadcasts on the National Broadcasting Company.[39] Poling found *The Screwtape Letters* "an extraordinary little book" with "real understanding of spiritual struggles," and he judged that *The Case for Christianity* "succeeds" in presenting "the vital and timeless proof of our universal Christian faith."[40]

The Christian Century, under the guidance of its long-time editor Charles Morrison, offered more reserved judgments. Its review of *The Case for Christianity* said that Lewis capitalized successfully on his status as a layman in stressing "the note of plain common sense," an effort that to this reviewer had not been particularly effective in *The Screwtape Letters* "in which his whimsicality was rather labored."[41]

More serious criticism came when the *Century* reviewed *The Problem of Pain*. Talmage C. Johnson, a North Carolina Baptist minister, noted what he called the "vogue" for Lewis in the U.S. but concluded that it was time to get past fascination with his "somewhat unusual style and penchant for twisting old doctrines into new and somewhat startling shapes." Then, while Johnson approved much that Lewis wrote early in that book, he did not at all like the chapter on

---

[38] James J. Maguire, CSP, Review of *The Case for Christianity*, by C. S. Lewis, in *The Catholic World*, 158 (Nov. 1943), 215-16.

[39] My thanks to Kirk Farney for the biographical information on Poling.

[40] Daniel Poling, Review of *The Screwtape Letters*, by C. S. Lewis in *The Christian Herald*, (April 1943), 58; Daniel Poling, Review of *The Case for Christianity*, by C. S. Lewis, in *The Christian Herald*, (December 1943), 70. *The Christian Herald* also included a short positive notice of *Out of the Silent Planet* by Frank S. Mead, long-serving editor of Revell Books and an editor of reference books on the American churches (December 1943), 68, 70.

[41] Charles Morrison, Review of *The Case for* Christianity, by C. S. Lewis, in *Christian Century*, 60.39 (29 September 1943), 1105.

animal pain, which he called "rather unconvincing," "hardly above superstition," and "meaningless, or else naïve." Johnson closed by criticizing Lewis for "low regard of the human race," a fault pardonable in the satire of *The Screwtape Letters* but not "in this more serious treatment of human suffering."[42] For the *Century*, these notices from 1943 represented the start of an ongoing ambiguous assessment.

One other mainline Protestant periodical expanded Lewis's American footprint when the Methodist-sponsored *Religion in Life* published Lewis's own paper, "The Poison of Subjectivism," Lewis's first writing to be published initially in this country.[43] Against all forms of modern relativism, this essay defended the objective character of moral values, which Lewis described as essential grounding for the personality traits of "virtue, knowledge, diligence and skill,"[44] It was an extension of the argument in the first half of *The Case for Christianity* that Lewis now advanced more generally through the pages of this Protestant periodical.

Finally, late in 1943 appeared the second published notice of Lewis in an evangelical outlet. A two-paragraph review in *The Moody Monthly* praised *The Case for Christianity* as "another stimulating and thought-provoking book" from an author who was "a master of analogy"; it also lauded some of the book's arguments, especially how "crystal clear [it was] in affirming the deity of Christ." Yet in a review where the tone was more welcoming than the *Christian Century*'s treatment of *The Problem of Pain*, this anonymous author nonetheless aired substantial reservations about aspects of the book that were "open to question." Those reservations are worth quoting in their entirety:

> Some Protestants would brand as sacramentalism the assertion that "baptism, belief, and . . . holy communion" are "conductors of the new kind of life" (p. 52). He speaks of losing the Christ-life (which he defines elsewhere as "Christ . . . actually operating through them," (p. 53). He seems to say that atonement consists of Christ's making our repentance possible (p. 50). Some elucidation of the following sentence is desirable:

---

[42] Talmage C. Johnson, Review of *The Problem of Pain*, by C. S. Lewis, in *Christian Century*, 60.48 (1 December 1943), 1400.

[43] Walter Hooper, *C. S. Lewis: A Complete Guide to His Life and Works* (New York: HarperSanFranciso, 1996), 817-23.

[44] C. S. Lewis, "The Poison of Subjectivism," in *Religion in Life*, 12 (Summer 1943), 365.

"We do know that no man can be saved except through Christ; we don't know that only those who know Him can be saved through Him."[45]

When the review from *Moody Monthly* joined the chorus of American responses to C. S. Lewis, the pattern was set that prevailed for the next several years. For all five categories of opinion—literary, mainline media, Roman Catholics, mainline Protestants, and conservative Protestants—analytical criticism would deepen and there would be more instances of negative criticism. Literary scholars continued to respond without making too many connections between Lewis's professional scholarship and his avocational Christian writing. The mainstream media continued to offer an extraordinary range of responses, with the positive far outweighing the negative. Catholics remained highly appreciative, though with some push-back on questions of substance and more on questions of church authority. Mainline Protestants would soon provide the most substantial recommendations of Lewis's work along with some of the sharpest criticisms. And conservative Protestants continued to respond with both appreciative enthusiasm and cautious wariness. As the volume of American Lewis criticism increased dramatically in the years after 1943 and the American publication of *The Screwtape Letters*, his appeal continued to elicit a widening range of important commentary; it also revealed intriguing hints about the character of American religious life in those same years.

The detailed attention that American periodicals devoted to Lewis from the last years of World War Two through the end of the decade deserves as much careful attention as this chapter has given to American criticism to that time. But a few speculative impressions will have to suffice.

Well after the war came to an end, favorable attention to Lewis's work showed that Christianity continued to occupy a large residual place among many segments of the American population. Exuberant reception of *The Screwtape Letters* and then of Lewis's space trilogy, with the last volume *That Hideous Strength* published in the United States in 1946, facilitated, and then accompanied, a mostly positive reception of his didactic Christian expositions in the public at large. From the standpoint of the twenty-first century, the wide and

---

[45] Review of *The Case for Christianity*, by C. S. Lewis, in *Moody Monthly*, 44 (December 1943), 239.

overwhelmingly positive attention to his works in the mainstream secular media now seems remarkable. The only parallel phenomenon in recent years might be the similarly positive reception given to the frankly Christian books of Marilynne Robinson.

In the years before 1950, mainstream Protestants continued to appreciate Lewis, even as some voices in these quarters criticized the naïveté of his theology. Significantly, during this period, the most determined and most extensive promotion came from a mainstream Protestant author, the Episcopalian Chad Walsh.[46] His own *Early Christians of the 21ˢᵗ Century* appealed for a version of "mere Christianity" that referenced Lewis a couple of times, even as it made a Lewis-esque defense of the moral law. In his bold appeals for racial justice and a general world government to restrain war-like nations, Walsh did, however, address social concerns more directly than did the British author he promoted so vigorously.

Roman Catholicism, though, continued to be the tradition that most enthusiastically recommended Lewis, with Joseph Brady's two-part *America* article from 1944 the first full-scale appreciation. After a great deal of enthusiastic response, however, a few Catholics eventually commented that Lewis's works fell short of standard Catholic instruction, and a few were really upset at the enthusiasm of other Catholics for works by a non-Catholic. Catholic responses seem to have been as extensive for Lewis's imaginative works as for his discursive writings, with only very light attention to his literary scholarship. Lewis's stress on the Tao, or natural moral law, remained a notable point of attraction for Catholics.[47]

Among conservative or evangelical Protestants, ambiguity towards Lewis continued, though increasing approval did finally appear in a growing number of publications, especially for the verve of his Christian writing. Yet with less and less serious attention to Lewis than among Catholics or mainline Protestants, the post-fundamentalist legacy of separatism seems to have remained strong. Conservative Presbyterians, like the authors of the earliest notices in the *Westminster Theological Journal*, showed more interest than other evangelicals, but they also objected to some of Lewis's ideas. Even

---

[46] See especially Chad Walsh, *C. S. Lewis: Apostle to the Skeptics* (New York: Macmillan, 1949).

[47] This judgment comes from surveying thirty-four articles in Catholic publications from 1944 through 1949.

as they applauded Lewis's general orthodoxy, these Presbyterians continued to worry about what they considered Lewis's overly optimistic account of sinful human nature and his lack of precision on the atonement and the order of salvation in general. Only as the decade of the 1950s rolled on would evangelicals and other conservative Protestants begin their love affair with Lewis that has never ceased.

Attention to Lewis's American critics before the post-war years, therefore, does not predict very well the nature of his ongoing American popularity over the last sixty years. It does, however, reveal a great deal about American public life during the 1930s and early 1940s when Roman Catholics, literary critics, and mainline Protestants made up the audiences that first hailed the writings of C. S. Lewis on American shores.[48]

---

[48] Research for this chapter was largely carried out by my wife, Maggie Noll, who with me joins Chris Mitchell's many friends in thanking God for his life and work. My many conversations with Chris during his time as director of Wheaton College's Wade Center often dwelt on the need to provide a fuller historical context for Lewis. This chapter, the first draft of which Chris solicited for a Wheaton conference, tries to do that.

Chapter 4

C. S. LEWIS AND THE OXFORD ENGLISH LITERATURE DISCUSSION GROUP

WALTER HOOPER

The flourishing of the English degree at Oxford University was due to C. S. Lewis and his friend Nevill Coghill to an extent neither could have foreseen when each decided to add a degree in English to the one he already had.[1] English Language and Literature did not become a subject at Oxford until 1904, with Professor Sir Walter Raleigh (1861–1922) as the first holder of the Chair of English. Raleigh, a Fellow of Magdalen College, had died at age 60 only a few months before Coghill and Lewis entered the English School. Lewis, a student at University College, had already read for the Classics degree, divided into *Honour Moderations*, in which the student concentrates on Latin and Greek language and literature, and *Literae Humaniores – or* "Greats" – mainly the study of philosophy and ancient history. He took First Class Honours in both of these, but as he could not find a Fellowship in Philosophy, he decided to tie a third string to his bow by trying for a degree in a "rising subject": English.

On 13 October 1922 Lewis began the study of English by meeting with Frank Percy Wilson (1889–1963), his Tutor in English. Wilson, after being wounded in World War I, returned to Oxford in 1920 as University Lecturer. In a few years' time, he was to become general editor of the *Oxford History of English Literature* and in 1935 asked Lewis to write a volume for that impressive series of books. Students of English at Oxford – unlike Cambridge – were required to

---

[1] Walter Hooper died on 7 December 2020. He was aware (he told me) that there were corrections to be made to this article, but he did not have the chance for a final revision. It has therefore fallen to me, as one of his executors, to edit the typescript, remove infelicities, and check references, so far as this has been possible during a pandemic. I am grateful to Simon Horobin for having collated transcriptions in this article against the original manuscript and to Gregory Lippiatt and the editor of this volume for logistical help. I am responsible for remaining errors. (A. T. Reyes, Wolfson College, Oxford)

study Old English, and Lewis's instructor in Old English was Edith Elizabeth Wardale (1863–1943), Tutor in Old English at St Hugh's College. Lewis was to use her *Old English Grammar* (1922).

Professor Raleigh had begun a Discussion Group on subjects of English Literature in 1906, and he passed this class to Professor George Gordon in 1922.[2] Each College could send one or two students reading English to join the Discussion Group as a member. The first meeting was not held until January 1923, and the group began with enormous enthusiasm.

I think it was the two Professors who had the idea of keeping minutes of their meetings, and this resulted in three notebooks which either Professor Gordon or his wife in the end gave to C. S. Lewis, and which he treasured for the rest of his life. Notebook A is divided into two parts. The first contains notes from Raleigh's Discussion Class of 1906–7. The second part is the work of Gordon's Discussion Class of 1925–6, continued in Notebooks B and C.

We see from the first part of Notebook A that the Discussion Group began on 13 November 1906. The notes begin:

> The 1st meeting of the class in the year 1906–7 was held in Magdalen on Tuesday Nov 13th at 5 p.m., the President being in the chair. At the nomination of the President Mr Colvile was appointed secretary. No paper was read at this meeting but subjects for papers were suggested and each member present selected one to write on. It was arranged that in future meetings should be held on Wednesdays at 5 p.m. in Magdalen. The *President* kindly undertook to read a portion of his forthcoming work on Shakespeare at the following meeting (Nov. 21st), and for Nov. 28th *Mr Mair* promised to read a paper on the *Autobiographical Aspects of Spenser's Poetry.*

We must here go to Notebook B to pick up where Professor Raleigh left off. Professor Gordon picks up the sequence with the Discussion Class in Hilary Term 1923. On 27 January 1923, Mr. Darlow of Magdalen read a paper on "England under Walpole's Ministry." He was followed by Nevill Coghill of Exeter College and

---

[2] George Stuart Gordon (1881–1942) began his career as Magdalen's first Fellow of English in 1907. He then became Professor of English Literature at the University of Leeds (1913–22) and later was Merton Professor of English Literature at Oxford (1922–8), President of Magdalen College (1928–42), Professor of Poetry (1933–38), and Vice-Chancellor (1938–41).

C. S. Lewis of University College – two men who were presently to become friends and to have a huge influence on English Literature in Oxford.[3]

On 2 February 1923, Coghill read a paper on "Realism from *Gorboduc* to *Lear*," and the next week, when Lewis read a paper on Edmund Spenser, Coghill in the Notebook introduced the speaker in Chaucerian verse, then summarized Lewis's paper in Spenserian stanzas, and finally reverted to Chaucerian style to describe the ensuing discussion:[4]

In Oxenford some clerkés of degree
Were gadréd in a goodlye companye
And I was oon, and here will yow devise
Our felaweshipe that worthy was and wys.
A noblé Professoúr, that Gordon hight,
There was, that soghte to guyde our talk aright
Ful oft he smil'd on our discussion class
Hys twynklynge eyen were as grey as glas
He couthe of auctours and of Poesye
Wel speken and hys voys was melodyc.
The seley clerkés lov'd him everichoon
Each stroof with ech his pleasure for to doon
A Scot he was; and yet he was not dour
Ne was there swich another Professour.
A clerke he hadde, ycleped *Martëleye*[5]
That kepte a boke about our companye.
His lokkes were crulle as they were laid in presse,

---

[3] Coghill was to become famous for his translation of Chaucer's *Canterbury Tales*: Geoffrey Chaucer, *The Canterbury Tales*, trans. by Nevill Coghill (Harmondsworth, England: Penguin Books, 1951).

[4] Part of the Chaucerian introduction and all five Spenserian stanzas were previously published in the preface to C. S. Lewis, *Selected Literary Essays*, ed. by Walter Hooper (Cambridge: Cambridge University Press, 1969), x–xii. A shorter selection appears in three footnotes to C. S. Lewis, *All My Road Before Me: The Diary of C. S. Lewis*, ed. by Walter Hooper (San Diego: Harcourt Brace Jovanovich, 1991), 192–3. In all transcriptions given here, the occasionally eccentric punctuation (or its lack) is maintained. Single words in parentheses at the end of two lines (i.e. "Kirk"; "Luce") are glosses that appear in the manuscript, presumably aids to pronunciation.

[5] Averell Robert Martley of Hertford College took his BA in 1923.

Of twenty yeer of age he was, I guesse.
Sober he was and pleasaunt of visage.
Daun Darlow[6] was there of a high corage
Whan he to speken wyslye wolde beginne
There was noon auditour coude on him wynne.
Ful byg he was, of brawn and eke of bones
Ful oft he spak in high and noblé tones
Of historye: he hadde a purplé tye
And in his button-hole a dayëseye.
Sir Payne[7] ther was: a Poet I dar seyn:
Gladly the companye wold suffer PAYNE.
Sir Lewis was ther; a good philosópher
He hadde a noblé paper for to offer.
Wel couthe he speken in the Greeké tongue;
And yet, his countenance was swythé yong.
And many otheres were there of oure route
A dozen or fifteene or thereaboute.
They liken to heare speken other twelve,
But sickerly they liken heare themselve.
Whan al our companye was gadred inne
Than dyde our noblé Professour beginne
To aske us all to feast with hym at tea
At ende of term with many a faire ladýe.
Our jolly faces lighted with pleasaunce
And hopes of intellectual dalliaunce
And gladly we accepted; then he bade
Our Poete read the verses he had made
Upon our second meetyng: so he read
And many a melodious rhyme he said.
Then to *Sir Lewis* turned the Professóur

---

[6] This colorful undergraduate was Thomas Sherrock Darlow (1901–39). His father was the Rev. Thomas Herbert Darlow (1858–1927), who published a number of theological works. Darlow matriculated at Magdalen College in 1920, where he read Natural Science before changing to English in 1922. He left the Discussion Class and Oxford fairly soon after this without a degree. At the outbreak of World War II, he became a very successful war correspondent for the *Daily Herald* in France. He was sent on an assignment to the RAF headquarters in France, became ill, and died shortly afterwards on 10 November 1939.

[7] Frederick Lewis Payne of Queen's College took his BA in 1923.

(That was our tale's juge and governour)
And cried unto hym "Now by Pigges bones,
"Thou shallt a noblé tale for the nones,
"Somewhat to quite Daun Darlow and the Cogge.
"Rede us of Spenser, by Seint Jamés dogge.
"Lordynges, attend, and hear our philosópher
"That hath both wit and beauty in his coffer!"
Anon turned Lewis to a bluë boke
He swalwed thrice; hys dewy fingers shooke
And he bigan with right a myrie cheere
His tale anoon; and spake in this mannere.

Heere bigynneth Sir Lewis'
TALE
OF
DAUN SPENSER.

"Desert the lesser groves of Poesy;
No more of Cuddie or the nuptial scene
All Spenser's magic and his melody
Find sweet perfection in the Faery Queene.
There, Elegy and Pastoral, I weene
And moral virtue chorus their full song;
The mind of Spenser grew not; it had been,
And still was, gentle; only a new throng
Of words more beautifully bear his verse along.

"And fifty years taught nothing more than this;
To bend his vowels to a gracious line;
Grandeur and thunder, magic, and the bliss
Of Heavenly Music, and the inner shine
Of γάνος, or the gleaming of divine
Moist, quiet woodland things; all these he found.
Distilled old myths and thoughts into new wine,
But not new thoughts; and though the Queene is crowned
With many beauties, oft she is most falsely gowned.

"But leave her faults admitted, leave his passion
Untrue, mere copy: Love, he did not know
But amorous reverie in a sensuous fashion

He well could sing, and make his verses grow
One to another, like a forest row
Of deepening trees; no drama, but a mood
Of queer archaic dream, and spacious flow
Of changing rhythms, till then not understood.
He was a pioneer, that did not cut, but plant a wood.

"And his sweet satisfying poesy
Offers no problem to the gnawing mind,
But pours the balm of pure simplicity
In allegories old as is mankind;
Vague and indefinite, they lie behind
The purpose of the poem; for all speech
Of men is allegory, ill-defined
Spenserian and dim: and who can teach
How fact and symbol are related each to each?

"So leave him, more than lovely, less than great;
He was a poet; he was nothing more:
Nay – but a poet's poet; and there sate
Milton and Keats within his forest door.
Young dreamy boys delight in Spenser's lore
And eat his satisfying faery food
And Wordsworth on his native mountain shore
Caught echoes from that dim enchanted wood;
Then enter ye who dare, ye who have understood."

OUR PROFESSOÚR gan swere as he were wood.
By Japes, Sir Lewis, that was mighty good
If other clerkés finden aught to say
Let them speke out, a twenty devel way.
DAUN DARLOW answerde "What of allegory,
What meneth swevnés in Daun Spenser's story
Why useth he swich women's artifice
Al vigourless, effeminate, and nice
As Daun Catullus doth in al his wirche?"
"I wold not end in the Byzantine Chirche" (Kirk)
Quod Lewis, "and Catullus, I dar seyn
Hath nought to do with Spenser, to be plain."

Quoth *Sing*,[8] "He wrote to please his suzerain
Four hundred pounds she yaf him for his payne."
Another saith "It stirred her to the bowels
When Spenser slashed on flatterye with trowels."
Daun Darlow then parformed a noblé speeche.
"There's contact with reality in each
Of Spenser's characters, whate'er their dresse.
The Red Crosse Knight is Becky Sharpe and Tess.
A spiritual explanatioún
He hath as hath the Popé's triple Crown
And eke as hath the Whore of Babyloún
We are a solemn generatioún,
Not flippant nor facete as men had beene
Under Victoria, that ydel Queene.
Even in swevnés, moderns are sincere....."
  (of this tale maketh Coghill na more)
Quoth *Burns*:[9] "In Spenser's nimblé verses swete
He yiveth us a picture too complete:
Too much he yiveth: fancy cannot roam
But Keats driveth the fancy far from home."
And then a slight digressïoún was made
War Poetes, Austynn Dobson, Boarde of Trade.
Daun Darlow saith "Tennyson faced not facts"
Then saith the Professoúr "He judged the acts
Of Mallory in the Divorcé-Court."
Then Lewis said, "In Spenser is a sorte
Of characterisation, faintly traced.
Justýse is just, and chastity is chaste."
Thus many wordes were bandied round the table
As many as we sely clarkes were able
And many more than I can yow rehearse
And some of hem were badde, and some were werse.
The moral Darlow, philosophical Lewis (Luce)
At length agreed to make an arméd truce;
And whan Daun Phoebus had ynogh y-heard
He sank to th'orizonte without a worde,
Thogh wexing redder than he was biforn.

---

[8] Fateh Singh of St John's College took his BA in 1923.
[9] Gilbert Talbot Burns of Christ Church took his BA in 1924.

Through Aries he passed, and Capricorn
And lastly sank beneath the worldé quyte.
This is as much to say that it was nighte.
Then rose we al, and wenten on our waye
In pleasaunt mood: There nis namore to saye.[10]

The fourth meeting of the term was held on 16 February 1923. Gilbert Talbot Burns of Christ Church was due to read his paper but was ill. In his place, Robert Macdonald of Lincoln College, who took his BA in 1925, read a paper on "Adaptations of Shakespeare." Lewis wrote the minutes for this paper and proved he could write Chaucerian verse almost as well as Nevill Coghill.[11]

But whan that Coghille had his tale ytold
Our Professoúr gan round about bihold
And lough and seyde "Unbokeled is the male!
Let see now who shal tell another tale;
And namély Sir Burns as thou art able
Telleth anon som matere profitable."
This seely man, this Burns, lift up his head,
He was al wan to see and nothing red,
And "Sir," he seyd, "By my devotioun
I shal yow nothing tell at this seasoún
For I have swyche a stounde of hevinesse,
It is the influenza as I guesse,
Another man shal tell. Hit am not I."
Ther was a Scottis clerké set thereby,
And he was wunder blak and wunder pale,
His vois was high upon the upper scale,
And he was cleped hende Macdonald.

---

[10] Lewis's own account of the debate following his paper is found in the entry for 9 February 1923 in Lewis, *All My Road* (above, n. 4), 192–4. Less than a week later, on Wednesday 14 February, he read an enlarged version of his paper on Spenser to the Martlets, a literary society which he had joined shortly after arriving in Oxford in January 1919. An account in dialogue form of the Martlets meeting is found in Lewis, *All My Road* (above, n. 4), 197–200. See also my essay "To the Martlets" in *C. S. Lewis: Speaker & Teacher*, ed. by Carolyn Keefe (Grand Rapids, Michigan: Zondervan, 1971), 37–62.

[11] Lewis briefly wrote a few lines about this meeting in his diary: Lewis, *All My Road* (above, n. 4), 200–1.

Whan that our Professoúr upon him cald,
He answerd, "Sir, I am beneath your yerde,
And tho' a sudden call to me is herde,
I wil you seye som lytel as I can,
Now herkneth al." Thereon this worthie man
Began to tellen us a noble storie
Whereof somdel we holden in memorie;
And it was all of oldé Shakéspire
The highé poet out of Warwickshire
And how he made ful manie a fayré pleye
And now was dead. But shortly for to seye
Ther came a rout of lewed borel men
As Davenaunt and Kean and Garrick then
And marr'd his pleys: for they had lerned thus
In their old auctor hight Bowdlerius.
But of the lewed bokes that they made
He tolde eek how a certayn one is layde
In Bodley. "But by Goddes trouth," quod he,
The olde monkes in the librairie
They know no more of it than min olde hat."
The Professour gan crien out at that,
And al the clerkes with hir sentens soon
Had shent those idel monkes everichoon.

    Thereafter swych a silence fell on us,
I thought it was the old god Morfëús
That made us sit about and slepen all,
Ye could have herde the little pinnes fall,
Till maistre Strick began to speke a word.
His vois was lowe, unnethe it might be herd;
He shook his handes two upon the table
As he to play piano tunes was able
In maner of V-fingre exercises,
And seyde anon that ther wer two devises
To make tragédies: and upon the one
Men tellen of som worthie wight fordone
And sorrwing after fashïon commune:
The other kind was cursing of fortune
In maner of the stark Prometheüs
And how fortúne, for al that, breketh us.
    Now at our table, ye shal understonde.

Ther was a paynim knight of ferne londe
Of Prester Iohn the kinges court of Ind,
Of whom in oldé bokés ye mai find.
A verie proper paynim knight he was,
And had by hert the plays of Kalidas.
"By Termagaunt," he seyde, "And Apollon,
We have dan Shakspere changéd long agon,
And turn'd the bok of Lear for a comédie,
For in our law ther mai be non tragédie,
We are so wearie for to speke of sorrwe.
And when a pley we gon about to borrwe
We make the sentens ever end in ioye,
Tho it wer Tristram or the Tale of Troye."
"Quak!" quod the duck, "Let be the bok of Lear,
I dar wel seyn it is a fool matere.
Who ever herde the like of swych a king?
By God there is no reasoun in the thing."
    "Have pees," seyd moral Darlow. "By my bonis,
Ye are not in the right as for the nonis.
The storie of Alissaundre is so commune
That everich wight, I thought, knew his fortune.
For, sothly, he let part his territorie
Among his sons, al-so as in the storie."
"What," quod the duck. "Hastow not red bifore
In Aristotle" – but he seyd no more,
For al our fellawship of oon accord
Gan risen al togeder from the bord
As they wer wood and crien out and seye
"Let be thin olde ensaumples we thee preye.
Of Aristotle and his philosophie
Telleth no more for Goddes dignitee."

• EXPLICIT • LIBER • DE • MACDONALDO •

There followed other papers in the remainder of Notebook B. All the papers in Notebook C are from pupils in women's Colleges.

For several years Lewis had tried to find a job in one of the Colleges teaching philosophy. He wondered how much longer he could hold on. Then a Fellowship in English was advertised at Magdalen. No doubt the good offices of Gordon helped his application.

On 20 May 1925, C. S. Lewis was elected a Fellow of Magdalen. His first reaction on gaining a Fellowship was to write to his father. It was a letter of gratitude for the faith and financial support that had made it possible to hold on at Oxford until he achieved his goal. He gave up philosophy for English with few regrets. Lewis wrote to his father on 14 August 1925:

> I have come to think, that if I had the mind, I have not the brain and nerves for a life of pure philosophy. A continued search among the abstract roots of things, a perpetual questioning of all the things that plain men take for granted, a chewing the cud for fifty years over inevitable ignorance and a constant frontier watch on the little tidy lighted world of science and daily life – is this the best life for temperaments such as ours? . . . At any rate I escape with joy from one definite drawback of philosophy – its solitude.[12]

What did Lewis think of George S. Gordon and his Discussion Class? Writing in Mary Gordon's biography of her husband, C. S. Lewis said:

> One of the pleasantest institutions in the English School as I first knew it was Gordon's weekly Discussion Class. Each tutor could send only one or two of his pupils to it, so we liked to regard ourselves as a *corps d'élite*. It was held sometimes in a Committee Room and sometimes in Gordon's house, and it was there that I first met Nevill Coghill. I don't remember the names of most of the others, though their faces, and indeed the whole scene, come back to me very clearly: specially Gordon himself, leonine and tolerant, at the head of the table looking very much less alert than he actually was. It was work that exactly suited him – to seem to be doing nothing and yet actually to guide the whole debate. He said surprisingly little: it was only afterwards one realized how his *exiguum clinamen* had, at several points, headed us all off from some blind alley, or how a few unemphatic words of apparent agreement had turned a half truth into a whole one and tacitly suppressed an error. It never crossed our minds that the papers we read and the arguments we had about them could be less interesting, novel and momentous to him than they were to us. This was partly, no doubt, because he had a real sympathy with youth: still more, as I now realize, because he was doing his job so

---

[12] C. S. Lewis, *The Collected Letters of C. S. Lewis*, 3 vols., ed. by Walter Hooper (San Francisco: HarperCollins, 2004–7), 1:648–9.

well that we never saw it was a "job" at all. It was doubtless his suggestion that inspired us to keep our Minutes in verse. Some of them (notably Coghill's, in the style of Chaucer) I re-read recently and thought them good.[13]

---

[13] Mary C. Gordon, *The Life of George S. Gordon: 1881–1942* (London: Oxford University Press, 1945), 77.

Chapter 5

HOW SHALL WE THEN READ?
GEORGE MACDONALD AND THE
BEGINNINGS OF A DISCIPLINE CALLED
"ENGLISH LITERATURE"

Kirstin Jeffrey Johnson

But I would rather assume office of master of the hearing,
for my aim shall be to cause the song to be truly heard;
to set forth worthy points in form, in matter, and in relation;
to say with regard to the singer himself, his time, its modes, its beliefs,
such things as may help to set the song in its true light –
its relation, namely, to the source whence it sprung,
which alone can secure its right reception by the heart of the hearer.

MacDonald, *England's Antiphon* 3

Seventeen months before C.S. Lewis died, at the end of a successful career as a Medieval and Renaissance scholar and professor, an apologist, and an author of popular fiction, he was asked to list the books which "did most to shape his vocational attitude and his philosophy of life."[1] At the very top of the list—before Boethius, Herbert, and Virgil—Lewis named George MacDonald's short novel *Phantastes, A Fairy Romance for Men & Women*. This is a surprising accolade for a short work of fantasy—yet the book's importance for Lewis was almost life-long. He claimed that when he was just seventeen years old *Phantastes* had "called him" across a "great frontier," that through his experience of reading that book "my imagination was, in a certain sense, baptized"[2] Even though Lewis was so explicit about the

---

[1] C.S. Lewis, "Booklists submitted in response to this department's query: 'What books did most to shape your vocational attitude and your philosophy of life?" in *The Christian Century*, 79.23 (June 6, 1962), 719.

[2] C.S. Lewis, *George MacDonald: An Anthology* (London: Geoffrey Bles, 1946), 21. It may be helpful to recall that Lewis is speaking as an Anglican, not out of an Anabaptist tradition—this "baptism" is a holy commencement of something unexpected, yet replete with promise. Once he finally did convert to Christianity, Lewis realized how he "was still

impact MacDonald had on his faith and work, many Lewis scholars remain unfamiliar with MacDonald's own faith and work and are thus unaware that his influence reaches far beyond *Phantastes* and the field of fiction. Lewis scatters many clues in the myriad of borrowed images and concepts in both his academic and fictional work as well as in more explicit examples, such as MacDonald epigraphs heading chapters of his literary criticism, MacDonald characters influencing his own literary creations, MacDonald appearing in person as a key character, as well as of course his anthology of MacDonald quotations (mostly drawn from MacDonald's non-fiction). Lewis explains:

> I have never concealed the fact that I regarded him as my master; indeed I fancy I have never written a book in which I did not quote from him. But it has not seemed to me that those who have received my books kindly take even now sufficient notice of the affiliation. Honesty drives me to emphasize it.[3]

Archived letters display evidence that Lewis spent his entire adulthood badgering friends and colleagues, students and strangers to read MacDonald; in writing to one friend about important teachers of faith, whilst referencing Augustine, Athanasius, Hooker, and more, Lewis explains that for himself, it is to George MacDonald that he owes his own "greatest debt."[4] Little has been published on how MacDonald's work shaped Lewis's reading, teaching, and critical studies. But before that can occur, MacDonald's own influential career and work must be better understood, which requires attention to MacDonald's own mentors. Lewis is directly indebted to two of the most significant of these, for they were founders of the discipline of English Literature and pioneers of Literary Criticism. Awareness of their work and how it shaped the man Lewis called "my master"

---

with MacDonald and that he had accompanied me all the way and that I was now at last ready to hear from him much that he could not have told me at that first meeting. But in a sense, what he was now telling me was the very same that he had told me from the beginning. There was no question of getting through to the kernel and throwing away the shell: no question of a gilded pill. The pill was gold all through." Lewis, *George MacDonald*, 21. Lewis reread *Phantastes*—and many other MacDonald texts—throughout his life. In 1933 he supervised quite possibly the first ever student thesis on MacDonald.

[3] Lewis, *George MacDonald*, 20.

[4] C. S. Lewis, *The Collected Letters of C. S. Lewis*, ed. by Walter Hooper, 3 vols. (London: HarperOne, 2004-7), 2:529.

will not only illuminate how MacDonald the literary critic, professor, and author influenced Lewis the literary critic, professor, and author, but it may also enable fuller exploration of Lewis's commitment to his vocation. Thus, this chapter attends not only to MacDonald but to his predecessors Alexander John Scott and Frederick Denison Maurice—three pioneers of Lewis's chosen profession. It is only an introduction but one that invites "new thoughts and directions," perhaps even reassessments, in Lewis studies.

MISCONCEPTIONS OF MACDONALD

Nineteenth-century Scot George MacDonald (1824-1905) is frequently identified, misleadingly, as a fantasist and a pastor. More accurately, he was one of the earliest teachers committed to the discipline of English Literature, a vocation to which he dedicated over forty years of his life. There is merit in the assignation "Grandfather of Fantasy," but, as with the Inklings who succeeded him, fantasy was but a portion of his work. A teacher from the page as well as from behind the podium, MacDonald began his published writing career with literary criticism and poetry. His short stories, realistic novels, hymns, sermons, essays, translations, and anthologies fill almost fifty books, with only a very minor percent of that literary output qualifying as obvious fantasy.[5] And although he is frequently caricatured as a pastor-forced-to-write, this is but one of the many misconceptions that populate his "received" biography. In reality—although in high demand as a guest preacher throughout his life—MacDonald served as minister in his parish at Arundel for only twenty-eight months.[6] By the beginning of that period he had already self-identified as a writer and had anticipated that his time in that pulpit would be short.[7] Long before this, his father had recognized

---

[5] For more on Lewis's favored MacDonald texts, see Kirstin Jeffrey Johnson, "The Storyteller," in *Christian History*, 113 (2015), 10-13.

[6] From October 1850 to May 1853. MacDonald "pastored" —guided, cared for, and counseled—many people throughout his life, including notorieties such as John Ruskin, Charles Dodgson, and Georgina Burne-Jones, but this was in his role as trusted friend and/or member of the community, not a paid occupation.

[7] Even before his ordination MacDonald wrote: "I don't think I am settled here for life . . .. I hope either to leave this after six or more years, or to write a poem for the good of my generation. Perhaps both." William Raeper, *George MacDonald* (Tring, Hertfordshire: Lion Publishing, 1987), 80.

in him and encouraged the beginnings of what would become a life-long vocation of teaching.[8] This passion to teach as manifested in MacDonald's writing as well as from behind the podium is a key factor in understanding both the man and his work. It helps explain his own "vocational attitude and philosophy of life" as well as how he influenced others. His decision to participate in this new discipline, teaching his students the works of English Literature and how to read and critique them, was at that time a choice to participate in social reform, a choice informed by the practical theology of his mentors, founders of the new discipline. These reformers, A. J. Scott (1805-1866) and F. D. Maurice (1805-1872), were MacDonald's personal, literary, and theological mentors and friends.[9] They fought numerous battles throughout their lives, but arguably their greatest inroads were in the field of education, and education through literature in particular. Their motivation, their pedagogy, and their output were directly shaped by their Trinitarian theology and its emphasis on relationship, revelation, and transformation, the manifestations of which deeply impacted MacDonald's own teaching and writing, and, in consequence, those *he* influenced.[10] Lewis is a clear beneficiary of and participant in that inheritance.

---

[8] Letter from George MacDonald, Sr. to George MacDonald, K/ PP82. 1/1/3, 19 March 1850, Papers of George MacDonald and the George MacDonald Society, Kings College, London.

[9] MacDonald named Scott as his greatest spiritual mentor and influence other than his father, and his greatest intellectual mentor. He wrote to Scott's widow: "All my prosperity in literary life besides has come chiefly through him and you." Greville MacDonald, *George Macdonald and His Wife* (London: Allenand Unwin, 1924), 359. MacDonald lived with Scott and his wife Ann for a short period; they were as foster parents to him and his wife Louisa. Maurice, long after becoming another of MacDonald's closest acquaintances, was his Anglican minister at St. Peter, Vere Street, London. MacDonald dedicated writings to both men, and named a child after each (his first, Lila Scott, and his ninth, Maurice).

[10] Scottish divine Thomas Erskine claimed that Scott (son of a Presbyterian minister) was more interested in a relationship with all three aspects of the triune God than anyone he had yet met. J. Philip Newell, *A. J. Scott and his Circle* (Edinburgh: Edinburgh University, 1981), 49.

FREDERICK DENNISON MAURICE, THE CAMBRIDGE APOSTLES, AND ALEXANDER JOHN SCOTT

At the beginning of the nineteenth century, access to education was very limited in England; it was the preserve of the privileged. Free public education even at the primary level was not mandated until 1899. Tertiary education was the domain of a very specific elite: the options were Cambridge or Oxford, and to both attend and graduate from either required having sufficient funds, being a member of the Church of England, and being male. A group of students at Cambridge were dissatisfied with this, not only because of the exclusiveness, which they deemed socially and ethically problematic, but also for how that exclusion negatively impacted their own education. Their culturally distinctive insistence upon the importance of respecting and learning from alternative voices set apart this group that became known as the "Cambridge Apostles," and their most influential member in shaping this ethos of "unity in diversity" was a student named Frederick Denison Maurice.[11] An articulated passion for holistic integrity marked their ambition: these students held that better and truer understanding— and consequential progress—could only come through respectful attention to multiple perspectives and ideas. With youthful idealism they championed a cohesive worldview that informed not only how one thought and spoke (and argued) but also how one acted in life; they held that what one believed theologically and philosophically, how one worked, and even how one played should all hold together, each aspect informing the other. Given the cultural status quo, a realization of their vision demanded facilitation of and participation in educational and civic reform for all peoples, regardless of class, religion, or gender. These students were convinced that one of the most effective mobilizers of such reform was the medium of literature.[12] Yet their conviction highlighted another dissatisfaction with the education system, for they felt that their university and Oxford as well sorely was lacking in literary curriculum. The literature discussed in classes was primarily

---

[11] Peter Allen, *The Cambridge Apostles: The Early Years* (Cambridge: Cambridge University Press, 2010), 4.

[12] Richard Deacon, *The Cambridge Apostles: A History of Cambridge University's Elite Intellectual Secret Society* (New York: Farrar, Straus, and Giroux, 1985), 9.

classical, not British. So, the Cambridge Apostles attempted to fill in the gap: assigning and reading essays on their own, discussing British Literature at length, and exploring recent European literary movements and reforms[13]

Maurice was not the only Apostle to remain committed to this idealism long after graduation, but he was arguably the most effective. For the remainder of his life he would write articles, chapters, and books that embodied these early Cambridge Apostle ideals. He helped found and taught at numerous institutions that provided tertiary education for the working classes, for women, for non-Anglicans, institutions that would eventually bear such names as University of London and University of Manchester. His enthusiasm drew others to participate in his education and reform projects, diverse personalities such as Carlyle, Thackeray, and Kingsley. While in London Maurice joined a growing number of equally diverse intellectual elites, such as Julius Hare, Erasmus Darwin, Francis Newman, Thomas Hughes, Karl Gützlaff, Anthony Norris Groves, Henry Crabb Robinson, the Gaskells, the Carlyles, and the Wedgewoods, all of them attracted to the lectures of a Scottish teacher with strikingly similar principles: Alexander John Scott. Like the Cambridge Apostles, Scott argued for an integrated holistic worldview (for him, as for Maurice, a Christian worldview), and he too was adamant that reform would come through historical and literary education, a belief he insisted was rooted in biblical precedence. Scott's own learning was astounding. He was an able lecturer in theology, philosophy, politics, history, languages, science, and literature; fluent in not only classical and biblical languages, but also able to read Middle and Old English, French, Italian, German, Old German, Sanskrit, and more; as regards his critical abilities Carlyle was one of many who called him the best Dante scholar of the age. Scott was also determinedly Trinitarian, which was of no small import to Maurice, who had carefully accepted that same doctrine despite being raised Unitarian. In A. J. Scott, Maurice found a compatriot, a teacher such as he had wished for at

---

[13] Deacon, *The Cambridge Apostles*, 9. Coleridge was a "primary source of inspiration. Members met him, talked with him." Some of these Apostles, and many of Scott's "disciples" were later recognized for their role in the revival of English medievalism and Renaissance scholarship, such as Maurice, Furnival, Tennyson, and the Rossettis. *Phantastes* itself was one of the first pieces of Victorian fiction based on Arthurian legend, pre-dating even Tennyson's *Idylls*.

Cambridge.

Despite their mutuality, Scott's background was very different from Maurice's. A Divinity graduate of Glasgow University, influenced by Thomas Chalmers' work in rehabilitating the community-oriented concept of parish, and inspired by theological, literary, and philosophical conversations with Thomas Erskine, Scott had come to London as a minister for expatriate Scots.[14] He carried on in that role for some years but almost immediately began giving concurrent lectures in his local parish (the Woolrich docklands) as well. As an immigrant, Scott had been shocked by many of the contrasts between England and Scotland, but perhaps most strikingly in the realm of education. Scotland's centuries old education system had not only resulted in a much higher literacy rate among both men and women (rural and urban) than in England, but Scottish schools were also much more integrated socially, and the Universities—twice as many as in England since the 1500s—were intentionally structured to facilitate a socially diverse student body. Nor did they restrict their degrees to one denomination.[15] Both within and without the education system, the sense of identity from a familiarity with one's own culture and literature was much stronger in Scotland, and Scott was deeply concerned by the consequences of its absence among *all* the classes that he met in London. He believed that to better know one's heritage—the stories of one's culture, one's faith, one's community— was to better know oneself, which would necessarily deepen and enrich one's relationship with God, in addition to improving relationships with one's neighbors. Struck that this lack of rootedness was not only endemic in the working classes of London (a predictable by-product of the Industrial Revolution) but amongst all classes—even those who had degrees from Oxford and Cambridge—Scott began to teach in the fashionable public lecture halls as well. Courses on

---

[14] A key element of Chalmers' parish work was his emphasis on unity in diversity, including theological diversity. When involved with the Cambridge Apostles, Maurice was closely studying the writings of Erskine, long a dialogue partner of Chalmers.

[15] In 1855 (the earliest such records are available), Scotland's literacy rate was 89% for men and 77% for women, compared with a respective 70% and 59% for England and Wales. In the majority of the Lowland counties, outside of the industrializing areas, male literacy was over 90%. Robert D. Anderson, *Education and Opportunity in Victorian Scotland: Schools and Universities* (Oxford: Clarendon Press, 1983), 1.

Britain's philosophers and theologians and British Literature and church history, from Medieval and Renaissance Literature right up to contemporary writers were offered. Scott spent hours delving through long forgotten texts in the British Library and translating them for his audiences. He introduced them to Bede and Aelfric, Beowulf and Chaucer, Milton and Wycliffe, Sidney and Spenser.[16] He argued that the better the English knew their own literature, the better readers they would become of other literatures, such as the works of Goethe and Dante.[17] Polymaths who considered themselves uniquely educated in literature, such as Ruskin, Southey, and Carlyle, numbered amongst Scott's most enthusiastic fans. Eventually MacDonald, when a student in his early twenties, would also attend such lectures by Scott, but long before that it was Maurice who found himself captivated. In Scott, Maurice found someone equally passionate, even more widely read, and just as convinced that these were matters deeply theological; they were kindred minds compelled to action.

Scott and Maurice ended up being involved in many projects together and supporting each other in many more. They would teach at each other's institutions; connect each other to fellow educators, artists, authors; and write on each other's behalf. Together they rallied colleagues to fight various ravages of the Industrial Revolution and the establishment upon the working class, women, and non-Anglicans, whether Christian or not. They did not agree on everything, but this did not impede their relationship, for diverse community bound together by the grace of and in obedience to the triune God was a shared central tenant. Arguably, their greatest collaborative effort was their mark upon the emerging discipline of English Literature. In 1840 Maurice was appointed to the new chair of English History and Literature at King's College, London. While the second to fill the position, he was the first to teach this course as it had been intended:

---

[16] His talks to the dockworkers also included science and introductions to recent technological advances.

[17] Working knowledge of German language and literature was rare at this point in Britain: Scott and Carlyle were in a select company, one that included Coleridge, Erskine, Sterling, and Julius Hare (Maurice's tutor). Newell, *A. J. Scott*, 197. Interest in Dante had been sparked by Coleridge and was reignited by Scott. Much to Carlyle's disappointment Scott never published his Dante scholarship, and it is now lost. Scott and Maurice were both convinced that understanding how other cultures had enriched England's own could ward off unhealthy nationalism.

integrated and contextual, history and literature each illuminating the other. He began with a lecture on "The Growth of the English Nation and its Literature." Maurice maintained that formal study of literature required the practice of literary criticism, and he drew his students into an engagement with not just the texts but the minds behind the texts that they studied.[18] Scott had been modeling and championing this same approach in his public lectures (those which Maurice attended) for years, and he soon would likewise follow suit in the classroom. In 1848, the same year Maurice founded Queen's College for Women, Scott was appointed Chair of English Literature at University College, London. Thomas Erskine had recommended him for the position, writing that not only would such an appointment be "a good service to your country" but that the position would be a "living vocation" to a "noble character."[19] Several others had already been appointed to this chair, but, as at King's, the overseeing committee had yet to be satisfied that the course they had envisioned was being taught. Scott exceeded their expectations. And while for others—even Maurice—the teaching of Literature had not been a full-time position, for Scott it was. He thus became the first ever full-time English Literature professor.[20]

---

[18] The accolade of the "father" of Literary Criticism or "the first modern critic" is sometimes given to Matthew Arnold. See Noel Annan in *Matthew Arnold: Selected Essays* (London: OUP, 1964). However, while possibly the most influential critic in England after the 1860s, Arnold was only fourteen when Maurice held his first chair and was teaching students how to compare and analyze texts. Scott's conception of the place of criticism in the study of culture anticipated Arnold's by several years. Additionally, Arnold never supported efforts to make English Literature an academic discipline. Franklin E Court, *Institutionalizing English Literature: The Culture and Politics of Literary Study, 1750-1900* (Stanford: Stanford University Press: 1992), 108.

[19] Joseph Thompson, *The Owens College: Its Foundation and Growth; and Its Connection with the Victoria University*, Manchester (Manchester: J.E. Cornish, 1886), 185.

[20] Although Scott eventually left this position to become the principal of Owens College (later University of Manchester), he continued to teach literature at Owens as well as in public lectures for the remainder of his life. Court thoroughly and adequately defends this title for Scott rather than for Henry Morely or Thomas Dale. Those prior to Scott viewed the discipline as either a vehicle for inculcating good conduct and fashionable taste or a platform for linguistics. The two established histories of the discipline of English Literature, D. J. Palmer, *The Rise of*

TRINITARIAN THEOLOGY AND THE
CONVERSATION OF ENGLISH LITERATURE

As mentioned, Scott and Maurice's impetus for teaching literature derived from their theological convictions. They believed that the study of literature would benefit individuals desirous of practicing the Christian faith as well as those who do not; they refused to bind institutional education to proselytization, though they always hoped that a deeper understanding of literature might draw skeptics to the faith. Contrary to a persistent belief that educating the working class was dangerous, Maurice argued that "literary study was a natural vehicle for both entertaining and educating the masses by appealing to the innate powers of sympathy that guided their conduct and formed their imagination."[21] He believed that Christians particularly had a social responsibility to make such education available. He concurred with Scott's argument that knowing one's story, one's lineage— scripturally, historically, and culturally in terms of the literature that is evoked by all three—could deepen one's self-understanding individually and communally as well as one's understanding of others and, therefore, enrich one's relationships both human and divine. And so, although uniquely positioned to teach multiple literatures, the focus of their efforts was upon the still relatively new teaching of England's literature. Learning how to conduct such careful engagement with literature, they maintained, better enabled a reader to discern

---

English Studies: An Account of the Study of English Language and Literature from Its Origins to the Making of the Oxford English School (Oxford: Oxford University Press, 1965) and Court's Institutionalizing English Literature (1992), give much time to tracing its development, from Juan Louis Vives in the sixteenth century through Adam Smith and into the twentieth century. But both conclude that English literature as a discipline is due to the collaborative work of Scott and Maurice. (Incidentally, both Palmer and Court are limited in their grasp of their theology behind this development, and Court mistakes Maurice as the mentor and Scott as the mentee). University College London opened in 1828 as an alternative to Oxford and Cambridge for those unable to adhere to traditional Church of England doctrine (Jews, Atheists, Roman Catholics, Presbyterians, Baptists, etc.) as well as for those simply unable to afford the traditional options. This inclusiveness earned it the disdain of a large portion of the British establishment. H. Hale Bellot, University College London, 1826-1926 (London: University of London Press, 1929), 315. The first Oxbridge program of English Literature began in 1878. Court, Institutionalizing English Literature, 38.

[21] Court, *Institutionalizing English Literature*, 91.

potentially transformative revelations in a text and thus evoke change on a personal level, a community level, and even possibly on a national level.[22]

Scott and Maurice encouraged initial attentiveness to and discussion of internal characteristics and devices employed in a text, such as theme, pattern, rhetoric, symbolism, irony, imagery, yet they suggested that preferential status should not be given to a work in and of itself, even if that is where the would-be critic begins. They were interested in a literary work as a *sub-creation*, to borrow Tolkien's term anachronistically. As such they taught that both its conception and inception should also be considered. For Scott and Maurice, that a text was not independent of the person from whose lived experience it originated was an essential aspect of criticism they taught. For them, it was a theological mandate: to know about the author and the circumstances of her creation is to understand that work better, just as to know something of God and of the creation of the world is to understand Creation better. They considered a text a unified whole but one that, like a human, could be even better understood by knowing its external relationships. They did not view any work as self-contained: both the words on the page as well as the contexts that produced and influenced them were important.[23]

---

[22] The careful thinking of Scott and Maurice about relationality, revelation, and transformation is evident throughout their various writings and transcribed lectures as well as in their letters, particularly those to Thomas Erskine and Thomas Chalmers.

[23] For further reading on A. J. Scott about these ideas, see: "A Lecture on Popular Education," in *The Woolwich Gazette, 10 October 1840, n.p.*; *Notes of Four Lectures on the Literature and Philosophy of the Middle Ages* (Edinburgh: T. Constable, 1857), "On University Education," in *Introductory Lectures on the Opening of Owens College, Manchester* (London: T. Sowler, 1852), and A. J. Scott, *Suggestions on Female Education: Two Introductory Lectures on English Literature & Moral Philosophy* (London: Taylor, Walton and Maberly, 1849). For more on F. D. Maurice, see *Mediaeval philosophy, or, A treatise of moral and metaphysical philosophy from the fifth to the fourteenth century* (London: Macmillan, 1870), and *The Friendship of Books and Other Lectures* (London: Macmillan and Co, 1874). Palmer and Court both claim that Scott and Maurice's emphasis upon the worldview brought by an author to the text—each with personal experiences and relationships as well as culture permeating the very turns of phrase—was not only unique, but a perspective surprisingly advanced for men living in what was then the world's most rapidly colonizing empire. More than a century later, Lewis would concur with this insight

While Scott and Maurice did not believe that pursuing critical study in this manner could ever lead to an exclusively correct reading of a text, they did believe that the effort would prove enlightening. They also taught that the inclusion of diverse readers could enable the apprehension of new truths since a text always contains more meanings than one reader can discover. They maintained that a text even holds more than its author intends, though that does not therefore render the declaration of intent by the author invaluable.[24] The reader is never more important than the author but is rather a participant in a conversation proffered by the author. The more respect and effort at understanding put into practice, the more successful the communication. This plea for attentiveness to the text and, when possible, to the wider corpus and even the biography of the author emphasizes Scott and Maurice's perspective that engagement with a text is communicating with another human being. It reflects their conviction that it is a Christian responsibility to try to understand those with whom one engages as best as possible. When teaching, Maurice frequently referenced Scott's adage that a book is "the expression of the living thoughts of living [persons]."[25] He himself wrote that "authors and readers exist together within an organic culture"; a close reading

---

that one can "go beyond the first impression that a poem makes on your modern sensibility. By study of things outside of the poem, by comparing it with other poems, by steeping yourself in the vanished period, you can then re-enter the poem with eyes more like those of the natives; now perhaps seeing the associations you gave to the old words were false, that the real implications were different from what you supposed, that what you thought strange was then ordinary and that what seemed to you ordinary was then strange . . . even if enjoyment alone were my aim I should still choose this way, for I should hope to be led by it to newer and fresher enjoyments, things I could never have met in my own period, modes of feeling, flavors, atmospheres, nowhere accessible but by a mental journey into the real past." C. S. Lewis, *Studies in Words* (Cambridge: Cambridge University Press, 1960), 3.

[24] MacDonald suggests that only God can know all the meaning held within a given text. This does not imply that MacDonald believed that *any* meaning could be evinced but that truths converge rather than conflict. "The truer its art, the more things it will mean . . . when such forms are new embodiments of Old Truths, we call them products of the Imagination." George MacDonald, "The Fantastic Imagination," in *A Dish of Orts* (Whitefish: Kessinger, 2004), 230.

[25] "Rev. F. D. Maurice at Owens," in *The Manchester Guardian*, 10 June 1868, n.p.

not only engaged with the text but with the mind of the person who wrote that text. *Attentive* reading was essentially an opportunity to "make contact with the great imaginations of the past."[26] Scott and Maurice both paraphrased Milton: "These books were not absolutely dead things, but the precious life-blood of master-spirits, embalmed and treasured to a life beyond life."[27] Thus, not only is a reader to probe the author's intent (whilst remaining aware that there may be more present in the text than intended), but to do so with the eschatological awareness that one may yet meet that author, even if no longer alive.

Maurice wrote that the best kind of literary criticism "delights to draw forth the sense and beauty of a book, and is able to do so because the heart of the critic is in sympathy with the heart of the writer."[28] Further, there is "a principle which I wish should always be taken for granted—and that is that if we read and interpret carefully in an attitude of cheerfulness and obedience to the Holy Spirit, our work can thrive—but if we are resistant to that obedience, or read with pride, [our] work will inevitably be marred."[29] According to Maurice, attentive reading and, thus, literary criticism itself should be conducted with graciousness. It is most successful, most insightful, if done under the guiding inspiration of the Holy Spirit, the potential "conversation" between author and reader being divinely mediated. Both men taught that practicing such an attitude in their engagement with other minds would increase the possibility of common understanding and unity generally, a consistent goal throughout their efforts at social reform as well as in their pulpit preaching.

The perspective that these "living thoughts of living authors" were calling for engagement had in part developed from Scott's decades of intense study of Dante Alighieri. In the *Commedia*, Dante skillfully modeled drawing upon literary voices of the past so that he might

---

[26] Palmer, *The Rise of English Studies*, 39.

[27] A. J. Scott, "Answer to the Question, What was the Reformation?" in *The Morning Watch: or, Quarterly Journal on Prophecy and Theological Review, Volume 1* (London: J. Nisbet, 1830), 632; F. D. Maurice, "On Critics," in *The Friendship of Books and Other Lectures* (London: Macmillan, 1886), 369.

[28] Maurice, "On Critics," 383. MacDonald's novel *Home Again* explores the struggles of a young literary critic who has yet to understand this.

[29] F. D. Maurice, *The Life of Frederick Denison Maurice Chiefly told in his own Letters, Vol. I* (London: Macmillan, 1884), 275.

speak into the present in a text he hoped might help prepare readers for the future. Scott believed that this intentionality is a significant part of why Dante's epic work continues to offer transformative insight to readers hundreds of years later. He and Maurice encouraged their students to likewise pay attention to confluences of ideas throughout literature, arguing that the better one knew Scripture and the voices that preceded and followed it, and the better one knew the voices that entered into intentional conversation such as Dante had, the better able one would be to identify these intersections of ideas and insights of timeless importance. Attending to such confluences in "the long conversation" within literature through the centuries could enable revelations of truth.

This proposal, that attentiveness to voices of those who had gone before, whether of distant or of immediate past, could better inform readers as they stepped into the future was a provocative concept in Victorian England, a culture so enamored with "progress." But Scott and Maurice believed that the willingness to apprehend and respond to perceived truths would necessarily invite transformation; the better equipped one was to understand the text as communication, the greater the possibility that one's insight would prove transformative. This might manifest in a seemingly simple change in perspective: finding trees more mysterious, *goodness* more attractive, or the hobbit-like more heroic. It might mean a broadening of one's theology or a shift in one's prejudice, sufficient to incite approval of education for women, the poor, or even pagans. It might evoke action, such as writing a response or changing a career-plan. It might even prove as radical as to provoke an acceptance of the Gospel.

The other very significant influence Dante had upon Scott as a teacher of Literature was Dante's choice of medium: the vernacular, the everyday language of the people. Dante was a pioneer in choosing to write an epic work in a language that could be read by more than just the educated elite. It was a very intentional decision; in *De Vulgari Eloquentia* Dante explains that he wanted his poem to be accessed by the greatest possible number of readers, without distinction of class or of sex (a limited number of females could read Latin). Scott argued that Dante's choice changed the course of Western Literature as subsequent authors began to follow suit. In his lectures Scott repeatedly discussed the decisions by Alfred, Chaucer, Milton, Wycliffe, Sidney, and Luther to make literature—stories of identity and faith, ideas of theological and philosophical import—accessible.

These examples fortified Scott's own argument for the importance of teaching the literature of the people in the language of the people, via the academic discipline of English Literature, but only insofar as it emulated a much older example: the Incarnation as the Vernacular Word of God. Scott declared, "the humanity of Christ is that which translates the ineffable language of the Most High into man's native tongue"[30] For Scott this precedence obliged him to translate the older, "once-vernacular" English Literature of *Beowulf* or Chaucer that was no longer accessible to the working classes who came to hear him teach, equipping them with modern translations, so that they would be able to read their own literature on their own someday, as well as providing academic assistance and establishing public lending-libraries and affordable magazines. Scott's precedence informed Maurice's establishment of Working Men's Colleges and crafting sermons, reminiscent of Ignatian exercises, that endeavored to help the listener/reader step into biblical stories. And although neither men published popular, vernacular fiction, their example informed the eager encouragement of their student MacDonald to do just that.[31]

GEORGE MACDONALD: TEACHER, SCHOLAR, WRITER

MacDonald had followed their lead in becoming a classroom teacher of Literature to all the categories of students previously excluded, as well as becoming a popular lecturer of English Literature to the general public in multiple countries.[32] But MacDonald additionally achieved what they had not: writing "vernacular literature" for the general public, popular literature that intentionally participated in the "long conversation" in the form of sermons, realistic novels, fairy tales, fantasies, essays, and poetry which consciously invited his "everyday" readers to join in. Like those of his predecessors and his true inheritors, his stories were richly

---

[30] A. J. Scott, *Two Discourses: The Kingdom of the Truth: The Ranges of Christianity* (London: Macmillan, 1866), 15. He adds, "the light of Godhead is reflected from him; but that is also the light of Godhead which is refracted through him." Scott, *Two Discourses*, 16.

[31] Maurice did write one novel, *Eustace Conway*, but, although praised by Coleridge, it had little public success. Maurice's use of "Ignatian imagination" was something MacDonald encouraged his novel readers to also consider, as explored in Chapter Seven of *The Seaboard Parish*.

[32] England, Scotland, Ireland, Italy, France, United States, Canada.

imbued, deliberate engagements with "the long conversation." While sufficient to entertain on a surface level, they contain layers of literary concepts and conversations for those who choose to read closely. Even the shortest of MacDonald's stories are abundant with literary legacy, referencing a multitude of texts. And they were remarkably successful.

In a foreshadowing of Lewis's accolades, the literature scholar MacDonald referred to Scott as both his "master" and his "teacher."[33] MacDonald was, like Scott, a polyglot, capable of reading and writing in numerous ancient and modern languages.[34] He was as intrigued by the sciences as by the arts.[35] Like Scott he was a gatherer of diverse persons. The MacDonald family picnics, with theatre and dancing, could include artists and activists, destitutes and socialites, princesses and priests. MacDonald was a counseling confidant of many, those struggling with faith and those who rejected it. Like Scott, he valued hospitality in his conversations and relationships as much as in his home.[36] MacDonald was, like Maurice, an adult convert to Anglicanism, and when asked to preach he wanted the entire service to cohere: the hymns, the scripture, the poetry (frequently Herbert), the sermon. Like Maurice, he taught fellow students when yet a student himself and supplemented his own education when the institute seemed lacking. He also, like Maurice, took on the editorship of different journals in an effort to disseminate affordable learning to the wider populace. Both Scott and Maurice were significant teachers, chosen mentors, and adult friends of MacDonald. They

---

[33] George MacDonald, "The Heart," in The Sunday Magazine, 1871, ed. by Alexander Strahan (London: Strahan, 1870), 14.

[34] Including Scots, English, German, Italian, French, Spanish, Latin, New Testament Greek, Classical Greek, and Hebrew. In his eighties he was learning Dutch. He started learning each new language with the New Testament. Ronald MacDonald, *From a Northern Window: A Personal Reminiscence of George Macdonald by His Son*, ed. by Michael Philips (Eureka, CA: Sunrise Books, 1989), 54-5). Ronald's essay is also reprinted in Dale Wayne Slusser, *In the Near Loss of Everything: George MacDonald's Son in America* (Hamden, CT: Winged Lion Press, 2009).

[35] Awarded M.A. prizes in Chemistry and Natural Philosophy, MacDonald's initial intent was to do graduate work in math or sciences. Thwarted by lack of finances, he nonetheless continued to tutor even colleagues in these subjects—for fun.

[36] MacDonald was, like Lewis, a hospitable counselor to many through correspondence, writing even to strangers who reached out to him for assurance and advice.

instilled in him a deep conviction of the importance of literature, and the theological need of a people to be storied, and so he willingly dedicated the majority of his life to the teaching of literature from the podium and the page.

Scott and Maurice's concern and passion that England learn her stories is reflected in MacDonald's choice of lecture topics, for, although all his work was shaped by authors of varied cultural backgrounds, in his hundreds if not thousands of lectures (many of which were written-up by journalists, thus increasing his audience exponentially), MacDonald always spoke on British writers (such as Chaucer, Shakespeare, Sidney, Tennyson, Hood, Coleridge, Burns, Milton, and Wordsworth) with the exception only of Dante.[37] True to the teaching of Scott and Maurice, his lectures never discussed the literature without considering the person who had penned it.[38] MacDonald's essays, including his commentary in his novels, reveal that he researched well the lives of these authors he admired and was eager to introduce. Like Scott, he lectured extempore, with one single and important exception, his seminal lecture on "The Imagination: Its Functions and Its Culture."[39] (The debt of not only Lewis but also

---

[37] The popular "English Romantics'" were but a small portion of MacDonald's subject matter; nor is there any record of his ever lecturing on German Romantics. In 1879 he wrote to the critic William Horder, "I could give you a lecture on Wordsworth, or Tennyson's Lyrics, but I much prefer lecturing on Hamlet or Macbeth." George MacDonald Collection, 1/2/2, Beinecke Rare Book and Manuscript Library, Yale University, New Haven, Connecticut. MacDonald was the first vice-president of Furnivall's Shakespeare society.

[38] Because he spoke without notes, there are no manuscripts of MacDonald's literary lectures; however, there are a plethora of journal transcriptions. John Ruskin, as much an admirer of MacDonald's literary prowess as he was Scott's, wrote in a testimonial of MacDonald for the Chair of Rhetoric at Edinburgh: "of all the literary men I know, I think you most love literature itself; the others love themselves and the expression of themselves; but you enjoy your own art, and the art of others, when it is fine." He added, "I am always glad to hear you lecture myself— and if I had a son, I would rather he took his lessons in literary taste under you than under any person I know, for you would make him more than a scholar, a living and thoughtful reader." George MacDonald Collection, 1/3/127, Beinecke Rare Book and Manuscript Library, Yale University, New Haven, Connecticut.

[39] In 1883 he writes again to Horder; "Would you like Hamlet & Julius Caesar or Tennyson & Sir Philip Sidney—or two upon

others such as Chesterton, Tolkien, and Barfield to the published version of this essay is profound.) All three of these pioneering professors of English Literature—Scott, Maurice, MacDonald—evoke the image of Ezra, the prophet who stood before the Israelites reminding them of the lost stories that gave rise to their laws, their culture, their worship, their identity, and their language, the teacher who then restoried his people (see Nehemiah 8).

MACDONALD'S REPUTATION AS A LITERARY CRITIC

MacDonald's written literary criticism of both classic and of contemporary works is largely overlooked in Inklings studies, but scholars in other literary fields have taken notice. Herbert scholar C. A. Patrides calls MacDonald's evaluation of "The Temple" in *England's Antiphon* "one of the most considerable essays in the history of Herbert criticism."[40] G. R. Hudson addresses the significance of MacDonald's Browning reviews in her *Robert Browning's Literary Life*.[41] A. J. Smith includes MacDonald's work in his *John Donne: The Critical Heritage*.[42] MacDonald's *Hamlet*,[43] which he himself considered one of his most important publications, has not been ignored in Shakespeare scholarship: e.g., Bernice W. Kliman (1988),[44] David Farley-Hills (1996),[45] Ann Thompson (2000),[46] Hardin L. Aasand (2003).[47] The

---

Wordsworth—or a read lecture on the Imagination? Choose." George MacDonald Collection, 1/2/7, Beinecke Rare Book and Manuscript Library, Yale University, New Haven, Connecticut. The lecture version was printed in newspapers at the time, the published version is in *A Dish of Orts*.

[40] C. A. Patrides, *George Herbert: The Critical Heritage* (London: Routledge, 1995), 27.

[41] G. R. Hudson, *Robert Browning's Literary Life: From First Work to Masterpiece* (Austin, TX: Eakin Press, 1992), 286.

[42] A. J. Smith, *John Donne: The Critical Heritage* (London: Routledge, 1996).

[43] George MacDonald, *Tragedie of Hamlet: A Study of the Text of the Folio of 1623* (Whitehorn, CA: Johannesen, 1995).

[44] Bernice W Kliman, *Hamlet: Film, Television, and Audio Performance* (Rutherford, NJ: Fairleigh Dickinson University Press, 1988).

[45] David Farley-Hills, *Critical Responses to* Hamlet, *1600-1900*, 4 vols. (New York: AMS Press, 1994-2006).

[46] Ann Thompson, "George MacDonald's 1885 Folio-Based Edition of Hamlet" in *Shakespeare Quarterly*, 51.2 (Summer, 2000), 201-5.

[47] Hardin L. Aasand, *Stage Directions in Hamlet: New Essays and New*

eminent Shakespearean Ann Thompson considers it "thoroughly scholarly," adding, "In addition to crediting George MacDonald for this innovative edition on textual grounds, I would recommend his commentary on literary grounds: the encounter between MacDonald and Shakespeare is always thoughtful and modest, often entertaining and original. I would also urge editors and publishers to consider his and Longman's elegant and reader-friendly layout as a possible model for modern editions of the two-text plays." She concludes that MacDonald's edition of *Hamlet* "deserves to be remembered."[48]

But MacDonald's explicit literary criticism does not appear solely in his expository works; it appears sometimes in much of his fiction as well. His fiction contains lectures on Sidney and translations of Dante (both authors are referenced in almost everything MacDonald wrote); discussions of *The Rime of the Ancient Mariner* and *Paradise Lost*; and entire chapters given over to exegetical discussions of Isaiah or to tracing the metaphor of metamorphosis from the Greek myth of Psyche through Paul and on up to Blake and Ruskin. Plato, Boethius, Langland, mystery plays, Mallory, Spenser, Shakespeare, Herbert, Bunyan, Goethe—these are a but a few of the writers/works that appear repeatedly, not just in expository passages but in the very fabric of MacDonald's fiction.[49] He pulls their phrases and images and ideas into conversation with each other, explicitly and implicitly. In his essay "The Imagination," MacDonald describes using a story as a "spiritual scaffolding or skeleton": "those main ideas upon which the shape is constructed, and around which the rest group, as ministering dependencies."[50] (39). The practice is one he utilizes often, explaining that such critical engagement with the art of previous sub-creators is itself high art and a key to understanding Lewis's use of the word *mythopoeic*, which he claimed "may even be one of the greatest arts" and

---

Directions (Madison, NJ: Fairleigh Dickinson University Press, 2003).

[48] Thompson, "Folio-Based Edition of Hamlet," 202, 205.

[49] In his first "realistic" novel *David Elginbrod*, for example, he explicitly mentions over ninety works of literature. This number does not include unreferenced quotations and allusions. Even the fantastical writing contains many direct quotations not always marked out by quotation marks and often directly names other literary titles.

[50] George MacDonald, "The Imagination: Its Functions and Its Culture," in *The British Quarterly Review* (London: Hodder and Stoughton, 1867), 39.

of which he said MacDonald "is the greatest genius."[51] MacDonald's position was that creativity could *only* occur relationally; art could not exist outside of a relational framework. The canon consisted of truly great literature that was born of highly informed and intentional engagement with the works of others. In his collection of English devotional literature, MacDonald calls it an antiphonal response.[52] In his own craft even a seemingly simple children's tale such as *The Princess and Curdie* proves to be, in addition to successful entertainment (never out of print), an exploration of a biblical narrative of Isaiah; a questioning of cultural ideologies, such as the newly formed self-help movement and Adam Smith's popular *laissez-faire*; a deft challenge to the literary and biblical criticism of Matthew Arnold, particularly as expressed in *Literature & Dogma* and Arnold's Isaiah commentaries; and a homage to typological convergences from Greek myth and Christian art traditions up through Coleridge and Shelley.[53] He even slips in nods to some recent geological treatises.[54] Throughout MacDonald's corpus is a clear awareness that, as Scott and Maurice emphasized, the precedence for this relational literature-craft is

---

[51] Lewis, *George MacDonald*, xviii.

[52] George MacDonald, *England's Antiphon* (Whitehorn, CA: Johannesen, 1996).

[53] For a fuller discussion, see Kirstin Jeffrey Johnson, "'The Curdie Books, Please': C. S. Lewis' Co-creative Reading in *That Hideous Strength*" in *Sehnsucht: The C. S. Lewis Journal*, 5/6 (2011-12), 43-66 and Kirstin Jeffrey Johnson, "Curdie's Intertextual Dialogue: Engaging Maurice, Arnold, and Isaiah" in *George MacDonald: Literary Heritage and Heirs*, ed. by Roderick McGillis, (Hamden, CT: Winged Lion Press. 2007), 153-82.

[54] In "The Fantastic Imagination" MacDonald writes: "When such forms are new embodiments of old truths, we call them products of the Imagination . . . genuine work of art must mean many things; the truer its art, the more things it will mean." George MacDonald, "The Fantastic Imagination," 230. He also argues that a successful tale should never depend on the apprehension of such elements and that they should not impede the reading. He explains that Shakespeare "will not spoil his art to show his art. It is there, and does its part: that is enough. If you can discover it, good and well; if not, pass on, and take what you can find. He can afford not to be fathomed for every little pearl that lies at the bottom of his ocean. If I succeed in showing that such art may exist where it is not readily discovered, this may give some additional probability to its existence in places where it is harder to isolate and define." George MacDonald, "St George's Day," in *A Dish of Orts* (Whitefish: Kessinger, 2004), 78, 92.

nowhere stronger than in Scripture itself.

MACDONALD AND THE COMMUNITY OF READERS

MacDonald intentionally entices his readership, even of his vernacular fiction, into deeper and broader reading of literature both contemporary and ancient, national and international. Whether the literature he references is familiar and easy to access or more obscure, he believed it would give shape and depth to his own printed communication. But because he was a consummate teacher, each text is also full of introductions. MacDonald sees his prime responsibility as teacher, critic, and author—for him, none distinct from the other— to be a facilitator of relationship. (It is little wonder that libraries are the setting for so many important relational engagements in the novels.) He writes in *England's Antiphon:*

> When we read rejoicingly the true song-speech of one of our singing brethren, we hold song-worship with him and with all who have thus at any time shared in his feelings, even if he have passed centuries ago into the "high countries" of song. My object is to erect, as it were, in this book, a little auricle, or spot of concentrated hearing, where the hearts of my readers may listen, and join in the song of their country's singing men and singing women.[55]

Ever a student of Scott and Maurice, MacDonald wanted his own students to remember that "the God of Abraham, of Isaac, and of Jacob" was also "the God of Sidney, of Hooker, of Herbert"[56] and of all readers since. He explained that in books one could find fellow pilgrims, kindred spirits, intellectual sparring partners . . . even "old friends," that is, a community of readers.

> Next to possessing a true, wise, and victorious friend seated by your fireside, it is blessed to have the spirit of such a friend embodied – for spirit can assume any embodiment—on your bookshelves . . .. Are they not likewise links connecting us with a future, wherein these souls shall dawn upon ours, rising again from the death of the past into the life of our knowledge and love? Are not these biographies letters of introduction, forwarded, but not yet followed by him whom they introduce,

---

[55] MacDonald, *England's Antiphon*, 2.

[56] George MacDonald, *The Seaboard Parish* (London: K. Paul, Trench, 1886), 162.

for whose step we listen, and whose voice we long to hear; and whom we shall yet meet somewhere in the Infinite?[57]

MacDonald shared the eschatological sense of community and readership suggested by his mentors. This long-term perspective heightened the demand not only of responsibility to the text but also to the very author upon whom one might presume to write or lecture. It kept to the fore that a book is a form of communication and, thus, of relationship.

MacDonald declared that his aim as a literary critic was to better facilitate the relationship "betwixt my readers and the writers from whom I have quoted."[58] This did not change in the writing of his vernacular fiction, in which he very explicitly followed the lead of those celebrated by Scott, such as Dante, Sidney, and Shakespeare. He entered the dialogue of the "long conversation" as but one of the participants, engaging in the truths he recognized and with which he resonated, perpetuating the communion, the conversation, the argumentation, his very participation inviting his readers to do the same. He renders it impossible to conduct the type of exclusive "close reading" encouraged by Matthew Arnold, one that only considers a text within itself in order to produce a single "clear sense,"[59] for he continuously drives the reader *out* with his frequent quotations and references, even in his fantasy books. MacDonald explains that a book draws the reader into a world envisioned by another in order that the reader may be better prepared for having related with the communications of that author to then venture out into yet other worlds. As the character in MacDonald's novel *Lilith*, Mr. Raven, croaks in exasperation to the protagonist: "A book is a door in, and therefore a door out."[60] MacDonald repeatedly attempts to show that no book can exist or come into existence in isolation from others. Writing is born out of the relationships which the author has formed, forged in community, literary and otherwise, whether in reaction,

---

[57] George MacDonald, "Essays on Some of the Forms of Literature: A Review," in *A Dish of Orts* (Whitefish, Montana: Kessinger, 2004), 229.

[58] MacDonald, *Antiphon*, 12.

[59] Matthew Arnold, *Literature and Dogma: An Essay Towards a Better Apprehension of the Bible*, Popular Edition (London: Smith, Elder, and Co, 1889), 2-15.

[60] George MacDonald, *Lilith* (Whitehorn, CA: Johannesen, 1995), 25.

response, or both. And a reader brings the same experiences to reading.

MacDonald declared that his prime intent in writing was to "wake up" his readers to the proffered revelation of the Divine Imagination.[61] His own Trinitarian theology led him to believe that an understanding of the intrinsically relational God cannot be grasped outside of a relational hermeneutic, that a list of dry propositions can never convey what vernacular poetry can.[62] He believed that it is in response to a revelation received as a result of relationship that transformation can occur, that, say, a reader might wake up, think new things, take new action. MacDonald obviously delighted in discovering intertextual interweavings of universal truths in great literature as much as did his literary mentors before him. From the lectures of Scott and from the literature of such as Dante, Sidney, and Spenser, he was schooled in the internal interplay of Scripture as well as in how it can engage with the ancient myths and great classics. To craft in this manner is to participate in a "literary conversation" that not only was his heritage but one that also embodied a relationality that he believed could transform those who chose to participate in it.

Unfortunately, C. S. Lewis did not have MacDonald as a teacher in person as MacDonald had Scott and Maurice, and Lewis's own fairly flawed biography of MacDonald indicates that he was unaware of MacDonald's actual profession. But Lewis still benefited from MacDonald's astonishing breadth and depth of literary knowledge as well as his embedded pedagogy. Throughout Lewis's oeuvre— his fiction, his criticism, his sermons, his talks—the influence of MacDonald's teaching is everywhere evident and, therefore, the legacy of Scott and Maurice as well. These pioneers were determined their students would comprehend that literature is—in its very conception

---

[61] MacDonald, "The Imagination: Its Functions and Its Culture," 28.

[62] MacDonald does not consider the terms poetry and story mutually exclusive, as articulated clearly in Antiphon in his discourse on the ballad. He uses the word poetry in the same manner as his literary guide, Philip Sidney, for whom *Aesop's Fables* and the biblical story of David and Nathan are proof of the educational power of "poetry." *Sir Philip Sidney, A Defense of Poesie and Poems* (London: Cassell, 1909), 61. MacDonald's Sidney quotation in his anthology clarifies this point further: "verse being but an ornament, and no cause to poetry; since there have been many most excellent poets that never versified . . . .. It is not riming and versing that maketh a poet [but] that feigning notable images of virtues, vices, or what else, with that delightful teaching . . . ." *Sir Philip Sidney, A Cabinet of Gems* (1891), ed. by George MacDonald (London: Elliot Stock, 1893), 149.

let alone in its transmission and apprehension—a communication born of relationship, one that invites participation and that may even evoke response. The attentiveness of a reader to this belief was central to their understanding of how to critique a text. And with the conviction that all humans deserve the opportunity to be such a reader, they founded the discipline of English Literature. Scott and Maurice thus taught MacDonald how to refine and practice his own reading, teaching, and writing. They advocated his translation of the literary tradition of the Christian faith into a cultural vernacular, imaginative collaborations with the antiphonal past to be heard by new audiences. Their investment was not misplaced, for MacDonald's textual teaching did—and does—wake up consciences, cause readers to think things for themselves, and baptize imaginations. This was the initial intent of the university discipline and the potential reward of every teacher of English Literature. If anyone is *not* prepared to take Lewis at his long professed, long repeated, and long considered insistence on MacDonald's influence, he or she needs merely to examine "the vocational attitude and philosophy of life" evident in the corpus of the Virgilian guide Lewis names once in *The Great Divorce* as George MacDonald and thereafter as "My Teacher."

No man could sing as he has sung, had not others sung before him.
Deep answereth unto deep, face to face, praise to praise.
To the sound of the trumpet the harp returns its own vibrating response
—alike, but how different!

MacDonald, *England's Antiphon* 3

II.

ASSESSMENTS AND REASSESSMENTS

Chapter 6

PLANET NARNIA REVISITED

MICHAEL WARD

Over many years Inklings scholars round the world came to know and value the encouragement that Dr. Christopher Mitchell would generously provide for their research projects. In my own case, he supported the work I undertook studying the theologically imaginative ways Lewis engaged with medieval cosmology. Chris gave very helpful feedback on early drafts of my book, *Planet Narnia*; he served as an official reader when Oxford University Press put it out for peer-review; and he hospitably made available the Wade Center for the American launch of the volume once it was published. When I was asked to contribute an essay to this collection in honor of his memory, these things came to mind, and the invitation presented itself as an opportune moment to revisit the research that he had fortified with his characteristic care, shrewdness, and warmth. That some of what I have to say in this paper results from insights or materials provided to me by other scholars is also fitting, for Chris, who was never proprietorial or territorial in his approach, taught me a lot about seeking to widen the scholarly circle and avoid the exclusive "inner ring" mentality. I offer this essay, then, not only as a continuation of the work to which he lent a hand, but also—I hope—as an example of the sort of scholarship that he himself so admirably modeled and promoted.

What follows is a gathering together of some of the choicest new discoveries that I have made, or that have kindly been brought to my attention by other people, in furtherance of the case argued in my book *Planet Narnia: The Seven Heavens in the Imagination of C. S. Lewis* since its initial publication in 2008.[1]

For readers who may not be familiar with its thesis, the central contention of the book is that Lewis constructed the Chronicles of Narnia out of the imagery of the "heptarchy," the seven planets of the pre-Copernican cosmos, which he described as "spiritual symbols" of "permanent value" and which he wrote about extensively, not only

---

[1] Michael Ward, *Planet Narnia: The Seven Heavens in the Imagination of C. S. Lewis* (Oxford: Oxford University Press, 2008).

in his academic work (see, for instance, the chapter entitled "The Heavens" in *The Discarded Image*), but also in the Ransom Trilogy (see especially chapter 15 of *That Hideous Strength*, "The Descent of the Gods") and in his long, complex poem, "The Planets," first published in the magazine *Lysistrata* in 1935. These seven symbols provided Lewis with his imaginative blueprint for each Narnia tale, governing both the "poiema" and the "logos" of the story, both what it is as "something made" and what it communicates as "something said."

Against those critics who have described the Chronicles as slap-dash[2], I maintain that the Narniad is an artistic specimen of the utmost intricacy and that this is what we should expect, given Lewis's well-attested interest in complexity and intentionality. This interest was born not only of his Christian belief in God's creative act but also of his guiding principles as a writer of fiction. About divine creativity, he held that God does not work by "general laws" but by a minute attention to the individual fittingness of every particular thing: "The great work of art was made for the sake of all it does and is, down to the curve of every wave and the flight of every insect."[3] As for the artistry involved in the composing of fairy tales, Lewis considered it a profound error to suppose that "everything is arbitrary." On the contrary, he said, "the logic of a fairy tale is as strict as that of a realistic novel, though different."[4] To imagine that Narnia is a mish-mash would be to suppose that Lewis discounted his deeply held beliefs about the intelligence behind the design of both the real world and successfully wrought sub-created worlds.

I should make it clear that, in what follows, I am not attempting any substantial argument, but only further illustrations in support of the argument developed at length in *Planet Narnia*. If readers have not already been persuaded of the Narniad's planetary design, they are unlikely to find the following essay convincing in and of itself. I suspect that the particulars enumerated here may seem nugatory in isolation from the parent book, as ineffective as coals when removed from the

---

[2] E.g., "Narnia is intentionally a hodge-podge collection of widely diverging elements, often with no relation to each other, giving it a dreamlike quality." Devin Brown, *Inside Narnia: A Guide to Exploring The Lion, the Witch and the Wardrobe* (Grand Rapids: BakerBooks, 2005), 42.

[3] C. S. Lewis, *Letters to Malcolm: Chiefly on Prayer* (London: Geoffrey Bles, 1964), 59.

[4] "On Stories" in *C. S. Lewis, Essay Collection and Other Short Pieces*, ed. by Lesley Walmsley (London: HarperCollins, 2000), 499.

fire in the grate. However, I dare to assume there will be some readers familiar with and sufficiently persuaded by the case propounded in *Planet Narnia*; it is for them that I write. I do so with the purpose in mind that Lewis himself describes in *Miracles* when talking about the discovery of an interpretative key for a novel. The only way to test the supposed key would be to read the novel in its light and see how well it illuminated the work. If the key were genuine, Lewis says, then at every fresh reading of the book, "we should find it settling down, making itself more at home, and eliciting significance from all sorts of details in the whole work which we had hitherto neglected."[5] As the Chronicles have been freshly read—by me and by others—in the light of the interpretative key provided by the seven heavens, the more they have yielded up their secrets and unveiled the intelligence and skill that went into their composition.

This planetary reading of the Narnia does indeed elicit significance from "all sorts of details," as we might have predicted, given Lewis's respect for intricacy and complexity, both as a Christian and as a writer. He believed that God's creative act was undertaken not just for each human soul but "perhaps for each beast. Perhaps even each particle of matter—the night sky suggests that the inanimate also has for God some value we cannot imagine."[6] And what is true of God's artistry in creation is also true, *mutatis mutandis*, of human artistry in sub-creation—assuming the work to be good. Lewis observes that "a man of genius composing a poem . . . has no mere by-products in his work . . . .. If each . . . word were conscious it would say: 'The maker had me myself in view and chose for me, with the whole force of his genius, exactly the context I required.'"[7] It is these kinds of considerations that should be alive in our minds as we examine the Narnian minutiae that follow. Rather than dismissing these details as unplanned by-products or random trivia, we should approach them with Puddleglum's bold claim ringing in our ears: "There *are* no accidents."[8]

---

[5] C. S. Lewis, *Miracles: A Preliminary Study* (London: Geoffrey Bles, 1947), 113.

[6] Lewis, *Letters to Malcolm*, 58.

[7] Lewis, *Letters to Malcolm*, 57.

[8] C. S. Lewis, *The Silver Chair* (New York: Collier, 1971), 134.

LUNA AND *THE SILVER CHAIR*

Let us start by examining the Chronicle in which Puddleglum himself first appears, *The Silver Chair*, for this, being Lewis's Lunar story, represents the lowest of the seven heavens: "her moist circle / Is nearest earth," as he says in "The Planets."[9] Having looked at Luna we will then examine the other planetary spheres, taking them in ascending order, one by one, in the manner of Dante's pilgrim in the *Paradiso*, proceeding from Luna to Mercury and thence to Venus, Sol, Mars, Jupiter, and Saturn.

Beginning with *The Silver Chair*, let us interrogate the title. The chair referred to is the piece of furniture found in the underground realm of the Lady of the Green Kirtle. But why should it be made of silver? Chairs are usually made of wood. A chair in a subterranean kingdom might be carved out of rock. But this chair is made of silver, and to a medievalist like Lewis, such a material would naturally connote the influence of Luna, for "her metal is silver."[10] Luna also produces "that periodical insanity which was first meant by the word *lunacy*,"[11] and it is therefore highly appropriate that the lost Prince Rilian should be bound to this chair each night during his (supposed) fit of madness.

What I have recently discovered is that the precise term, "silver chair," is used in a poem by Ben Jonson (1572-1637) as a way of describing the Moon herself.[12] The phrase occurs in a poem entitled "Hymn to Cynthia", Cynthia, of course, being another name for the Lunar goddess.

Lewis did not much like Jonson's work[13], but he could admire the literary talent it displayed. We see this from the way Lewis holds up Jonson as a relevant standard of comparison when discussing the poetry of Alexander Montgomerie (1550-98) in his *English Literature*

---

[9] C. S. Lewis, *The Collected Poems of C. S. Lewis*, ed. by Walter Hooper (London: Fount, 1994), 26.

[10] C. S. Lewis, *The Discarded Image: An Introduction to Medieval and Renaissance Literature* (Cambridge: Cambridge University Press, 1964), 109.

[11] Lewis, *Discarded Image*, 109.

[12] I am indebted to a former student of mine, Betsy Howard, for pointing me to this poem.

[13] See his letter to Martin Kilmer of 29 September 1958, in C. S. Lewis, *The Collected Letters of C. S. Lewis*, ed. by Walter Hooper, 3 vols. (London: HarperCollins, 2004-7), 1:974-5.

in the Sixteenth Century. Lewis gives his opinion of Montgomerie's oeuvre as follows:

> The *Solsequium* is perhaps the best, or else the *Address to the Sun* . . .. [Montgomerie] would have enjoyed, though he would never have learned to imitate, Ben Jonson's lyrics.[14]

Lewis considers Montgomerie incapable of imitating Jonson's lyrics. This is an implicit ranking of the two poets: Jonson has the greater skill, Lewis is quietly suggesting. But why compare the two authors at all? What leads Lewis to mention Montgomerie and Jonson in the same breath? There are scores of sixteenth-century lyric poets who could have been held up for comparison. There must be something about Montgomerie's content and style that is especially redolent of Jonson. And when we take a look at the two poems by Montgomerie that Lewis names and then turn to Jonson's "Hymn to Cynthia," we can see why Lewis should have made this literary critical judgement, for all three are concerned with what happens when the Sun disappears.

In one of Montgomerie's poems that Lewis mentions, "Address to the Sun," the poet appeals to Sol to "withdrau thy bemes" so as not to burn the beauty of his beloved. If the Sun won't oblige, his mistress will take revenge by closing her "cristall ees" (crystal eyes), which have "a brightnes far surmounting thyne," and thus the Sun shall be ashamed and lose his credit in the skies.

The other Montgomerie poem "Solsequium" (literally "sun-follower") is about the marigold, a flower that opens at the rising and closes at the setting of the sun. The poet likens himself in the absence of his beloved to the marigold "when the sun goes out of sight": he "Hings doun his head, / And droups as dead, / And will not spread." He prays for his mistress's presence, which will be to him as revivifying as the sunlight shed by Apollo: "O happie day! / Go not auay. / Apollo! Stay / Thy chair from going doun into the west."

It is with these two poems in mind that Lewis adverts to Jonson's lyrics. He does not specify "Hymn to Cynthia" as the point of comparison (he mentions no particular titles at all), but this is surely among the poems that bring Jonson to his mind, making it natural for him to say that Montgomerie "would have enjoyed" such works. Jonson's "Hymn to Cynthia" runs as follows:

---

[14] C. S. Lewis, *English Literature in the Sixteenth Century, Excluding Drama* (Oxford: Clarendon, 1954), 110.

Queen and huntress, chaste and fair,
Now the sun is laid to sleep,
Seated in thy silver chair,
State in wonted manner keep.
Hesperus entreats thy light,
Goddess excellently bright.

Earth, let not thy envious shade
Dare itself to interpose;
Cynthia's shining orb was made
Heaven to clear, when day did close.
Bless us then with wishèd sight,
Goddess excellently bright.

Lay thy bow of pearl apart,
And thy crystal-shining quiver;
Give unto the flying hart
Space to breathe, how short soever;
Thou that mak'st a day of night,
Goddess excellently bright.[15]

Just as Montgomerie had written of Apollo's "chair," so here Jonson pictures Cynthia enthroned upon her "silver chair," the very term Lewis adopts for the title of his fourth-published Narnian tale. We may therefore legitimately conclude that his chair is a "silver chair" not just because it denotes the piece of furniture to which a lunatic is bound each night, but also because it more subtly connotes the Moon herself, for the Moon *is* the silver chair in which Cynthia reclines. Scholars who have wondered about the origins of Lewis's title have previously got as far as identifying the "silver seat" or "silver stool" that Edmund Spenser mentions in *The Faerie Queene*.[16] Jonson's poetry takes us to a deeper source.

It will be worth staying with the poetry of Montgomerie and Jonson for a moment as we mull over *The Silver Chair* further. Montgomerie's poems depict what happens when the Sun withdraws his beams and his "chair" goes down into the west; Jonson's poem

---

[15] Ben Jonson, "Hymn to Cynthia," in *The Complete Poems* (London: Penguin Classics, 1988), 287.

[16] See, e.g., John D. Cox, "Epistemological Release in *The Silver Chair*," in Peter J. Schakel, ed., *The Longing for a Form: Essays on the Fiction of C. S. Lewis* (Kent, OH: Kent State University Press, 1977).

extols the excellence of the Moon "now the Sun is laid to sleep." *The Silver Chair* likewise refers to the fading of the Sun, or its absence, or its weakness, or its paleness, throughout the middle fourteen chapters of the tale. In the second chapter, for instance, we read that:

> The sun which had been high overhead when [Jill] began her journey was now getting in her eyes. This meant that it was getting lower . . . . Jill . . . didn't think much about the points of the compass. Otherwise she would have known, when the sun began getting in her eyes, that she was travelling pretty nearly due west.[17]

The window of her room in the castle of Cair Paravel "looked west into the strange land of Narnia, and Jill saw the red remains of the sunset still glowing behind distant mountains."[18] As the story progresses, we find references to "sunset light,"[19] "pale winter sunlight,"[20] a "sunless sky,"[21] "pale sunlight,"[22] a "sunless sea";[23] we meet an owl who is not quite himself "till the sun's down"[24] and an Earthman who repeatedly states "Many fall down and few return to the sunlit lands."[25]

All of this downplaying of the sun is already familiar to the attentive reader of *The Silver Chair*. What will be less well known is that, on page 117 of the typescript of *The Silver Chair* (which the late, lamented Walter Hooper kindly brought to my notice), Lewis amended the title of chapter 10, changing it from "The Sunless Sea," which he perhaps thought too redolent of Coleridge's "Kubla Khan,"[26] to "Travels without the Sun."[27]

---

[17] Lewis, *Silver Chair*, 23.

[18] Lewis, *Silver Chair*, 36.

[19] Lewis, *Silver Chair*, 27-8.

[20] Lewis, *Silver Chair*, 68.

[21] Lewis, *Silver Chair*, 82.

[22] Lewis, *Silver Chair*, 115.

[23] Lewis, *Silver Chair*, 164.

[24] Lewis, *Silver Chair*, 32.

[25] Lewis, *Silver Chair*, 122.

[26] "In Xanadu did Kubla Khan / A stately pleasure-dome decree: / Where Alph, the sacred river, ran / Through caverns measureless to man / Down to a sunless sea": the opening lines of Samuel Taylor Coleridge's poem "Kubla Khan" (1797). http://www.poetrybyheart.org.uk/poems/kubla-khan-2/

[27] The typescript may be consulted in the Bodleian Library, University of Oxford. Page 48 of the typescript is also of interest: it shows

One other detail from Jonson's "Hymn to Cynthia" is helpful to keep in mind as we attempt to discern the poetic skill that has gone into the construction of *The Silver Chair*. In the third stanza of his poem, Jonson beseeches the Moon to forgo her role as the goddess of hunting and give a chance to the "flying hart" (i.e., running deer) In this connection, we would do well to recall Puddleglum's horror on discovering at Harfang that he has eaten a Talking Stag.

Furthermore, we should give close attention to the way Lewis portrays Puddleglum's response to this abomination. Puddleglum does not dismiss the incident as meaningless or simply pass the buck by placing the blame on the Harfang giants. As we have already noted, Puddleglum believes "there are no accidents." In this he resembles his creator, Lewis, who says elsewhere that "for a Christian, there are, strictly speaking, no chances."[28] To Puddleglum's mind the grievous mistake of consuming a Talking beast "comes of not attending to the signs."[29] We readers, likewise, should attend to the Lunar signs that gleam and glimmer throughout this silvery tale.

MERCURY AND *THE HORSE AND HIS BOY*

In addition to Puddleglum, another melancholy character in the Narniad is Shasta; or at any rate, he is glum when we first encounter him in the opening chapter of *The Horse and His Boy*. His life with his cruel stepfather, Arsheesh, is little better than slavery, making Shasta so unhappy that he decides to run away from home.

A question we ought to ask ourselves is why Lewis made Arsheesh a fisherman. For Shasta to have a motive for running away, all that we need know about Arsheesh is that he is cruel. If, for the sake of verisimilitude, Lewis felt a need to give Arsheesh an occupation, why not make him a cruel wood-cutter, a cruel blacksmith, a cruel keeper of Dalmatians? But Lewis makes this cruel character a fisherman and bothers to develop the sketch with two or three further strokes of the pen: Arsheesh "went out in his boat to fish" each morning; each afternoon he "loaded the cart with fish" to sell it in a nearby village; and when Shasta day-dreams about absconding he thinks of the residents in a great lord's house who "eat meat every day," meat no

---

Lewis to have amended "the blood of gods flowed in her veins" so that it reads "the blood of the stars flowed in her veins."

[28] C. S. Lewis, *The Four Loves* (Glasgow: Collins, 1982), 83.

[29] Lewis, *Silver Chair*, 112.

doubt being a rare luxury in his own experience.[30]

The significance of fish recurs on the morning following Shasta's escape, when he awakens to an unexpected olfactory sensation:

> . . . what Shasta chiefly noticed was the air. He couldn't think what was missing, until at last he realized that there was no smell of fish in it. For of course, neither in the cottage nor among the nets, had he ever been away from that smell in his life. And this new air was so delicious, and all his old life seemed so far away, that he forgot for a moment about his bruises and his aching muscles.[31]

As I point out in *Planet Narnia*,[32] the word *air* is nearly always used by Lewis with an astrological double meaning, for the sublunary realm contains air (as distinct from the translunary ether) that carries the influences of the planets. Lewis notes in *The Discarded Image* that the planetary influences do not work upon us directly but by first modifying the air of earth's atmosphere:

> Hence when a medieval doctor could give no more particular cause for a patient's condition he attributed it to 'this influence which is at present in the air'. If he were an Italian doctor he would doubtless say *questa influenza*. The profession has retained the word ever since.[33]

---

[30] C. S. Lewis, *The Horse and His Boy* (New York: Collier, 1971), 1, 8. It may be pointed out, quite fairly, that one reason for the emphasis upon fishing is that it subtly connotes the calling of the first disciples. In the second paragraph of the story we learn that Shasta spends his time "mending and washing the nets;" in the third paragraph, we are told that he sits out of doors, "mending the nets." The echo of James and John "mending their nets" (Matthew 4:21; Mark 1:19) and of "fishermen" (presumably Simon and Andrew) "washing their nets" (Luke 5:2) is unmistakable. But there is no need to pit these Biblical echoes against the Mercurial structure of *The Horse and His Boy*. We do not have to choose between them. Part of Lewis's genius was his interest in, and capacity for, seeing points of compatibility between Holy Scripture and a wider tradition of Christian humanism. Making Arsheesh a fisherman kills two birds with one stone: Shasta can be "desolate in Pisces"; he can also be a proto-disciple. For more on this, see my "The Good Serves the Better and Both the Best: C. S. Lewis on Imagination and Reason in Apologetics," in *Imaginative Apologetics: Theology, Philosophy and the Catholic Tradition*, ed. by Andrew Davison (Grand Rapids, MI: Baker Academic, 2012), 59-78.

[31] Lewis, *Horse and His Boy*, 18.

[32] Ward, *Planet Narnia*, 26.

[33] Lewis, *Discarded Image*, 110.

Since publishing *Planet Narnia*, I have discovered, thanks to Bernard O'Donoghue, Fellow of Wadham College, Oxford, that the fishy air of Shasta's childhood represents part of the overarching Mercurial design of *The Horse and His Boy*. Professor O'Donoghue owns a complete edition of the works of Chaucer that was previously in the possession of Lewis himself.[34] O'Donoghue kindly lent me these volumes so I could peruse Lewis's hand-written notes, and it was striking how many of these underlinings, markings, and marginal comments highlighted astrological details.[35]

In medieval astrology it was believed that the *influenza* of the planets varied according to the zodiacal house in which the planet found itself in its passage across the heavens. The place of maximum influence was known as the "exaltation" of the planet; the place of minimal influence was known as the planet's "desolation." In "The Wife of Bath's Prologue" (lines 703f), Chaucer writes:

> And thus, God woot [knows], Mercurie is desolat
> In Pisces.

In his edition of Chaucer, Lewis marked the phrase "Mercurie is desolat / In Pisces;" it evidently caught his attention and struck him as noteworthy. Pisces is the sign of the zodiac between Aquarius and Aries, and, of course, means "Fish." Undoubtedly, the fishy smell that has dominated the air of Shasta's upbringing is meant to represent a Piscean "desolation." Shasta is being raised in a land of "southern jargon,"[36] surrounded by people "talking to one another very slowly about things that sounded dull"[37] and where all the animals are "dumb and witless."[38] The Mercurial influence is low, weak, almost imperceptible in the fisherman's hut and its environs. But as the story progresses and Shasta heads towards "Narnia and the North,"[39] he comes increasingly under the influence of Mercury and discovers a

---

[34] Having acquired them from Lewis's former student, friend, and eventual biographer, George Sayer.

[35] Astrology, it must be emphasized, does not necessarily mean something un-Christian. For more on the long tradition of Christian astrology, see *Planet Narnia*, 28-9, 247-9.

[36] Lewis, *Horse and His Boy*, 11.

[37] Lewis, *Horse and His Boy*, 2.

[38] Lewis, *Horse and His Boy*, 11.

[39] Lewis, *Horse and His Boy*, 16.

"new air" that is "delicious."[40] He is no longer desolate, but on his way to being exalted by an encounter in the mountain pass with the divine Word, the "lord of language," as "The Planets" puts it, the Mercurial Aslan.

"Who are you?" [Shasta] said, scarcely above a whisper.

"One who has waited long for you to speak."[41]

VENUS AND *THE MAGICIAN'S NEPHEW*

From fish we turn to mutton. Digory's London home in *The Magician's Nephew* is described as "one of those houses that get very quiet and dull in the afternoon and always seem to smell of mutton."[42] This is a curious description and could perhaps have been dismissed as insignificant if it were not for the fact that mutton is mentioned again later in the story, during the journey that Digory, Polly, and Fledge make to the Western Garden. They pause for a rest overnight and when they become hungry, Fledge, the flying horse, suggests they all eat grass:

> "Oh, don't be silly," said Polly, stamping her foot. "Of course humans can't eat grass, any more than you could eat a mutton chop."
>
> "For goodness' sake don't talk about chops and things," said Digory. "It only makes it worse."[43]

Mutton and chops never appear in any of the other Narnia Chronicles, yet they receive these repeated mentions in *The Magician's Nephew*. Mutton is not the sort of thing that one would necessarily associate with Venus, Our Lady of Cyprus, the beautiful Aphrodite. It seems out of place, quirky. Yet we should also remember that Venus, in addition to producing "amorousness,"[44] is "a partly comic spirit."[45] She is "the laughter-loving goddess."[46]

Lewis is having fun, and not just random fun. The joke is appropriate to the Venereal influence that the whole story is designed

---

[40] Lewis, *Horse and His Boy*, 18.

[41] Lewis, *Horse and His Boy*, 157.

[42] C. S. Lewis, *The Magician's Nephew* (New York: Collier, 1971), 85.

[43] Lewis, *Magician's Nephew*, 150.

[44] Lewis, *Discarded Image*, 107.

[45] Lewis, *Four Loves*, 92.

[46] C. S. Lewis, *The Allegory of Love: A Study in Medieval Tradition* (Oxford: Oxford University Press, 1958), 237.

to communicate. He is playfully alluding, I believe, to a popular music-hall song from "a serio-comick bombastick operatick interlude" entitled *Amoroso, King of Little Britain*,[47] in which the protagonist, Amoroso, sings as follows:

> Love's like a mutton-chop,
> Soon it grows cold.
> All its attractions hop,
> Ere it grows old.

Venus is "the planet of love" and, weirdly enough, "love's like a mutton-chop." Love warms up, and then, all too soon, cools down. It can be very frustrating. Mutton quite rightly, therefore, has a place in the Narnia Chronicle that is irradiated with Venus symbolism: what is ostensibly odd is actually apt. As Doris Myers has noted, *The Magician's Nephew* is "lighter and more humorous than the other Chronicles"[48] and the comparison of soaring, iridescent, passionate Venus to a humble chop would undoubtedly have appealed to Lewis, who could write elsewhere about the way the laughter-loving goddess often "makes game of us," increasing desire even as she takes away opportunity: "She herself is a mocking, mischievous spirit, far more elf than deity."[49]

The connection between love and mutton would, incidentally, help explain another peculiar moment in Lewis's output, from *Mere Christianity*, where he wryly observes that the inordinacy of the sexual urge would be clearer to us if we thought about indulging our appetite for food in a similar way. He writes:

> You can get a large audience together for a striptease act . . . . Now suppose you come to a country where you could fill a theatre by simply bringing a covered plate on to the stage and then slowly lifting the cover so as to let every one see, just before the lights went out, that it contained a mutton chop or a bit of bacon, would you not think that in that country something had gone wrong with the appetite for food? And would not anyone who had grown up in a different world think there was something equally queer about the state of the sex

---

[47] By James Robinson Planché, *Amoroso, King of Little Britain* was first performed at the Theatre Royal, Drury Lane, London, in 1818.

[48] Doris Myers, *C. S. Lewis in Context* (Kent, OH: Kent State University Press, 1998), 174.

[49] Lewis, *Four Loves*, 92.

instinct among us?[50]

Alan Jacobs finds this passage "rhetorically miscalculated" and "just strange,"[51] but with Venus as our interpretative key, it becomes more understandable. We might agree with Jacobs that the passage is a little ham-fisted[52] in execution, but in intent at least, Lewis is doing nothing more extraordinary that drawing a moral from the ancient association between food and sex.[53]

To return to *The Magician's Nephew*: the proverbial old woman who dresses too young is said to be "mutton dressed as lamb." In this Chronicle, Lewis, for comic effect, momentarily dresses lamb—the youthful, alluring Venus—as mutton. There is, then, if we have ears to hear it, a hilariously involved note of suppressed desire in Digory's desperate wish: "For goodness sake don't talk about chops and things," said Digory. "It only makes it worse."

---

[50] C. S. Lewis, *Mere Christianity* (Glasgow: Collins, 1980), 86-7. See also letter to Mary Willis Shelburne, 10 March 1954: "Verily 'He that but looketh on a plate of ham and eggs to lust after it, hath already committed breakfast with it in his heart.'" Lewis, *Collected Letters*, 1:439.

[51] "I have met several people over the years who remember nothing that Lewis says about sex except this bizarre metaphor and who therefore go about with the conviction that all Lewis's ideas about sexuality are perverse or inexplicable." Alan Jacobs, *The Narnian: The Life and Imagination of C. S. Lewis* (San Francisco: HarperSanFrancisco, 2006), 256n.

[52] Lewis feared he had committed "the sin of Ham" by uncovering his father's nakedness (Genesis 9:20-3). C. S. Lewis, *Surprised by Joy: The Shape of My Early Life* (New York: Harcourt Brace and World, 1955), 101. See his letter of 10 December 1955 in Lewis, *Collected Letters*, 1:681. Colin Hardie reassured him that he had been "not at all Ham-handed." See letter of Lewis to Dorothy L. Sayers, 27 November 1955, in Lewis, *Collected Letters*, 1:676.

[53] When Mr. Bultitude and his mate start devouring food, including "half the ham," in the kitchen at St. Anne's (in the chapter entitled "Venus at St. Anne's"), Ransom says, "*Sine Cerere et Baccho*, Dimble" (C. S. Lewis, *That Hideous Strength* [New York, Scribner, 2003], 375), alluding, inaccurately, to the comedy Eunuchus (IV.v.6) by the Roman dramatist Terence (second century B.C.). He meant "*Sine Cerere et Libero friget Venus*": "without Ceres and Libero [= Bacchus], Venus freezes," i.e., without food and drink, love is cold. It is for this reason that "food and wine" await Mark and Jane at their connubial reunion in the Lodge at the end of the novel. See God is "Bacchus, Venus, Ceres all rolled into one," Lewis, *Miracles*, 118.

SOL AND *THE VOYAGE OF THE "DAWN TREADER"*

Rather like the dialogue between Digory and Fledge in *The Magician's Nephew*, there is a little exchange between King Caspian and Lucy Pevensie in *The Voyage of the "Dawn Treader"* that is oddly detailed and, on the face of it, wholly unnecessary. Nothing comes of it, it is entirely superfluous to the plot; yet it becomes explicable in the light of the planetary imagery out of which this Chronicle is constructed—in this case, Solar imagery.

After the children from England have joined the ship, they are told that the "Dawn Treader" has already visited the island of Galma where the local Duke was hoping that Caspian would marry his daughter. But the King did not care for her looks. Why?

> "Squints, and has freckles," said Caspian.
> "Oh, poor girl," said Lucy.[54]

The daughter of the Duke of Galma has evidently been too much in the Sun: that's why she squints and has freckles. Freckles, we should remember, are also known as "sun-kisses," and squinting is what everyone does, freckled or not, when looking in a sunward direction. Caspian, rather ungallantly, seems not to care for the girl's appearance, and Lucy evidently deems it unfortunate, but what Lewis himself thinks about it we do not know. It is a mistake automatically to equate, as John Goldthwaite equates, Lewis's views with the views of Lewis's characters. Goldthwaite becomes greatly exercised by what he takes to be an outrageous slur on girls with freckled faces[55] but fails to see that this tiny detail is present as evidence of Solar influence

---

[54] C. S. Lewis, *The Voyage of the "Dawn Treader"* (New York: Collier, 1971), 17.

[55] Goldthwaite cites this exchange between Caspian and Lucy as an example of Lewis's "smug" and "snide" disparagement of girls. John Goldthwaite, *The Natural History of Make-Believe* (New York: Oxford University Press, 1996), 227-9. Goldthwaite not only falls into the trap of equating characters' views with authorial views, he mistakenly extrapolates from the particular to the general. He would benefit from reading Lewis's letter to Laurence Krieg, 24 October 1955: "I don't dislike Panthers at all, I think they are one of the loveliest animals there are. I don't remember that I have put any bad panthers in the books (there are some good ones fighting against Rabadash in [*The Horse and His Boy*] aren't there?) and even if I had that wouldn't mean that I thought all Panthers bad, any more than I think all men bad because of Uncle Andrew, or all boys bad because Edmund was once a traitor." Lewis, Collected Letters, 3:666.

bringing about a less than wholly desirable effect.

While Goldthwaite leaps to the defense of freckled squinters, he has no such concern, apparently, for one-legged idiots. Yet the monopods or dufflepuds or duffers come in for far more criticism than the Duke of Galma's daughter. Randy Klassen has done expert work tracing the way that the duffers connect to the Solar theme, and as Sol makes men liberal and generous, I will quote from Klassen's work liberally, trusting to his generosity as I do so.[56]

Lewis derives his monopods from Pliny's account (*Natural History* 7.23) of the "Monocoli" who "have only one leg, and who move in jumps with surprising speed; the same are called the Umbrella-foot tribe [*Sciapodae*] because in hotter weather they lie on their backs on the ground and protect themselves with the shadow of their feet."

Sciapodae means those who are "shade-footed" or "shadow-footed," and, as Klassen notes, they "represent the total inversion of every Solar quality . . . .. They use the most non-rational part of their bodies, the one furthest from their head, to shut out the light of the Sun. In the hierarchical medieval worldview, which is Lewis's native air, this is the posture of foolishness." Though Sol "makes men wise,"[57] he cannot confer wisdom on a benighted soul with an upraised sole.[58]

Klassen goes on to make a particularly enlightening observation about the way Lewis characterizes the monopods. He notes how, in Dante's *Paradiso* (cantos X-XIV), Beatrice leads the pilgrim through the sphere of the Sun, "the Heaven of theologians and philosophers,"[59] where they meet the wisest figures from Holy Scripture and Church history, including Solomon, Chrysostom, Anselm, and Aquinas:

> One of the key episodes, told by Thomas Aquinas in Canto XI, deals with the life of St. Francis. In what must surely be one of the most remarkable tales of the Crusades, Francis . . . journeyed into enemy territory in Egypt, and sought to share the gospel and make peace with Sultan Al-Malik al-Kamil,

---

[56] Randy Klassen, "Monopods, Magic, and Mission: C. S. Lewis's 'Spell for Making Hidden Theology Visible,'" in *Direction: A Mennonite Brethren Forum*, 39.2 (Fall 2010), 204-19. http://www.directionjournal.org/39/2/monopods-magic-and-mission-cs-lewiss.html#Note29

[57] Lewis, *Discarded Image*, 106.

[58] Pun intended. Lewis quibbles on "Sol" and "soul" in the Solar section of "The Planets" poem. *The Voyage of the "Dawn Treader"* is the only Chronicle that features the word "console."

[59] Lewis, *Discarded Image*, 106.

who was indeed a wise and generous leader. Francis had a genial visit, but failed to convert the sultan. Dante says the following about Francis and his mission: "he found that folk unripe to be / converted."[60]

Klassen then invites us to compare that passage from *The Divine Comedy* with the following exchange between Coriakin and Aslan in *The Voyage of the "Dawn Treader"* when the Magician asks,

> "Do you intend to show yourself to them [the Duffers]?"
>
> "Nay," said the Lion . . .. "I should frighten them out of their senses. Many stars will grow old . . . before your people are ripe for that."[61]

This, Klassen contends, is "an unmistakable allusion to Dante's words about Francis, whose offer of the gospel was to a 'people' (Dante's word is *gente*) that were spiritually 'unripe' (*acerba*)." *Ripe* is never used of people in any other place in the Narniad, and given Lewis's great love for and knowledge about the *Comedy* (he described the *Paradiso* as "the highest point" poetry had ever reached[62] and studied its imagery in minute detail[63]), it is surely this passage from Dante's Solar cantos that is the source for his unusual vocabulary here. To the modern imagination, sunshine ripens fruit, but in the Middle Ages it was believed that Sol also ripened people. While the Duke of Galma's daughter has seen too much of the Sun, the Duffers have seen too little.

---

[60] Klassen, "Monopods, Magic, and Mission," 214. The translation of Dante is by Dorothy L. Sayers. See Dante Alighieri, *The Comedy of Dante Alighieri. The Florentine. Cantica III, Paradise (il Paradiso)*, trans. by Dorothy L. Sayers and Barbara Reynolds (Harmondsworth, England: Penguin, 1962), XI.103-4.

[61] Lewis, *Dawn Treader*, 138.

[62] C. S. Lewis, "Shelley, Dryden and Mr Eliot," in *Selected Literary Essays*, ed. by Walter Hooper (Cambridge: Cambridge University Press, 1969), 203.

[63] See, for example, "Dante's Similes," "Imagery in the Last Eleven Cantos of Dante's Comedy," and "Dante's Statius" in C. S. Lewis, *Studies in Medieval and Renaissance Literature*, ed. by Walter Hooper (Cambridge: Cambridge University Press, 1966).

MARS AND *PRINCE CASPIAN*

Lewis's knowledge of Dante and of European literature in general can sometimes seem so vast as to be utterly comprehensive. However, even Homer nods, and Lewis's expertise had its limits. In *Planet Narnia*, I quoted a rare confession of ignorance on Lewis's part. Commenting upon Chaucer's *Compleynt of Mars*, he said that "the astronomical allusions are, I confess, too hard for me." I went on to confess the fact that some of the Martial connections of his own *Prince Caspian* were likewise too hard for me, acknowledging that I could not explain the Mars-related significance of the name of the eponymous hero, Caspian.[64]

Thanks to the draft of "The Planets" that Charlie Starr has helpfully brought to my attention, I now think it is possible to give a reason for Lewis's choice of the name "Caspian" because, in that draft, Lewis describes the heaven of Mars as "the sky's Scythia."[65]

According to the ancient Greek historian Herodotus, whose work Lewis, as an Oxford-trained classicist, knew intimately,[66] the Scythians—the tribe of people prominent in Eurasia from about the ninth till the first century before Christ—had a peculiar devotion to the god Mars. They were among the first peoples to master mounted warfare and appear to have had a reputation for being especially barbaric. (This helps explain, by the way, St. Paul's statement in Colossians 3:11 that "Here there is no . . . barbarian, Scythian, slave or free".) It was only in the cult of Mars that the Scythians used images, altars, and temples; the rites they paid to Mars were unique; and they made more sacrifices to Mars "than to all the rest of the gods."[67] With these facts in mind we can better understand Lewis's description in "The Planets" of the sphere of Mars as "the sky's Scythia," but it also helps explain why he chose to name his protagonist "Caspian," given that the realm of Scythia consisted of the Pontic-Caspian steppe, the plains that stretch from the north coast of the Black Sea all the way east to the Caspian.

---

[64] Ward, *Planet Narnia*, 274, n44.

[65] I borrow this Martial section from my essay "Return to Planet Narnia," in *An Unexpected Journal*, 1.4 (Advent 2018), 90-107.

[66] See, for example, his parody, C. S. Lewis, "Xmas and Christmas: A Lost Chapter from Herodotus," in *God in the Dock* (Grand Rapids, MI: Eerdmans, 1970), 301-3.

[67] Herodotus, *The Histories*, Book IV.

But having shown a link from Mars, via Scythia, to the name "Caspian," we must ask a further question: of all the places within the borders of Scythia that might have supplied Lewis with a name for his eponymous hero, what was it about the word "Caspian" that particularly claimed his attention?

One possibility is that Lewis has in mind the Caspian Pass, which, according to Pliny (vi.17), was a very narrow defile in the Caspian mountains and which perhaps Lewis is glancing at in his description of the almost invisible "steep and narrow path going slant-wise down into the gorge between rocks"[68] through which Aslan guides the children at a critical juncture in the tale.

Another possibility is etymological. "Caspian," like the term "Caucasian," was originally a native self-designation, meaning "white," by extension from "snow" or "ice."[69] Whiteness, in a Martial context, would usually suggest fear or even cowardice. Hence, "Tough-looking warriors turned white" when the Awakened Trees come hurtling towards them.[70] Lewis as a young man during the Great War would have heard about and perhaps known personally certain male contemporaries of his who for refusing to serve in the armed forces were "given the white feather," to signify their supposed cowardice. Such feathers were literally attached to the clothing or sent to the homes of able-bodied young men who decided not to sign up. The intention, of course, was to shame them into action.

According to "The Planets," "white-feathered dread / Mars has mastered." Given that "Caspian" appears to mean "white," it would follow that Lewis chose this name for the hero of his story in order to denote a character whose chivalric spirit is so pure, so perfectly "hardened" by Martial influence,[71] one who has so completely mastered dread, that he has nothing to fear even from bearing a name, *white*,

---

[68] C. S. Lewis, *Prince Caspian: The Return to Narnia* (New York: Collier, 1971), 144.

[69] Pliny the Elder in his *Natural History* (Book 6, chapter 17) derives "Caucasus" from the Scythian term "Croucasis," meaning "white with snow." *Pliny the Elder, Natural History: In Ten Volumes*, trans. by W. H. S. Jones (Cambridge: Harvard University Press, 1949-54).

[70] Lewis, *Prince Caspian*, 190.

[71] Mars produces "sturdy hardiness" in Lewis, *Discarded Image*, 106; "the hard virtue of Mars" from "The Adam at Night," in Lewis, *Collected Poems*, 59. Accordingly, Caspian begins "to harden" as he sleeps "under the stars" in Lewis, *Prince Caspian*, 79.

that would otherwise be suggestive of timidity or pusillanimity.[72]

On the other side of the coin, King Miraz and his men are fearfulness personified and can hardly even bear to hear the word "coward." In this connection, it is worth noting that in the draft of "The Planets" poem, "white-feathered dread" appears as "white-*livered* fear" (my emphasis). Lewis is here drawing on the tradition of medieval thought that assigned virtues to certain bodily organs. In this tradition the liver was believed to be the seat of courage; a truly Martial liver would give warriors stomach for the fight. It should come as no surprise, then, that the only time in the Narniad where the liver is ever mentioned is in *Prince Caspian* when the cowardly Miraz, fretting over his "martial policy," scorns his courtiers for being "lily-livered."[73] The Telmarines' whiteness is not the whiteness that comes from having mastered dread through pureness of heart, as Caspian has done, but from being morally anemic, insufficiently hardened by the iron of Mars.

JUPITER AND *THE LION, THE WITCH AND THE WARDROBE*

We meet another kind of negative whiteness in the White Witch, the antagonist of *The Lion, the Witch and the Wardrobe*. Her whiteness in this context bespeaks winter, paralysis, death, and her preferred mode of murder is petrification. Among the creatures she turns to stone are many standard characters from the realms of faery and myth, such as dwarfs, dryads, centaurs and fauns. But there is one victim who stands out and doesn't seem to belong, namely "a poor kangaroo."[74] A *kangaroo*, forsooth! It is never mentioned anywhere else in *The Lion*, and kangaroos never feature in any of the other Chronicles either. Ever since I was a boy, I have wondered why an antipodean marsupial should crop up in *The Lion, the Witch and the Wardrobe* but appear nowhere else in the Narniad.

We will find an answer to this little puzzle, I believe, by keeping the spiritual symbol of Jupiter steadily before us as the imaginative

---

[72] "Fear Him, ye saints, and you will then / Have nothing else to fear." Lewis described this line from the hymn "Through All the Changing Scenes of Life" as "perfection." C. S. Lewis, *Image and Imagination: Essays and Reviews* (New York: Cambridge University Press, 2013), 164.

[73] Lewis, *Prince Caspian*, 178.

[74] C. S. Lewis, *The Lion, the Witch and the Wardrobe* (New York: Collier, 1970), 168.

key to the book. We know a great deal of what Jupiter meant to Lewis because of the numerous times he wrote about him explicitly. One such example is his 1947 poem, *"Le Roi S'Amuse"* ("The King Amuses Himself"), in which *le Roi*, Jupiter, amuses himself by creating the universe. In the first stanza we learn that

> [Jove's] glance turned
> Into dancing, burning
> Colour-gods who rushed upon that sullen world,
> Waking, re-making, exalting it anew –
> Silver and purple, shrill-voiced yellow, turgid crimson, and virgin blue.[75]

This Jovial palette should put us in mind of the scene in *The Lion* when Aslan de-petrifies the Witch's victims, "burning" them into color again:

> Everywhere the statues were coming to life. The courtyard looked no longer like a museum; it looked more like a zoo . . . Instead of all that deadly white the courtyard was now a blaze of colours; glossy chestnut sides of centaurs, indigo horns of unicorns, dazzling plumage of birds, reddy-brown of foxes, dogs, and satyrs, yellow stockings and crimson hoods of dwarfs; and the birch-girls in silver, and the beech-girls in fresh, transparent green, and the larch-girls in green so bright that it was almost yellow.[76]

The deadly pallor that the Witch had cast over all her victims becomes, under the revivifying warmth of Aslan's breath, a riot of colour, akin to what Jove achieves in the poem with his "Silver and purple, shrill-voiced yellow, turgid crimson, and virgin blue."

The similarities between poem and Chronicle continue. In *The Lion*, the sepulchral silence of the Witch's court erupts into a cacophony of "roarings, brayings, yelpings, barkings, squealings, cooings, neighings, stampings, shouts, hurrahs, songs and laughter."[77] In *"Le Roi S'Amuse,"* Jove bursts with laughter that is positively creative, bringing to birth a large cast of characters, the last of whom should particularly interest us:

---

[75] C. S. Lewis, *The Collected Poems of C. S. Lewis*, ed. by Walter Hooper (London: Fount, 1994), 39.

[76] Lewis, *The Lion*, 166.

[77] Lewis, *The Lion*, 166.

Like cloven-shafted
Lightning, his laughter into brightness broke.
From every dint
Where the severed splinters
Had scattered a Sylvan or a Satyr woke;
Ounces[78] came pouncing, dragon-people flew,
There was spirited stallion, squirrel unrespectful, clanging
raven and kangaroo.[79]

In the poem, Jove wakes the kangaroo, just as Aslan takes special care of that poor kangaroo in *The Lion, the Witch and the Wardrobe*. And it is not just in *"Le Roi S'Amuse"* and *The Lion* where a link between Jupiter and this particular animal is to be observed but also in *That Hideous Strength*, where Ransom, having turned by that stage of the trilogy into a human embodiment of the Jovial spirit,[80] summons mice into his room, mice that "when they sat up" looked "like tiny kangaroos."[81]

Evidently, the kangaroo is one of Lewis's favorite animals when he wishes to evoke the fecundity and variety of God's creation. In *Miracles*, where he argues for monarchical (and therefore Jovial) Supernaturalism,[82] he writes: "It will be agreed that, however they came there, concrete, individual, determinate things do now exist: things like flamingoes, German generals, lovers, sandwiches, pineapples, comets and kangaroos."[83] The fact that he ends the list with the kangaroo in both *Miracles* and *"Le Roi S'Amuse"* suggests that this animal held a special place in his personal iconography; and it is worth pointing out that, even in *The Lion*, the kangaroo is the last of the creatures to be de-petrified.[84]

Both his fascination with marsupials and his recurrent decision to place them last are connected, I suspect, with one of the peculiarities

---

[78] "Ounces" in this context means snow leopards.

[79] Lewis, *The Collected Poems*, 39.

[80] Jane emerges from her audience with Ransom "in the sphere of Jove." For more on Ransom's Jovial transformation, see Ward, *Planet Narnia*, 47-53.

[81] Lewis, *That Hideous Strength*, 149.

[82] For more on the link between Joviality and *Miracles*, see Ward, *Planet Narnia*, chapter 10.

[83] Lewis, *Miracles*, 90

[84] Last, that is, among the crowd of general, unnamed characters. The very final character to be de-petrified is Mr. Tumnus.

of his Christian conversion. It is well known that Lewis came to believe in the divinity of Christ during a journey to Whipsnade Zoo in the side-car of his brother's motorcycle: "When we set out I did not believe that Jesus Christ is the Son of God, and when we reached the zoo I did."[85] What has received less attention is the fact that, after he arrived at the zoo, he found himself in an enclosure called Wallaby Wood having a near-paradisal experience: "Wallaby Wood, with the birds singing overhead and the bluebells underfoot and the wallabies hopping all round one was almost Eden come again."[86] Is it too fanciful, I wonder, to ask whether Lewis did not ever afterwards smile on both wallaby and kangaroo[87] alike as a private, somewhat comic, token of himself as a Christian convert? Is there even a humorous little glance at St. Paul in his decision always to put the kangaroo at the end of his lists: "Last of all, as to one untimely born, he appeared to me . . ."?[88]

Be that as it may, I can imagine a reader objecting that the link I have traced between Jovial imagery and kangaroos is extremely involved and that the Narnian marsupial is an insignificant ingredient in the story in any case. Does it really matter? I would counter by contending that smallness and intricacy are the very points at issue. It is part of the message of *"Le Roi S'Amuse"*—and much of Lewis's other work—that God (here figured as Jove) delights in "patterned atoms" and "woven mazes." The divinely creative act, like Lewis's sub-creative act, covers all creatures great and small.

SATURN AND *THE LAST BATTLE*

From the bounding kangaroo we turn our attention to the shambling ape and the Saturnine spirit of *The Last Battle*. The very word "shambling" is our first point of focus here.

In the published version of "The Planets" poem, Lewis described Saturn as walking round the heaven "Stoop'd and stumbling, with staff groping." In the draft of the poem, which Charlie Starr has brought to my attention, Lewis used a slightly different form of words:

---

[85] Lewis, *Surprised by Joy*, 237

[86] Lewis, *Surprised by Joy*, 237-8. See also the yellow wallabies in *Perelandra*, chapters 5 and 12.

[87] Wallabies and kangaroos belong to the same taxonomic family (*macropodidae*) and sometimes to the same genus.

[88] 1 Corinthians 15:8.

"Stoop'd and stumbling, with staff *shambling*" (my emphasis). It is significant that, in *The Last Battle*, Lewis uses that verb, to shamble, a couple of times, though never even once in the entire remainder of the Narniad: "Shift went shambling along . . . he came down the tree and shambled across to the lion-skin."[89]

The verb is well-chosen for Saturnine purposes, given its etymology. A *shamble* was originally a trestle-table on which animals would be butchered or meat displayed for sale. By extension, it came to mean a slaughter-house, a place of carnage or confusion: hence the modern phrase "a complete shambles" and even "omni-shambles." The verb *to shamble*, suggesting a straddling, ungainly gait, seems to derive from the wide-set legs of the trestle. Thus, Shift's shambling walk, while denoting an awkward way of moving, also connotes something much more ominous: pain, blood, and death.

A much happier connection between the draft of "The Planets" poem and *The Last Battle* is to be found not in the Saturn section of the poem, as might be expected, but in the Jupiter section. As I argue in *Planet Narnia*,[90] the atmosphere at the end of *The Last Battle* shifts away from the gravity of Saturn and becomes deliberately Jovial. Indeed, Lewis subtly signifies this lightening mood in the exchange between Lucy and Eustace, after they have both died and gone to the Narnian equivalent of the outskirts of heaven:

> "Isn't it wonderful?" said Lucy. "Have you noticed one can't feel afraid, even if one wants to? Try it."
>
> "By Jove, neither one can," said Eustace after he had tried.[91]

It is "by Jove" that they are unable to feel afraid. Jupiter has regained his happy seat, and now it is time for all the redeemed characters to enter into joy. The pace quickens and the heavenly ecstasies become more and more intense, so that the normal restraints are left behind— even gravity itself:

> [Jill] saw something white moving steadily up the face of the Waterfall. That white thing was the Unicorn. You couldn't tell whether he was swimming or climbing, but he moved on, higher and higher. The point of his horn divided the water just above his head, and it cascaded out in two rainbow-coloured

---

89 C.S. Lewis, *The Last Battle* (New York: Collier, 1971), 7-8.

90 Ward, *Planet Narnia*, 207-13.

91 Lewis, *The Last Battle*, 173.

streams all round his shoulders. Just behind him came King Tirian. He moved his legs and arms as if he were swimming but he moved straight upwards: as if one could swim up the wall of a house . . .. It was the sort of thing that would have been quite impossible in our world . . .. But in that world you could do it. You went on, up and up, with all kinds of reflected lights flashing at you from the water and all manner of coloured stones flashing through it, till it seemed as if you were climbing up light itself . . ..[92]

In the published version of "The Planets," the Jovial influence is described in this way:

Soft breathes the air
Mild, and meadowy, as we mount further
Where rippled radiance rolls about us . . .

In the draft version of the poem, Lewis had inserted an extra line:

Soft breathes the air
Mild and meadow-sweet as we mount further
Diving upward mid dancing light
Where rippled radiance rolls about us . . .

Diving upward mid dancing light. This picture of a gravity-defying plunge into water and light, from the draft Jupiter section of "The Planets," is a nice summary of the Jovial passage from the end of *The Last Battle* quoted above. Though Lewis dropped the line from the published version of the poem, he did not forget the imagery and made sure to retrieve it at the happy climax of his final Chronicle.

CONCLUSION

In *Planet Narnia*, I assessed the Chronicles both in fine detail and on a larger scale. This present essay has focused solely on points of fine detail. Properly understood, I believe, these details reveal themselves to be the literary equivalent not of dandruff but of breadcrumbs, which, like those left behind by Hansel and Gretel, Lewis dropped intentionally; they are clues, not detritus. If we follow their lead, they will take us to some of Lewis's core theological convictions and to the heart of his plan for the Narniad.

Theologically, Lewis held to a belief in a God who was both Creator of the world and the Author of history. The divine being has

---

[92] Lewis, *The Last Battle*, 173-4.

not just made the stage, the props, and the cast, He has also written the play. God has "intricately wrought" us in the womb and "in thy book were written, every one of them, the days that were formed for me" (Psalm 139:15-16). Christianity teaches, according to Lewis, that "God made the world—that space and time, heat and cold, and all the colors and tastes, and all the animals and vegetables, are things that God 'made up out of His head' as a man makes up a story."[93] And this story is intelligible, designed, internally coherent; it is not a hodge-podge or a mishmash but has a discernible theme and a logic derived from the Logos who spoke it into being:

> Death and resurrection are what the story is about; and had we but eyes to see it, this has been hinted on every page, met us, in some disguise, at every turn, and even been muttered in conversations between such minor characters (if they are minor characters) as the vegetables.[94]

The hero of the story is the dying and rising Son, whose dramatic trajectory is reflected even in the insensate corn that dissolves into the ground and re-emerges in the crops.

If we had eyes to see it, we could perceive God working His purposes out in every single thing, and, just occasionally, Lewis confesses, he believes he gains an inkling of the divine Author's fine-grained purposes:

> I trust no one will call me a mystic . . . but . . . all sorts of objects, animate and inanimate, natural and artificial . . . seem to me . . . like Jane Austen's niece, 'so odd and all the time so perfectly natural'.[95] They respond, like chords of music, to some want within, unnoticed till the moment of its fulfilment. They fit the senses and imagination like an old glove. Momentary as they are, they seem (I hardly know how to say it) to have been prepared from all eternity for their precise place in the symphony of things.[96]

The medieval imagination reflected this divine creativity and authorship especially well in Lewis's view. There is an impulse in

---

93 Lewis, *Mere Christianity*, 41.

94 Lewis, *Miracles*, 102.

95 See Jane Austen's letter to her niece, Fanny Knight (20 February 1817).

96 E. M. W. Tillyard and C. S. Lewis, *The Personal Heresy: A Controversy* (London: Oxford University Press, 1939), 79-80.

much medieval art that we may call

> the love of the labyrinthine; the tendency to offer to the mind
> or the eye something that cannot be taken in at a glance,
> something that at first looks planless though all is planned.
> Everything leads to everything else, but by very intricate
> paths.[97]

As a medievalist himself, Lewis naturally enough reflected this imaginative grasp of reality in his own writings. We see this love of the labyrinthine, for instance, in the grand cosmic dance at the end of *Perelandra*: "All that is made seems planless to the darkened mind, because there are more plans than it looked for . . .. There seems no plan, because it is all plan."[98] And Lewis's own poetry, likewise, is often fantastically complex, and those poems which the uneducated "would mistake for *vers libre*" are often in "the strictest and most complicated metres of all."[99]

When, at the height of his career, he came to write the Chronicles, Lewis's theological insights were so matured and his world-building skills so refined that he deliberately created Narnia with a superficial appearance of randomness, while secretly working to an imaginative blueprint of the utmost sophistication and complexity. The apparent hodge-podge betokened the supposed planlessness of the real world as perceived by "the darkened mind": his authorial intent betokened the intelligent design that he perceived in God's creative act:

> A supreme workman will never break by one note or one
> syllable or one stroke of the brush the living and inward law of
> the work he is producing. But he will break without scruple any
> number of those superficial regularities and orthodoxies which
> little, unimaginative critics mistake for its laws. The extent to
> which one can distinguish a just "license" from a mere botch or
> failure of unity depends on the extent to which one has grasped
> the real and inward significance of the work as a whole.[100]

Humphrey Carpenter describes the Chronicles as "very hastily written," claiming they borrow "indiscriminately from other

---

[97] Lewis, *Discarded Image*, 194.

[98] C. S. Lewis, *Perelandra* (London: London Bodley Head, 1977), 202.

[99] Lewis, *Collected Poems*, xx.

[100] Lewis, *Miracles*, 100.

mythologies and narratives."[101] A. N. Wilson calls them a "jumble .
.. full of inconsistencies."[102] Brian Sibley claims Lewis composed the
Narniad "glibly" in a "whizz-bang, easy-come-easy-go, slap-it-down
kind of way."[103] In naming these three figures, I do not mean to imply
that they are among the "little, unimaginative critics" whom Lewis
lambasts, still less that they suffer from the "darkened mind" he
critiques in *Perelandra*. But I do believe they are mistaken and that
they have dismissed Narnia prematurely.

As I hope this essay has confirmed, the "real and inward
significance" of each Chronicle is keyed to one of the seven "spiritual
symbols" that Lewis considered of "permanent value" in the human
imagination. Like the pilgrim in the *Paradiso*, Lewis rises up through
these heavens—Luna, Mercury, Venus, Sol, Mars, Jupiter, Saturn—
turning the influences of each planetary personality to world-building
effect. It is to their symbolic logic that he owes not only the large-scale
architectonics of each tale but also all manner of minor ingredients,
including the jots and tittles we have been inspecting here: chairs,
fish, chops, freckles, livers, kangaroos, and shambling apes.

Admittedly, these details are tiny. So small are they that one
might be inclined to dismiss them as entirely negligible. On further
consideration, however, these paltry trifles turn out not to be chicken-
feed but rather "patterned atoms," basic and essential components of
those "woven mazes" that were so vitally important to Lewis, both as
a Christian and as a writer. "It is just on such apparent *minutiae* that
the total effect of a poem depends,"[104] he declared, speaking of Dante's
microscopically fine artistry in *The Divine Comedy*. And we may take
poem to include also the genre of fairy-tale, to which the Narnia
Chronicles belong. Their poetry, like their theological meaning, rests
in no small part on their smallest parts.

---

[101] Humphrey Carpenter, *The Inklings: C. S. Lewis, J. R. R. Tolkien,
Charles Williams, and Their Friends* (London: HarperCollins, 1997), 224-7.

[102] A. N. Wilson, *C. S. Lewis: A Biography* (New York: W.W. Norton
& Co., 1990), 225.

[103] Brian Sibley, *Cover Stories*, BBC Radio 4 (11.30 a.m., 13 June
2002).

[104] C. S. Lewis, "A Note on Comus," in C. S. Lewis, *Studies in
Medieval and Renaissance Literature*, ed. by Walter Hooper (Cambridge:
Cambridge University Press, 1966), 181.

Chapter 7

THE FIGURE OF MERLIN IN
THAT HIDEOUS STRENGTH

David C. Downing

That Hideous Strength is Lewis's only work of fiction set in the time and place in which he lived, and its principal concerns continue to have currency and relevance. In this novel, we find an Orwellian anxiety about the all-pervasive powers of the modern State, a satire on uncritical reverence for technology as the cure for all human ills, a concern for the rights of animal and human subjects in the laboratory, and an examination of contemporary attitudes toward sex and marriage. In general, *That Hideous Strength* offers a searching critique of what has been called The Modern Temper. How curious then, and how very like Lewis, that this story should also be considered a major twentieth-century contribution to the heritage of Arthurian literature.

Nathan Comfort Starr in *King Arthur Today* speaks for many readers when he declares that the third novel of the Ransom trilogy "deserves an honored place in the Arthurian legend, for it is a highly original restatement of old truths applied to our violent, distraught world, and it is conceived in terms of vaulting imagination."[1] Indeed, it would take a vaulting imagination to set forth a tale of space travelers, totalitarian schemers, and ruthless technocrats, and then bring Merlin the magician onto the stage, newly awakened from fifteen centuries of enchanted slumber. On one side of the story's conflict are those at the National Institute of Coordinated Experiments (NICE) who propose to combine the powers of modern Science with those of ancient Magic. On the other side are Ransom and his company at St. Anne's, who hope to recruit Merlin if they may, stop him if they must. And then there is Merlin himself, awakened not only for the service of his secret arts, but also that he himself may find redemption.

Merlin is unquestionably one of the most revered characters in Arthurian lore. In Geoffrey of Monmouth's *History of the Kings of*

---

[1] Nathan Comfort Starr, *King Arthur Today: The Arthurian Legend in English and American Literature, 1901-1953* (Gainesville: University of Florida Press, 1954), 187.

Britain,[2] Merlin is the one who puts Arthur on the throne and who sustains him there. In Sir Thomas Malory's *Le Morte d'Arthur*,[3] he is chief advisor not only to Arthur and his father before him, but also to the Archbishop of Canterbury. *Idylls of the King* by Alfred, Lord Tennyson refers to Merlin as a "gentle wizard" of "vast wit" and "high purpose."[4] Even Dante makes a glancing reference to Merlin as a "good enchanter."[5] For some readers then, it may come as something of a shock in *That Hideous Strength* when Lewis has Ransom tell Merlin bluntly, "Because Our Lord does all things for each, one of the purposes of your reawakening was that your soul should be saved."[6]

Why would C. S. Lewis, that great admirer of Camelot and all it stood for, present its chief sponsor and sustainer as a soul in need of saving? To answer that question, readers must consider Lewis's work not only as novelist, but also as critic, cultural historian, and Christian essayist. Such a project casts new light upon Merlin's appearance in *That Hideous Strength*; it also uncovers one of the bedrock convictions upon which Lewis's life and writings were founded.

For those familiar with Merlin's role in Arthurian tradition, it is not hard to discover clues as to why he might be seen as one in need of redemption. Recounting the lore of Bragdon Wood (Merlin's supposed resting place in *That Hideous Strength*), Lewis invents a historical character, "the fabulously learned and saintly Richard Crowe," who lauds Arthur's wizard for being "a true King's man as ever ate bread," even though he is "the Devil's son."[7] The first half of this formula fits our usual image of Merlin; the second half may come as a surprise—yet it is a tradition of long standing in the Matter of Britain.

In the first great Arthurian work, Geoffrey of Monmouth's *History of the Kings of Britain*, completed in 1137, Merlin is described as

---

[2] Geoffrey of Monmouth, *The History of the Kings of Britain*, trans. by Lewis Thorpe (New York: Viking Penguin, 1987).

[3] Sir Thomas Malory, *King Arthur and his Knights*, ed. by Eugene Vinaver (Oxford: Oxford University Press, 1975).

[4] Alfred Lord Tennyson, *Idylls of the King* (New York: Signet, 1961), 121, 137.

[5] Norris J. Lacy, ed., *The New Arthurian Encyclopedia* (New York: Garland, 1991), 128.

[6] C. S. Lewis, *That Hideous Strength: A Modern Fairy Tale for Grown-Ups* (New York: Macmillan, 1968), 289.

[7] Lewis, *That Hideous Strength*, 22.

the offspring of an incubus and a Welsh princess.[8] Despite his sinister origins, Merlin is a stout-hearted figure in Geoffrey's pseudo-history, one who consistently uses his preternatural powers in the service of king and country. Consequently, writers who came after Geoffrey seemed to want to soften the story of Merlin's origins as described in this early source. Robert de Boron, a French priest whose *Joseph of Arimathea* comes about a half century after Geoffrey's monumental work, concedes that Merlin is the son of a devil, but suggests that both he and his mother are innocent of any wickedness. In Robert's version, the infant Merlin is a prodigy of eloquence and clairvoyance, who, even while a babe in arms, proves his mother's blamelessness in court and secures her acquittal by telling the judge that he knows of that official's own dubious parentage.[9] The English poet Layamon goes a step further in *Brut* (1205) declaring that Merlin's father was not a demon at all, but one of the mischievous creatures who dwells in the sky.[10]

Both as a scholar and as a story-teller, Lewis followed Layamon's lead. In *The Discarded Image*, Lewis notes that in the early Middle Ages, it was believed there were creatures of the air who could be either good or bad, like humans, but that gradually these beings, called Daemons, became associated with fallen angels, or demons.[11] Lewis's mouthpiece in *That Hideous Strength*, Dr. Dimble, comments more fully on the mystery of Merlin's origins and character:

> Has it ever struck you what an odd creation Merlin is? He's not evil; yet he's a magician. He is obviously a druid; yet he knows all about the Grail. He's 'the devil's son'; but then Layamon goes out of his way to tell that the kind of being who fathered Merlin needn't have been bad after all. You remember, 'There dwell in the sky many kinds of wights. Some of them are good, and some work evil.'[12]

Later in the novel, Dimble coins the term "Neutrals" in talking to his wife about beings which do not fall into any convenient theological

---

[8] Geoffrey, *Kings of Britain*, 20.

[9] Norma L. Goodrich, *Merlin* (New York: Harper and Row, 1988), 43-6.

[10] Eugene Mason, trans., *Wace and Layamon: Arthurian Chronicles* (London: J. M. Dent and Sons, 1962), 145.

[11] C. S. Lewis, *The Discarded Image* (Cambridge: Cambridge University Press, 1964), 118.

[12] Lewis, *That Hideous Strength*, 31-2.

category:

> There used to be things on this Earth pursuing their own business, so to speak. They weren't ministering angels sent to help fallen humanity; but neither were they enemies preying upon us. Even in St. Paul one gets glimpses of a population that won't exactly fit into our two columns of angels and devils. And if you go back further . . . all the gods, elves, dwarves, water-people, *fate, longaevi*. You and I know too much to think they were just illusions.[13]

As he so often does, Lewis in this passage uses his fiction to provide an imaginative embodiment for ideas which he elucidates in his scholarly works. In *The Discarded Image*, he offers a fuller discussion of Dimble's "Neutrals," as well as those unusual terms *fate* and *longaevi* (though in that context he is not so free as Dr. Dimble to speculate about the veracity of ancient folk traditions). There he surveys all of these varieties of *Longaevi*, "long-livers," explaining that Fairies were much more splendid and fascinating beings in the Middle Ages than the modern notion of fairies as toy angels. He says that the Italian *Fata Morgana* was fully Fairy, whereas the elusive, almost playful Morgan le Fay in Malory and other English writers is much more humanized. Lewis goes on to suggest that Merlin belongs to this order of beings, better understood as half-fairy than half-devil.[14] So when Merlin proclaims near the end of *That Hideous Strength* that he is no devil's son,[15] we may take him at his word.

If rumors of Merlin's demonic descent are false, then the question remains why he is in need of redemption. It does not take more than a cursory survey of Arthurian lore to reveal a number of stains on his scutcheon. Again, it is the early source, Geoffrey of Monmouth's *History*, which recounts some of his most dubious deeds. In Geoffrey's version, Merlin is a faithful servant to the royal family, but one whose service is not cluttered by any moral idealism. When Arthur's uncle Aurelius wants a battle monument for Salisbury, Merlin suggests they go over Ireland and take a circle of giant stones that he has seen there. This they do without any compunctions, defeating the Irish king and carrying the stone pillars back to England by Merlin's magic to create Stonehenge. After Aurelius' death, his brother Uther falls in love with

---

[13] Lewis, *That Hideous Strength*, 284-5.

[14] Lewis, *The Discarded Image*, 130.

[15] Lewis, *That Hideous Strength*, 289.

Ygerna, the wife of one of his most loyal vassals, Gorlois, Duke of Cornwall. Again, Merlin works the king's will without any thought to morality, transforming Uther into the likeness of Gorlois, so that he can make a midnight visit to Ygerna, who later begets Arthur. (Again, we see later writers taking care to spruce up Merlin's image: in Malory, he is ignorant of Uther's seduction scheme. In Tennyson, this episode is left out entirely.)

But in presenting Merlin as one who stands in need of salvation, Lewis does not seem to have in mind any particular misdoings on his part. After all, as an orthodox Christian, Lewis would certainly affirm that salvation comes by faith, not by perfection of works. In *That Hideous Strength*, Lewis does not refer to Merlin's questionable actions as recorded by various romancers. He is less interested in what Merlin has done than in who he is. And, ultimately, we see that the soul of Merlin the Magician has not been sullied by this or that misdeed, but by the very fact that he *is* a magician.

One of the paradoxes Dr. Dimble expressed about Merlin is that "he's not evil; yet he's a magician,"[16] implying, of course, that by definition magicians are generally evil. For Lewis, their sin is not just that they dabble in forbidden arts; more seriously, they have succumbed to the serpent's oldest temptation, "Ye shall be as gods." Those who read widely in Lewis's books will notice certain key words that take on personal meanings in his work, terms which retain the same specialized connotations in a variety of contexts. Words such as *joy, pagan, comfort,* and *taste* all have specific and philosophically-rich colorings in the Lewis lexicon. *Magic* and *magician* are words of this sort, both in Lewis's fiction and his non-fiction. Andrew Ketterley in *The Magician's Nephew* is typical, one who wants to manipulate occult forces for his own gain; who feels exempt from ordinary morality because of his "high and lonely destiny";[17] who disregards the sanctity of life, whether human or animal. Though he is essentially a comic character, Andrew's "magic" shares a great deal with "science" as practiced at Belbury in *That Hideous Strength*.

It is not anomalous, then, in *That Hideous Strength*, for twentieth-century technocrats to seek the services of a reputed wizard. In *The Abolition of Man*, Lewis makes explicit his sense of the connection

---

[16] Lewis, *That Hideous Strength*, 31.

[17] C. S. Lewis, *The Magician's Nephew* (New York: Scholastic, 1988), 18.

between ancient magic and modern science:

> I have described as a "magician's bargain" that process whereby man surrenders object after object, and finally himself, to Nature in return for power. And I meant what I said. The fact that the scientist has succeeded where the magician failed has put such a wide contrast between them in popular thought that the real story of the birth of Science is misunderstood. You will even find people who write about the sixteenth century as if Magic were a medieval survival and Science the new thing that came to sweep it away. Those who have studied the period know better. There was very little Magic in the Middle Ages: the sixteenth and seventeenth centuries are the high noon of magic. The serious magical endeavour and the serious scientific endeavour are twins: one was sickly and died, and the other strong and throve. But they are twins. They were born of the same impulse.[18]

Some readers of Lewis have dismissed such equations of science and magic as facile and reactionary. Lewis's contemporary, J. B. S. Haldane, the Marxist ideologue who bears more than a little resemblance to Edward Weston, complained that Lewis was contemptuous of scientists in general and that he parodied their research methods.[19] More recently, Philip Deasy called the Ransom trilogy "a total and unrelenting attack on science."[20] But Lewis argued that the main target of his satire was not science, but Scientism, the quasi-religious hope of using technology to help humans evolve into some new species of divinity. He pointed out that the one real scientist in *That Hideous Strength* was murdered when he tried to leave NICE, having discovered its work was not really about science.[21]

Lewis's concern is not so much with magic in itself or science in itself as with the deeper impulse which unites the two. As he goes on

---

[18] C. S. Lewis, *The Abolition of Man* (New York: Macmillan, 1965), 87.

[19] J. B. S. Haldane, "Auld Hornie, F. R. S.," in *Modern Quarterly* 1 (Autumn 1946), 33-4. Reprinted in *Shadows of Imagination: The Fantasies of C. S. Lewis, J. R. R. Tolkien, and Charles Williams*, ed. by Mark R. Hillegas (Carbondale, IL: Southern Illinois University Press, 1969).

[20] Philip Deasy, "God, Space, and C. S. Lewis," in *Commonweal*, 68 (25 July 1958), 422.

[21] C. S. Lewis, "A Reply to Professor Haldane" in Of Other Worlds: Essays and Stories, ed. by Walter Hooper (New York: Harcourt Brace Jovanovich, 1966), 78.

to explain in *The Abolition of Man*:

> There is something which unites magic and applied science while separating both from the "wisdom" of earlier ages. For the wie men of old the cardinal problem had been how to conform the soul to reality, and the solution had been knowledge, self-discipline, and virtue. For magic and applied science alike the problem is how to subdue reality to the wishes of men: the solution is a technique.[22]

Here Lewis touches on one of the themes that was closest to his heart: learning to accept what is given and to conform one's will to reality, rather than insisting on one's own way and trying to bend reality to one's will. Apart from the intrinsic dangers of the occult, the practice of Magic also betokens an underlying attitude of not accepting one's creatureliness, of trying to escape the intractable vulnerability of being human. Lewis expresses this thought most succinctly in "The Inner Ring," where he observes, "It is the very mark of a perverse desire that it seeks what is not to be had."[23]

This idea recurs frequently in the Ransom trilogy, a lesson which must be learned over and over. In *Out of the Silent Planet*,[24] Ransom seeks safety in avoiding the Malacandrians, the very ones whose help he will need to survive. In *Perelandra*,[25] he comes to understand that the fundamental nature of evil, the sin by which the Bent One fell, is to cling to what is desired rather than accepting what is given. He must learn to live like the unfallen creatures of Perelandra, who abide in a perpetual state of trust and obedience, throwing themselves into each wave as it comes and not trying to dwell on the Fixed Land. By the time we meet Ransom in *That Hideous Strength*, he has learned that deep-seated desires for safety or comfort are not things to be grasped: he refuses Merlin's offer to mend his wounded heel, knowing by then that he has been destined to bear in his flesh the wound of the Serpent Slayer (Gen. 3:15).

Lewis's frequent warnings about the danger of trying to dominate nature, of trying to assert one's will over reality, take on a particular poignancy in *Surprised by Joy* where he discusses the death

---

[22] Lewis, *Abolition of Man*, 87-8.

[23] C. S. Lewis, "The Inner Ring," in *The Weight of Glory and Other Addresses* (Grand Rapids, MI: Eerdmans, 1977), 63.

[24] C. S. Lewis, *Out of the Silent Planet* (New York: Macmillan, 1943).

[25] C. S. Lewis, *Perelandra* (New York: Macmillan, 1944).

of his mother when he was nine. There, he explains that as a child he had prayed that she might be miraculously restored to him, but that his prayers were essentially "irreligious" in nature:

> I had approached God, or my idea of God, without love, without awe, even without fear. He was, in my mental picture of this miracle, to appear neither as Savior nor as Judge, but merely as magician; and when He had done what was required of Him I supposed He would simply—well, go away.[26]

Here again, that keyword *magician* is associated with the desire to make reality conform to one's will instead of accepting that which cannot be changed. Lewis adds that children often pray in such a spirit, but that is one of the childish things which must eventually be put away.

But even if Merlin is a magician, aren't there different kinds of magic? Most students of the occult distinguish between white magic, used only for constructive purposes such as healing or enhancing fertility, and black magic, the casting of spells and curses.[27] Lewis, of course, was aware of the distinction, but he doubted whether it were as clear-cut as sometimes maintained. In his volume of the *Oxford History of English Literature*, he explains the difference between *magia*, high or "white" magic, such as we encounter in Merlin or Bercilek, which is associated with the world of Faerie, and *goeteia*, black magic, associated with witchcraft and Faustian contracts with the devil. But having made the distinction, Lewis adds that most sixteenth-century writers, including King James himself (who published his *Demonology* in 1597) condemned all kinds of magic as a snare, warning that even "white magic" was a danger to the soul.[28]

In *That Hideous Strength*, it is Dr. Dimble who insists on the contrast between Merlin's magic and the magic of sorcerers: "What common measure is there," he asks, "between ceremonial occultists like Faustus and Prospero and Archimago with their midnight studies, their forbidden books, their attendant fiends or elementals, and a figure like Merlin who seems to produce his results simply by

---

[26] C. S. Lewis, *Surprised by Joy: The Shape of My Early Life* (New York: Harcourt Brace Jovanovich, 1955), 21.

[27] W. B. Crow, *A History of Magic, Witchcraft, and Occultism* (London: The Aquarian Press, 1968), 127.

[28] C. S. Lewis, *English Literature in the Sixteenth Century, Excluding Drama* (Oxford: Clarendon Press, 1954), 7-8.

being Merlin?"[29] Later Dimble argues that Merlin's source of power is utterly different from the technological approach at NICE:

> Merlin is the reverse of Belbury. He's at the opposite extreme. He is the last vestige of an old order in which matter and spirit were, from our modern point of view, confused. For him every operation on Nature is a kind of personal contact, like coaxing a child or stroking one's horse. After him came the modern man to whom Nature is something dead—a machine to be worked, and taken to bits if it won't work as the way he pleases.[30]

Dimble concludes that the leaders at NICE will never be able to enlist Merlin as an ally:

> They thought the old *magia* of Merlin, which worked in with the spiritual qualities of Nature, loving and reverencing them and knowing them from within, could be combined with the new *goeteia*—the brutal surgery from without. No. In a sense Merlin represents what we've got to get back to in some different way.[31]

Ransom agrees that there is a difference, believing that Merlin's magic is descended somehow from lost Atlantean magic, not from the sorcery of the Renaissance. He recognizes this as a much more potent magic than that of the sixteenth century (and perhaps the twentieth century), but doubts that it is any less guilty.[32] Ultimately, Ransom, like Prospero, rejects all magic, even the "good" magic of Atlantis.

In Lewis's books, Merlin, Morgan le Fay, and Atlantis are all associated with ancient mystery and power, more innocent than Faustian magic, but still to be avoided. For the great fact of Atlantis is that it is lost and irrecoverable, one of those "things not to be had." Andrew Ketterley, the magician in *The Magician's Nephew*, is impotent himself as a sorcerer, but he conjures up worlds of trouble with rings he has obtained from his godmother, significantly named Mrs. Lefay.[33] Again, the most poignant expression of this image pattern comes in Lewis's autobiography, where he discusses his childhood bereavement:

> With my mother's death all settled happiness, all that was tranquil and reliable, disappeared from my life. There was to

---

[29] Lewis, *That Hideous Strength*, 200.

[30] Lewis, *That Hideous Strength*, 285.

[31] Lewis, *That Hideous Strength*, 285-6.

[32] Lewis, *That Hideous Strength*, 201.

[33] Lewis, *The Magician's Nephew*, 16.

be much fun, many pleasures, many stabs of Joy; but no more of the old security. It was all sea and islands now; the great continent had sunk like Atlantis.[34]

In *That Hideous Strength*, even Dr. Dimble, the one who senses so great a contrast between Merlin and Faust, recognizes that ultimately Merlin has worked wonders to his own spiritual injury:

> Even in Merlin's time . . . though you could still use that sort of life in the universe innocently, you couldn't do it safely. The things weren't bad in themselves, but they were already bad for us. They sort of withered the man who dealt with them. Not on purpose. They couldn't help doing it. Merlinus is withered. He's quite pious and humble and all that, but something has been taken out of him. That quiet of his is just a little deadly, like the quiet of a gutted building. It's the result of having laid his mind open to something that broadens the environment just a bit too much. Like polygamy. It wasn't wrong for Abraham, but one can't help feeling that even he lost something by it.[35]

That phrase about "broadening the environment a bit too much" is an enigmatic one, but it suggests going beyond the natural bounds of one's station. Here again Lewis the scholar provides the most valuable gloss on Lewis the novelist. In *The Discarded Image*, he argues that one of the most persistent habits of the medieval mind is what he calls the "Principle of the Triad," the sense that two things often need "some wire, some medium, some introducer, some bridge—a third thing of some sort" in between them.[36] Often this relationship of three may be defined as agent-mean-patient, one acting, one being acting upon by way of an intermediary. Between the king and the commons are the nobility; between reason and the appetites, sentiment; between God and humans, first Christ and then nine ranks of angels.[37] In this view, humans are most often patients, acted upon by God, the means or instruments of divine agency. Too often, though, they seek god-like powers of agency in situations where it is not theirs to be had.

As with terms already discussed, words associated with The Principle of the Triad—*agent*, *mean*, and *patient*—often have specialized connotations in Lewis's writings. In *That Hideous*

---

34 Lewis, *Surprised by Joy*, 21.

35 Lewis, *That Hideous Strength*, 285.

36 Lewis, *The Discarded Image*, 43-4.

37 Lewis, *The Discarded Image*, 74.

Strength, Macphee, the resident skeptic at St. Anne's, complains that the leaders at NICE will take over the country by the time Ransom and his company have taken any countermeasures. One of the others at St. Anne's answers with a line from Charles Williams's *Taliessen through Logres*: "All lies in a passion of patience, my Lord's rule."[38] For Williams, as for Lewis, the patience referred to here is not just a willingness to let time pass, but a willingness to submit to the agency of someone in whom you have utter and serene trust.

The besetting sin of the magician is to usurp divine agency, to act upon others using nature as the instrument. Ironically, Merlin's magic, if the source of his spiritual injury, eventually becomes the source of his spiritual recovery. Once Merlin has submitted himself to Ransom's authority as Pendragon, Ransom explains to him the means by which Maleldil's agents will destroy the conspiracy at NICE: "I have become a bridge," begins Ransom simply—a term which suggests he intuitively understands his role in the triad. Merlin objects that if heavenly powers put forth all their strength, they will destroy the entire planet. "That is why they will work only through a man," answers Ransom, going on to explain why Merlin himself is that man:

> I will take Our Fair Lord to witness that if it were my task, I would not refuse it. But he will not suffer a mind that still has its virginity to be so violated. And through a black magician's mind their purity neither can nor will operate. One who has dabbled . . . in the days when dabbling had not begun to be evil, or was only just beginning . . . and also a Christian and a penitent. A tool (I must speak plainly) good enough to be so used and not too good.[39]

Of course, Merlin accepts the task and he becomes the channel through which the heavenly powers are able to defeat the forces of spiritual darkness which have gathered at Belbury. This is his last deed on earth, for Jane Studdock, who is gifted with second sight, witnesses Merlin's final moments in a dream-vision:

> It looked as if he was on fire . . . .. I don't mean burning, you know, but light—all sorts of lights in the most curious colours shooting out of him and running up and down him. That was the last thing I saw: Merlin standing there like a kind of pillar

---

[38] Charles Williams, "The Crowning of Arthur," in *Taliessen Through Logres* (London: Oxford University Press, 1938), 194.

[39] Lewis, *That Hideous Strength*, 291; ellipses Lewis's.

and all those dreadful things happening all round him. And you could see in his face that he was a man used up to the last drop, if you know what I mean—that he'd fall to pieces the moment the powers let him go.[40]

Several times in the trilogy the eldila, ministering angels, are associated with pillars of light,[41] and here Merlin is seen as the candlewick for their flame. Jane's last sight of Merlin suggests that he has learned to become the medium, the bridge by which higher powers are able to accomplish their ends on earth. And, according to Ransom, in so losing his life, he saves it.

Merlin's redemption in *That Hideous Strength* is only one story among many, one victory in a titanic conflict which has come thundering down the centuries. Ransom told Merlin that Maleldil "does all things for each"—for Merlin, for Mark and Jane Studdock, for the whole company who have chosen to follow Ransom. In a wider circle still, the clash between Belbury and St. Anne's is *sub specie aeternitatis*. Near the end of the novel, some of the younger members of Ransom's circle aren't quite sure what the battle has been all about. The ever-obliging Dr. Dimble explains to the neophytes that their struggle has been part of an ongoing conflict, a centuries-old duel between forces of light and darkness in England:

> 'It all began,' Dimble explains, 'when we discovered that the Arthurian story is mostly true history. There was a moment in the Sixth Century when something that is always trying to break through into this country nearly succeeded. Logres was our name for it—it will do as well as another. And then gradually we began to see all English history in a new way. We discovered the haunting . . .. Something we may call Britain is always haunted by something we may call Logres.'[42]

As he so often does, Lewis here assigns special, spiritually evocative meanings to words that were not nearly so richly laden before they were touched by his imagination.

The term "Logres" is taken from the Welsh word for "England." Traditionally, Logres represents the Britain of King Arthur; the term appears in Spenser and Milton with about the same connotations as

---

[40] Lewis, *That Hideous Strength*, 361.

[41] Lewis, *Out of the Silent Planet*, 79; Lewis, *Perelandra*, 18; Lewis, *That Hideous Strength*, 321.

[42] *That Hideous Strength*, 368-9.

the word "Camelot." Lewis's friend Charles Williams lent the word more mystical overtones in his Arthurian books, using Logres to denote the spiritual side of England, the combination of Christian and Celtic ideals to stand against the tides of worldliness and corruption. In *Taliessen through Logres*, Williams goes so far as to compare Logres to the Logos. As his Merlin watches the coronation of Arthur, amid splendid heraldic pageantry, the prophet actually sees "the glory of Logres, patterns of Logos in the depths of the sun."[43]

In Lewis's paradigm, borrowed from Williams, Logres becomes a form of the divine Word seeking to be enfleshed in human hearts and in the culture they create. Such a definition strikes a familiar chord: for many people, Logres, or more familiarly Camelot, has come to represent the fragile ideal of a society governed by chivalric virtues of goodness, fairness, courage, and love. We find this note sounded in Geoffrey of Monmouth as early as the twelfth century; it becomes a leitmotif in Malory's fifteenth-century *Morte*; and, in the nineteenth century, Tennyson's *Idylls* derive more poetic power from their underlying moral idealism than from the narrative itself. Clearly, there is a long-standing sense that Arthur and Camelot stand for more than just romance, bravery, or adventure. The legends have become intertwined with an enduring mystique of transcendent values emboldening human valor and engendering human virtue.

Yet, surely, it would almost seem idolatrous to thus equate Logres with Logos, to confuse the spiritual ideals of the Britons with the Divine Word itself. Of course, both Williams and Lewis knew better. In that same vision of the coronation depicted in *Taliessen through Logres*, Merlin also sees coming disaster, the Dolorous Stroke, one brother striking down another. Merlin muses to himself that "the spark of Logres fades, glows, fades."[44] And Lewis might have Dr. Dimble speak of a time when Logres nearly broke through, but in that seemingly casual word "nearly" is all the drama and heartbreak of human history.

Though Logres, like any spiritual ideal, may never be fully incarnated in fallen men and women, it may still have redemptive power for an awakened enchanter, for anchorless modern intellectuals like the Studdocks, for a world increasingly defined by efficacy of technique over clarity of moral vision. Writing about the Arthurian

---

[43] Williams, "The Crowning of Arthur," lines 44-5.

[44] Williams, "The Crowning of Arthur," line 72.

romances of the twelfth-century French poet Chretien de Troyes, Lewis concludes that Golden Ages like Camelot never were, and always are:

> For it is interesting to notice that [Chretien] places his ideal in the past. For him already 'the age of chivalry is dead.' It always was: let no one think the worse of it on that account. These phantom periods for which the historian searches in vain— the Rome and Greece that the Middle Ages believed in, the British past of Malory and Spenser, the Middle Age itself as it was conceived by the romantic revival—all these have their place in a history more momentous than that which commonly bears the name.[45]

Part of the enduring fascination of *That Hideous Strength* is Lewis's ability to evoke this "momentous history" not visible in daily newspapers or scholarly tomes. The novel shows Mark and Jane Studdock just beginning their spiritual journey, as Ransom nears the end of his. And then out of time steps Merlin, not only as magician and prophet but also as fellow pilgrim. Their combined strength overcomes even "That Hideous Strength," as each of their lives is woven into a resplendent tapestry of imagined redemption history.

In studying Lewis's treatment of Merlin the magician and Logres the lost kingdom, one cannot help but notice his remarkable unity of vision. In *Surprised by Joy*, Lewis reported that throughout his teens and twenties his intellect and his imagination were almost like separate and isolated hemispheres of his brain.[46] But in the books which flowed from his pen from the time of his conversion until his death, he sustained an extraordinary consistency of viewpoint. Whether reading his fiction, his apologetic and devotional books, or his scholarly masterworks, we encounter each time a mind, heart, and imagination all working as one, offering ingenious supposals about the substance of things hoped for, and finding in new, unexpected places the evidence of things unseen.

---

[45] C. S. Lewis, The *Allegory of Love* (Oxford: Oxford University Press, 1938), 23-4. See Chretien de Troyes. *Arthurian Romances*, trans. by W. W. Comfort (London: J. M. Dent and Sons, 1976).

[46] Lewis, *Surprised by Joy*, 170.

Chapter 8

THE THEOLOGICAL IMAGINATION:
C. S. LEWIS AS READER AND AUTHOR

MARJORIE LAMP MEAD

Once C. S. Lewis became a Christian, he very quickly attempted to combine his desire to be a writer with his new understanding of life. This impulse initially prompted him to write an allegorical tale, *The Pilgrim's Regress* (1933). Issued two years after his conversion, Lewis's first published prose work was an attempt to explain how he had come to faith; however, he later acknowledged that his personal experience was much less common than he had first assumed, and as a result, the volume was too obscure in its meaning for many readers.[1] In spite of this less than satisfactory beginning, Lewis's aspiration to write about his Christian belief remained strong. His next faith-based literary venture, *Out of the Silent Planet* (1938), was even more bold in terms of its imaginative approach and much more successful; for in crafting this story set in the heavens, Lewis had found a literary genre that suited *both* his artistic voice and his religious vision. Indeed, this science fiction novel was the first momentous step in what would become for Lewis a lifelong enterprise: the creative embodiment of Christian truths in fictional form.

Given Lewis's deep enjoyment of fantasy and mythological writings *and* the key role that these works played in his own spiritual journey, it should be no surprise that he found this type of story to be especially conducive to the expression of belief. In fact, several decades later, in attempting to describe the common element that wove throughout his entire life as a writer, Lewis sent the following assessment to the Milton Society of America in October of 1954:

---

[1] For those who are interested in a better understanding of Lewis's intention when writing this first prose work on his Christian faith, C. S. Lewis, *The Pilgrim's Regress: A Wade Annotated Edition*, ed. by David C. Downing (Grand Rapids, MI: Eerdmans, 2014) offers helpful notes, including Lewis's background commentary on various elements of his own conversion story.

The list of my books . . . will, I fear, strike you as a very mixed bag. [Nonetheless] I may point out there is a guiding thread. The Imaginative man in me is older, more continuously operative, and in that sense more basic than either the religious writer or the critic. It was he who made me first attempt (with very little success) to be a poet. It was he who, in response to the poetry of others made me a critic . . .. It was he who after my conversion led me to embody my religious belief in symbolic or mythopoeic [i.e., myth-making] forms, ranging from *Screwtape* to a kind of theologized science fiction; and it was of course he who has brought me, in the last few years, to write a series of the Narnian stories for children.[2]

That Lewis was intentional about the integration of his faith within his imaginative writings is not in doubt. But this intentionality was not always perceived by everyone—nor was it always perceived accurately. For example, when *Out of the Silent Planet* was first published, Lewis learned to his astonishment that many reviewers failed to discern the theological underpinnings of the story.[3] As he wrote to Sister Penelope, an Anglican nun: "You will be both grieved and amused to learn that out of about 60 reviews, only 2 showed any knowledge that my idea of a fall of the Bent One was anything but a private invention of my own. But if only there were someone with a richer talent and more leisure, I believe this great ignorance might be a help to the evangelization of England: any amount of theology can now be smuggled into people's minds under cover of romance without their knowing it."[4]

Significant as this is, misunderstanding the place and purpose of the theological element in Lewis's imaginative writings is just as critical an error as missing the theological element altogether. Unfortunately, this is a common mistake. Too often readers assume that Lewis began his writing with an express moral or value-driven objective, and *then* crafted a story to express his meaning. This was decidedly not the case. As he asserted towards the end of his life: "One thing I am sure of. All my seven Narnian books, and my three

---

[2] C. S. Lewis, *The Collected Letters of C. S. Lewis*, ed. by Walter Hooper, 3 vols. (London: HarperCollins, 2004-7), 3:516-17.

[3] See for example David C. Downing, *Planets in Peril* (Amherst: University of Massachusetts, 1992), 36, for a brief discussion of critical responses to Lewis's first science fiction novel.

[4] Lewis, *Collected Letters*, 2:262.

science-fiction books, began with pictures in my head."[5] In other words, Lewis began writing his fantasy stories as the result of an imaginative impulse—"seeing pictures"—and not with a didactic purpose in mind. We can find instances of this assertion in numerous places throughout his writings. For example, in a recorded conversation with fellow science fiction authors, Lewis described his literary creation of *Perelandra* as the result of seeing an image of floating islands which he then turned into an entire imaginative world; it was only later that he incorporated the idea of an averted fall. One of the other writers expressed surprise at this order of composition (mental image → creative story → theological idea), rather than the other way around with the theological idea triggering the book. Lewis responded:

> "Yes, everyone thinks that. They are quite wrong . . .. [Nonetheless] the story of this averted fall came in very conveniently. Of course it wouldn't have been that particular story if I wasn't interested in those particular ideas on other grounds [i.e., because of his Christian belief]. But that isn't what I started from. I've never started from a message or a moral, have you?"[6]

READING FOR ENJOYMENT

Why is a proper understanding of the relationship between imagination and moral purpose in Lewis's fiction so significant? Simply because, if one believes that an author's primary purpose in writing a story to be the conveyance of religious ideas, then there is an obvious temptation to begin reading by scouring the text to search for this "hidden" message. In so doing, one risks distorting not only what theological meaning is present but also presents the hazard of missing the wonder of the narrative itself.

In an essay on John Bunyan's *Pilgrim's Progress*, Lewis illustrates this inherent danger of distorted reading when he describes the wrong way of reading an allegory as being "the pernicious habit of reading allegory as if it were a cryptogram to be translated." Instead, Lewis maintains, the correct method is to stop thinking about what an image

---

[5] C. S. Lewis, "It All Began with a Picture," in *On Stories and Other Essays on Literature*, ed. by Walter Hooper (New York: Harcourt Brace Jovanovich, 1982), 53.

[6] C. S. Lewis, "Unreal Estates," in *On Stories and Other Essays on Literature*, ed. by Walter Hooper, (New York: Harcourt Brace Jovanovich, 1982), 144-5.

means, since this has the negative effect of causing you to move out of the story into the "conception you started from and would have had without reading it."[7] To put it another way, each time the reader stops to consider what something "means," the narrative thread is lost and the enchantment of the story is broken. As Lewis's friend and former pupil, George Sayer, explained: "Jack wanted the moral and spiritual significance of his works to be assimilated subliminally, if at all, and he was annoyed when his publisher outlined the theme of *Out of the Silent Planet* in the blurb on the dust jacket. Over and over again in talking about his fiction, he would say, 'But it's there for the story.'"[8]

To truly benefit from the theological imagination, one must begin by first *delighting* in the narrative itself. Once this premise is understood, then it is easier to guard against viewing stories as an alternative type of theological primer or as a means of instruction that has been presented in another guise. Rather, first and foremost, stories are to be savored and experienced. This approach has its own rewards, for if we allow ourselves to imaginatively enter the story—to look, listen, surrender, and receive, as Lewis himself counseled—then "we shall be deliciously surprised by the satisfaction of wants we were not even aware of till they were satisfied."[9]

It is important to note that while Lewis desired that his readers enjoy the story, in and of itself, he also valued employing more analytical approaches to the text on subsequent readings. Indeed, even though he placed great significance upon the experiential aspect of receiving the story through the baptized imagination, he knew that not all stories had the mythopoeic touch that would enable the reader to receive in this special way. Further, as a literary critic, himself, Lewis understood well the importance of employing different ways to read. In other words, Lewis is not saying that the only way to read story is for enjoyment, but rather that he saw this as the necessary first step.

---

[7] C. S. Lewis, "The Vision of John Bunyan," in *Selected Literary Essays*, ed. by Walter Hooper, (Cambridge: Cambridge University Press, 1969), 149.

[8] George Sayer, *Jack*. (Wheaton: Crossway, 1994), 256.

[9] C. S. Lewis, *An Experiment in Criticism* (London: Cambridge University Press, 1969), 134.

LEWIS'S LOVE OF STORY

This ability to receive freely and fully from the narrative marked C. S. Lewis from an early age. As a child, his love of reading was expansively nurtured by both of his parents. In his memoir, *Surprised by Joy*, Lewis recalls that Little Lea, his Belfast family home, was filled with "endless books . . . [that reflected] every transient stage of my parents' interests, books readable and unreadable, books suitable for a child and books most emphatically not. Nothing was forbidden me. In the seemingly endless rainy afternoons, I took volume after volume from the shelves. I had always the same certainty of finding a book that was new to me as a man who walks into a field of finding a new blade of grass."[10]

Growing up in a family of readers was a great gift that deepened Lewis's own innate love of reading. In *Surprised by Joy*, he devotes considerable space recalling his parents' taste in reading, noting that his mother loved good novels, while his father was drawn to dramatic verse and humorous works such as those by Dickens and W. W. Jacobs. Even though their family home was filled to over-flowing with books, Albert Lewis took his two sons on regular visits to Mullan's bookshop in Belfast. For more than half a century, Albert was such a frequent customer that he became great friends with the owner, and shopping trips to Mullan's bookshop were notable social occasions. Each Christmas featured an especially enjoyable visit for the two Lewis brothers as their father allowed both of them the privilege of choosing a new book as a present.

A devoted bibliophile, Lewis not only learned to love story and the words that he read, but he also developed a great appreciation for the physical book that he held in his hands. In writing to Arthur Greeves, a lifelong friend from his boyhood days in Belfast, Lewis avidly discussed the substance of what he was reading, though at times, he would also describe the binding of a new book that he found especially appealing. For example, when Clarendon Press accepted his own book, *The Allegory of Love*, Lewis wrote to Arthur that once published, he would be receiving a copy as a gift, while self-deprecatingly declaring: "I hope . . . binding, paper, etc will be – in our old formula – excellent, exquisite and admirable. In other words, if you can't read it, you will enjoy looking at it, smelling it and

---

[10] C. S. Lewis, *Surprised by Joy* (London: Geoffrey Bles, 1955), 17.

stroking it. If not a good book, it will be a good pet!"[11]

As with most readers, Lewis returned again and again to books that had impacted him in terms of both enjoyment and understanding. Indeed, he described the mark of a literary man to be the desire to read the same work even "ten, twenty or thirty times during the course of their life."[12] The quality of Lewis's reading can also be gleaned by looking through volumes from his personal library.[13] The careful marginalia and precisely written indices on the endpapers of many of these books reveal both what Lewis garnered from the text as well as his intention to return to various tomes for future readings.[14]

THE BAPTIZED IMAGINATION

As much as Lewis valued the sheer delight of story, it was by no means the only reason that he chose to embody his Christian faith in fantasy and myth. Even as a young boy, part of what had drawn him to story was the way in which certain fictional tales awakened within him "an unsatisfied desire which is itself more desirable than any other satisfaction"—a longing that he termed Joy.[15] Perhaps the most powerful instance of this awakening occurred in Lewis, when as a teenager, he first encountered George MacDonald's fantasy novel, *Phantastes*. Lewis later came to understand that what he found so

---

[11] C. S. Lewis, *They Stand Together: The Letters of C. S. Lewis to Arthur Greeves (1914-1963)*, ed. by Walter Hooper (London: Collins, 1979), 474.

[12] C. S. Lewis, *An Experiment in Criticism* (London: Cambridge University Press, 1969), 2.

[13] The bulk of Lewis's personal library was acquired by the Marion E. Wade Center in 1986 from Wroxton College in Banbury, England. The collection contains over 2000 titles and includes many volumes with Lewis's own annotations. The Lewis Library listing may be viewed on the Wade Center's website.

[14] Humorously, there are several titles to be found in Lewis's personal library with the declaration: "Never again"—which of course only underscores the fact that he did reread other books without fail. One might also ask why he kept the "never again" books in his library, if not to at least have them close at hand if the need to consult them should arise.

[15] Lewis, *Surprised by Joy*, 23-4. Lewis's experience of Joy was not confined to story alone (e.g., the beauty of nature as found in the landscape of his native County Down, the music of Wagner, or the illustrations of Arthur Rackham). However, given his own inherent impulse to write, it was natural that he would be drawn to share his faith through fantasy and myth.

compelling in this imaginative depiction was in fact "the quality of the real universe, the divine, magical, terrifying and ecstatic reality in which we all live . . . what I learned to love in *Phantastes* was goodness."[16] So profound was this experience that Lewis described it as having his imagination baptized. By this, Lewis meant that his imagination was now opened up to the divine meaning and transcendence always present in the world around him but previously "unseen" by him.

Of course, not all stories have this almost sacramental impact or potency. Those that do are tales that provide a new vision of reality, pointing us towards divine attributes such as beauty, truth, and holiness. Such stories also touch our hearts in a deep way with longing for something other or greater than the physical world in which we live—Lewis's concept of Joy. As Lewis experienced, these types of story have the power to not only break the spell of materialism that masks awareness of transcendent realities but also to re-enchant our daily existence by awakening the reader to a longing for and perception of the divine.

UNDERLYING PURPOSE ("PAST WATCHFUL DRAGONS")

Drawing upon his own profound experiences as a reader, Lewis understood that even though he intended the primary aim of his own writings to bring enjoyment, this did not preclude a second and equally significant purpose: to awaken his readers to theological truths by helping them experience spiritual realities in a deeper and more meaningful way. Specifically, in terms of his Narnian stories, Lewis described his goals this way:

> I thought I saw how stories of this kind could steal past a certain inhibition which had paralysed much of my own religion in childhood. Why did one find it so hard to feel as one was told one ought to feel about God or about the sufferings of Christ? I thought the chief reason was that one was told one ought to. An obligation to feel can freeze feelings . . . .. But supposing that by casting all these things into an imaginary world, stripping them of their stained-glass and Sunday school associations, one could make them for the first time appear in their real potency? Could one not thus steal past these watchful dragons?

---

[16] C. S. Lewis, *George MacDonald: An Anthology* (London: Geoffrey Bles, 1946), 21.

I thought one could.[17]

Elsewhere, Lewis affirms that this intentionality of purpose—to aid others in overcoming their own emotional barriers to faith—was something he saw as necessary and worthwhile for *both* his young and his adult readers.[18] In other words, Lewis was not simply "packaging" theology in the form of fantasy in order to reach those too young to read works of apologetics, but rather he saw the power and value of this genre to reach *all* ages—independent of educational background or intellectual ability. That he was effective in accomplishing this purpose for many who read his stories is clear. But some might well ask, why go to stories at all for religious insight? What is it about this type of writing—specifically fantasy, fairy tale, and myth—which enables it to overcome certain inhibitions to faith and thereby inform us of spiritual realities which we cannot easily apprehend in other ways? I would suggest that there are several key reasons why these type of stories are unusually effective in communicating theological truths—and even, as Lewis suggests, "baptizing the imagination."

HEIGHTENED AWARENESS

As a Christian, C. S. Lewis firmly believed that there is an unseen transcendent world encompassing us which we cannot apprehend through our senses alone. However, because of our finite nature, the majority of people (including many Christians) live their daily lives as though the physical world—which we *can* see and touch—is, in fact, our only true reality. Before his conversion, Lewis himself had fallen victim to this spiritual blindness, but he gradually came alive to a new view of the world around him, in part through the reading of certain mythopoeic stories, such as those by George MacDonald. Indeed, Lewis believed that myth and fantasy have a unique ability to alert us to transcendent realities:

[This type of story] goes beyond the expression of things we have already felt. It arouses in us sensations we have never had

---

[17] C. S Lewis, "Sometimes Fairy Stories May Say Best What's to be Said," in *On Stories and Other Essays on Literature*, ed. by Walter Hooper, (New York: Harcourt Brace Jovanovich, Publishers, 1982), 47.

[18] C. S. Lewis: "The inhibitions which I hoped my stories would overcome in a child's mind may exist in a grown-up's mind too, and may perhaps be overcome by the same means." Lewis, "Sometimes Fairy Stories," 48.

before, never anticipated having, as though we had broken out of our normal mode of consciousness and 'possessed joys not promised to our birth'. It gets under our skin, hits us at a deeper level than our thoughts or even our passions, troubles oldest certainties till all questions are re-opened, and in general shocks us more fully awake than we are for most of our lives.[19]

Or to put it another way, story by its very nature speaks to us through our non-rational (*not* irrational) intuitions and understandings. In such reading, we encounter theological truths with our *heart* first of all and only later with our intellect, which is very different from the informational way in which we approach theology.

Lewis did not see this distinction between how we receive truth intellectually in apologetic works versus how we receive it experientially through story as either unimportant or inadvertent. Rather he felt that narrative was uniquely effective in communicating spiritual realities because it was part of God's own intentional design. As Lewis explained: ". . . I do not think the resemblance between the Christian and the merely imaginative experience is accidental. I think that all things, in their way, reflect heavenly truth, the imagination not least. 'Reflect' is the important word."[20] Elsewhere, Lewis describes myth as "a real though unfocused gleam of divine truth falling on human imagination."[21] In other words, just as viewing the grandeur of nature can point us back to God the Creator, so too, can fantasy or myth serve as a pointer to God and His divine love for all people. But, as Lewis was careful to clarify, in understanding this function of story, one must keep in mind that such tales are a *reflection of unfocused* truth, which is why the theological imagination speaks primarily (or at least initially) to the heart and not to the head. This distinction does not make such insight a lesser function, simply a different one. We need stories to "teach" us, as well as theological texts.

ENHANCED CLARITY OF VISION

When we truly experience a story by entering the secondary world created by the author, we begin to respond imaginatively in ways that free us from our usual preconceptions. As a result of this new perspective, we are enabled to observe even our own temporal world

---

[19] Lewis, *George MacDonald: An Anthology*, 16-7.

[20] Lewis, *Surprised by Joy*, 159.

[21] C. S. Lewis, *Miracles* (London: Geoffrey Bles, 1948), 161.

with "new eyes." In this way, story can teach us greater discernment by helping us to look outside ourselves and our usual surroundings. Lewis described the benefits of this increased understanding in this way: "Each of us by nature sees the whole world from one point of view with a perspective and a selectiveness peculiar to himself . . .. [But] we want to see with other eyes, to imagine with other imaginations, to feel with other hearts, as well as with our own . . .. We demand windows."[22]

J. R. R. Tolkien also uses the image of windows as a way of describing how story aids us in understanding our own experiences. He maintains that fantasy stories can help us "clean" our windows and thereby recover a clear view of the world around us:

> Recovery [is a function of fantasy literature and] . . . is a re-gaining—regaining of a clear view. I do not say 'seeing things as they are' . . . though I might venture to say 'seeing things as we are (or were) meant to see them'—as things apart from ourselves. We need in any case, to clean our windows; so that the things seen clearly may be freed from the drab blur of triteness or familiarity—from possessiveness . . .. Of course, fairy-stories are not the only means of recovery . . .. Humility is enough.[23]

In other words, story clears away some of the distractions and unconscious assumptions of our daily existence, and thereby aids us in perceiving those transcendent realities that are *always* present but previously *were hidden* from our sight.

INCREASED DEPTH OF UNDERSTANDING

However, simply becoming increasingly aware of spiritual truths is not enough; we must also begin to see them rightly. In part, this is accomplished in mythopoeic tales through the storyteller's creative ability to depict. Literary depictions, at their best, are a powerful means that bring theological doctrines and beliefs alive in ways which mere didactic statements cannot. We can understand this distinction better by looking at an example: for instance, reading about attributes of the nature of God (e.g., omnipotent, omnipresent, omniscient) can be very instructive, but it cannot produce the same depth of

---

[22] Lewis, *An Experiment in Criticism*, 137-8.

[23] J. R. R. Tolkien, "On Fairy-Stories," in *The Tolkien Reader* (New York: Ballantine Books, 1974), 57-8.

understanding or response that results from a literary encounter with the great lion Aslan in the Narnian chronicles. Or as Lewis's friend and former pupil, Dom Bede Griffiths, explained:

> "The figure of Aslan tells us more of how Lewis understood the nature of God than anything else he wrote. It has all the hidden power and majesty and awesomeness which Lewis associated with God, but also the glory and the tenderness and even the humor which he believed belonged to him, so that children could run up to him and throw their arms around him and kiss him . . .. It is 'mere Christianity.'"[24]

This deeper understanding is a direct result of the creative act itself. When writing a book on theology, the author's own training and background mark the limits of what can be successfully communicated to the reader. But in writing a story, the process of inspiration results in the creation of something that may extend beyond even the author's own comprehension. In other words, as Lewis suggests:

> 'Creation' as applied to human authorship . . . seems to me an entirely misleading term . . .. [W]e re-arrange elements [God] has provided. There is not a *vestige* of real creativity . . . in us. Try to imagine a new primary color, a third sex, a fourth dimension, or even a monster which does not consist of existing animals stuck together! Nothing happens. And that is surely why our works . . . never mean to others quite what we intended: because we are re-combining elements made by Him and already containing *His* meanings. Because of those divine meanings in our materials it is impossible we should ever know the whole meaning of our own works, and the meaning we never intended may be the best and truest one. Writing a book is much less like creation than it is like planting a garden or begetting a child: in all three cases we are only entering as *one* cause into a causal stream which works, so to speak, in its own way.[25]

Lewis reiterates his belief in the fluid nature of literary creation in the following comment to a former pupil, Father Peter Milward: "My view would be that a good myth (i.e., a story out of which ever varying meanings will grow for different readers and in different ages) is a higher thing than allegory (into which *one* meaning has already

---

[24] Dom Bede Griffiths, "Letter–26 November 1983," in *The Canadian C. S. Lewis Journal*, 47 (Summer 1984), 1-2.

[25] Lewis, *Collected Letters*, 2:555.

been put). Into allegory a man can put only what he already knows: in a myth he puts what he does not yet know and could not come to know in any other way."[26] In this statement, Lewis is contrasting the limitations of an intentional, moral-driven, didactic approach (allegory) with the more open-ended potentialities of a mythopoeic story (whether fantasy, fairy tale or myth). It is these creative potentialities which allow an author to write a story that possesses meaning that he *does not yet know*; thus enabling Lewis to make the following extraordinary statement about one of his own mythic tales, *Till We Have Faces*: "An author doesn't necessarily understand the meaning of his own story better than anyone else."[27]

OUR LONGING FOR THE TRANSCENDENT

However, simply becoming aware of another reality is not enough for most people. We live in a hectic, noisy world which surrounds us with numerous compelling attractions; we are easily distracted and pulled in many directions. Accordingly, in order to keep our eyes focused on the unseen transcendent, we need some assistance; our desire for spiritual realities must be *nurtured*. Lewis puts it this way:

> If I find in myself a desire which no experience in this world can satisfy, the most probable explanation is that I was made for another world . . .. Probably earthly pleasures were never meant to satisfy it, but only to arouse it, to suggest the real thing. If that is so, I must take care, on the one hand, never to despise, or be unthankful for, these earthly blessings, and on the other, never to mistake them for something else of which they are only a kind of copy, or echo, or mirage. I must keep alive in myself the desire for my true country, which I shall not find till after death.[28]

In all of his writings, but most especially his fiction, Lewis attempted to fulfill this objective: first of all, to arouse this sense of longing whenever it is dormant—and then, to nurture this longing and keep it alive once it has been awakened.

C. S. Lewis believed that this ability to both awaken and nurture the desire for the transcendent is something that story does powerfully

---

[26] Lewis, *Collected Letters*, 3:789-90.

[27] Lewis, *Collected Letters*, 3:830.

[28] C. S. Lewis, *Mere Christianity* (New York: Macmillan, 1952), 106).

and uniquely. As Lewis put it, "This is the most remarkable of the powers of Poetic Language: to convey to us the quality of experiences which we have not had, or perhaps can never have, to use factors within our experience so that they become pointers to something outside our experience—as two or more roads on a map show us where a town that is off the map must lie."[29] Thus, even though we don't look to imaginative works for the primary explication of theology, we must recognize that rational exposition alone is not enough for full understanding either. We need the added insight that stories uniquely provide.

Award-winning children's author Katherine Paterson eloquently illustrates the way in which the theological imagination works on the hearts and minds of readers by describing the effect of Lewis's Narnian tales in her own life:

> I was once very much involved with a young man who, when I tried to share with him my love for C. S. Lewis's *Chronicles of Narnia*, said earnestly that he felt it was wrong of Lewis to distort the Bible in this way. I should have known at that moment that the relationship was doomed. Aslan is not a distortion but a powerful symbol of the Lion of Judah,[30] which can nourish our spirits as the reasoned arguments of a thousand books of theology can never do. We can dare face the dark, because we've had a shining glimpse of the light.[31]

And indeed, this is what story—what the theological imagination as Lewis understood it—does best: it awakens us to the transcendent light shining all around; the bright gleam of reality which we could not perceive as effectively through our reason alone. Story helps us to experience, and thereby to understand, spiritual truth in a deeper and more immediate way. C. S. Lewis, as both reader and author, would firmly declare that story, at its best, helps us to actually "taste and see" the transcendent reality surrounding us.

---

[29] C. S. Lewis, "The Language of Religion," in *Christian Reflections*, ed. by Walter Hooper (Grand Rapids, MI: Eerdmans, 1967), 133.

[30] Interestingly, Lewis stated that: "Only after Aslan came into the story—on His own; I never called Him—did I remember the scriptural 'Lion of Judah.'" Letter of 2 December 1962 in James E. Higgins, "Five Authors of Mystical Fancy for Children: A Critical Study." Doctoral dissertation, Columbia University, New York, 1965), 376.

[31] Katherine Paterson, *Gates of Excellence: On Reading and Writing Books for Children* (New York: Dutton, 1981), 60.

Chapter 9

RECOVERING THE MYTHICAL IMAGINATION

Mark Neal

C. S. Lewis possessed a robust understanding of the imagination. Scattered throughout his literary corpus are obscure references to more than thirty nuances. We shouldn't be surprised, since any deeper understanding of a particular reality takes nuances into account. For example, he describes the *penetrating imagination* as a way to understand a thing from many different angles, or the *satisfied imagination* that seeks satisfaction and re-enchantment in the familiar and the mundane. The *material imagination* attempts to accurately depict the material world. Each is a specific strategy to intentionally engage with reality.

The *mythical imagination* is the focus of this essay. Lewis defined myth as a "real though unfocussed gleam of divine truth falling on human imagination."[1] Thus, he writes, the ancient pagans who created the dying god myths of Balder or Osiris did so because the divine light given to all men enabled their imaginations to envision and prefigure, though darkly, the fruition of these myths in the factual person of Christ, the myth become fact.

Clyde Kilby maintains that "myth is the name of a way of seeing, a way of knowing in depth, a way of experiencing—a way that in being disinterested contains the freedom of unending and vital interest."[2] Myth also inspires longing. Good myth draws it from us as parched earth draws rain. Lewis writes that the tragic human dilemma is either to know a thing intellectually or to experience it viscerally—never both at once. Lewis believed that myth partially solved this dilemma by enabling us to experience concretely principles that are in fact abstractions. We experience an ardent longing when we taste the myths in this way, a longing for something unnamed and often unknown; an elusive, ephemeral grasping that recedes and vanishes when we move from tasting to thinking. Lewis believed these

---

[1] C. S. Lewis, *Miracles: A Preliminary Study* (New York: Macmillan, 1953), 161.

[2] Clyde Kilby, "Foreword," in Rolland Hein, *Christian Mythmakers* (Chicago: Cornerstone Press, 1998), xii.

longings found their true object in God. Perhaps we may blend the three definitions, thus: myth is a way of seeing, an unfocused gleam of divine truth providing an unending vital interest and depth to human imagination that inspires longing.

Lewis identifies three distinctions of the word "imagination": reverie or wish fulfilling fantasy, invention, or experiences of what he terms "joy," that ineffable desire or longing that grips us at times with visions too deep for words. And it is this third category that Lewis marks as the truest apotheosis of the imagination.[3] Thus, one of the primary goals of the mythical imagination is to receive myths anagogically in order to understand supernatural reality and connect with this longing. It also reorients us to its proper object through the unique way of seeing described by Kilby and Lewis.

FACETS OF THE MYTHICAL IMAGINATION

The mythical imagination was native to the medieval period of history. This essay, then, will examine five selected attributes or facets characteristic of the medieval mind that are also characteristic of the mythical imagination. They are not its sole characteristics, but they are bellwethers of the whole, which may be likened to an old telescope: each section extends out into the next to reveal a clearer picture.

The medieval cosmology was beloved of medieval man. He had built it painstakingly in a great work of syncretism; harmonizing the texts that he possessed, he created a beautiful model of the universe. It was ordered, crowded with a dizzying amount of reiteration and followed the principle of plenitude, or a full exploitation of the universe. To understand his passion, one must recall that medieval man had lost most of his books. Of the few he possessed, he was reticent to acknowledge that some were right and others wrong. His solution was to harmonize them, to make their data fit into the overall pattern, to crowd the heavens even more. His mind loved to dwell on the model because his mind loved repetition and order.

Despite this love, he recognized that its status as a model was provisional. It was subject to revisions as new knowledge and understanding superseded old. For example, if a new work of history or literature was found, he would have to accommodate that knowledge to the whole. He would have accepted as necessary what Lewis

---

[3] C. S. Lewis, Surprised by Joy: The Shape of My Early Life (New York: Harcourt Brace and World, 1955), 15-16.

terms "saving the appearances," that is, any theory must preserve the phenomena it deals with in the sense of including them and doing justice to them. Plenitude is an outworking of this theory.

In order to determine which supposal (for there could be many) saves the appearances most effectively, a problem-solving theory called Occam's razor must be appended. This principle states that among competing hypotheses, the one with the fewest assumptions would most effectively save the appearances.[4] But all models, even scientific ones, are metaphorical. Just as medieval man understood gravity to be the desire of an object to return to its home, we understand it to be a force whereby objects possessing mass are drawn together. Both understandings are equally metaphorical. We cannot actually comprehend what is happening. And medieval man, who had exercised plenitude and filled the universe with innumerable beings and creatures, was comfortable with this metaphorical understanding.

This would allow and indeed enable the second facet, an absence of skepticism or credulity, specifically toward the literature of the period. Lewis wonders how medieval man could have believed in such things as the clearly mythical animals or creatures described in the bestiaries of the time, what he calls pseudo-zoology.[5] He writes that the medievals were not necessarily concerned with the question of fact as moderns would be. Even their historians wrote almost nothing of the impersonal, as modern historians might pride themselves on doing. What mattered were the stories of great people and the legends and deeds which sprung from them. History was a story to be passed on, with few changes. The medievals were merely caretakers. The question of belief or disbelief in a particular history wouldn't have likely occurred to their minds. The story was what mattered.[6]

In a culture where story is thus valued, one could assume that the world and universe hold anagogical significance. In the medieval cosmological model of the universe there existed two divisions. Everything above the sphere of the moon was considered to be immutable and non-contingent. The heavens thus moved in perfect accord in their eternal attempt to imitate the nature of God. All below the sphere of the moon was subject to randomness and decay.

---

[4] C.S. Lewis, *The Discarded Image* (Cambridge: Cambridge University Press, 1974), 15.

[5] Lewis, *Discarded Image*, 151.

[6] Lewis, *Discarded Image*, 180-2.

The heavens were seen to be ordered and perfect, a pattern which mankind on earth should attempt to emulate. Thus, the visible world reflected an invisible pattern based on the perfection of the heavens. This enabled a built-in moral sense in the created order. And it required a response to the significance of the universe. And so, we return to the importance of story in history. It wasn't the factual truth of the story that mattered but its moral significance to its hearers and promulgators. They wanted the established models of the past, Lewis writes, for poetry, conversation, and a pattern or model for imitation.

The created order may also be explained etiologically, in terms of myth. For example, the planets revolve because they are associated with an Intelligence, an angelic being whose desire is to most closely approximate God. In the minds of the ancient Greeks, the circle was considered to be the closest approximation to perfection; thus, the planets revolve because of their desire for the one true perfection. Another example would be the influence of the planets on humanity. The moon was thought to produce wandering, both in terms of traveling and wandering of the mind. The sun's influence was thought to make men wise and liberal and to produce gold in the ground. And so on. Each planet had particular positive or negative influences on humanity. The etiological or anagogical explanation gave meaning to the heavens.

The fourth facet is the medieval belief in devolution or declination. Though earth was the center of the universe all movement toward it was considered to be downward. In the scheme of the heavens, earth was understood to be on the fringe, the outer edges of darkness. It was furthest removed from the splendors of the heavens. Each sphere of the heavens passed its knowledge of God to the sphere beneath it by way of an intermediary, as noted. As one moved downward through the heavens, all impulse, light, dynamics, and knowledge of God grew weaker until reaching its nadir on the earth. This prompted the belief in devolution, that all life moved from perfection to imperfection. It was indeed the job of mankind to mimic as best he could the perfection of the heavens in his earthly rituals and celebrations. And these rituals included the passing on of great stories of the past, in which the earthly patterns mirror the heavenly and its outcomes when men either align with or work against the patterns. And naturally, a desire to emulate the invisible pattern would create longing. The old myths and stories helped to fuel it.

A devolutionary belief also contributed to medieval man's

understanding of history. The past was a glorious pageant far superior to the present. It was a brilliant spectacle, packed with the stories and heroes of old. And due to a lack of a sense of historical period, medievals had a more immediate access to that past, on which the pattern of the present was built.[7] Contrast this with the modern understanding of evolution where all moves from imperfection to perfection. Lewis called this the deepest habit of the contemporary mind. It is one which we can readily imagine and engage with as it presents a picture of man triumphing over nature.[8]

The fifth facet is an outworking of the anagogical or moral understanding of the universe. The historians of the time were concerned with passing on the great traditions and stories of history written by the great *auctours* of the past. In this sense, they were not concerned with invention or originality as a modern would be. They made slight adjustments here and there, but it would have been contrary to their nature to have any ambition to take credit for having written or created a particular work. The point, Lewis writes, was not self-expression, but a desire to hand on the history in a worthy manner. To this end, then, art and genius did not matter. It was simply the continuance of the story that was important. To the medievals, originality would have seemed preposterous. There were so many deeds, tragedies, adventures, and glorious escapades in the world yet to be set down that to be inventive would have smacked of paucity rather than richness.[9] A modern can scarcely understand this mentality. As Lewis notes, we would likely scorn anyone that tried to rewrite someone else's book. But medievals did not think this way; they thought only of the content of the story itself.

SEEING BEYOND: SATISFIED, CLASSICAL, AND ROMANTIC IMAGINATION

The five facets outlined above are vital to the mythical imagination, but three subsets of this imagination contribute to and inform it even more fully. These are the *satisfied, classical* and to a lesser degree, *romantic* nuances of the imagination, again identified by Lewis.

---

[7] Lewis, *Discarded Image*, 184-5.

[8] C. S. Lewis, *The Weight of Glory and Other Addresses* (New York: Macmillan Publishing, 1980). 90.

[9] Lewis, *Discarded Image*, 211.

The *satisfied imagination* finds pleasure in the mundane and the repetitive. Its goal is to re-enchant the familiar, that which has been seen so repetitively it is now subject to the old adage "familiarity breeds contempt." G. K. Chesterton famously wrote, "Now, there is a law written in the darkest of the books of life and it is this: if you look at a thing nine hundred and ninety-nine times you are perfectly safe; if you look at it the thousandth time, you are in frightful danger of seeing it for the first time."[10] This is what is meant by re-enchanting the familiar. The passion of the medieval scholastics to utilize plenitude, a highly ordered and reiterative universe, is an example of it. As noted, their minds loved to dwell on its material. Their stories repeated it. They never grew tired of it.

The *classical imagination*, writes Lewis, "loves to embrace its object completely, to take it in at a single glance, and see it as something harmonious, symmetrical, and self-explanatory."[11] It is crowded, yet ordered. The Parthenon or the *Summa* of Thomas Aquinas or *The Divine Comedy* are examples of this. Similarly, the whole universe of the medievals was classical by design.

Conversely, the *romantic imagination* loves to wander in a labyrinth and succumb to the inextricable. It revels in mystery. Lewis suggests that the Italian epic poem *Orlando Furioso* is an example of it. This subset of the mythical imagination makes up a smaller part of the whole. We see it principally in the medieval belief in the *longaevi*, or long livers: the fauns, satyrs, nymphs and so on that would later come to be known as fairies. Lewis writes that the value of the romantic imagination was to soften the classical severity of the medieval cosmology. It added an element of danger and uncertainty into a universe where everything had been mapped out.[12]

These three nuances or subsets contribute a synergistic effect to the mythical imagination by enabling us to recognize how any given thing can help us to see beyond itself; it acts as a conduit for the mythical vision that is informed by our own history, preferences, reading—everything. For example, when I sit around a bonfire, I am not simply seeing a bonfire. I am seeing the bonfire through a lens of

---

[10] G. K. Chesterton, *The Napoleon of Notting Hill*, in *The Collected Works of G. K. Chesterton*, ed. by Denis J. Conlon (San Francisco: Ignatius Press, 1991), 227.

[11] Lewis, *The Weight of Glory*, 76.

[12] Lewis, *Discarded Image*, 122.

the many other bonfires I have sat around, the bonfires I have read about, seen pictures of, heard stories of. There is satisfaction in the fire itself, there is a desire to see its meaning in relation to all other moments of meaning, to view them as a whole, and there is mystery. These three subsets work together to inform a mythic vision in which associations, mental images, feelings, and a whole host of other things work to affect my perception of this fire. This fire is a symbol of some perfect fire I long for. It is a visible pattern of some invisible, archetypal fire. This mythical vision arrives through the mythical imagination and points to something beyond: the invisible pattern that I cannot see, yet long for.

RESERVATIONS

While the mythical imagination was beneficial to medieval man, it also possessed drawbacks. But even these drawbacks contained certain benefits that preserved him from making mistakes to which moderns might be prone. Again, we'll examine reservations that emerge from the five facets outlined earlier.

Since medieval man was dispassionate about facts and possessed a somewhat negligent attitude toward verifiable truth, he was prone to wrong interpretations of reality that led to some negative historical consequences. He was not purposely blind, but he was certainly overly credulous. And he had reason for being so. As has been noted, he had lost most of his books. Of the ones he did possess, he was unwilling to call any merely fiction.

Of this inability to distinguish between truth and fiction in books, Lewis writes, "The poet is ranked with the scientist as authority for a purely scientific proposition. This astonishing failure or refusal to distinguish—in practice, though not always in theory—between books of different sorts must be borne in mind whenever we are trying to gauge the total effect of an ancient text on its medieval readers."[13] In this instance, historical and fictional accounts are thrown together, and both are believed as truth. Of the harm engendered by this credulity, Lewis cites the Roman poet Lucan, who in his epic poem *Pharsalia*, describes the heinous practices of the witch Erictho. Lewis states that this work may have had a disastrous impact when it came to the witch-hunting tribunals of the time.[14]

---

[13] Lewis, *Discarded Image*, 31.

[14] Lewis, *Discarded Image*, 32.

The inability of medievals to distinguish historical reality and fiction could also be attributed to a lack of invention. Historians were not even aware, writes Lewis, that the old myths and stories were fiction or that what they wrote to keep the story alive were more fictions. To them it was simply truth to be passed on. Its worth was highly valued, but writers did very little to make it palatable to readers.

Thus, another potential drawback is what Lewis calls the "sheer, unabashed, prolonged dullness" of medieval literature. In a world of built-in meaning, the writers feel that their subject matter is so interesting that they need do nothing further to make it more interesting for their readers.[15] This might lead to a narrowness of mind that was unwilling to step outside of its inherited worldview.

Closely associated with lack of invention is a lack in the sense of historical period. The glorious past is interpreted—regardless of the timeframe of history—in terms of the medieval age. Lewis writes that moderns grow up with a sense, though often erroneous, of the difference between historical periods. It is difficult for us to conceive of a time when this would not have been so. Medieval man would have believed that all of history was like his present time. Not only did they not possess a sense of period, they would not have even considered the additional differences of temper or mental climate that arise from different ages.[16] However, there is a benefit to this drawback. Lewis writes that this kind of ignorance enabled the artists and poets of the day to bring life to any historical matter. And it excluded a vice particular to the modern age: historicism, a belief that man can discover a meaning in the historical process.[17]

A final problem resulted from the etiological interpretation of the universe. The heavens were immutable and non-contingent, outside of man's ken. But the heavens could influence men in the realms of mutability, as has been discussed. They produced both positive and negative influences, which resulted in a belief in astrological determinism among the medievals. If one is subject to the whims of the planetary influences, then free will is a ridiculous notion and one might as well succumb to the randomness that will be all one knows.

---

[15] Lewis, *Discarded Image*, 212,

[16] Lewis, *Discarded Image*, 183.

[17] C. S. Lewis, *Christian Reflections*, ed. by Walter Hooper (London: Geoffrey Bles, 1967), 100.

THE EMPTIED WORLD:
HOW THE MYTHICAL IMAGINATION WAS LOST

According to Lewis, the mythical imagination was lost when the old medieval cosmology was discarded for a newer one based on science, primarily mathematics. This methodological revolution was ushered in by Johannes Kepler and Galileo who both verified the heliocentric theory that Copernicus had put forth. Kepler, writes Lewis, explained planetary motion animistically at the beginning of his career. By the end, he was able to explain it scientifically.[18] What mattered was not that the picture of the universe had changed, but that the process whereby that change was verified by scientists could now be precisely measured by observed phenomena. Lewis writes,

> By reducing Nature to her mathematical elements it substituted a mechanical for a genial or animistic conception of the universe. The world was emptied, first of her indwelling spirits, then of her occult sympathies, and antipathies, finally of her colours, smells, and tastes . . . .. The mind, on whose ideal constructions the whole method depended, stood over against its object in ever sharper dissimilarity. Man with his new powers became rich like Midas but all that he touched had gone dead and cold. This process, slowly working, ensured during the next century the loss of the old mythical imagination . . . .. Later still, as a desperate attempt to bridge a gulf which begins to be found intolerable, we have the Nature poetry of the Romantics.[19]

If we return to our definition of myth as a way of seeing as well as providing depth to human imagination, this development was a severe loss of meaning as well as vision. If "myth is a lane down which we walk to repossess our soul,"[20] as Kilby writes, this change would equate to a certain amount of soul unmaking. It was destined to have ramifications in every sector of medieval belief, but we will again limit our examination of its impact to several of the five facets of the mythical imagination.

The advent of new scientific knowledge and language would help to destroy the characteristic of plenitude through discoveries that disproved what the model had always represented. To explain a

---

[18] C. S. Lewis, English Literature in the Sixteenth Century, Excluding Drama (Oxford: Oxford University Press, 1968), 3.

[19] Lewis, *English Literature in the Sixteenth Century*, 3-4.

[20] Kilby, "Foreword," xiii.

planet's movement mechanically, where it had once been understood animistically as moved by an Intelligence, is a metaphorical as well as a spiritual loss. And as science gradually came to understand how empty, vast, and isolated the heavens actually were, this belief would have been completely shattered. Thus, too, the satisfied imagination would have been lost because a delight in the universe would no longer be possible in the same way.

A preference for story over facts, for the bequeathing of the great stories and histories of the past, would suffer a similar fate at the hands of the methodological revolution that brought factual evidence as the new way to understand and interpret reality. If a universe was emptied of all its deities and animistic conceptions, one could no longer circulate as history what had been proven to be false. Take merely one instance of medieval belief, that of planetary influence on human life and events. The planets were seen to determine human affairs and to produce certain effects on the human psyche. Remove this belief and the old stories cease to have the same impact. They would now be seen to be *merely* stories, inaccurate, yet still entertaining. Once the old mythic understanding is gone, their meaning has been emptied and their power lost.

If material reality can be explained by way of analogy, the world possesses a built-in significance. And analogy is perhaps the primary way we understand spiritual realities. They are, by definition, outside of our experience. Humans are finite beings. God is infinite. Therefore, He breaks the category of definition, because definition means *of the finite*. By definition, we describe things using comparatives and superlatives; we essentially define things by their limitations. God is limitless; He is completely other. The medieval scholastics understood this. The only way to apprehend God was at many removes, through comparisons with defined realities that provided a sense of the infinite. Once material reality was scientifically verified, the significance was lost. Things no longer meant or resonated in the same way.

The loss of a mythic understanding of the universe and its anagogic significance would also result in a loss of spiritual belief. If the heavens can be explained scientifically, mystery has been banished and the romantic imagination stripped out. It is ironic that even though scientific understanding helped to destroy the medieval conception of the universe, scientific language itself is nothing more than another metaphor. But it is a metaphor emptied of meaning.

Finally, the displacement of a centuries-old geocentric model by a heliocentric one would drastically change or more likely destroy the medieval notion of devolution, and of course, with it, the accepted structure and hierarchy of the heavens. This reordering places earth in a position that is distinctly not the nadir of the universe. When earth was comfortably situated at the fringe, man longed to participate in the perfection of the heavens. He possessed an abundance of wonder and a fitting humility at his place in the created order. Scientific verification would destroy this humility. With their new knowledge, men had become like gods. As Lewis writes, "Nature was delivered into our hands."[21]

While all these changes were not instantaneous, and indeed, writes Lewis, took many years to wend their way into mainstream thought, they gradually led to the loss of the mythical imagination as a way of comprehending nature and the universe. Lewis believes the nature poetry of the Romantics, which came much later, to be an outbreak of this mythological imagination, to repeat,[22] an effort "to bridge a gulf which begins to be found intolerable."[23] Lewis doesn't elucidate what he means, but it can perhaps be inferred that man relinquished a significant relationship to nature as the old mythical imagination and its associated meanings ebbed away. The Romantics felt this loss deeply and tried to rectify it in their poetry.

CAPTURING THE NON-SUCCESSIVE: MYTHICAL IMAGINATION IN THE WRITINGS OF C. S. LEWIS

Lewis, who loved the imaginative splendor and imaginative viability of the medieval cosmology, embodied the mythical imagination in his own writing. In his book *Planet Narnia*, Michael Ward has suggested that a great imaginative secret is to be found in Lewis's Chronicles of Narnia. Ward states that each of the seven books in the series is associated with one of the seven planets of medieval cosmology and that Lewis has woven into each an abundance of images, metaphors, and atmosphere related to medieval understandings of those planets. The casual reader who enjoys these books but is unfamiliar with medieval cosmology will not realize that

---

[21] Lewis, *English Literature in the Sixteenth Century*, 3.

[22] See the block quotation referenced by footnote 19.

[23] Lewis, *English Literature in the Sixteenth Century*, 4.

Lewis has followed the example of plenitude; he has crowded his books with hidden meanings.

For example, *The Lion, the Witch, and the Wardrobe* is associated with the planet Jupiter. Recall that each of the medieval planets exerted influences on humans. Ward refers to a poem Lewis wrote entitled "The Planets" that enumerates the planetary influences of medieval belief. Thus, Jupiter is connected with the coming of spring, kingliness, revels, and so forth. The lion, Aslan, is associated with kingliness, and the romp he has with the children is suggestive of revel. The waning power of the White Witch— reflected in the melting of the snow that has for so long held Narnia in its thrall—is connected to the coming of spring.[24]

Similarly, *The Horse and His Boy* is connected with the planet Mercury. Mercury is the god of speed, he inspires the studious, and he is the patron of pilferers. Throughout this chronicle, we see the idea of swiftness repeated again and again. The constant cry of "Narnia and the North," the fleeting trip across the desert, and the swift race of the horses to the hermit's enclosure each illustrate speed, writes Ward. Shasta, once he is reunited with his family learns that he will be educated; this is the influence of Mercury's studiousness. Shasta also steals a number of times in the book; Mercury as the patron of pilferers would approve.[25] This is but a fraction of what Ward suggests Lewis worked into each book. There are many more examples, but these will suffice to briefly show how Lewis followed the pattern of plenitude by filling The Chronicles with medieval cosmology.

The idea of credulity, not in its negative sense, but in its beneficial sense, as a willingness to find significance in both factual and fictional narratives, is a bit more difficult to discover in Lewis. It would perhaps be more pertinent to describe how Lewis understood it rather than how he employed it in his own work. We might find it in the idea of atmosphere, which, particularly in fiction, was of the highest importance to Lewis. In thinking about why people return again and again to certain stories or narratives, Lewis suggests it "is like going back to a fruit for its taste; to an air for its . . . what? for *itself*; to a region for its whole atmosphere—to Donegal for its Donegality and

---

[24] Michael Ward, *Planet Narnia: The Seven Heavens in the Imagination of C. S. Lewis* (New York: Oxford University Press, 2008), 57-64.

[25] Ward, *Planet Narnia*, 155.

London for its Londonness."[26] It is this sense of evoked atmosphere that was prized by Lewis in stories as well as in the medieval cosmos.

In "On Fairy-Stories," J. R. R. Tolkien writes of the four things offered by fairy tales. One of them is escape. Now, there are positive escapes and negative escapes. Positive escapes give us imaginative satisfaction, often of such ancient desires as the desire to swim with the fish, soar with the birds, and converse with animals. But it can also offer us an escape from the ugliness of modernity or from pain, or ultimately, from death. In other words, they satisfy some longing which has always been innate within us. And the key word here is longing. We return to certain stories again because of the atmosphere that creates a longing within us. And with what do both Tolkien and Lewis ultimately associate our longings as humans? It is a longing to which everything else points us, a true object, that is, God. All good stories remind us of this in the end. In Lewis, it is the idea of the myth become fact. In Tolkien it is the *eucatastrophe*, the gospel as fairy tale.[27]

For Lewis, the problem is that in stories, we grasp at this atmosphere, but all we get is a succession of events where we can never quite enter in. This occurs in life as well. We are always searching for the essence of something; it is always in our thoughts that if we can just attain this, we will finally arrive and be enfolded in the essence we were seeking. One place it takes shape is in our dreams of happiness that always seems to be waiting just over the next hill. But the reality never matches up to the vision. Lewis writes, "In life and art both, as it seems to me, we are always trying to catch in our net of successive moments something that is not successive."[28] Lewis concludes by saying that this union we seek is sometimes accomplished in stories.

In speaking of literature, he also writes of "receivers" versus "users" of art. The users attempt to do things to the art; the receivers wait for the art to do something to them. In Lewis's words, users don't cross the frontier into a new region where the art has enabled an enlargement of the world, but receivers do.[29] And what are we

---

[26] C. S. Lewis, *Spenser's Images of Life*, ed. by Alastair Fowler (Cambridge: Cambridge University Press, 1967), 115.

[27] J. R. R. Tolkien, "On Fairy-Stories," in *Essays Presented to Charles Williams*, ed. by C. S. Lewis (Grand Rapids, MI: Eerdmans, 1973), 78-82.

[28] C. S. Lewis, *Of Other Worlds: Essays and Stories*, ed. by Walter Hooper (New York: Harcourt Brace Jovanovich, 1966), 20.

[29] C. S. Lewis, *An Experiment in Criticism* (Cambridge: Cambridge University Press, 2008), 21-2.

attempting to receive but the essence of the work itself, to get in past the longings and be united to that which the longings point to? A beneficial credulity, receiving from a work of fiction nourishment, sustenance, and spiritual growth, frames the core of Lewis's own fiction as well.

As already noted, the medieval writers loved to repeat the stories of the past. So did Lewis. We should not, perhaps, be surprised that an Oxford don specializing in medieval studies loved to include elements of his area of expertise in his fiction. It is obvious that he loved to repeat elements of the medieval cosmology. They can be found hidden or overt in The Chronicles of Narnia, in Lewis's poetry, and in the Ransom Trilogy tradition of passing along the old tales, just because their substance is worthy to pass on.

Devolution can be found in Lewis's portrayal of earth in *Out of the Silent Planet*, called Thulcandra or Earth by the inhabitants of Malacandra or Mars. To them it is a dark and silent planet, and their leader Oyarsa says this to Ransom: "Thulcandra is the world we do not know. It alone is outside the heaven, and no message comes from it."[30] *Outside the heaven* is the key phrase. If we return to medieval cosmology, each of the seven planets is above the region of the moon and thus immutable and non-contingent, caught up in the perfection of the heavenly dance. And of course, the spheres of the heavens in their movement create music, which we cannot hear because paradoxically, we have always heard it. They are animated and harmonious in their sound. Earth, the sublunary planet, outside the heavenly realms, alone is silent. Lewis likens the inhabitants on earth who gaze into the heavens as animals staring at the fires of an encampment they cannot enter or rustics gazing into the distance at a city. We are outside the city wall, looking in.[31] We long to enter and participate, but we cannot. The perfection and order of the heavens gradually spirals down to the weakest impulse: the imperfection, randomness, and silence of earth.

In any place where longing is to be found, we can hypothesize that devolution is the principle at hand. We realize that things are not as they should be, that the world seems to grow steadily more evil and chaotic. The medieval belief that the past was more glorious than the

---

[30] Ward, *Planet Narnia*, 120.

[31] C. S. Lewis, *Studies in Medieval and Renaissance Literature*, ed. by Walter Hooper (Cambridge: Cambridge University Press, 1966), 59.

present is an example of this. In the Chronicles especially, there is a repeated theme of longing for the adventures that took place in the past. Edmund and Lucy share it in *The Voyage of the "Dawn Treader,"* as they sit in the bedroom, talking earnestly of Narnia before they are sucked into the painting of a sailing ship hanging on the wall. When Susan, in *Prince Caspian*, discovers the solid gold chess knight in the overgrown ruins of what later turns out to be Cair Paravel, she is overwhelmed by longing for the past when she ruled as a queen of Narnia. "It brought back—oh, such lovely times. And I remembered playing chess with fauns and good giants, and the mer-people singing in the sea, and my beautiful horse . . . ."[32] Just as Jill Pole and Eustace long to escape the bullying of Experiment House in *The Silver Chair*, we on earth are products of devolution; we long for the beauty and order of the heavens, of the other reality toward which we are drawn all our lives, whether we are aware of it or not.

If as Ward suggests, each Narnia chronicle is associated with a planet, then the whole, in a sense, is a glimpse of the heavenly realms. As we read, we stand outside this heaven, looking in. Just about each tale begins with a longing to get in:

The Lion, the Witch, and the Wardrobe: Getting into Narnia through a wardrobe

Prince Caspian: Caspian loves tales of old Narnia, the mythic world he has been told doesn't exist, yet he longs to find it

The Voyage of "Dawn Treader": Getting in through the painting of the sailing ship

The Silver Chair: The longing to escape school, getting in through the door in the high stone wall

The Horse and His Boy: The longing to know what is over the green hill

The Magician's Nephew: Getting into other worlds via magic rings and pools in the wood between the worlds

The Last Battle: Getting in through the stable to the source of all longings

In a sense, Lewis's characters do get in, though it is not a world of perfection. But it is a world of meaning and color and myth come

---

[32] C. S. Lewis, *Prince Caspian: The Return to Narnia* (New York: Harper Trophy, 1994), 18.

to life. And in nearly every book, they must leave this world at the end. The final fulfillment and satisfaction and union are not yet to be. Longing is the response to living in a state of devolution, that is, living apart from God. All our desires to get in, to become one with the beauty we see, to attain that particular thing or regain that particular feeling are indicators of it. And Lewis writes that all the leaves of the New Testament are rustling with the fact that one day, we will get in.[33]

TAKING THE THOUSANDTH LOOK: RECOVERING THE MYTHICAL IMAGINATION

The mythical imagination has much to teach, but we live in an age that does not encourage its use. The irony of its loss to scientific understanding is that evolution, our current understanding of the universe, is every bit the myth that the ancient cosmology was. Any scientific explanation of facts is metaphorical, and therefore mythical. We can never get deep enough to the ultimate truth of any given matter unless we could actually see reality created as it springs from the fingers of God.[34] All our theories and understandings must therefore be provisional. We can never say we've found the explanation for anything. Everything can really only be explained in terms of something else. Simple items we take for granted like tables and walls are things we can't even begin to understand. Perhaps, then, part of recovering the mythical imagination is a realization that its use is not completely banished to history, that aspects of it still linger. To enact a fuller recovery will take a willingness on our part to shift our perceptions and see the world with new eyes.

The mythical imagination enables us to enter fully into the significance of ancient stories and myths, if not for their literal truth, then for the truths they suggest. Lewis writes that what flows into us from myths is not truth, but reality; thus, myth becomes the parent of many truths at the abstract level. "Myth is the mountain whence all the different streams arise which become truths down here in the valley."[35] We should hold our disbelief lightly, with a willingness to

---

[33] Lewis, *The Weight of Glory*, 13.

[34] C. S. Lewis, *Letters to Malcolm, Chiefly on Prayer* (London: Geoffrey Bles, 1964), 105-6.

[35] C. S. Lewis, "Myth Became Fact," in *God in the Dock: Essays on Theology and Ethics*, ed. by Walter Hooper (Grand Rapids, MI: William B.

learn, to be immersed in a myth and be fed by it. At this level its historical accuracy is irrelevant. It is the story that matters.

The ancient stories and myths give us strength, meaning, and color and a sense of direction and purpose in a world that has become in many ways directionless and meaningless. Chalcidius, a fourth-century philosopher who translated portions of Plato, believed that sight begets philosophy. We won't search for God or aspire to a moral life unless we have first observed the heavens or nature.[36] The idea of plenitude may seem farcical to a modern because the theories of the medieval model have been disproven, yet still, as the poet Gerard Manley Hopkins reminds us, "The world is charged with the grandeur of God." Plenitude is a principle of the universe, even from a scientific view. We will never get to the end of what's there. All scientific knowledge to date has barely scratched the surface. We merely exchange one model for another, equally as metaphorical in describing the observed phenomena. It takes a willingness to carefully observe the world, to notice instead of merely to see, to take G. K. Chesterton's thousandth look and see as if for the first time. This takes a native wisdom and an ability to be receptive to the universe that is crowded with God's grandeur.

If sight begets philosophy, in a world so crowded, it should not be difficult to detect or infer an invisible pattern from the visible world. As previously noted, there really isn't any excuse for not inferring a God or a Christ from the visible data. The pagan writers who created dying god myths saw an invisible pattern in the visible. Their stories were the forerunners of the one true story. In an age that is constantly distracted, learning to see the invisible pattern in the visible is arduous. To acquire the anagogical mindset, we must be present to the created world, to notice, not just to see, and then to engage our mind with what we see.

But the odds are against us. As screen technologies continue to proliferate and hold our attention captive, the natural world and our relationships with others fade. It will take a powerful effort on our part to labor against this trend, to engage this aspect of the mythical imagination. This is where the myths can help us; by presenting an etiological understanding of the created order, they activate the satisfied imagination, re-enchant our world, and help us find delight

---

Eerdmans, 1970), 66.

[36] Lewis, *Discarded Image*, 55.

in the familiar. They reawaken meaning. Through the myths we capture, though faintly, glimmers a truth, signifying the true story behind all of creation. Again, Lewis defines myth as an unfocused gleam of divine truth. *Divine truth*. God, as the iconoclast, breaks into our lives to begin enabling us to see the invisible reality we are so adept at ignoring.

A delight in a world crowded with God requires a certain humility. Medieval man had it. Lewis writes, "Historically as well as cosmically, medieval man stood at the foot of a stairway; looking up, he felt delight. The backward, like the upward, glance exhilarated him with a majestic spectacle, and humility was rewarded with the pleasures of admiration."[37] In a worldview that embraced devolution, the past would have been glorious. It was the present time that was negligible. History was a long push from perfection to imperfection. In our own age, we believe in evolution; movement from imperfection to perfection. The case could be argued either way. The perfection of the garden of Eden and the fall of man created a devolutionary sense of history in which the outworking of sin continues to grow.

But at the same time, as believers in Christ, we understand that there is a sense in which our trajectory on this earth is evolutionary, not in the scientific and popular sense, but in that we are spiritual beings on a growth trend we believe will result in final union with God. Meanwhile, our world continues to decay. We must strike a balance between the two ideas. To embrace the humility of taking part in the glorious scheme of history and being content is certainly laudable; in the same way, we cannot neglect to seek and grow towards our spiritual fulfillment. In the cosmological sense of devolution, we can also learn a lesson; in this life we are indeed outside the city wall, and it is our responsibility to imitate those high pomps of heaven, that is, the high ideals of Christ. Just as the medievals could only imagine the revels of the heavenly bodies, we see through a glass darkly. But we long for these glories, nonetheless.

---

[37] Lewis, *Discarded Image*, 185.

Chapter 10

FROM SUFFERING TO SERVICE: EDMUND'S SPIRITUAL FORMATION

WAYNE MARTINDALE

Edmund Pevensie winds his way through four of the seven Narnia books, making his first appearance along with Peter, Susan, and Lucy in *The Lion, the Witch and the Wardrobe*, where he gets his fullest and most important development, then in *Prince Caspian, The Voyage of the "Dawn Treader,"* and at the end of *The Last Battle*. Few characters in the Chronicles are more central to the main story line, especially in *The Lion, the Witch and the Wardrobe*, where Edmund creates the crucial conflict (on the human side), precipitates Aslan's death, and illustrates the transformative power of union with Christ as represented by Aslan. We get to know Edmund as he plays a rainy day game of hide-and-seek with his siblings in their uncle's house. The game may be an intentional metaphor of the spiritual journey the children take, especially Edmund, who hides from the truth and is sought and found by Aslan. The game and its aftermath in Narnia are the occasion of Edmund's sin of pride. To put his brother and sisters in their place—humiliated and beneath him—Edmund lies, betrays, and imperils his siblings' lives and his own soul in a deal with the White Witch, who offers the pleasures of Turkish Delight and lordly rule. It appears certain that his deal with the "Devil" will cost him and perhaps all Narnia their lives.

The journey of transformation will lie through physical and emotional pain, deep conviction of sin, renunciation of the sinful self, hope in the exclusive claims of Aslan's power, and ultimate transformation into a faithful servant. Lewis found great insight into this thoroughly biblical process as analyzed by Evelyn Underhill, a leading voice in spiritual formation, whom Lewis much admired. Edmund develops through Underhill's classic stages of spiritual formation: 1) "awakening of the Self to the consciousness of Divine Reality"; 2) "Purgation," which is the effort to draw close to God by "Discipline and Mortification"; 3) "Illumination" or moral clarity and knowledge of God; 4) the "Purification of Spirit," in which the will chooses obedience to God even when He seems absent; and 5) the

"Unitive" stage, at which the love of God flows over into the love of others in active service.[38] The emphasis here is on the "Unitive" stage, that challenge in spiritual formation that daunts us all apart from the empowering Holy Spirit, for here God demands nothing less than all. Lewis puts it this way in his address called "A Slip of the Tongue":

> [God] has, in the last resort, nothing to give us but Himself; and He can give that only insofar as our self-affirming will retires and makes room for Him in our souls. Let us make up our minds to it; there will be nothing "of our own" left over to live on, no "ordinary" life . . . .. He claims all, because He is love and must bless. He cannot bless us unless He has us. When we try to keep within us an area that is our own, we try to keep an area of death. Therefore, in love, He claims all. There's no bargaining with Him.[39]

Underhill says that we may expect several results from a direct encounter with God: "a total change and reorientation of life, a long, hard discipline and inward growth, an immense transformation of personality, great creative power."[40] All of these happen to Edmund in the course of our long acquaintance with him as he progresses from a spiteful kid in need of a good spanking to a humble and self-sacrificing—even lovable—young man of true nobility. According to Underhill, a person who has truly met God in Christ will be the opposite of otherworldly, a person whose head is in the clouds and of no practical use to anyone else. Rather, a follower of Jesus, *must* be a good neighbor and a good citizen. As Underhill reminds us, a disciple's "love of God and thirst for God have been cleansed by long discipline from all self-interest; and the more profound his contemplation of God, the more he loves the world and tries to serve it as a tool" of God.[41]

Her statement is fully biblical and richly illustrated in the lives of those detailed in Scripture, from Moses to Isaiah to Paul and, of

---

[38] Evelyn Underhill, *Mysticism: A Study in the Nature and Development of Man's Spiritual Consciousness* (London: Methuen, 1967). It was first published in 1911.

[39] C. S. Lewis, "A Slip of the Tongue" in *The Weight of Glory and Other Addresses*, ed. by Walter Hooper (New York: Simon and Schuster, 1996), 141.

[40] Evelyn Underhill, *Collected Papers of Evelyn Underhill*, ed. by Lucy Menzies (New York: Longmans, Green and Co., 1946), 109.

[41] Underhill, *Collected Papers*, 115-16.

course, preeminently modeled in Christ. "It means renouncing the hotel-life of religion with its comforts and conveniences," Underhill continues, "and setting our face towards the snows; not for any personal ambition or enjoyment, but driven [to the summit] by the strange mountain of love."[42] There are two characters who achieve union with God/Aslan in the fullest sense, whose old nature seems to have been "crucified with Christ" so that they can say with Paul, "It is no longer I who live, but Christ who lives in me" (Galatians 2:20 ESV). These two are Lucy and, preeminently, Reepicheep. But when we look for someone most like ourselves, it may be to someone like Edmund, who is moving in that direction, but whose progress is painfully slow, and whose old nature emerges yet from time to time.

JOINED WITH CHRIST

> We do not have a high priest who is unable to sympathize with our weaknesses, but one who in every respect has been tempted as we are, yet without sin. Let us then with confidence draw near to the throne of grace, that we may receive mercy and find grace to help in time of need. (Hebrews 4:15-16)

> Let steadfastness have its full effect, that you may be perfect and complete, lacking in nothing. (James 1:4)

What God is up to in Edmund and in each of us who place our destiny in his hands is making us perfect, in the image of his Son. God makes us "permanently into a different sort of thing; into a new little Christ, a being which, in its own small way, has the same kind of life as God; which shares in His power, joy, knowledge and eternity."[43] We are not invited to a formula for successful Christian living, a set of behaviors that can wring from God favors and prosperity. As with Edmund meeting Aslan, we are invited to an encounter with a living person. We are invited, not to follow a map, but a guide. To embody that living presence is the fulfillment of our creaturely destiny, the thing we were born for.

Jesus gives us his life as surely and as radically as Aslan gives new life to the dead creatures made into stone statues by the White Witch. Aslan breathes into them the breath of life. The symbolism is quite compact, combining as it does the initial creation of man—formed

---

[42] Underhill, *Collected Papers*, 118-19.

[43] C. S. Lewis, *Mere Christianity* (New York: Macmillan, 1960), 164.

THE UNDISCOVERED C. S. LEWIS

of clay but lifeless until God "breathed in him the breath of life and he became a living soul"— the giving of the Holy Spirit, symbolized by tongues and wind in the New Testament ("wind" and "breath" are the same word in Greek). In *Mere Christianity*, Lewis uses the same symbolism, of stone statues coming to life, for talking about salvation and becoming sons and daughters of God.

> A man who changed from having *Bios* [physical life] to having *Zoe* [spiritual life] would have gone through as big a change as a statue which changed from being a carved stone to being a real man.
>
> And that is precisely what Christianity is about. This is a great sculptor's shop. We are the statues and there is a rumour going round the shop that some of us are some day going to come to life.[44]

While joining with Christ's life is in one sense the whole aim of our lives and destiny, that moment of new birth is in another sense only the beginning of a pilgrimage that leads to "Union," here meaning complete conformity to the will of God. The evidence that we are on this pilgrimage is a changed life—a radically different thing from behaving a certain way to earn this life. It is always the other way around; we receive the new life, then do things that were previously not in our nature: things that please God, that are intrinsically good because they flow out of God's character. What does a life moving in this direction look like?

THE FELLOWSHIP OF SUFFERING

> We are children of God, and if children, then heirs—heirs of God and fellow heirs with Christ, provided we suffer with him in order that we may also be glorified with him. (Romans 8:16-17)

This section could go almost anywhere, since suffering runs like a leitmotif through the solemn music of our lives. In Edmund's case (a not uncommon one), suffering awakens him to his sinful nature and opens him to a sense of need and longing for Aslan. After coming to Aslan for salvation, in suffering Edmund serves, and in suffering he grows, throughout the Chronicles—though, crucially, the pain is bathed in joy as his hope is now in Aslan's country and his chief pleasure to do Aslan's bidding and receive his "well done." This is the promise of Scripture to all who pursue Christ—the Unitive way: joyful

---

[44] Lewis, *Mere Christianity*, 140.

service, though suffering in its many forms will often accompany the faithful pilgrim. We may call to witness the example of Christ, Paul's listing of hardships in 2 Corinthians 11, the roll call of sacrificial heroes of the faith in Hebrews 11, and the martyrdom of virtually all the apostles.

That Jesus will make us perfect, as he promised, we cannot doubt. But he warned us to "count the cost." In one of his many recognitions of this fact, Lewis says in *Mere Christianity*: "Though our feelings come and go, His love for us does not. It is not wearied by our sins, or our indifference; and, therefore, it is quite relentless in its determination that we shall be cured of those sins, at whatever cost to us, at whatever cost to Him."[45] Citing St. John of the Cross, Underhill affirms the observation that most people stop at the Illuminative stage. Lewis agrees. They have left the valley of worldliness and have in sight the "mysterious region of the everlasting snows,"[46] the summit representing union with God, of conforming our will to his, of "doing the right thing for the right reason."[47] Meditating on Jesus is a necessary and satisfying part of the Unitive way, and while we never grow beyond it (nor will we through eternity), we must not think that is our complete earthly calling.

We are mostly content to stay on the easy plateau where Edmund found himself after being forgiven by Aslan, and with Edmund, we would look continually at that face which is the Beatific Vision, the source of all our hope and joy. Because from this point to Union, there are no paths. "No one can tell the climber how to tackle the precipice. Here he must be led by the Spirit of God; and his success must depend on his self-abandonment and his courage—his willingness to risk, to trust, and to endure to the very end. Every one suffers on the precipice,"[48] Here Reepicheep, Jewel, Tirian, and Edmund dare to go. "It is a rare experience," Underhill concludes, "but the only way to the real summit; the supernatural life of perfect union with the self-giving and outpouring love of God."[49]

---

[45] Lewis, *Mere Christianity*, 118.

[46] Lewis, *Mere Christianity*, 119.

[47] T. S. Eliot, *Murder in the Cathedral* (New York: Harcourt Brace & Company, 1963), 44.

[48] Underhill, *Collected Papers*, 119-20.

[49] Underhill, *Collected Papers*, 120.

FROM MEDITATION TO ACTION

> Let us run with endurance the race that is set before us, looking to Jesus, the founder and perfecter of our faith. (Hebrews 12:1-2)

After Edmund is saved at the last minute from a grisly execution at the Witch's hand, Aslan and he have a conversation that we never hear, but which "Edmund never forgot." Aslan then brings Edmund to his siblings and reconciles them, with instructions not to bring up past misdeeds. "'Here is your brother,' he said, 'and—there is no need to talk to him about what is past.'"[50] In a most poignant episode, the White Witch has asked for an audience with Aslan, which he grants. The White Witch has come to claim Edmund's life as hers by right, since he is a traitor. Much is at stake and mysterious things are afoot. The others are whispering their observations and questions. "But Edmund had got past thinking about himself after all he'd been through and after the talk he'd had that morning. He just went on looking at Aslan. It didn't seem to matter what the Witch said."[51] While the Witch is bargaining for Edmund's life, Edmund was "looking all the time at Aslan's face."[52] Edmund here shows us the first priority of our lives: to know Christ, to gaze on his face, to begin to comprehend his consuming love for us.

In the New Testament, and in the lives of believers at all times, contemplation is followed (as in the life of Jesus himself) by action. That action aims at the spiritual good of others, under the lordship of Christ and at his direction, though it cost us suffering or life itself. After the Witch leaves, in an event meant to recall Jesus's last supper before his crucifixion, they have a meal. Then the narrative shifts to detail Aslan's death and resurrection as witnessed by Susan and Lucy, just as it was some of his women followers who cared for Jesus's body and first witnessed the resurrection. The next time we meet Edmund, he is "fighting desperately," side by side with Peter in the grueling battle against the forces of evil.[53] Contemplation has given way to action, knowing to doing, faith to works. That is the right order. And

---

[50] C. S. Lewis, *The Lion, the Witch and the Wardrobe* (New York: HarperCollins, 1994), 153.

[51] Lewis, *The Lion*, 155.

[52] Lewis, *The Lion*, 156.

[53] Lewis, *The Lion*, 193.

what heroic and singular service Edmund has given. In a sign of his own maturity, Peter praises his brother to Aslan.

> "It was all Edmund's doing, Aslan," Peter was saying. "We'd have been beaten if it hadn't been for him. The Witch was turning our troops into stone right and left. But nothing would stop him. He fought his way through three ogres to where she was just turning one of your leopards into a statue. And when he reached her he had the sense to bring his sword smashing down on her wand instead of trying to go for her directly and simply getting made a statue himself for his pains. That was the mistake all the rest were making. Once her wand was broken, we began to have some chance—if we hadn't lost so many already. He was terribly wounded. We must go and see him."[54]

UNION AND THE BODY OF CHRIST

> We, though many, are one body in Christ, and individually members of one another. Having gifts that differ according to the grace given us, let us use them. (Romans 12:5-6)

The next thing we observe is that no one serves alone, and no one gift or person is sufficient to win the battle against evil. We were created for fellowship, to be members of a single organism, symbolized as the body, of which Jesus is the head. Life in the body of Christ, to the extent that we observe it, is also action, but with that special biblical focus so at odds with our modern Western view of such things as heroism, individualism, and rights as distinctly self-focused. Summarizing this key New Testament teaching in *Mere Christianity*, Lewis says, "Christianity thinks of human individuals not as mere members of a group or items in a list, but as organs in a body—different from one another and each contributing what no other could."[55] The spiritual gifts, which all need, are spread among believers as a way of promoting our unity.

All of the creatures the Witch had turned to stone but were breathed back to life by Aslan are eager to join the battle on his side, and each has a particular place. Some can give rides to the battle and some need to take the rides. Those who have a keen sense of smell must lead the party and are commanded up front "with us lions to

---

[54] Lewis, *The Lion*, 195-6.
[55] Lewis, *Mere Christianity*, 159.

smell out where the battle is."[56] The lions are ecstatic: "Did you hear what he said? *Us Lions?*" That is the feeling of wonder proper to each of us when we are welcomed into the body of Christ, discovering that we are at once needy and needed. Once at the battle scene, Lucy must use her gift to bring healing to Edmund. She had been given a magic (read "spiritual" and "miraculous") bottle, a single diamond containing a potion that will heal nearly any wound. Lucy applies a drop to each of Edmund's wounds, and he is restored.

The unity of service continues as the Witch and her main force are defeated. Together, the four children serve long and well as kings and queens of Narnia, mopping up the remnants of evil, giving rewards and feasts, ensuring peace, making just laws and good alliances, and taking each other's counsel (as in whether to hunt the White Stag). Their new position of honor and service is accompanied by new names: Peter the Magnificent, Susan the Gentle, Lucy the Valiant, and Edmund the Just.[57]

MATURITY: *PRINCE CASPIAN, THE VOYAGE OF THE DAWN TREADER*, AND *THE LAST BATTLE*

Let us offer to God acceptable worship, with reverence and awe, for our God is a consuming fire. (Hebrews 12:28-29)

Prince Caspian, the book following *The Lion, the Witch and the Wardrobe* in composition order, takes up the further adventures of the Pevensie kids. After only a year in our world since returning from their first visit to Narnia, the siblings are sitting at a train station when, unknown to them, Susan's magic horn is blown in Narnia, calling them back. They are pulled out of this world, vanishing "into thin air," landing in a Narnian wood. Though only a year has passed in this world, Narnian time, which runs differently, has covered several generations. The great need for which the children were summoned is Miraz's usurpation of the Narnian throne. The Pevensies, early kings and queens of Narnia, discover that their task, through hardships and battles, is to see the rightful Prince Caspian enthroned as king of Narnia.

From the very beginning, we see that the changes wrought in Edmund by his encounter with Aslan are still much in evidence. He

---

[56] Lewis, *The Lion*, 119.

[57] Lewis, *The Lion*, 201.

is the one who discerns that some magic is at work pulling on them in the train station, and at his suggestion, all join hands to be sure they are in the adventure together. Then, in Narnia, while their task is yet unknown and the going gets a bit rough, Edmund trades off carrying Peter's great coat, though his own was left behind, and readily shares his sandwich, though it is only one of two among four kids. These are small things, but they signify enormous spiritual growth from self-centeredness to other-centeredness.

Here they receive the usual benefits of cooperation in making life not only more pleasant, but to a large extent even possible. When they become thirsty after the sandwiches, Edmund knows that fresh water can be found by looking for streams because that's the way it is done in the books. Reading the right books, the ones that cultivate the imagination (the organ of meaning), is always a positive sign in the Narnia books; remember that Eustace, when we meet him in his "stinker" stage, had read all the wrong books—those with information. As Lewis insists, cultivating the imagination is the hallmark of a good education.

Of course, the most important marks of spiritual growth are how we relate to Christ—or in Narnia, to Aslan. As they have all learned, Lucy is the one most likely to see Aslan. On the tangled and perilous journey to Aslan's How, Edmund is the only one to support Lucy, even though it means admitting he was wrong about directions, and anyone who has been in an argument about directions knows how much maturity this simple admission of error requires. Neither Edmund nor any of the others besides Lucy has yet seen Aslan, but he comes to trust what we recognize in Lucy as the spiritual gifts of faith and discernment. Edmund must conquer not only his own pride in admitting that he was wrong, but he must also support Lucy in the face of opposition by the two older siblings, Peter and Susan, and the ever-skeptical Dwarf, Trumpkin—the very type of the hard-headed pragmatist who thinks "seeing is believing," when faith always works the other way around.

Trumpkin has trouble taking any of the Pevensies seriously because they are, after all, only kids. This suggests another aspect of Lewis's constant symbolism in the Narnia books. Jesus said that unless our faith is like that of a child, we will not see the kingdom of God. It is the children who trust Aslan first, and the smallest and simplest, Lucy, who is most trusting of all. Edmund's trust in Aslan and in Lucy's sighting of him results in their getting to the battle at Aslan's

How by the shortest route—one they would never have guessed and one opposite their direction of travel. For his faith, Edmund receives Aslan's "well done," the reward all followers of Christ most seek.[58]

We see further evidence of progress on the Unitive way in Edmund and Lucy's relationship in the next book, *The Voyage of the "Dawn Treader."* Edmund is stuck sharing a bedroom with the "stinker" Eustace, who is more like the unregenerate Edmund than any other character in Narnia. Of course, they wouldn't have liked each other if Edmund had still been a stinker, too, except when (banish the thought) they might have ganged up on Lucy. But now, as the story opens, Edmund and Lucy are "stealing a few precious minutes alone together."[59] At the opening of *The Lion, the Witch and the Wardrobe,* the animosity between Edmund and Lucy was as palpable as that now between Eustace and his cousins, but we see in a flash that the sibling rivalry is over, replaced by a spiritual kinship deeper even than blood.

When Eustace comes into the room where Edmund and Lucy are enjoying looking at a picture that reminds them of Narnia, Eustace, who has no imagination (and is hence a moral cripple), all too naturally begins finding fault with both the picture and his cousins. The old Edmund begins to flare up again. This is no surprise because he sees clearly what he himself has recently been and doesn't like being reminded. Nevertheless, when they fall through the picture into the Narnian sea, Edmund helps to save the floundering Eustace, who can't do anything really useful, like swim.

But at last, with all the other adventurers from Narnia, we do come to love Eustace. After his selfishness and laziness get him turned into a dragon and he suffers a good deal, he becomes genuinely repentant. At this point, several of the more mature Narnians step up to help Eustace. Lucy and Reepicheep help him the most while he is still a dragon. Reepicheep, who was most often the butt of Eustace's sarcasm and physical abuse, becomes Eustace's "most constant comforter."[60] Edmund shows his maturity through his humility and identification with Eustace as a sinner. After Aslan undragons Eustace, he admits

---

[58] C.S. Lewis, *Prince Caspian* (New York: HarperCollins, 1994), 162.

[59] C.S. Lewis, *The Voyage of the "Dawn Treader"* (New York: HarperCollins, 1994), 3-4.

[60] Lewis, *"Dawn Treader,"* 108.

that he's "been pretty beastly."[61] It is literally true of Eustace as dragon, but we have heard that name ("beastly") a good deal before, as it was often applied to Edmund in *The Lion, the Witch and the Wardrobe*. Both applications of the term fit at the time. Knowing what Edmund has been and seeing what he has become, his exchange with Eustace is one of the most moving in the Chronicles:

> "That's all right," said Edmund. "Between ourselves, you haven't been as bad as I was on my first trip to Narnia. You were only an ass, but I was a traitor."
>
> "Well, don't tell me about it then," said Eustace. "But who is Aslan? Do you know him?"
>
> "Well—he knows me," said Edmund. "He is the great Lion, the son of the Emperor-beyond-the-Sea, who saved me and saved Narnia. We've all seen him. Lucy sees him most often. And it may be Aslan's country we are sailing to."[62]

Several things about this passage illustrate Edmund's spiritual growth. He has become the "father confessor" for Eustace, as well as his comforter. Edmund has mastered his pride and in humility (that is, truth) acknowledges his own great sin, but not to wallow in it; rather, to give glory to Aslan. Edmund has also come to realize that the crucial element of the relationship is Aslan's initiative and what Aslan knows. To be known and approved of by Aslan is Edmund's goal and the source of his new-found contentment in who he is.

To finish Edmund's story, we have to leap ahead to *The Last Battle* and the end of time, the end of the Old Narnia, and the entrance of the "good characters" into Aslan's Country: the New Narnia, Heaven. In theological terms, Aslan's (Christ's) followers have passed from the earthly process of sanctification (becoming more like Christ) to glorification—fully transformed into what Jesus intended each to be, free from sin, and loving all and each in perfect harmony—or, in the language of spiritual formation, they have progressed from Purgative to Illuminative to Unitive. At this stage, Edmund becomes one of the interpreters of last things to new arrivals in the New Narnia. It is a place full of wonder, yet Edmund is at home in it, even though he is making new discoveries, too.

In Lewis's fiction, even small details can tell us a great deal about

---

61 Lewis, *"Dawn Treader,"* 117.
62 Lewis, *"Dawn Treader,"* 117-18.

a character when we read it in light of the whole. Here is such a detail about Edmund. He knew which train his parents would be on, thus, that they were all killed in an accident. Lewis describes him as "the sort of person who knows about railways."[63] This is, of course, useful information, and everyone is happy to have it, but there is in this parenthetical description a sly grin and recognition of where Edmund has come from. It is a kind of summary of Edmund's whole spiritual pilgrimage. Though not a sin, this is no compliment. And remember, this is before they are all taken to the New Narnia in a "frightful roar" and a "bang."[64] Recall the first time we met Eustace in *The Voyage of the "Dawn Treader"*? [consistency of citation] He has read all the wrong books: none imaginative, all informational.

This is part of Lewis's portrayal of those who don't believe and don't take the imaginative and childlike leap of faith essential to true knowledge. Imagination is the organ of meaning, Lewis has said straightforwardly. The Calormene soldier and, pre-eminently, the Dwarfs (who are for the Dwarfs) can't, or won't, see spiritual reality. They are inside the stable, like those who follow Aslan, but they can't see the blue sky, the green grass, and beautiful fruit. They can't taste the deliciousness of Aslan's food. While others sip a wondrous wine, the Dwarfs taste only trough water. "'You see,' said Aslan. 'They [the Dwarfs] will not let us help them. They have chosen cunning instead of belief. Their prison is only in their own minds, yet they are in that prison, and so afraid of being taken in that they cannot be taken out.'"[65]

But for all who have been spiritually awakened, the same sight presents a radically different prospect. "The earth trembled. The sweet air grew suddenly sweeter. A brightness flashed behind them. All turned. Tirian turned last because he was afraid. There stood his heart's desire, huge and real, the golden Lion, Aslan himself."[66] As with Tirian, so with all who eagerly await Aslan's return. They are rewarded with the Beatific Vision: They see the glorified Aslan/ Christ and are invited into that glory, while those who had chosen against Aslan see his face in judgment, the Miserific Vision. All of the rational creatures "ran up to the doorway where Aslan stood":

---

[63] C. S. Lewis, *The Last Battle* (New York: HarperCollins, 1994), 173.

[64] Lewis, *Last Battle*, 173.

[65] Lewis, *Last Battle*, 173.

[66] Lewis, *Last Battle*, 183.

The creatures came rushing on, their eyes brighter and brighter as they drew nearer and nearer to the standing Stars. But as they came right up to Aslan one or other of two things happened to each of them. They all looked straight in his face, I don't think they had any choice about that. And when some looked the expression of their faces changed terribly—it was fear and hatred: except that, on the faces of Talking Beasts, the fear and hatred lasted only for a fraction of a second. You could see that they suddenly ceased to be *Talking* Beasts. They were just ordinary animals. And all the creatures who looked at Aslan in that way swerved to their right, his left, and disappeared into his huge black shadow, which (as you have heard) streamed away to the left of the doorway. The children never saw them again. I don't know what became of them. But the others looked in the face of Aslan and loved him, though some of them were very frightened at the same time. And all these came in at the Door, in at the door on Aslan's right. There were some queer specimens among them. Eustace even recognized one of those very Dwarfs who had helped to shoot the Horses . . .. Among the happy creatures who now came crowding round Tirian and his friends were all those whom they had thought dead.[67]

Even Puzzle is in the New Narnia, but not now as the poor deluded beast he has been for most of the book: for a "whole ten seconds," no one recognizes him, then a half dozen voices say at once, "'Why, it's old Puzzle!'" "He was himself now," the narrator comments, "beautiful" and "with an honest face" and so attractive in his renovated, true self that Queens Jill and Lucy run up and put their arms around his neck and kiss his nose.[68] This is the essence of Heaven: We are all, at last—with Puzzle and Edmund and "all who love his appearing"—our true selves.

SUMMARY OF LESSONS
ON SPIRITUAL FORMATION FROM EDMUND

From Edmund's journey of spiritual formation through the Purgative, Illuminative, and Unitive, we draw many lessons. First of all, spiritual formation takes time. Second, it involves challenge and often suffering; we rarely choose (or would if we could) the circumstances which ultimately do us good. The circumstances

---

[67] Lewis, *Last Battle*, 191-3.
[68] Lewis, *Last Battle*, 207-8.

by themselves do not assure growth. Susan is no longer a friend of Narnia by the end, though she shared the adventures and privileges of her faithful brothers and sister. The oft repeated formulation about suffering applies here: We will get bitter or better. Suffering may be our only hope, but it is God's "megaphone to rouse a dead world," not the whip he uses to drive us like slaves.[69] Third, spiritual formation requires an encounter with Christ that is never neutral: It always involves choice and consequence. Additionally, it has positive consequences, including a shift from being self-centered to being other-centered; a willingness to sacrifice—or, in other words, a new capacity for love, defined as the willingness to give of self or substance for another's spiritual good—genuine humility. Spiritual formation also results in discovering the source of all our longings. And last, it culminates in the joy of being known by God, being completed in Him, and receiving His "well done."

The transformation of Edmund and his spiritual formation are the radical norm for Christ-followers of all ages. It is for this very thing that we were in the mind of Christ from before the foundation of the world that, complete in Christ, we might "glorify God" and "enjoy him forever."

---

[69] C. S. Lewis, *The Problem of Pain* (New York: Macmillan, 1962), 93.

Chapter 11

THE SHORTER PLANETARY FICTION OF C. S. LEWIS

BRUCE R. JOHNSON

C. S. Lewis had a lifelong fascination with the medieval imagery of the heavens: seven planets circling the earth in a grand celestial dance. Of course, we now know this model is not true. Lewis nevertheless believed it was instructive in its geocentric simplicity and its hierarchical complexity. Moreover, he valued the planets, and the pagan gods associated with them, as spiritual symbols. As he once wrote to Ruth Pitter, "It was beautiful, on two or three successive nights about the Holy Time, to see Venus and Jove blazing at one another, once with the Moon right between them: Majesty and Love linked by Virginity—what could be more appropriate."[1] For Lewis, the cast of celestial bodies would play recurring roles in his poetry, his trilogy of space novels, and in his introduction to medieval and Renaissance literature, *The Discarded Image*.

Michael Ward has stirred popular interest in Lewis and medieval cosmology through his BBC television documentary "The Narnia Code," based on his seminal book, *Planet Narnia*. In both accounts, Ward advances the theory that each of the seven books of The Chronicles of Narnia was deliberately written to embody the qualities of one of the seven medieval planets. An intriguing aspect of this theory is what Lewis meant to say about God and God's intent for humanity through the sevenfold lens of these planetary gods. As Ward writes:

> This theological disposition is worked out in each of the Chronicles as the children, who by the common grace of 'nature' are already part of a planetary world, become more so by special grace as they follow the planetary deity's leading. Thus, in *The Lion* they become monarchs under sovereign Jove; in *Prince Caspian* they harden under strong Mars; in *The 'Dawn Treader'* they drink light under searching Sol; in *The*

---

[1] Letter of 2 January 1953, in C. S. Lewis, *The Collected Letters of C. S. Lewis*, ed. by Walter Hooper, 3 vols. (San Francisco: HarperCollins, 2004–7), 3:273.

Silver Chair they learn obedience under subordinate Luna; in *The Horse and His Boy* they come to love poetry under eloquent Mercury; in *The Magician's Nephew* they gain life-giving fruit under fertile Venus; and in *The Last Battle* they suffer and die under chilling Saturn.[2]

As the debate surrounding Ward's theory continues—all the more so with the release of a book version of *The Narnia Code*[3]—a reexamination of Lewis's shorter planetary fiction seems in order. In his lunar tale, "Forms of Things Unknown," and in his Martian story, "Ministering Angels," what aspects of the older cosmological model can be discerned? Are they in keeping with what Ward claims are the essences of Luna and Mars, as Lewis understood them? And what, if any, theological points may Lewis be making in these two tales? The present study will address each of these three issues. It will also attempt to answer the two main objections put forward about these stories: whether "Ministering Angels" is misogynistic, and whether "Forms of Things Unknown" is an authentic Lewis tale.

What aspects of the medieval model can be discerned in these two stories? "Ministering Angels" was first published in 1958 and deals with an outpost of scientists on Mars who receive a surprise visit from two self-selected "comfort women." This space farce was written in direct response to Robert Richardson's controversial article, "The Day after We Land on Mars," in which no role for women in space was foreseen outside of prostitution.[4] Lewis tackles Richardson's bad idea head on, exposing the flawed logic of his chauvinistic male fantasy. Lewis wrote with a Martian militancy; like the persona "MARS mercenary" in his poem "The Planets," he "flaunts laughingly" while he attempts to see "The wrong righted."[5]

The story itself reflects a tone that seems fitting for the god of war. All the astronauts based on Mars are battling discords of one sort or another. The meteorologist, nicknamed "the Monk," is seeking to right the internal wrong in his soul. The botanist is pressed for

[2] Michael Ward, *Planet Narnia: The Seven Heavens in the Imagination of C. S. Lewis* (New York: Oxford University Press, 2008), 237.

[3] Michael Ward, *The Narnia Code: C. S. Lewis and the Secret of the Seven Heavens* (Carol Stream, IL: Tyndale House, 2010).

[4] Robert S. Richardson, "The Day after We Land on Mars," in *The Magazine of Fantasy and Science Fiction*, 9.6 (December 1955), 44–52.

[5] C. S. Lewis, "The Planets," in *Poems*, ed. by Walter Hooper (New York: Harcourt Brace Jovanovich, 1977), 13–14.

time and battling interruptions. Paterson and Dickson face discord arising out of the former's unrequited homosexual advances towards the latter. The Captain resists accepting his worst fears, as he thinks of his new bride back on earth. A different Martian quality is found in the Thin Woman, who drops the not-so-enticing pick-up line, "immorality . . . must no longer be regarded as unethical."[6] This describes the indifference of Mars the mercenary, whom Lewis poetically portrayed as a "hired gladiator / Of evil and good. All's one to Mars."[7] Elsewhere, Lewis explained how "sturdy hardiness" was also part of the Martian temperament.[8] This attribute seems most characteristic in the Monk. He is the steadiest character, the one most able to adjust to changing circumstances. It is he who suggests a meal when the conversation becomes awkward, who speaks with grace to the rejected Fat Woman, and who eventually adjusts his outward focus in light of changed reality. The story set on Mars is appropriately Martian.

The lunar tale, "Forms of Things Unknown," was published posthumously in 1977 as part of the collection of short fiction by Lewis, entitled, *The Dark Tower and Other Stories*. It is the story of the fourth of four manned voyages to the moon, all of which end in disaster. The reason for this—and the surprise ending to the story—is the presence of a lunar Gorgon, whose hair of writhing snakes transforms each astronaut into stone as he turns to look backward. The classic tales of Medusa and the other Gorgons associate them with marine rather than lunar deities. Their lunar quality is rather found in the Gorgons' ability to change one thing into another. For ancient writers, Luna bordered the realm of mutability. Her sphere is "the great frontier between air and aether," between Aristotle's everchanging "Nature" and never-changing "Sky."[9] The lunar cycle itself appears more like corruptible earth than the eternal heavens. Luna's influence on people was thought to be related to change. Hence, Lewis wrote, "In men she produces wandering, and that in two senses. She may make them

---

[6] C. S. Lewis, "Ministering Angels," in *The Dark Tower and Other Stories*, ed. by Walter Hooper (New York: Harcourt Brace Jovanovich, 1977), 112–23.

[7] Lewis, "The Planets," 13–14.

[8] C. S. Lewis, *The Discarded Image: An Introduction to Medieval and Renaissance Literature* (Cambridge: Cambridge University Press, 1970), 106.

[9] Lewis, *The Discarded Image*, 32.

travelers . . .. But she may also produce a wandering of the wits."[10] Luna both charms and deceives, often hiding her true nature. She "Enchants us—the cheat!"[11] She is also associated with liquidity: Lewis waxes that Luna "Cruises monthly; with chrism of dew / And drenches of dream, a drizzling glamour."[12]

All these lunar qualities are present in "Forms of Things Unknown." Lieutenant Jenkin is wandering, cut adrift from a relationship with "that girl" (even her proper name was crossed out by Lewis in the original manuscript). Jenkin has rejected the influence of Venus (love) and come under the influence of Luna (virginity). He also distances himself from his friend Ward. Ward offers to come along on the lunar voyage, but Jenkin insists on making the trip alone, believing isolation will keep him safe. Of course, Jenkin wanders physically—as far from home as humanly possible. The lunar theme of liquidity makes the briefest of appearances through the two pints of draught Bass, ordered up by Jenkin at a pub. Lewis believed Bass to be "the lowest level surely that beer can attain,"[13] and perhaps meant this to be, tongue-in-check, a harbinger of upcoming madness. In his lunar voyage, and as he walks on the Moon's surface, Jenkin struggles against lunacy and fear. The prose is peppered with expressions like *claustrophobia, agoraphobia, terror, terrors, terrifying, fear,* and *frightening.* Earlier on, Jenkin speculates, "Might there be something on the Moon—or something psychological about the experience of landing on the Moon—which drives men fighting mad?"[14] Later, he misquotes Pascal's line about "the silence of those eternal spaces," leaving off his closing point: it "frightens me."[15] Terror is approaching. Like Luna herself, the lunar Gorgon lulls the doomed astronaut into a false sense of euphoria. For a few moments, he believes a race of lunar artisans has sculptured three lifelike tributes to the astronauts who preceded him. The truth is far different. When on the moon the name of one previous astronaut, Fox, is mentioned three times, perhaps

---

[10] Lewis, *The Discarded Image,* 109.

[11] Lewis, "The Planets," 12.

[12] Lewis, "The Planets," 12.

[13] Letter of 3 September 1927, in Lewis, *Collected Letters,* 1:730.

[14] C. S. Lewis, "Forms of Things Unknown," in *The Dark Tower,* 126.

[15] Lewis, "Things Unknown," 127. Pascal's actual line from *Pensées,* section III, 206, was *Le silence éternel de ces espaces infinis m'effraie,* "The eternal silence of these infinite spaces frightens me." See Blaise Pascal, *Pascal's Pensées* (New York: E. P. Dutton, 1958), 61.

recalling the Teumessian fox that was changed into stone and set among the stars. Jenkin's own fate is prefigured by prior appearances in the story of the words "petrified" and "animated stones." In the last sentence, his doom is sealed: "His eyes met hers."[16] The story set on the Moon is appropriately lunar.

To what extent do these interpretations coalesce with Ward's assessment of Lewis's approach to medieval cosmology? The breadth of Ward's scholarship on Lewis is impressive, drawing on his fiction, nonfiction, poetry, literary criticism, essays, letters, and diary. So, it may be more productive to ask what parts are missing. More specifically, which parts of Lewis's medieval model for Luna and Mars, as understood by Ward, are not reflected in "Ministering Angels" and "Forms of Things Unknown"? Additionally, do these inconsistencies present a problem for Ward's theory of a planetary scheme for The Chronicles of Narnia?

Ward is able to make good use of the metals associated with the gods in classical and medieval writing. In discussing *Prince Caspian*, he is able to point out important references to the Martian metal iron.[17] He also demonstrates that the lunar metal silver appears repeatedly throughout *The Silver Chair*.[18] Neither metal, however, appears in Lewis's shorter planetary stories. Nor can the animals Ward associates with Mars be found there, including the wolf, woodpecker, and horse.[19] Of course, terrestrial animals are not likely to appear in stories set in other worlds, except by such clever devices as using "Fox" as a surname. Verticality, a pervasive Martian quality in *Out of the Silent Planet*,[20] is absent from "Ministering Angels." The reflective and subordinate quality of Luna[21] is hard to discern in "Forms of Things Unknown," unless the opening voice of Jenkin's "instructor" is meant to imply that it emanates from his commanding officer. Yet this is nitpicking. Any of these absences is more than offset by the presence of numerous other planetary qualities. In fact, Ward is not only able to delve into qualities cited previously in this article, he expands the list.

Ward notes, for example, that "Necessity is a major feature of

---

16 Lewis, "Things Unknown," 132.

17 Ward, *Planet Narnia*, 92.

18 Ward, *Planet Narnia*, 130–1.

19 Ward, *Planet Narnia*, 93.

20 Ward, *Planet Narnia*, 78.

21 Ward, *Planet Narnia*, 139.

the symbolic value that Lewis, as a poet, located on Mars. The god of war is 'necessity's son,' as he put it in 'The Planets.'"[22] The Thin Woman in "Ministering Angels" speaks of sex as an "indispensable function"[23] and believes her presence on Mars is a logical necessity. "Part of the Martian spirit," says Ward, "is a ranked and patterned orderliness."[24] The Monk in "Ministering Angels" is committed to the "slow, perpetual rebuilding" of his "inner structure," keeping the discipline of the Divine Hours and looking to God as his "Gentle and patient Master."[25] Ward also looks at the range of incarnations of Mars and Luna for more symbolic clues. An early conception of the Martian deity was Mars Silvanus, a tutelary spirit of woods, flocks, and fertility.[26] References to vegetation abound in *Prince Caspian*, while in "Ministering Angels" the Botanist is feverishly cataloguing Martian flora, from "hardy organisms" to the deathly "Martian cress." Indeed, in the subplot, where two deaths stem from the consumption of Martian cress, Lewis may be trying to combine Mars Silvanus, the god of the forest, with Mars Gradivus, the god of war (since war brings on death). Ward lays out the range of Lunar goddesses who appear in Lewis's early poetry, including Artemis, who helps the "hunted,"[27] and Diana, "the pure Huntress riding low."[28] In "Forms of Things Unknown," Jenkin begins to "hunt" on the lunar surface, unaware that the female Gorgon lies behind him, hunting him.

Through connecting Mars with the ideal of the medieval Christian knight and the whole range of chivalry, Ward's ideas shed particular light on the Monk. He quotes Lewis in *Mere Christianity*: "The idea of the knight—the Christian in arms for defence of a good cause—is one of the great Christian ideas."[29] Soon after, he adds, "knightliness is

---

[22] Ward, *Planet Narnia*, 78.

[23] Lewis, "Ministering Angels," 116.

[24] Ward, *Planet Narnia*, 92.

[25] Lewis, "Ministering Angels," 112.

[26] Ward, *Planet Narnia*, 82.

[27] From "The Queen of Drum," Canto IV, line 9, in C. S. Lewis, *Narrative Poems*, ed. by Walter Hooper (New York: Harcourt Brace Jovanovich, 1972), 156.

[28] From "The Queen of Drum" Canto V, line 126, in Lewis, *Narrative Poems*, 170. The full list of lunar deities in the *Poems of C. S. Lewis* is found in Ward, *Planet Narnia*, 126.

[29] C. S. Lewis, *Mere Christianity* (San Francisco: HarperSanFrancisco, 2001), 119. Quoted by Ward, *Planet Narnia*, 93.

evident as much in gentleness as in hardiness."[30] Those well-disposed to God's refining work, as filtered through the lens of the Mars persona, are characterized by discipline, obedience, faithfulness, strength, and growth.[31] These traits are consistent with the character whose prayer concludes the story of "Ministering Angels": "Oh Master . . . forgive—or can you enjoy?—my absurdity also. I had been supposing you sent me on a voyage of forty thousand miles merely for my own spiritual convenience."[32] Far from being a stumbling block, Lewis's shorter planetary fiction lends more credence to Ward's underlying premise: "Lewis's love of the Ptolemaic cosmos"[33] led to his repeated use of the planets as symbols in his writing.

Before turning to consider the other spiritual lessons embedded in Lewis's shorter planetary fiction, it may be helpful to consider some of the objections raised by these stories. Shortly after publication of *The Dark Tower and Other Stories*, reviewers began to raise the claim of misogyny, especially regarding aspects of "Ministering Angels." The writer and poet Ursula LeGuin, perhaps illustrating the deep chasm that had by then opened up between her generation of "second wave" American feminists and Lewis's earlier—and more traditional— British view of women's roles, firmly disliked the story: "The spitefulness shown to women in these tales is remarkable," she wrote, "but the authentic Inside Club (MCP [Male Chauvinist Pig] branch) tone is at its braying clearest in 'Ministering angels,' a humorous piece." She was particularly offended by the portrayal of the Thin Women:

> However petty, this is hate; the depth of it is proved in the final paragraph, where the Christian member of the team blissfully contemplates the conversion and salvation of the decrepit whore, but never gives a thought to the soul of 'the lecturer at a redbrick university.'[34]

The American Roman Catholic writer Charles Andrew Brady, though sympathetic to Lewis and his writings, nevertheless pointed out that the end of the story, "hardly absolves Lewis from the charge

---

[30] Ward, *Planet Narnia*, 96.

[31] Ward, *Planet Narnia*, 99.

[32] Lewis, "Ministering Angels," 123.

[33] Ward, *Planet Narnia*, 28.

[34] Ursula K. LeGuin, Untitled review, in *New Republic*, 16 April 1977, 29–30.

of a bachelor's misogyny which is one of his few flaws, and one not to be found in his major books."[35] Even Katherine Harper's more recent (and favorable) treatment of Lewis's shorter fiction finds serious flaws. "'Ministering Angels'," she writes, damningly, "is decidedly misogynistic; as were so many male scholars of his time (and before, and since), Lewis was unconvinced of women's ability to reason."[36]

Given the nature of the criticism that surrounds them, it can be hard to remember that Lewis originally composed this story in defense of women. He was, he believed, engaged in chivalrous, literary combat. His weapon was satire. When the reprinting of "Ministering Angels" was being considered in 1961 for inclusion in a larger collection of his stories and essays, Lewis wrote to his publisher, "You wd. need to reprint their headnote to make it fairly intelligible."[37] That headnote, by Anthony Boucher, who served as the editor of *The Magazine of Fantasy and Science Fiction*, reads as follows:

> Dr. Robert Richardson's controversial article, *The Day after We Land on Mars*—first published in the *Saturday Review* and later expanded for *F&SF* (December 1955)—contained the provocative prediction that "we may be forced into first tolerating and finally openly accepting an attitude toward sex that is taboo in our present social framework . . .. To put it bluntly, may it not be necessary for the success of the project to send some nice girls to Mars at regular intervals to relieve tensions and promote morale?" C. S. Lewis takes it from there in his first short story of space travel—a tale of the First Martian Expedition which is perceptive, human, and warmly comic.[38]

Richardson worked at the Mount Wilson Observatory in the San Gabriel Mountains above Los Angeles and wrote science fiction under the pen name Philip Latham. His article, "The Day after We

---

[35] Charles A. Brady, "Some Notes on C. S. Lewis's *The Dark Tower and Other Stories*," in *CSL: The Bulletin of the New York C. S. Lewis Society*, 95 (September 1977), 1.

[36] Katherine Harper, "C. S. Lewis's Short Fiction and Unpublished Works," in *C. S. Lewis: Life, Works, and Legacy*, ed. by Bruce L. Edwards, 4 vols. (Westport, CT: Praeger, 2007), 2:160.

[37] Letter of 20 April 1961, in Lewis, *Collected Letters*, 3:1258.

[38] Anthony Boucher, ed., *The Magazine of Fantasy and Science Fiction*, 13.7 (January 1958), 5.

Land on Mars,"[39] was, however, a work of nonfiction. Richardson was completely serious in his belief that women should periodically be sent into space to relieve the sexual needs of male astronauts—in a ratio of one woman to quite a few men. Boucher's 1955 headnote declared the article to be "an admirable brief refresher course on the probable first steps of interplanetary travel, which leads, with deceptive simplicity, to certain highly provocative conclusions."[40] Apparently, Boucher also smelled an opportunity for publicity. The following January, the same magazine contained a story by the American historian and science fiction writer Paul A. Carter, which explored in fiction the very conclusions which the astronomer suggested. Boucher publicized it as "possibly the first honest fictional study of human sexual mores on another planet."[41] Perhaps ironically, the February 1956 issue of that same magazine contained the story "The Shoddy Lands" by Lewis.[42]

With the publication of this final story—a fantasy tale of a man seeing the world through the mind of a woman—Lewis had a problem. It appeared in the same magazine whose two previous issues contained articles promoting a view of men and women in space that he found morally reprehensible. "Ministering Angels" was his response and was directed at Richardson in particular. Many elements of the setting and plot of "Ministering Angels" were taken directly from "The Day after We Land on Mars." Richardson envisioned a colony on Mars consisting entirely of "young unmarried men."[43] The trip from earth to Mars and back would take many months to complete.[44] Once they arrived, only a few men could work outdoors at a time.[45] Biologists would be busy examining maria,[46] but much of the other

---

[39] Robert S. Richardson, "The Day after We Land on Mars," in *The Magazine of Fantasy and Science Fiction*, 9.6 (December 1955), 44–52.

[40] Boucher, *The Magazine of Fantasy and Science Fiction*, 9.6 (December 1955), 44.

[41] Boucher, *The Magazine of Fantasy and Science Fiction*, 9.6 (December 1955), 52. See Paul A. Carter, "Unbalanced Equation," in *The Magazine of Fantasy and Science Fiction*, 10.1 (January 1955), 105-21.

[42] C. S. Lewis, "The Shoddy Lands," in *The Magazine of Fantasy and Science Fiction* 10.8 (February 1956), 68–74.

[43] Richardson, "The Day after We Land on Mars," 47.

[44] Richardson, "The Day after We Land on Mars," 47.

[45] Richardson, "The Day after We Land on Mars," 48.

[46] Maria, Latin for "seas," are darker features on the planetary surface. "If the *maria* consist of vegetation he would be in much the same

work would be monotonous.[47] Conflicts arising from close contact were, he concluded, sure to arise,[48] and it was certainly possible that some astronauts would be tempted to engage in homosexual activity.[49] Lewis, in making his Captain a newly married man, departs from Richardson's scheme of exclusively unmarried astronauts. In every other respect, the conditions in "Ministering Angels" match those found in "The Day after We Land on Mars." At the beginning of the story, Clifford Paterson, one of the young male technicians and a homosexual, is trying to attract the interest of Bobby Dickson, the other male technician. "The only part of any woman that interested him was her ears. He liked telling women about his troubles; especially the unfairness and unkindness of other men."[50] At the end of the story, Paterson is attempting to talk through his male troubles with the Thin Woman, who is comically trying to flirt with him at the same time. The irony of her addressing the one man on Mars completely immune to her propositions symbolizes the fruitlessness Lewis saw in Richardson's entire scheme. As he remarked in regards to his own Space Trilogy, "I wanted farce as well as fantasy."[51]

Within this context, it is not surprising that Lewis made the Thin Woman such an unsympathetic character. In the story, she is the main proponent of Richardson's new morality (or lack thereof). What remains strange, however, is where Lewis locates the earth-bound proponents of the scheme: "the idiots on the Advisory Council," namely, "a pack 'o daft auld women (in trousers for the most part) who like onything sexy, onything scientific, and anything that makes them feel important."[52] Because Lewis was challenging a male fantasy composed and published by two male writers, one wonders why the Advisory Council was not filled with "daft auld men"? If a charge of sexism is to be leveled at the story, it would be stronger to focus

---

situation as Galileo with his first telescope—wherever he looked he would be sure to make an important discovery." Richardson, "The Day after We Land on Mars," 49.

[47] Richardson, "The Day after We Land on Mars," 49.

[48] Richardson, "The Day after We Land on Mars," 49–50.

[49] Richardson, "The Day after We Land on Mars," 51.

[50] Lewis, "Ministering Angels," 120.

[51] C. S. Lewis, "A Reply to Professor Haldane," in *Of Other Worlds: Essays and Stories*, ed. by Walter Hooper (San Diego: Harcourt Brace & Company, 1975), 77.

[52] Lewis, "Ministering Angels," 122.

criticism on this aspect. Lewis, however, may have responded in a similar fashion to his reply to Professor Haldane:

> It was against this outlook on life, this ethic, if you will, that I wrote my satiric fantasy, projecting in my Weston a buffoon-villain image of the 'metabiological' heresy. If anyone says that to make him a scientist was unfair, since the view I am attacking is not chiefly rampant among scientists, I might agree with him: though I think such criticism would be over sensitive.[53]

Substitute "the Thin Woman," "new ethics," and "women" for the words "Weston," "metabiological, and "scientists," and one is probably closer to the views of Lewis. But perhaps a better way forward has been laid out by Diana Glyer in her aptly titled essay, "'We Are All Fallen Creatures and All Very Hard to Live With': Some Thoughts on Lewis and Gender":

> It seems to me that the principal text in any discussion of Lewis's views toward women is not to be found in a private statement made in a letter, an isolated public statement made in an essay, or a comment that issues forth from a character in his fiction. As position statements, these myriad bits and random pieces are simply unreliable . . . .. [M]ore significant weight should be placed on the fuller and more telling "text" of how Lewis lived his life.[54]

Employing this broader and more inclusive standard, Glyer finds Lewis to be a model in promoting unity, liberty, and love among women and men.

The principal objection to "Forms of Things Unknown" is of an entirely different nature. Did Lewis actually write it, or is it a clever forgery? Kathryn Lindskoog, the primary advocate for doubting its authenticity, offered three main reasons for her position. First, it is "an awkward, amateurish, rather mean-spirited story that doesn't sound like Lewis."[55] Second, she believed the inspiration behind the story

---

[53] Lewis, "A Reply to Professor Haldane," 77.

[54] Diana Pavlac Glyer, "'We Are All Fallen Creatures and All Very Hard to Live With': Some Thoughts on Lewis and Gender," in *Christian Scholar's Review*, 36.4 (Summer 2007), 483. For the quotation from Lewis, "We are all fallen creatures and all v. hard to live with," see letter of 8 November 1962 in Lewis, *Collected Letters*, 3:1379.

[55] Kathryn Lindskoog, *Sleuthing C. S. Lewis: More Light in the Shadowlands* (Macon, GA: Mercer University Press, 2001), 104.

was Virgil Finlay's cover illustration for the October 1958 issue of *Fantastic Universe* magazine. If that is the case, she asks, "Why would he [Lewis] waste his time turning Finley's first-rate pictorial idea into a third-rate story?"[56] Third, she rejects Walter Hooper's purported claim that "he had rescued it along with the *Dark Tower* fragment from Warren's January 1964 bonfire."[57]

As to Lindskoog's first point, she may have meant that "Forms of Things Unknown" is simply not as good as Lewis's major writings. Few would disagree. In this regard, however, it is instructive to remember that Lewis believed not every line of Shakespeare's was "good,"[58] and that Tolkien astutely observed that not every work by Lewis was either. Lindskoog becomes more specific in labeling one word and one phrase found in the story as "unlikely" to have come from Lewis. Yet, the hints of the medieval model of Luna—change, wandering, virginity, madness, deception, hunting and, perhaps, liquidity—all seem characteristic of Lewis.

Lindskoog's second objection, that the story was based on an illustration from a magazine, is difficult to verify or dismiss. If the story could be dated with certainty prior to October 1958 (the date of Finlay's cover illustration for *Fantastic Universe*), then, obviously, the theory would be false. Absent that information, the theory remains intriguing. But why would this lead to the conclusion that the story is a forgery? Charles Brady, who first mentioned the connection to Finlay's illustration, remained convinced that Lewis was the author of "Forms of Things Unknown."[59] In the early 1950s, Alastair Fowler observed Lewis reading from *Astounding Science Fiction*,[60] and later in the same decade Lewis both read and wrote stories for *Fantasy and Science Fiction*. Clearly, Lewis "wasted" a fair amount of time consuming a variety of science fiction, some of which he regarded as "abysmally bad" and some which contained "real invention."[61]

---

[56] Lindskoog, *Sleuthing C. S. Lewis*, 106.

[57] Lindskoog, *Sleuthing C. S. Lewis*, 105.

[58] See, for example, the lines from Shakespeare's sonnets quoted in C. S. Lewis, *English Literature in the Sixteenth Century, Excluding Drama* (New York: Oxford University Press, 1954), 489.

[59] Brady, "Some Notes," 1–10.

[60] Alastair Fowler, "C. S. Lewis: Supervisor," in *C. S. Lewis Remembered*, ed. by Harry Lee Poe and Rebecca Whitten Poe (Grand Rapids: Zondervan, 2006), 105.

[61] Letter of 3 February 1953, in Lewis, *Collected Letters*, 3:288.

Lindskoog's third charge stems from her doubt that Hooper actually rescued Lewis's manuscripts from the flames of his brother's bonfire. She also challenged the authenticity of other writings attributed to Lewis but published posthumously, including "After Ten Years" and *The Dark Tower*. Significantly, however, Alastair Fowler has since revealed that Lewis let him read both of these unfinished stories, among others, prior to his death in 1963.[62] Fowler's testimony lends considerable credence to Hooper's account. His statement in 1977 thus seems reasonable enough: that the manuscript of "Forms of Things Unknown" was "discovered among the papers given me by Major [Warren] Lewis."[63]

Having addressed the objections raised about these two stories, we can now turn to the particular theological lessons inherent in them. The Martian tale begins with a man at prayer and is designed, as a whole, to defend the Christian ideals of chastity against those who would objectify women sexually. Sanctification is at work as the Monk prays for God's help in the rebuilding of his soul. He both receives and holds out to another the promise of God's forgiveness. There is grace present as he refers to the old prostitute as "daughter," and the hope of redemption can be found in his words, "you are not far from the Kingdom." The Monk's closing prayer displays growth, charity and humility.

The theme of humility is played out a second way. The Thin Woman's besetting sin is not fuzzy thinking but pride. Pharisees are in more spiritual danger than harlots. As Lewis puts it, "Prostitutes are in no danger of finding their present life so satisfactory that they cannot turn to God: the proud, the avaricious, the self-righteous, are in that danger."[64]

The Monk also acts as a spiritual director to the Fat Woman, and there are several other characters in Lewis's writings who take on a similar role. Most notable of these are Ransom to Jane Studdock in *That Hideous Strength*, the character of George MacDonald to the persona of Lewis in *The Great Divorce*, and the persona of Lewis to Malcolm in *Letters to Malcolm: Chiefly on Prayer*. Yet the Monk's advice does not sound very similar to the words of these other three fictional spiritual directors, whose counsel is delivered at

---

[62] Fowler, "C. S. Lewis: Supervisor," 105.

[63] Walter Hooper, "Preface" in Lewis, *The Dark Tower*, 12.

[64] C. S. Lewis, *The Problem of Pain* (New York: Macmillan, 1948), 86.

an appropriately high intellectual level. The Monk's words, on the other hand, are very different—and appropriately so, given that the Fat Woman, unlike these other spiritual apprentices, has not had the advantages of a privileged education. She has, in fact, experienced very few advantages. So, the Monk's words to her are humble, simple without being simplistic. Typical of Lewis, there is a brief and vivid illustration to drive home the point being made. "Daughter . . . you are not far from the Kingdom. But you were wrong. The desire to give is blessed. But you can't turn bad bank-notes into good ones just by giving them away."[65]

These words are more similar in style to the actual spiritual advice Lewis occasionally proffered in his correspondence. People who read his books often sought his counsel. Lewis displayed the patience of a saint in responding to the many hundreds of letters he received each year from admirers and spiritual seekers throughout the world. The following counsel sent to an American girl, Joan Lancaster, is illustrative of these efforts: "Duty is only a substitute for love (of God and of other people), like a crutch at times; but of course it's idiotic to use the crutch when our own legs (our own loves, tastes, habits etc) can do the journey on their own!"[66]

The theology contained in "Ministering Angels," especially that found in the character of the Monk, reflects Lewis's ongoing concern for the spiritual welfare of others. When attention is shifted to the lunar story, "The Forms of Things Unknown," the overt theology disappears. Consequently, critical evaluation of the story's theological nature must remain tentative. However, like Luna herself, deeper meanings may be embedded in the story. If so, the theological key for this lunar story may lie in the internal reference to the Cretan labyrinth and in the external discussion by Lewis of the Hippolytus myth.

"The Forms of Things Unknown" can, in fact, be read as a warning against cutting oneself off from others. As Jesus and St. Paul (among others) repeatedly emphasized, no one is spiritually self-sufficient. To believe otherwise is madness. As Lewis inquired of Dom Bede Griffiths, "Is any pleasure on earth as great as a circle of Christian friends by a good fire?"[67] In commenting on Hamlet, a play

---

[65] Lewis, "Ministering Angels," 119.

[66] Letter of 18 July 1957, in Lewis, *Collected Letters*, 3:872.

[67] Lewis, *Collected Letters*, 2:501.

haunted by madness, Lewis observed, "The next best thing to being wise oneself is to live in a circle of those who are."[68] Before reaching the moon, Lieutenant Jenkin has already discerned many pieces of the lunar puzzle: fight madness, do not look behind you, and report on what you see. Yet, he fails to assemble these pieces in time. He has not learned the lessons of the old stories. He recalls the Cretan labyrinth,[69] but forgets that Theseus was unable to survive his perils on his own. He had the assistance of Ariadne and her ball of string, which, after battling the Minotaur, helped Theseus find his way out of the labyrinth. Jenkin, however, cut off from friend and lover, will not survive the perils that await him on the Moon. He will never find his way home.

In 1954, Katherine Farrer, wife of the famous Oxford theologian and preacher Austin Farrer, sent Lewis a story she had written in which the moon was described, "like the white face of an idiot lost in a wood." Lewis chided her severely for denigrating "the high creation of God," suggesting that as penance she should memorize Psalm 136, which praises God who created "The moon and the stars to govern the night" (136:9). He continued, "Not safe, either, to be rude to goddesses—Artemis still owes Aphrodite a come-back for the Hippolytus affair and we shd. hate you to be the target."[70] In Greek mythology Hippolytus, the son of Theseus, found himself in the middle of a love triangle with these two goddesses. Hippolytus preferred Artemis. Aphrodite was not pleased, and her trickery eventually led to the death of Theseus' young wife Phaedra and of Hippolytus himself.

In the end, the revenge of the moon maiden, Artemis, would not fall on Katherine Farrer. In his next letter to her, Lewis apologized for "mounting too high a horse about the 'idiot-moon.'"[71] The revenge falls instead on Lieutenant Jenkin. To cut off one's self from others is not to find safety; it is to invite disaster. It is not isolation but love which casts out fear.

Lewis once complained to Arthur C. Clarke, the English science fiction writer, futurist, and inventor, "What's the excuse for locating

---

[68] C. S. Lewis, "Hamlet: The Prince or the Poem," in *Selected Literary Essays*, ed. by Walter Hooper (Cambridge, 1969), 99.

[69] Lewis, "Things Unknown," 127.

[70] Letter of 3 February 1954, in Lewis, *Collected Letters*, 3:423–4.

[71] Letter of 9 February 1954, in Lewis, *Collected Letters*, 3:426.

one's story on Mars unless 'Martianity' is through and through used," explaining in a footnote that he meant used "Emotionally & atmospherically as well as logically."[72] In "Ministering Angels" and "Forms of Things Unknown," Lewis produced stories fit for their settings. His Martian story is militant in its defense of a good cause. His lunar tale both enchants and deceives to the very last sentence. Ward's pioneering work on Lewis and medieval cosmology adds considerably to our understanding of these shorter planetary tales. Lewis drew on a long history of traditions about Mars and Luna, hoping that his readers would not only be entertained but enlightened. Above all else, he hoped one day they would end up "bright in the land of brightness."[73]

---

[72] Letter of 20 January 1954, in Lewis, *Collected Letters*, 3:412.

[73] Lewis, "Ministering Angels," 123.

Chapter 12

SILENT NO MORE
LEWIS'S COSMOLOGICAL VIEW
OF CHRIST'S ATONING WORK

ADAM J. JOHNSON

According to C. S. Lewis's Ransom Trilogy, our home is "Thulcandra—the silent world or planet,"[1] for "it alone is outside the heaven, and no message comes from it."[2] That is to say, no message *came* from our planet until Ransom was kidnapped and brought to Malacandra (or Mars). At a certain point in the story, Ransom learns that Oyarsa, the "angel" of Mars, knows that God (or Maleldil) "would not give [the earth] up utterly to the Bent One, and there are stories among us that He has taken strange counsel and dared terrible things, wrestling with the Bent One in Thulcandra. But of this we know less than you; it is a thing we desire to look into."[3] Shortly after this, Oyarsa asks Ransom: "Now tell me of Thulcandra. Tell me all . . .. Tell me what Maleldil has done in Thulcandra."[4] But Ransom's answer is interrupted before it begins, and we are left to wonder: what would he have said? The problem is exacerbated when we learn that Ransom spent that afternoon answering Oyarsa's questions—a conversation to which we are not privy. What was Ransom's answer? And why are we kept from overhearing it?[5]

In correspondence, Sister Penelope asked C. S. Lewis: "Could

---

[1] C. S. Lewis, *Silent Planet* (London: Macmillan, 1947), 69.

[2] Lewis, *Silent Planet*, 130.

[3] Lewis, *Silent Planet*, 131. See 1 Peter 1:12.

[4] Lewis, *Silent Planet*, 133-4.

[5] Downing comes as close as anyone I know of in noting Lewis's cosmological theory of the atonement, but he stops too short: "The wonders Ransom told the Oyarsa about were the life, death, and resurrection of Christ, which atoned for the sin of Adam and broke the power of the Bent One . . .. Here Lewis cleverly takes theological doctrines that readers might find dull or unpalatable and reshapes them into an interplanetary battle scenario more compelling than most of the science fiction available in the pulps." David C. Downing, *Planets in Peril: A Critical Study of C. S. Lewis's Ransom Trilogy* (Amherst: University of Massachusetts Press, 1992), 42.

you not, for believers only, perhaps as a *Theology* article, write the scene where Ransom tells Oyarsa about the Incarnation?" Jack's response: "I don't think, even 'for believers only' I could 'describe' Ransom's revelation to Oyarsa: the fact that you want me to really proves how well advised I was merely to *suggest* it."[6] Jack's demurral notwithstanding, in what follows, we will attempt to sketch a rough outline of "Ransom's revelation."

Two reasons come to mind for why we do not overhear Oyarsa and Ransom's conversation. First, we find Lewis's answer scattered throughout his works, such that in certain regards he need not repeat himself here, burdening his account with what would amount to a lecture on Christian doctrine. Second, Lewis in fact gives us an answer throughout the book—if we have the eyes to see.[7] We will explore each possibility in turn. First, we will briefly canvass the range of Lewis's views on Christ's atonement. Second, we will explore one of Lewis's most unique developments in this doctrine, which to my knowledge has no known precedent in the history of theology: a cosmological theory of Christ's saving work, in which *God became man and died and rose again in order to re-establish the earth within the music of the spheres.*[8]

In essence, this is the doctrine of the atonement turned inside out, an account of the cosmological implications of the *Christus victor* theory (an account of the atonement in which God became man in

---

[6] C. S. Lewis, *The Collected Letters of C. S. Lewis*, ed. by Walter Hooper, 3 vols. (San Francisco: HarperCollins, 2004-7), 2:261-2.

[7] See Fiddes's account, which is quite earthly in scope. Paul S. Fiddes, "On Theology," in *The Cambridge Companion to C. S. Lewis*, ed. by Robert MacSwain and Michael Ward, (Cambridge: Cambridge University Press, 2010), 90-101. The idea that Lewis would embed such an interesting thesis in a novel has been carefully explored in Michael Ward, *Planet Narnia: The Seven Heavens in the Imagination of C. S. Lewis* (Oxford: Oxford University Press, 2008), 3-22.

It is worth noting that a certain improbability attends this thesis. After all, most initial reviews of the trilogy failed to notice *any* theological significance to the books, let alone discern one of the most creative and expansive explanations of the doctrine of the atonement ever attempted. See Downing, *Planets in Peril*, 35-36. Lewis, however, clearly intended the books to be theological in nature, stating so himself.

[8] In this paper, I use the word "theory" in a non-competitive sense, such that the work of Christ allows for multiple complimentary "theories." For a fuller account, see chapter 2 of Adam Johnson, *Atonement: A Guide for the Perplexed* (New York: T & T Clark, 2015).

order to free us from the power of Satan) from the perspective of the unfallen angels, rather than from that of fallen human beings.[9] In this line of thought, the earth—which had become the "silent planet" through the fall of its ruling power, Satan—is restored to its proper role and dignity, fulfilling its role within the music of the spheres through the work of Christ. Lewis's passion for ancient and medieval cosmology is well documented, but to my knowledge his integration of this passion with the Passion of Christ in the Ransom Trilogy is yet to be explored. Through this integration, Lewis offers the gift of creative theology: saying something which may be true, where something must surely be true. That is to say, he ventures into some of the obscure corners of Scripture, filling out an incomplete picture with an imaginative account saturated in ancient and medieval cosmology and theology.

LEWIS ON THE ATONEMENT: A RANGE OF PERSPECTIVES

One of the more striking features of Lewis's account(s) of the atonement is a certain reticence. In his *Preface to Paradise Lost*, for instance, he writes: "It may, of course, be asked why Milton did *not* write a poem on the Crucifixion. For my own part, I think the answer is that he had more sense."[10] And this demurral is no exception, for we find much the same thought expressed in *The Problem of Pain*, which claims that the work of Christ, "in some manner incomprehensible to human thought, has effected a real change in our relations to the 'awful' and 'righteous' Lord, and a change in our favor"[11]; and again, in *Miracles*: "To penetrate the whole of this mystery is, of course, far beyond my intention. If the pattern of Descent and Re-ascent is (as looks not unlikely) the very formula of reality, then in the mystery of

---

[9] As such, this belongs with my earlier reflection on the role of the atonement for the unfallen angels: "Where Demons Fear to Tread: Venturing into an Obscure Corner of the Doctrine of the Atonement Concerning the Un-Fallen Angels," *Journal of Reformed Theology*, 9.1 (2015). The mere fact that the angels and heavens are unfallen need not imply that they stand not to benefit from Christ's work: "there is no limit to the future glories of the world which, needing no redemption itself, yet profits by the Incarnation." Lewis, *Collected Letters*, 2:667.

[10] C. S. Lewis, *A Preface to Paradise Lost* (New York: Oxford University Press, 1961), 91; see Lewis, *Collected Letters*, 2:261-2.

[11] C. S. Lewis, *The Problem of Pain* (New York, Macmillan, 1948), 12.

Death the secret of secrets lies hid. But something must be said in order to put the Grand Miracle in its proper light."[12] Perhaps the most famous such statement comes from *Mere Christianity*: "The central Christian belief is that Christ's death has somehow put us right with God and given us a fresh start. Theories as to how it did this are another matter. A good many theories have been held as to how it works; what all Christians are agreed on is that it does work . . .. No explanation will ever be quite adequate to the reality."[13]

That being said, we had best not overplay this card, lapsing into an apophatic silence—for this is a specific form of reticence: the kind that takes its shape and meaning from a genuine encounter with a great reality, to which we cannot do full justice. But note the conclusion to the passage from *Miracles*: "But something must be said in order to put the Grand Miracle in its proper light"—and indeed, Lewis did say something, a great many things, to help put this, the greatest of all miracles, in its proper light.

The Lion, The Witch and the Wardrobe is arguably Lewis's most influential foray into the doctrine of the atonement, a story saturated with *Christus victor* themes, though not limited to such an account. However, as others have explored this material, we largely bypass the Chronicles of Narnia in this essay.

In *Mere Christianity*, we find an altogether different mode of thought. After a tepid endorsement of penal substitution,[14] Lewis explains the atonement in terms of repentance. For ourselves, repentance "means unlearning all the self-conceit and self-will that we have been training ourselves into for thousands of years. It means killing part of yourself, undergoing a kind of death. In fact, it needs a good man to repent."[15] And this, of course, is precisely what we have in Christ: "He could surrender His will, and suffer and die, because He was man; and He could do it perfectly because He was God."[16]

---

[12] C. S. Lewis, *Miracles: A Preliminary Study* (New York: Macmillan, 1973), 130.

[13] C. S. Lewis, *Mere Christianity* (New York: Macmillan, 1953), 42-3.

[14] To frame this tepidity, see Lewis, *Collected Letters* 2:976-7. Note also Lewis's retraction of certain claims in this context, regarding "discarding" theories of the atonement, when he meant merely to affirm that they "need not be used." Lewis, *Mere Christianity*, 502.

[15] Lewis, *Mere Christianity*, 45.

[16] Lewis, *Mere Christianity*, 45.

And this is no mere example, no mere guide to Christian behavior:

> Our attempts at this dying will succeed only if we men share in God's dying, just as our thinking can succeed only because it is a drop out of the ocean of His intelligence: but we cannot share God's dying unless God dies; and He cannot die except by being man. That is the sense in which He pays our debt, and suffers for us what He Himself need not suffer at all.[17]

To be sure, this is fascinating, but it is not unprecedented—for Lewis is working with the thought of John McLeod Campbell and R. C. Moberly.[18] Essentially, this view argues that sinners needed to repent, but that repenting entails a very real form of death—the removal of that part of ourselves of which we must repent, and that "part" is in fact pervasive. To repent, we must die. But only a good man could want this, which we surely are not. God, in his love and grace, takes upon himself our debt, our condition, and becomes man that he might repent of human sin in our place as one of us. We, in turn, are free to participate in this repentance, death, and ensuing transformation. While much of the language sounds foreign at first, the mode of thought is fundamentally substitutionary and representative.

We see this all the more clearly in Lewis's *Miracles*, which drops the repentance language, while retaining the substitutionary/representative framework:

> Humanity must embrace death freely, submit to it with total humility, drink it to the dregs, and so convert it into that mystical death which is the secret of life. But only a Man who did not need to have been a Man . . . only one who served in our sad regiment as a volunteer, yet also one who was perfectly Man, could perform this perfect dying; and thus (which way you put it is unimportant) either defeat Death or redeem it. He tasted death on behalf of all others. He is the representative "Die-er" of the universe: and for that very reason the Resurrection and the Life . . .. Because Vicariousness is the very idiom of the reality He has created, His death can become ours.[19]

---

[17] Lewis, *Mere Christianity*, 46.

[18] Fiddes traces vicarious repentance to Moberly. Fiddes, "On Theology," 99. Chris Mitchell had tracked down another influence (neither Campbell nor Moberly), but I failed to take note of the name, before he passed away.

[19] Lewis, *Miracles*, 135.

The representation, the vicarious tasting of death,[20] our own death freely tasted, in which we participate . . . the fundamental features of Campbell's thought are present, with the absence of the "repentance" language. While Lewis is free to adopt Campbell's approach to the atonement, he is just as free to dispense with it—all the while affirming a constellation of themes broadly characterized in terms of vicarious representation.[21]

While these three books offer what are likely Lewis's most developed contributions to the doctrine of the atonement, each demonstrating a creative appropriation of the history of the doctrine, it is worth noting that partially developed hints and statements about Christ's death and resurrection appear throughout Lewis's works. He writes of the world as "a dance in which good, descending from God, is disturbed by evil arising from the creatures, and the resulting conflict is resolved by God's own assumption of the suffering nature which evil produces,"[22] speaking of this great work as being funded by a disinterested love which the demons cannot fathom.[23] But disinterested does not mean ignorant or uninvolved, for "God, who needs nothing, loved into existence wholly superfluous creatures in order that He may love and perfect them. He creates the universe, already foreseeing . . . the buzzing of flies about the cross."[24] Continuing with the interrelation of God and time, Lewis writes:

'Only One has descended into Hell.'

'And will He ever do so again?'

'It was not once long ago that He did it. Time does not work

---

[20] Lewis, *Miracles*, 122-3.

[21] It is worth noting that Lewis connects this line of thought to the *Christus victor* theory in this chapter in *Miracles*. It is likewise noteworthy that Lewis begins this chapter with a theme borrowed from Irenaeus, known as recapitulation (see Lewis, *Miracles*, 115). The point seems to show that Lewis draws widely and deeply from the history of theology in unpacking the doctrine of the atonement. Ironically, however, he persistently misreads Anselm's *Cur Deus Homo*, interpreting Anselm as a proponent of Christ bearing punishment in our place, rather than offering an alternative to this view. See Lewis, C. S. Lewis, *A Preface to Paradise Lost* (New York: Oxford University Press, 1961), 90-91; *The Problem of Pain* (New York: Macmillan, 1962), 86.

[22] Lewis, *Problem of Pain*, 84.

[23] C. S. Lewis, *The Screwtape Letters* (New York: Macmillan, 1943), 97.

[24] C. S. Lewis, *The Four Loves* (New York: Harvest/HBJ, 1960), 176.

that way once ye have left the Earth. All moments that have been or shall be were, or are, present in the moment of His descending. There is no spirit in prison to Whom He did not preach.'[25]

These matters are no mere speculative game for Lewis—he faces the trinitarian challenge underlying the doctrine, noting, "sometimes it is hard not to say, 'God forgive God.' Sometimes it is hard to say so much. But if our faith is true, He didn't. He crucified Him."[26] Taking such a line of thought to its extreme (anticipating current feminist and womanist interpretations of the cross), Lewis writes: "[Jesus] had found that the Being He called Father was horribly and infinitely different from what He had supposed. The trap, so long and carefully prepared and so subtly baited, was at last sprung, on the cross. The vile practical joke had succeeded"[27]—something we wish we could do for others, but was allowed only for One, who "has done vicariously whatever can be so done. He replies to our babble, 'You cannot and you dare not. I could and dared.'"[28]

Elsewhere Lewis shows himself eager, for instance, to point out or interact with false or perverse views of the atonement in *The Pilgrim's Regress*,[29] *The Problem of Pain*,[30] *The Great Divorce*,[31] and *Till We Have Faces*.[32] And on the flip side of this, Lewis connects the atonement to the Christian life,[33] marriage[34] and spiritual formation,[35] among other topics. Lewis also develops an account of divinization or *theosis*

---

[25] C. S. Lewis, The Great Divorce (Glasgow: Collins, 1974), 114.

[26] C. S. Lewis, *A Grief Observed* (San Francisco: HarperSanFrancisco, 1994), 44.

[27] Lewis, *Grief Observed*, 46. Lewis does not here answer the dilemma he has posed in his time of grief—a fuller answer must be pieced together from his other works, with special emphasis upon "bait" and "trap," hinting at a *Christus victor* theme underlying this powerful statement.

[28] Lewis, *Grief Observed*, 61.

[29] C. S. Lewis, *The Pilgrim's Regress* (Grand Rapids, MI: Eerdmans, 1979), 135.

[30] Lewis, *Problem of Pain*, 84.

[31] Lewis, *Great Divorce*, 77-8.

[32] It is difficult to even know where to begin with this marvelous book, but the sacrifice of Psyche to Ungit serves as good beginning.

[33] Lewis, *Great Divorce*, 57.

[34] Lewis, *Four Loves*, 148.

[35] Lewis, *Four Loves*, 187.

throughout his works—a theme he integrates with the atonement, as did the church fathers.[36] In short, the atonement is a lively, fertile, and ubiquitous doctrine throughout Lewis's writings.[37] But in surveying this wonderful material, which easily merits sustained treatment of its own, we have not touched on the most creative and radical insight Lewis offers into the doctrine of the atonement. For this, we must broaden our frame of reference, asking questions that few theologians (but some philosophers) ask, but which Lewis returned to again and again.

In 1947, Lewis briefly considered whether other planetary races could be affected by Christ's atonement.[38] In 1958, he returned to the topic, and once more in 1963, showing a continued interest in the cosmic implications of the work of Christ.[39] But the richest and most provocative development of this theme he reserved for his Ransom Trilogy, Lewis's cosmological theory of the atonement.

In and of itself this fecundity of thought is of great interest, warranting further study of Lewis as a theologian of the cross (and empty tomb). For our purposes, however, this preamble is a warrant for our inquiry, establishing strong precedent for the theory that Lewis developed an innovative and perhaps altogether unique understanding of the atonement in his Ransom Trilogy. For this would be entirely in keeping for a man who repeatedly developed this doctrine in new and interesting ways, across a wide range of genres and in the most surprising of contexts.

---

[36] Myk Habets, "Walking *in Mirabilibus Supra Me*: How C. S. Lewis Transposes *Theosis*," *Evangelical Quarterly*, 82.1 (2010), 15-27; David Meconi, "Mere Christianity: Theosis in a British Way," *Journal of Inklings Studies*, 4.1 (2014), 3-18.

[37] For an article devoted to Lewis's view of the atonement, see: P. H. Brazier, "C. S. Lewis on Atonement: A Unified Model and Event, the Drama of Redemption—Understanding and Rationalizing the Tradition," in *Heythrop Journal*, 56.2 (March 2015), 285-305.

[38] Lewis, *Miracles*, 127.

[39] C. S. Lewis, "The Seeing Eye" in The Seeing Eye, (New York: Ballantine, 1967), 235-7; "Religion and Rocketry," in *Fern-Seed and Elephants, and Other Essays on Christianity*, ed. by Walter Hooper, (Glasgow: Collins, 1975), 88-9.

ATONEMENT AND THE RANSOM TRILOGY:
A COSMIC PERSPECTIVE

Turning our attention to the Ransom Trilogy, we find the confluence of two of Lewis's most treasured topics: Christ's atonement and cosmology. We have already surveyed the former; concerning the latter, Lewis sought "to challenge modern cosmology and offer an alternative view of the universe."[40] In short, he rehabilitated the ancient and medieval view of the cosmos within a modern heliocentric model. The ancient and medieval view, he noted

> is nothing if not religious. But is the religion in question precisely Christianity? Certainly there is a striking difference between this Model where God is much less the lover than the beloved and man is a marginal creature, and the Christian picture where the fall of man and the incarnation of God as man for man's redemption is central. There may perhaps, as I have hinted before, be no absolute logical contradiction . . ..
> But there remains, at the very least, a profound disharmony of atmospheres. That is why all this cosmology plays so small a part in the spiritual writers, and is not fused with high religious ardour in any writer I know except Dante himself.[41]

Precisely this disharmony, or, put more positively, this logical possibility entailed in the lack of absolute logical contradiction, is what Lewis sought to explore, developing the central theme of Christianity upon a stage set by a largely ancient and medieval cosmology. By so doing, he wove together 1) a person and work so sublime as to fully and rightfully call for our worship, and 2) an object the likes of which "the human imagination has seldom had before it . . . so sublimely ordered as the medieval cosmos."[42] To properly appreciate Lewis's vision, we will break it down into three parts, considering: 1) the *Christus victor* background for the view, 2) the cosmology Lewis develops, and 3) Lewis's cosmological theory of the atonement.

---

[40] T. A. Shippey, "The Ransom Trilogy," in *The Cambridge Companion to C. S. Lewis*, ed. by Robert MacSwain and Michael Ward (Cambridge: Cambridge University Press, 2010), 239.

[41] C. S. Lewis, *The Discarded Image: An Introduction to Medieval and Renaissance Literature* (Cambridge: Cambridge University Press, 1998), 119-20.

[42] Lewis, *Discarded Image*, 121. See C. S. Lewis, *Out of the Silent Planet* (New York, Macmillan, 1947), 32-3, 39, 145.

CHRISTUS VICTOR BACKGROUND

Lewis adopts a *Christus victor* understanding of the atonement, such as we find in *The Lion, the Witch, and the Wardrobe*, to ground his thesis. Elwin Ransom, is, after all, a ransom—the kidnapped human sacrifice offered to the natives of Mars, the price to be paid by evil men to appease the evil they feared and gain the benefits they sought.[43] Behind this, of course, is a much deeper and more evil logic: the conflict between the "Bent One" and the purposes of Maleldil, partly for Malacandra but more generally for the cosmos as a whole.[44] But the shape is quite unfamiliar to us—for in effect this is a *Christus victor* theory turned inside out. Just as Ransom had his understanding of the universe turned "rather oddly inside out" (102),[45] so with the atonement, for rather than being held captive in enemy territory, in these books we refugees find ourselves for the first time on land occupied by the rightful king, where wars and rumors of wars are distant matters, though important to be understood.

Ironically, because Ransom was brought to Malacandra as a perverse or demonic ransom, he can now serve as a divine ransom, the bridge connecting the heavens, providing an entry-point for the heavenly powers to thwart the Bent One's schemes on Earth (this

---

[43] See Downing, *Planets in Peril*, 52. But Ransom is not the only one to bear this name: "'My name also is Ransom,' said the Voice. It was some time before the purport of this saying dawned upon him. He whom the other worlds call Maleldil, was the world's ransom, his own ransom, well he knew. But to what purpose was it said now? Before the answer came to him he felt its insufferable approach and held out his arms before him as if he could keep it from forcing open the door of his mind. But it came. So that was the real issue. If he now failed, this world also would hereafter be redeemed. If he were not the ransom, Another would be. Yet nothing was ever repeated. Not a second crucifixion: perhaps—who knows—not even a second Incarnation . . . some act of even more appalling love, some glory of yet deeper humility. For he had seen already how the pattern grows and how from each world it sprouts into the next through some other dimension. The small external evil which Satan had done in Malacandra was only as a line: the deeper evil he had done in Earth was as a square: if Venus fell, her evil would be a cube - her Redemption beyond conceiving. Yet redeemed she would be." C. S. Lewis, *Perelandra* (London: John Lane, 1948), 154.

[44] Lewis, *Silent Planet*, 130-3, 152.

[45] "The Malacandrians . . . have an odd habit, sometimes, of turning the solar system inside out," Lewis, *Silent Planet*, 174.

is the key to the third book in the series, *That Hideous Strength*).[46] Everything here hinges on the role of authority, which is central to discussions of the *Christus victor* theory.[47] The question is why God did not simply destroy Satan and his works, for Satan had sinned against God. The answer throughout the history of the church seems to be a matter of loving authority, rooted in law and justice. Just as God loves us and in so doing gives us some small, relative authority within our sphere of influence, so God also acknowledges and upholds the (always relative) authority of his other creatures, including the angels (thus the "Seventh Law").[48] Ransom provides the bridge between the heavens, so that the angelic powers of other planets can have influence on Earth without simply violating the Bent One's authority. But as noted before, this is the mere framework, or background, to Lewis's development. We turn now to the heart of the matter: cosmology.

LEWIS'S COSMOLOGY

Lewis's cosmology, at least that portrayed within his Ransom Trilogy, was thoroughly Miltonian, in that it bridged the gap between ancient and modern conceptions.[49] "Careless readers of *Paradise Lost*," Lewis writes:

> . . . sometimes fail to notice Milton's careful and sensitive use of *world* and *earth*, and thereby miss some of the greatest achievements of his visual imagination. Milton felt a strong

---

[46] We learn in *That Hideous Strength* that there was a "Seventh Law:" that the Lord "will not send down the powers to mend or mar in this Earth until the end of all things." But the evil men, and the demons, "had brought about, even as Judas brought about, the thing he least intended. For now there was one man in the world—even myself—who was known to the Oyéresu and spoke their language . . .. Our enemies had taken away from themselves the protection of the Seventh Law. They had broken by natural philosophy the barrier which God of His own power would not break." Ransom, in short, had become a "bridge" between the worlds. C. S. C. S. Lewis, *That Hideous Strength* (New York: Macmillan, 1968), 290-294. Cf. 352.

[47] Lewis, *Silent Planet*, 130-1.

[48] Lewis, *That Hideous Strength*, 290

[49] For a delightful treatment of this broad theme throughout Lewis's works, see Ward, *Planet Narnia*, chap. 2. As Ward notes, "the subject [of celestial bodies] is pervasive, for Lewis's whole imaginative outlook was enamoured of the medieval, or Ptolemaic, or Aristotelian, view of the heavens" (26).

need to express the new sort of space-consciousness. But he also wanted to retain a good deal from the old walled and elegant *kosmos* which is so much richer in plasticity, in associations, and indeed in everything except one particular (and romantic) species of sublimity. His solution was to enclose his *world* (*kosmos* or *mundus*) in an opaque spherical shell, hang this from the floor of his *Heaven* by a golden chain, and surround it with illimitable *Chaos*.[50]

This might seem to be of relatively little consequence to any but Milton scholars, but in fact the point is revolutionary, giving Lewis the conceptual resources for a synthesis of ancient and modern cosmologies. Since Copernicus, the universe has been understood as vast and inherently shapeless. There is no meaningful reference standing as the "center," "perimeter," or any other point from which an overall shape or structure could be affirmed. Our solar system wanders among a host of stars, suns, and other solar systems, with no particular claim to significance.

Of course the ancient and medieval models were altogether different:

> The central (and spherical) Earth is surrounded by a series of hollow and transparent globes, one above the other, and each of course larger than the one below. These are the 'spheres', 'heavens', or (sometimes) 'elements'. Fixed in each of the first seven spheres is one luminous body. Starting from Earth, the order is the Moon, Mercury, Venus, the Sun, Mars, Jupiter and Saturn; the 'seven planets'. Beyond the sphere of Saturn is the *Stellatum*, to which belong all those stars that we still call 'fixed' because their positions relative to one another are, unlike those of the planets, invariable. Beyond the *Stellatum* there is a sphere called the First Movable or *Primum Mobile*.[51]

Such a cosmos saturated the ancient world and imagination with structure, order, symmetry and shape, which modern cosmology

---

[50] C. S. Lewis, *Studies in Words* (Cambridge: Cambridge, 1967), 254-5.

[51] Lewis, Discarded Image, 96. See "The Planets" in *The Collected Poems of C. S. Lewis: A Critical Edition*, ed. by Don W. King, (Kent, OH: Kent State University Press, 2015), 316-19. In this paper I do not explore the possibility that the character of each planet in some way represents Christ, in effect portraying him "under seven veils, seven kinds of iconography: King, Commander, Light, Son, Word, Life, Mystery." Ward, *Planet Narnia*, 238.

replaced with space, distance, infinity, and chaos.[52] But shape and order are just the beginning, for according to Pythagoras, who was followed by Plato and many others, this structured movement of the spheres was naturally accompanied by music and harmony.[53]

We find this poignantly expressed in Cicero's *Dream of Scipio*. After describing the heavens, much as Lewis does, Scipio asks: "What is this sound, so strong and so sweet, which fills my ears?" "That," Africanus replies,

> is the music of the spheres. They create it by their own motion as they rush upon their way. The intervals between them, although differing in length, are all measured according to a fixed scheme of proportions; and this arrangement produces a melodious blend of high and low notes, from which emerges a varied harmony. For it cannot be that these vast movements should take place in silence, and nature has ordained that the spheres utter music.[54]

It is worth noting that there was some range of diversity on the question of whether the spheres produce music. Aristotle, for instance, thought the whole idea ridiculous,[55] while Plato, more importantly for our purposes, posited that "up above on each of the rims of the circles stood a Siren, who accompanied its revolution, uttering a single sound, one single note. And the concord of the eight notes produced a harmony," thus personalizing what had been a purely physical

---

[52] As Plato says, "the god wanted everything to be good and nothing to be bad so far as that was possible, and so he took over all that was visible—not at rest but in discordant and disorderly motion—and brought it from a state of disorder to one of order, because he believed that order was in every way better than disorder." Plato, "Timaeus," in *Complete Works*, (Indianapolis: Hackett, 1997), 30a.

[53] Robin Waterfield, ed. *The First Philosophers: The Pre-Socratics and Sophists* (Oxford: Oxford University Press, 2009), T16, and Plato, "Republic," 530d. On the music of the spheres, see Robert R. Reilly, "The Music of the Spheres, or the Metaphysics of Music," *The Intercollegiate Review Fall* (2001); Ward, *Planet Narnia*, chap. 11. For other works of fiction that heavily utilize music in the cosmologies and creation stories, I recommend J. R. R. Tolkien's *Ainulindale*, and Calvin Miller's trilogy *The Singer, The Song*, and *The Finale*.

[54] Marcus Tullius Cicero, "Dream of Scipio," in *On the Good Life: Selected Writings of Cicero*, (Harmondsworth: Penguin, 1971), 348.

[55] Aristotle, "Heavens," in *Works*, ed. by W. D. Ross, (Chicago: Encyclopædia Britannica, 1955), 290b-291a.

phenomenon in Pythagoras.[56]

Lewis adopted a Miltonian approach to this tension, standing with a foot in each cosmology, while heavily favoring the ancient/medieval view. With regard to the modern view, he adopted a heliocentric model of the solar system, allowing for the space and scope of the modern universe.[57] But that is about as far as he goes in that direction, placing all his emphasis upon the order, beauty, structure, and harmony of the solar system (just as Milton did, with his "golden thread"), and the way that the planets play a powerful role in influencing affairs upon earth. And one of the most profound implications of his cosmological thesis was a problem that the ancients and medievals could never have fathomed: the silence of the planet Earth. More on that shortly.

THE COSMOS AND THE ANGELS

Cosmology is just the beginning, for even as we saw with Plato, the hierarchy of the spheres could not long be kept distinct from the hierarchies of intelligences, whether they be gods, sirens, or angels. Note, for instance, Aquinas' survey of the relevant opinions as to whether the planets were living beings:

> Philosophers have differed on this question. Anaxagoras, for instance, as Augustine mentions (*De Civ. Dei* xviii, 41), "was condemned by the Athenians for teaching that the sun was a

---

[56] Plato, "Republic," 617b. Apparently, Lewis got this idea from "Bernardus Silvestris, a twelfth-century Platonist. The Oyarsa is the tutelary spirit of the planet, a higher order of angel responsible to rule that sphere (*Silent Planet*, p. 152)"; see David C. Downing, "Rehabilitating H.G. Wells: C. S. Lewis's *Out of the Silent Planet*," in *C. S. Lewis: Life, Works, and Legacy*, ed. by Bruce L. Edwards, (Westport: Praeger, 2007), 21.

[57] Lewis, *Silent Planet*, 120. See T.A. Shippey, "The Ransom Trilogy," in *The Cambridge Companion to C. S. Lewis*, ed. by Robert MacSwain and Michael Ward, (Cambridge: Cambridge University Press, 2010), 240. This is not entirely clear, however, for in *That Hideous Strength*, Ransom tells Merlin that the moon "walks in the lowest sphere"—a point taken from ancient cosmology (p. 273). Notwithstanding, it seems evident that *That Hideous Strength* presumes a heliocentric cosmology, as suggested by the point that the earth is "not the bottom of the universe, but . . . a ball spinning, and rolling onwards, both at delirious speed, and not through emptiness but through some densely inhabited and intricately structured medium." Lewis, *That Hideous Strength*, 320.

fiery mass of stone, and neither a god nor even a living being." On the other hand, the Platonists held that the heavenly bodies have life. Nor was there less diversity of opinion among the Doctors of the Church. It was the belief of Origen (*Peri Archon* i) and Jerome that these bodies were alive, and the latter seems to explain in that sense the words (*Ecclesiastes* 1:6), "The spirit goeth forward, surveying all places round about." But Basil (*Hom.* iii, vi *in Hexaem.*) and Damascene (*De Fide Orth.* ii) maintain that the heavenly bodies are inanimate. Augustine leaves the matter in doubt, without committing himself to either theory, though he goes so far as to say that if the heavenly bodies are really living beings, their souls must be akin to the angelic nature (*Gen. ad lit.* ii, 18; *Enchiridion* lviii).[58]

Lewis, it seems, took the view that the planets themselves were inanimate, but that each planet had a governing power: "each sphere, or something resident in each sphere, is a conscious and intellectual being . . .. These lofty creatures are called Intelligences. The relation between the Intelligence of a sphere and the sphere itself as a physical object was variously conceived."[59] This is precisely what we find in Dante, who writes:

> As from the blacksmith springs the hammer's art,
> so power and motion in each holy wheel
> breathe from the blessed beings that move the sphere;
> So too that heaven so many lights adorn.
> From the deep Mind that turns it, it receives
> Its image, and it makes itself the seal.[60]

Though hesitant to refer to these Intelligences as "angels,"[61] it seems clear that this is precisely what Lewis meets in the Oyarsa of Malacandra, the same being true of the Bent One, who rules our own Thulcandra. And in *That Hideous Strength*, Lewis refers to the "five excellent Natures," and the "*Gloria*" which they "perpetually sing."[62]

---

[58] Thomas, *Summa Theologica*, trans. Fathers of the English Dominican Province (Westminster: Christian Classics, 1981), Ia.LXX.3.

[59] Lewis, *Discarded* Image, 115.

[60] Dante Alighieri, *Paradise*, trans. Anthony M. Esolen (New York: Modern Library, 2004), II.127-132.

[61] Lewis, *Silent Planet*, 171.

[62] Lewis, *That Hideous Strength*, 327.

Lewis, then, posits not merely an ordered and harmonic cosmos or solar system but one filled with intelligent spiritual beings, some of which hold power or sway over whole planets, without quite being said to reside in them. Though Lewis does not connect these intelligences to Plato's "Sirens,"[63] it is a short step to bind together the angelology and cosmology of this view with the Pythagorean music of the Spheres, in the *Gloria* Lewis says they perpetually sing.[64] We see something akin to this in *The Great Divorce*, where the planet itself, "the Nature or Arch-nature of that land rejoiced to have been once more ridden, and therefore consummated, in the person of the horse."[65] This may have been behind Dante's synthesis of the spheres, angelic hierarchies, and the song proper to each of the spheres. Dante may have replaced Plato's Sirens with angelic beings who sang not a single note but a whole song unique to that sphere or planet.[66]

Ransom first hears this song by understanding Malacandrian song:

> Now first he saw that its rhythms were based on a different blood than ours, on a heart that beat more quickly, and a fiercer internal heat . . .. A sense of great masses moving at visionary speeds, of giants dancing, of eternal sorrows eternally consoled, of he knew not what and yet what he had always known, awoke in him with the very first bars of the deep-mouthed dirge, and bowed down his spirit as if the gate of heaven had opened before him.[67]

For this is precisely what was happening: Ransom, through Malacandrian song, was beginning to hear the music he had always known but never heard, the music of the Spheres, the "central music

---

[63] Plato, "Timaeus," 29e-41.

[64] Despite a chapter by this title, Michael Ward does relatively little with this theme (though one might expect it given his delightful treatment of Lewis's cosmology), probably because the theme is far more prominent in the Ransom Trilogy than in the Chronicles of Narnia. See Ward, *Planet Narnia*, chap. 11, 223-43.

[65] C. S. Lewis, *The Great Divorce* (Glasgow: Collins, 1974), 94. The song which the planet sings in the following paragraphs is worth noting, though it escapes the limited scope of our project.

[66] Alighieri, *Paradise*, XXVIII.87-139.

[67] Lewis, *Silent Planet*, 142. See C. S. Lewis, *The Magician's Nephew* (New York: Macmillan, 1964), 88.

in every pure experience which had always just evaded memory."[68]

THE GREAT EXCEPTION: OUR SILENT PLANET

The great exception to all this is the Thulcandra—our own planet Earth. While the ancients well knew that the Earth was a sphere as to a supposed "flat earth" ("Bless me, what *do* they teach them at these schools?"),[69] it does not mean that they thought it was a planet, for the planets were the moving stars, the "wanderers."[70] The Earth, on the other hand, was still. Plato had it winding "around the axis that stretches throughout the universe."[71] Along these lines, Cicero writes: "there below the Moon is the earth, the ninth and lowest of the spheres, lying at the centre of the universe. The earth remains fixed and without motion; all things are drawn to it, because the natural force of gravity pulls them down."[72] Dante, looking down upon the earth from the heavens, sees:

> this globe so small
> I smiled at how it appeared;
> And I approved that counsel best of all
> that scorns it—but to think of something higher
> truly bespeaks a spirit brave and tall.[73]

Shortly thereafter, Dante speaks of the other planets, "shifting their places," each "in its size, in its velocity," in contrast with the "little winnowing floor," our planet Earth.[74]

For the ancients and medievals, then, the earth was silent but for a quite simple reason: it was still. That is to say, it did not wander through the heavens, making a sound in keeping with its movement.

---

[68] Lewis, *The Screwtape Letters*, 159. Elsewhere, Lewis writes: "And secondly, as that vast (though finite) space is not dark, neither is it silent. If our ears were opened we should perceive, as Henryson puts it, every planet in his proper sphere In moving makand harmony and sound (*Fables*, 1659) as Dante heard it (*Paradiso*, I, 78) and Troilus (v, 1812)." Lewis, *Discarded Image*, 112.

[69] C. S. Lewis, *The Lion, The Witch and the Wardrobe* (New York, Collier, 1976), 186.

[70] Plato, "Timaeus," 38c.

[71] Plato, "Timaeus," 40c.

[72] Cicero, "Dream of Scipio," 347. On the earth as the lowest point of the universe, see Aristotle, "Heavens," 269b.

[73] Alighieri, *Paradise*, XXII.133-138.

[74] Alighieri, *Paradise*, XXII.148-152.

Fixed, still, heavy: it lay at the weighty center of the universe, in contrast to the eternally and perfectly moving heavens. The earth was a silent, motionless winnowing floor, best scorned for the higher things.

Lewis, following a Miltonian cosmological synthesis, provides an altogether different reason for the silence of the Earth. In his heliocentric cosmology,[75] the earth becomes a planet, a wanderer, but remains silent: "Thulcandra—the silent world or planet,"[76]something unfathomable to the ancient and medieval mind.[77] Why then is our planet silent? Because Lewis attributes the music of the spheres not merely to the physical movement but to the Muse, Siren, or angelic being governing and moving that planet. Our planet is silent not because it is still but because its governing intelligence is silent, has broken communion with God and the heavens: we are a planet under siege.[78] As Shippey puts it, "the presiding Intelligence of earth is Satan. That is why earth is the 'silent planet', cut off from the everlasting harmony of the planetary and stellar spheres . . . the universe's cold dregs, its inhabitants a prey to demonic temptation and delusion, in a word, 'fallen' – though not beyond salvation."[79]

The key to this vision lies in the Intelligence or governing angel of Earth, the Bent One: "Once we knew the Oyarsa of your world—he was brighter than I," says Oyarsa:

> And then we did not call it Thulcandra. It was the longest of all stories and the bitterest. He became bent. That was before any life came on your world. Those were the Bent Years of which we still speak in the heavens, when he was not yet bound to Thulcandra but free like us. It was in his mind to spoil other worlds besides his own . . . .. We did not leave him at large for long. There was great war, and we drove him back out of the heavens and bound him in the air of his own world as Maleldil taught us. There doubtless he lies to this hour, and we know no

---

[75] Lewis, *Silent Planet*, 120.

[76] Lewis, *Silent Planet*, 69, 102-3.

[77] For Dante, Christ opened our access to the heavens (Alighieri, *Paradise*, VII.46.). The thought that Christ would in some way perfect or save the heavens from some problem would be utterly foreign to him, given his cosmology.

[78] Tolkien goes a different route, positing cacophony rather than silence in his *Ainulindale*.

[79] Shippey, "The Ransom Trilogy," 241.

more of that planet: it is silent.[80]

And this brings us full circle, for we are back in the narrative, where the dominant concern is to account for Christ's defeat of Satan. But the picture has radically changed, for the stage has been turned inside out, and we view Satan's fall and tyranny not from the perspective of the earth and its treacherous inhabitants but from Mars and, later, Venus. From this vantage point, Satan has been quarantined as a matter of cosmological precaution for the other planets.[81] The church's teaching, "implied in several Dominical, Pauline, and Johannine utterances—. . . that man was not the first creature to rebel against the Creator, but that some older and mightier being long since became apostate and is now the emperor of darkness and (significantly) the Lord of this world," still stands true.[82] But its implications have been given a cosmic rather than merely earthly scope.

A COSMIC THEORY OF THE ATONEMENT

We now have all the key components in place to appreciate Lewis's brilliant development of Christ's atoning work. The basic scheme is that of *Christus victor*, such as developed in *The Lion, the Witch and the Wardrobe*, where the problem is firmly focused on Satan and the havoc he unleashes in creation. But Lewis has expanded the stage to a cosmic scope. The plight is not merely that of traitors such as Edmund; the plight is that of the heavens themselves. For while the angels and beings of other planets may not have fallen, and Satan has been quarantined within the confines of this earthly atmosphere[83] to protect those planets from further harm, the consequences of his rebellion nonetheless touch upon the heavens as a whole. What to the ancients and medievals was a simple and unproblematic given, the silence of the earth, has now become a cosmic problem: the silence of our planet, within the music of the spheres.

Why did God become man? In part, to overthrow the rule of Satan and bring deliverance to the captives. But the solution is as big or bigger than the problem itself. After all, where sin abounds, grace abounds all the more (Rom. 5:20). So, once more, why did God

---

[80] Lewis, *Silent Planet*, 130.

[81] Lewis, "Religion and Rocketry," 93.

[82] Lewis, *Problem of Pain*, 134.

[83] He is, after all, the prince of the power of the air (Ephesians 2:2).

become man? *He became man to end the siege of Thulcandra and overthrow the rule of Satan, that through his Lordship over the planet Earth, it might once more rejoin the heavenly song, bringing completion and perfection to the music of the Spheres.* God became man that the heavens might once more, or perhaps even for the first time, perfectly proclaim the glory of God by means of their heavenly song. The heavens do indeed proclaim the glory of the Lord (Psalm 19:1), but through the work of Christ, our own planet now joins in that song.

We see the fullest expression of this line of thought in Lewis's poem, "The Turn of the Tide," in which he tells of a wave of silence, beginning with the breathless air over Bethlehem when Christ was born, sweeping around the earth and out into the heavens:

> . . . From the Earth
> The signal, the warning, went out,
> Away beyond the air; her neighbors were aware
> Of change, they were troubled with doubt.[84]

Was this the end? The divine Ousiarchs, the "Great Galactic Lords" whispered:

> . . . Is this perhaps the last
> of our story and the glories of our crown?
> —The entropy worked out?

No!

> Like a stab at that moment over Crab and Bowman,
> Over Maiden and Lion, came the shock
> Of returning life, the start, and burning pang at heart,
> Setting galaxies to tingle and rock.
> The Lords dared to breathe, swords went into sheathes
> A rustling, a relaxing began;
> With rumor and noise of the resuming of joys
> Along the nerves of the universe it ran.
> Then, pulsing into space with delicate dulcet pace,
> Came a music infinitely small,
> But clear; and it swelled and drew nearer, till it held
> All worlds with the sharpness of its call,
> And now divinely deep, ever louder, with a leap
> And quiver of inebriating sound,
> The vibrant dithyramb shook Libra and the Ram,
> The brains of Aquarius spun round—
> Such a note as neither Throne nor Potentate had known

---

[84] C. S. Lewis, *Poems* (New York: Havest/HBJ, 1977), 49.

Since the Word created the abyss.
But this time it was changed in a mystery, estranged,
A paradox, an ambiguous bliss.
Heaven danced to it and burned; such answer was returned
To the hush, the *Favete*, the fear
That Earth had sent out. Revel, mirth and shout
Descended to her, sphere below sphere,
Till Saturn laughed and lost his latter age's frost
And his beard, Niagara-like, unfroze;[85]
The monsters in the Sun rejoiced; the Inconstant One,
The unwedded Moon, forgot her woes;
A shiver of re-birth and deliverance round the Earth
Went gliding; her bonds were released . . ..[86]

Of course this is but a beginning, the first onslaught. As in Milton's *Paradise Regained*,[87] this Incarnation is but a prelude to the second, greater and colder wave of silence that will sweep heavens on Good Friday and the far greater shock of triumphant, resurrected life that will resound and echo through the heavens, filling them with a song to this point unheard, un-guessed, a song that will swell unending throughout the heavens, leading them in their glorious dance. Not only will the earth be delivered, released from her bonds, she will be in her glory, radiant before her Lord, crowning the heavenly dance, fulfilling the music of the spheres.

---

[85] Recall that in "The Planets," Lewis describes Saturn as sickly, uncertain, a vault severe of vast silence, the last planet old and ugly, in tattered garment, weak with winters. His eye fathers pale pestilence, pain of envy, remorse and murder. C. S. Lewis, "The Planets," in *The Collected Poems of C. S. Lewis: A Critical Edition*, ed. by Don W. King (Kent: The Kent State University Press, 2015), 318-9, lines 101-122. In this poem the Nativity, not to mention the resurrection of Creation's Lord, brings healing not merely to sinners but the heavens and planets themselves, melting Saturn's beard and making him young again.

[86] Lewis, *Poems*, 50-1.

[87] Lewis notes in "The Planets" that at this point, despite the song in the heavens:

... at Bethlehem the bless'd
Nothing greater could be heard
Than sighing wind in the thorn, the cry of One new-born,
And cattle in stable as they stirred. (lines 81-4)
That "thorn" remains to be borne by its sighing Lord, before the song can be heard in the Silent Planet.

CONCLUDING IMPLICATIONS

Why bother asking whether Christ's death impacted aliens, planets, and supposed heavenly music?[88] After all, isn't the death and resurrection of Jesus primarily about reconciling men and women to God? Yes, but one of the great and unique things about the Jewish and Christian faiths is that "their gusto, or even gratitude, embraces things that are no use to man," of "creatures useless or hurtful or wholly irrelevant to man," for these are the creatures of God, the "Creator and sustainer of all," and are therefore "our fellow-dependents . . . and mention of all equally redounds to his praise."[89] But this is no mere matter of creation or the Old Testament alone. The Bible clearly anticipates "a 'redemption' or 'remaking' of Nature which could not stop at Man, or even at this planet. We are told that 'the whole creation' is in travail, and that Man's re-birth will be the signal for hers."[90] In short, redemption, just as with creation, is a matter that includes but far transcends our own being and concerns, stretching to encompass the whole of God's creation.

Lewis's thesis concerning the atonement and the music of the spheres is thus partly a matter of re-enchanting the cosmos, converting "space" to "the heavens," refashioning the whole of the universe into God's good creation.[91] But doing this requires so much more than a doctrine of creation, as though this could or should stand independently of the work of Christ. Lewis's genius lies partly in his commitment to accomplishing this grand synthesis through the death and resurrection of Jesus Christ, binding the periphery to the center. From this center, from the atoning work of Jesus Christ, Lewis works outward, filling the whole universe with meaning or, rather, witnessing to the meaning with which God, in his wisdom,[92] filled

---

[88] It is worth taking some care not to fall into the fate of the student in Chaucer's *Miller's Tale*, who, abandoning his study of theology and the arts, fell "with this here 'astromy,' into a fit, or lunacy maybe." Geoffrey Chaucer, *The Canterbury Tales*, trans. Nevill Coghill (New York: Penguin, 2003), 95.

[89] C. S. Lewis, *Reflections on the Psalms* (London: Collins, 1972), 72-3.

[90] Lewis, *Miracles*, 125 and 127.

[91] This is one of the primary concerns of *Silent Planet*, as seen in chapters 3 and 5, and especially pp. 158-59, which is an expansion of the experiment proposed in Lewis, *Discarded Image*, chapter 5.

[92] Lewis, *Silent Planet*, 155.

his creation.

In precisely this wisdom of God Lewis helps us delight, reminding us that "it might turn out that the redemption of other species differed from ours by working through ours. There is a hint of something like this in St Paul (Romans 8:19-23) when he says that the whole creation is longing and waiting to be delivered from some kind of slavery, and that the deliverance will occur only when we, we Christians, fully enter upon our sonship to God and exercise our 'glorious liberty.'" Lewis proceeds to speculate that even though Paul was probably "thinking only of our own earth," it is "perhaps possible—it is not necessary—to give his words a cosmic meaning," a meaning as cosmic as creation was in the first place (Genesis 1-3).[93] This possibility is profoundly important to us, for it vindicates the doctrine of creation, casting us up into the sphere of God's own concerns.

We do well to dwell on the breadth and scope of these concerns: "As our Earth is to all the stars, so doubtless are we men and our concerns to all creation; as all the stars are to space itself, so are all creatures, all thrones and powers and mightiest of the created gods, to the abyss of the self-existing Being." But lest we find ourselves lost in this immensity, Lewis immediately affirms the identity of this self-existing Being, "who is to us Father and Redeemer and indwelling Comforter."[94] Why dwell on the cosmic work of Christ? Because it expands the horizons of our understanding and worship of God as Creator, giving us a far greater framework for knowledge and action, without the danger that mere cosmic speculation might have of making us insignificant before the scope of the universe. Our introduction to this scope is precisely through the work of the incarnate Maker, who *for us* as for creation as a whole, *and for our salvation* and the perfection of the interplanetary song, became man. And this "union between God and Nature in the Person of Christ admits no divorce. He will not *go out of* Nature again and she must be glorified in all ways which this miraculous union demands."[95] Among these glories is that sacred music of the spheres, the joyful and triumphant song of the heavens in praise of their Maker and Redeemer.

One final question: should we believe this? Should we preach a cosmic theory of the atonement, replete with the music of the spheres?

---

[93] C. S. Lewis, "Religion and Rocketry," 90-1.

[94] Lewis, *Problem of Pain*, 153-4.

[95] Lewis, *Miracles*, 128.

First, I believe it is worth noting that there have been pastors and theologians throughout the history of the church that could have and would have affirmed and preached such an account of Christ's atoning work. Our own impoverished cosmology is no excuse for an impoverished faith. But there are perhaps too many hypotheticals, too many assumptions in this account to call forth a resounding "amen" from many today.

But that is not all we can say, for Lewis's account, I suggest, says *what may be the case*, where *something must be the case*. His is creative theology at its best, venturing into the borders and shadows of the Christian faith. But not into darkness. Scripture has paved the way forward here, not clarifying precisely what must be said or casting a dim light but making room for *something* to be said. Could someone believe this or some similar account? Indeed. Something like this must be true: that the maker of heaven and earth reconciled all things to himself, the heavens included (Colossians 1:20), in the person and work of Jesus Christ. To shy away from such an account, imaginative as it may be, is to shy away from the invitation of Scripture.[96]

[96] My family and I would like to express our love for Chris and Julie, for the delightful time we had with them during the year we taught together at Biola. Chris and I had each spoken to a mutual colleague about co-writing an essay on Lewis and the atonement but had not gotten around to talking about it with each other, when he so suddenly became an expert on all things pertaining to salvation (and so unable to share that expertise with us in manuscript form). Alone, I write what was meant to be a joint project, to the great loss of the reader. I would also like to thank Biola University's Torrey Honors College, including its faculty, staff, and students, for support and encouragement in writing this paper. Rachael Smith, my research assistant, was particularly helpful, as she tracked down some exceptionally rich material of great use to this argument, as was Josh Steele with his keen editorial eye. Uche Anizor, Jason McMartin, Ryan Peterson, Gabe Renfro, Jennifer Snell, Kyle Strobel, and Michael Ward were all kind enough to offer helpful comments and critique.

III.

INTERACTIONS WITH CONTEMPORANEOUS OR CURRENT WRITERS

Chapter 13

C. S. LEWIS: COMMUNICATION PROFESSOR

STEVEN A. BEEBE

C. S. Lewis was often introduced at speaking events or described on the dust jackets of his books as "Professor Lewis." It was only during the last nine years of his life, however, that he officially acquired the title "professor," a prestigious rank bestowed by British colleges and universities on a select few. When at Magdalen College in Oxford, Lewis lost the election for Professor of Poetry to C. Day Lewis in 1951. But three years later, in recognition of his outstanding academic accomplishments, he was appointed Chair of Medieval and Renaissance Literature at Cambridge, a position that also included the coveted title "Professor." Lewis was well qualified for his professorial rank. Although he did not hold an earned doctorate, he had received honorary doctorates from several universities.[1] His triple first at Oxford, along with his voluminous output as an author and scholar, and his skill as a tutor and lecturer, had firmly established his academic credentials. C. S. Lewis clearly deserved the title Professor.

Although Lewis was Professor of Medieval and Renaissance Literature, he had eclectic academic interests. His formal education included not only classical Greek and Roman literature, typical curricular components of an Oxford education, but also philosophy and English literature. His writing reflects his diverse interests and broad scope of knowledge. As a result, several academic disciplines claim him as their own. Literary scholar Doris Myers argues that Lewis should be recognized for his expertise primarily as a literary scholar: "It is literary craftsmanship, after all, that will ensure for Lewis a permanent placed in the canon."[2] On the other hand, given the popularity of his apologetic work, Christians claim Lewis as an

---

[1] Lewis's honorary degrees include: Doctor of Divinity from the University of St. Andrews (1946), Doctor of Letters from Laval University (1952), Doctor of Literature from the University of Manchester (1959), a Doctorate from the University of Dijon (1962), and a Doctorate from the University of Lyon (1963).

[2] Doris T. Myers, *C. S. Lewis in Context* (Kent: Kent State University Press, 1994), xvi.

important theologian. Lewis scholars Jerry Root and Mark Neal count seventeen different literary genres in which Lewis wrote: apologetics, autobiography, educational philosophy, essays, fairy stories, journals, letters, literary criticism, literary history, lyric poetry, narrative poetry, novels, religious devotion, satire, science fiction, short story, and translations.[3] In addition to this extensive list of academic interests, Lewis can also be explicitly linked with the discipline of communication.

Students majoring in "communication studies," the most often used label to describe the contemporary discipline of communication (previously known as "speech"), rarely, if ever, read his works as communication literature or find references to Lewis's ideas or his writing in communication textbooks. It is highly unusual to find a course about Lewis taught in a communication department. Although he once described himself in a letter as "a born rhetorician . . . I love to 'ride like a cork on the ocean of eloquence,'"[4] there is no evidence that he ever referred to his professional expertise as "communication" or "speech." However, the purpose of this chapter is to suggest that C. S. Lewis *should* be considered for his knowledge, insight, and expertise as a communication scholar. His life's work, both what he wrote about as well as his application of communication principles, provides evidence of his communication expertise.

THE COMMUNICATION DISCIPLINE

To make the case that Lewis should be embraced for his knowledge of human communication, it is useful to understand how the communication discipline and Lewis's interests intersect. The communication discipline is interdisciplinary; it embraces several academic traditions, some as ancient as the study of rhetoric and others more contemporary, including social media and mediated messages. Mirroring the multifaceted nature of the communication discipline, Lewis, too, had interdisciplinary interests; his study and writing ventured into literature, literary history, theology, psychology, philosophy and other topics found in both the humanities and social sciences.

---

[3] Jerry Root and Mark Neal, *The Surprising Imagination of C. S. Lewis: An Introduction* (Nashville, TN: Abingdon Press, 2015), 3.

[4] C. S. Lewis, *The Collected Letters of C. S. Lewis*, ed. by Walter Hooper, 3 vols. (San Francisco: HarperCollins, 2004-7), 1:713.

The National Communication Association, the oldest and largest professional academic communication association in the U.S., defines communication as "how people use messages to generate meanings within and across various contexts" and "the discipline that studies all forms, modes, media, and consequences of communication through humanistic, social scientific, and aesthetic inquiry."[5] The U.S. Department of Education defines the academic domain of communication as including "instruction in the theory and practice of interpersonal, group, organizational, professional, and intercultural communication; speaking and listening; verbal and nonverbal interaction; rhetorical theory and criticism; performance studies; argumentation and persuasion; technologically mediated communication; popular culture; and various contextual applications."[6] C. S. Lewis was not just mildly interested in these topics, but as this chapter documents, he had insightful and detailed observations about the theory and practice of human communication.

The academic discipline of communication studies has most fully developed in the United States in the years since World War II, as evidenced by the plethora of organized departments and schools of communication established in that interim. There were no U. S. departments of "speech" in 1900.[7] By 1930, when Lewis was coming into his own as a tutor at Magdalen College, Oxford, a survey of selected U. S. institutions found more than twenty-five U. S. departments included the word "speech" in their titles. As Lewis's career began to soar, a 1948 survey reported 256 U. S. colleges and universities included the word "speech" in a department title; 51 were titled "speech and drama," 18 "public speaking," 48 "English and speech," and 5 "communication"[8] Today, there are approximately 2,000 U.S. departments that include a study of what used to be encompassed by the word "speech" and what today is more often

---

[5] National Communication Association, "What is Communication." https://www.natcom.org/about-nca/what-communication.

[6] U. S. Department of Education, Classification of Instructional Programs: 2000 Edition (Washington D.C.: National Center for Education Statistics, 2002), x.

[7] D. K. Smith, "Origin and Development of Departments of Speech," in *History of Speech Education in America: Background Studies*, ed. by Karl Richards Wallace (New York: Appleton-Century-Crofts, 1954), 447.

[8] Smith, "Origin and Development," 462.

labeled "communication" or "communication studies."[9]

What is the central focus of the contemporary communication discipline? Communication scholars and educators continue to have an ongoing conversation about the central tenets of communication study. Over the past few decades, communication scholars have suggested various concepts as the focal point of the discipline:

Speech: The oral nature of communication[10]

Message: The written, spoken, and unspoken elements of communication to which people assign meaning[11]

Human symbolic activity: The use of symbols to represent a thought, concept, object, or experience[12]

Text: Words and images that create meaning[13]

Meaning and messages: An emphasis on messages and the resulting co-creation of the meaning of messages[14]

Relationships: The connections made with another person in a variety of contexts through communication.[15]

---

[9] Everett M. Rogers, *A History of Communication Study: A Biographical Approach* (New York: Free Press, 1997).

[10] Walter J. Ong, *Ramus, Method, and the Decay of Dialogue: From the Art of Discourse to the Art of Reason* (Cambridge, MA: Harvard University Press, 1958); Frank E. X. Dance, *Speech Communication: Concepts and Behavior* (New York: Holt, Rinehart and Winston, 1972), and *Speaking Your Mind: Private Thinking and Public Speaking* (Dubuque: Kendall/ Hunt, 1974); Horace G. Rahskopf, "Speech at Mid-Century" in *Quarterly Journal of Speech*, 37 (1951): 147-52.

[11] John H. Powers, "On the Intellectual Structure of the Human Communication Discipline," in *Communication Education*, 44 (1995): 191-222.

[12] Gary Cronkite, "On the Focus, Scope, and Coherence of the Study of Human Symbolic Activity," in *The Quarterly Journal of Speech*, 72.3 (August 1986): 231-46.

[13] Joshua Gunn, "Gimme Some Tongue (On Recovering Speech)," in *Quarterly Journal of Speech*, 93 (2007): 361-4.

[14] D. Zarefsky, "The State of the Discipline," Address presented to the National Communication Association national convention, San Francisco, California, November 2010. https://www.natcom.org/.

[15] Steven A. Beebe, "It's A Wonderful Discipline," National Communication Association Presidential Address, 23 November 2014.

Given C. S. Lewis's academic interests and expertise and the interdisciplinary nature of contemporary communication studies, what are the key arguments for considering C. S. Lewis a Professor of Communication?

THE EVIDENCE FOR C. S. LEWIS AS COMMUNICATION PROFESSOR

There are at least five reasons to consider C. S. Lewis a communication educator and scholar. First, applications of communication ideas and principles, as well as explicit observations about words, meaning, messages and human behavior, can be found in virtually everything he wrote. His friends and colleagues, J. R. R. Tolkien and Owen Barfield, were both celebrated philologists, and Lewis was a philological scholar in his own right, as evidenced by his work *Studies in Words*.[16] Second, communication scholars historically tend to emphasize oral communication; Lewis was interested in writing *and* speaking, both in theory and in application, but gave special attention to the oral nature of messages. Third, Lewis wrote extensively about how to communicate effectively; he offered several strategies for making messages, both written and oral, clear, interesting, and memorable. Fourth, he was a skilled communicator, known not only for his prolific output of books and essays but also for his abilities as a captivating speaker, teacher, and broadcaster. He modeled the communication principles about which he wrote. Finally, C. S. Lewis was not only interested in rhetoric and dialectic but discussed applications of communication principles in several contexts, including interpersonal and small group communication. He was a "catholic communicator" in the sense that he was interested in a variety of communication contexts and genres, from friendship to classical rhetoric.

Language, symbols, and meaning were consistent themes that permeated Lewis's life's work

The central focus of the communication discipline, according to former National Communication Association president David

---

https://www.natcom.org/.

[16] C. S. Lewis, *Studies in Words* (Cambridge: Cambridge University Press, 1960).

Zarefsky, is the relationship between meaning and messages.[17] Meaning, messages, and the importance of language are also consistent and pervasive themes running throughout Lewis's work. Lewis possessed a sophisticated understanding of the nature of meaning and the centrality of using language to develop human connections: "This book has grown out of a practice which was at first my necessity and later my hobby; whether at last it has attained the dignity of a study others must decide."[18] The study he is talking about is his interest in words. This thesis sentence from *Studies in Words,* published in 1960, offers evidence of Lewis's life-long love of language and how words affect and reflect human nature. Lewis believed that through language we articulate our longing for joy and acknowledge objective truth. Therefore, a prime argument for viewing Lewis as a communication professor is both his "necessity" and "hobby" of thinking and writing about language and meaning.

Lewis's understanding of the importance of language and meaning in everyday life had practical implications for him: "I have an idea of what is good and bad language . . .. Language is an instrument of communication. The language which can with the greatest ease make the finest and most numerous distinctions of meaning is best."[19] As additional evidence of his practical applications of language principles, he illustrated what General Semanticists call the communication problem of *bypassing,* when one word has two meanings, with this example from *Studies in Words*:

> When I spoke of supper after the theatre, I meant by *supper* a biscuit and a cup of cocoa. But my friend meant by *supper* something like a cold bird and a bottle of wine. In this situation both parties might well have agreed on the lexical (or dictionary) meaning of supper; perhaps a supernumerary meal which, if taken at all, is the last meal before bed.[20]

Lewis knew that language could unite us with a common understanding or divide us when we use words that mean different things to different people. In his essay "On Criticism," he further comments about the importance of a common meaning between communicators:

> The ideally false or wrong 'meaning' would be the product in the

---

[17] Zarefsky, "The State of the Discipline."

[18] Lewis, *Studies in Words,* 6.

[19] Lewis, *Studies in Words,* 6.

[20] Lewis, *Studies in Words,* 14.

mind of the stupidest and least sensitive and most prejudiced reader after a single careless reading. The ideally true or right 'meaning' would be that *shared* (in some measure) by the largest number of the best readers after repeated and careful readings over several generations, different periods, nationalities, moods, degrees of alertness, private preoccupations, states of health, spirits, and the like cancelling one another out when (this is an important reservation) they cannot be fused so as to enrich one another.[21]

Lewis's practical insights about language and meaning were anchored in his belief about the link between language and subjectivism. In *The Abolition of Man*, Lewis makes his argument for objectivism and the existence of Natural Law by pointing to the power of language in his challenge to the conclusion of what he calls *The Green Book* by "Gaius" and "Titius." (According to Walter Hooper, the actual title of "*The Green Book*" is *The Control of Language*, authored by Alex King and Martin Ketley.)[22] "Gaius" and "Titius" suggest that when someone describes a waterfall as "sublime," the utterance is really a statement about the person's feelings rather than a description of the waterfall. Lewis disagrees. He notes, "If the view held by Gaius and Titius were consistently applied it would lead to obvious absurdities. It would force them to maintain that *You are contemptible* means *I have contemptible feelings*: in fact that *Your feelings are contemptible* means *My feelings are contemptible*."[23] Lewis logically argues for the existence of "the doctrine of objective value, the belief that certain attitudes are really true, and others really false." Language, for Lewis, was a means to discover and describe truth.

Additional evidence of Lewis's insights about language and meaning is found in the planned, but never published, C. S. Lewis and J. R. R. Tolkien book about the nature of language and its link to human behavior. The existing fragment that Lewis started provides a brief yet tantalizing glimpse of his over-arching approach to the importance of language in influencing our behavior. He told Chad Walsh, who visited him in the summer of 1948, that this book was

---

[21] C. S. Lewis, "On Criticism," in *C. S. Lewis: Essay Collection & Other Short Pieces*, ed. by Lesley Walmsley (London: HarperCollins, 2000), 56-7.

[22] Walter Hooper, *C. S. Lewis, Companion and Guide* (San Francisco: HarperSanFrancisco, 1996), 332.

[23] C. S. Lewis, *The Abolition of Man* (New York: Macmillan, 1944), 15.

to be called *Language and Human Nature* and was to be published the following year by the Student Christian Movement Press, but this publication never happened.[24] In 1950, Lewis wrote to a friend, "My book with Tolkien—any book in collaboration with that great, but dilatory and unmethodical man—is dated I fear to appear on the Greek Calends."[25] Walter Hooper adds a footnote, clarifying that the reference to the "Greek Calends" means "never." The manuscript fragment, found in the University of Oxford Bodleian Library and published in 2010, includes a detailed definition of language and a discussion of the nature of meaning.[26]

Additional evidence for Lewis as a "Professor of Communication" is found in his essay "The Language of Religion." He offers insightful and detailed commentary about descriptive language and its poetic power to stimulate the imagination. Specifically, Lewis discussed the advantages and disadvantages of three kinds of language: Ordinary, Scientific, and Poetic. Each kind of language has its place. Ordinary language, or everyday language, is an appropriate style in which to express the basic, day-to-day aspects of life. There are instances, however, when more precise, scientific language is needed, not only for scientists, but also for anyone who needs to provide a specific, detailed, and accurate summary of facts and events. Poetic language uses metaphor and other figurative words to express sensations or implicit meaning that may lie "between the words."[27]

Throughout his writing, whether in *Studies in Words*, *The Abolition of Man*, a planned book that was to be called *Language and Human Nature*, or numerous other books and essays, Lewis was keenly interested in language, meaning, and the importance of human

---

[24] See: Joe R. Christopher, "A Note on an Unpublished (and Probably Unwritten) Collaboration," in *Mythlore*, 10. (May 1975), 29. Also see Diana Pavlac Glyer, *The Company They Keep: C. S. Lewis and J. R. R. Tolkien as Writers in Community* (Kent, Ohio: The Kent State University Press, 2007), 146.

[25] Lewis, *Collected Letters*, 3:6.

[26] C. S. Lewis, "Language and Human Nature (Manuscript Fragment)," in *VII: An Anglo-American Literary Review*, 27 (2010), 25-8; Steven A. Beebe, "C. S. Lewis on Language and Meaning," in *VII: An Anglo-American Literary Review*, 27 (2010), 7-24.

[27] C. S. Lewis, "The Language of Religion," in *Christian Reflections*, ed. by Walter Hooper (London: Geoffrey Bles, 1967), 127.

expression. His ideas about language are pervasive and original.[28]

Lewis viewed language as a holistic process emphasizing both oral and written messages

Lewis's academic training focused on English literature and the written word, but he was equally interested in oral communication, a central and historical focus of the communication discipline. Traditionally, U.S. college and university academic English departments focus on written messages, while communication departments emphasize oral messages. Reflecting Lewis's holistic interest in communication and supporting his Professor of Communication title, he was interested in both.

Spoken rhetoric was a specialized area of study by the ancient Greeks and Romans. Lewis most definitely studied rhetoric. In fact, the classical roots of communication and rhetoric are what Lewis knew best, although he did not always enthusiastically embrace rhetorical study. During his pre-Oxford education he wrote to his father,

> In Greek we have begun Demosthenes. Of course oratory is not a sort of literature that I appreciate or understand in any language, so that I am hardly qualified to express an opinion on our friend with the mouthful of pebbles. However, compared with Cicero, he strikes me as a man with something to say, intent only upon saying it clearly and shortly.[29]

As a renowned expert on literary criticism, Lewis was well versed in the classical approaches to words and meaning. Lewis scholar Bruce Edwards concludes,

> In his scholarly career and his imaginative writing, Lewis understood "rhetoric" in its traditional, classical sense—a compendium of tools that equipped an artist or essayist with strategies to communicate truth more memorably, to express difficult ideas more accessibly, to appeal to the imagination with greater aplomb and delight, and, certainly, to make confrontation with the deeper facthood of transcendent reality less avoidable. His canon of compelling texts are an enduring legacy that point to his own mastery of these venerable strategies of persuasion, instruction, and engagement.[30]

---

[28] Steven A. Beebe, *C. S. Lewis and the Craft of Communication* (New York: Peter Lang, 2020).

[29] Lewis, *Collected Letters*, 1:137.

[30] Bruce L. Edwards, "Language/Rhetoric," in *The C. S. Lewis*

C. S. Lewis clearly understood and applied principles of rhetoric in his writing and practice.

At Malvern College Lewis had the benefit of being taught by Harry Wakelyn Smith, an influential teacher dubbed "Smewgy" by his students, who nurtured his communication performance instincts. Smewgy had a considerable talent for reading poetry, giving Lewis an early role model who demonstrated effective techniques of oral interpretation. According to Lewis biographer and personal friend George Sayer, Lewis credited Smewgy with teaching him two key communication skills: how to analyze the grammar and syntax of a poem, and how to read poetry with a focus on the sounds and rhythms of the poem. Sayer reports that Lewis enjoyed good animated conversations ("How I like talking!")[31] and adds, "Although he did not have Smewgy's lovely musical voice and could not read romantic poetry with Smewgy's power to enchant, [Lewis] excelled in reading heroic verse and such poetry as Milton's that required a grand style."[32] Lewis's talent for holding an audience with his speaking acumen perhaps began with Smewgy's attention not only to the substance of a message but also its performance.

Lewis's Oxford education would certainly refine and add to his rhetorical competencies, but without William T. Kirkpatrick (a.k.a. "The Great Knock"), it is questionable that Lewis would be the communicator we know today. Although Lewis thought orators Demosthenes and Cicero were "The Two Great Bores," he nonetheless fine-tuned his dialectical (debate) and rhetorical (persuasion) skills when studying with Kirkpatrick.[33] Lewis acknowledges both Smewgy and Kirkpatrick for their skill in speaking, analytical thinking, and writing: "Smewgy and Kirk were my two greatest teachers. Roughly, one might say (in medieval language) that Smewgy taught me Grammar and Rhetoric and Kirk taught me Dialectic."[34] Lewis notes, "If Kirk's ruthless dialectic had been merely a pedagogic instrument I might have [resented it]," adding, "A pure agnostic is a fine thing.

Readers' Encyclopedia, ed. by Jeffrey D. Schultz and John G. West (Grand Rapids: Zondervan, 1988), 231-2.

[31] George Sayer, *Jack: A Life of C. S. Lewis* (Wheaton, IL: Crossway Books, 1994), 123.

[32] Sayer, *Jack: A Life*, 88.

[33] Sayer, *Jack: A Life*, 166.

[34] Sayer, *Jack: A Life*, 171.

I have known only one and he was the man who taught me how to think."[35] Lewis also valued his education in challenging ideas: "We have both learnt our dialectic in rough academic arena where knocks that would frighten the London literary coteries are given and taken in good part."[36] By the winter of 1916 Lewis was prepared to seek an Oxford education.

Rhetorician and Lewis scholar James Como notes Lewis's contributions to the study of rhetoric but found that Lewis's copy of Aristotle's *Rhetoric*, housed in the Marion E. Wade Center at Wheaton College, contains no marginal annotations or markings.[37] On the other hand, Greg Anderson, another rhetoric and Lewis scholar, who also examined Lewis's personal library of books at the Wade Center, discovered that Lewis's 1665 copy of Quintilian's *Institutionum Oratorium* is "heavily underscored,"[38] as are Hugh Blair's *Lectures on Rhetoric and Belles Lettres*, and I. A. Richards's *The Philosophy of Rhetoric*. Anderson speculates that Lewis's copy of *Rhetoric* deposited at the Wade Center may have been a replacement copy from Lewis's office library at Cambridge.[39] At any rate, Lewis's existing well-annotated rhetoric books view oral and written rhetoric as inextricably linked.

Lewis's definition of language places considerable emphasis upon the *oral* nature of communication. In *Language and Human Nature*, Lewis writes, "A language in the simplest sense, is a system of signs. Thus there is a language of flags (used in the navy) a 'language of flowers' and so forth."[40] He goes on to say, "But there is one such system of signs so widely used and so much richer than all the others that it generally is called simply 'language.' This is the system in which the signs are the various noises made by a human mouth. It is language in this sense, which is the subject of the present book."[41]

---

[35] Lewis, *Collected Letters*, 2:444.

[36] C. S. Lewis and E. M. W. Tillyard, *The Personal Heresy* (London: Oxford University Press, 1939), 69.

[37] James Como, *Branches to Heaven: The Geniuses of C. S. Lewis* (Dallas: Spence Publishing Company, 1998), 27.

[38] Greg M. Anderson, "A Most Potent Rhetoric: C. S. Lewis, 'Congenital Rhetorician,'" in *C. S. Lewis: Life, Works, and Legacy*, ed. by Bruce L. Edwards (Westport, CT: Praeger, 2007), 198.

[39] Anderson, "A Most Potent Rhetoric," 218.

[40] Lewis, "Language and Human Nature," 25.

[41] Lewis, "Language and Human Nature," 25.

Why is it significant that Lewis describes language as an *oral* process ("the various noises made by a human mouth"), and not just a *written* system of signs? Because Lewis knew that although the oral and written elements of language use different communication channels, they are holistically integrated.

Reflecting the oral style of his work, many of Lewis's books and articles began as lectures or speeches presented to a group of academics, students, or the public. He was an efficient communicator in that he often got double duty out of his work. What would first be a speech or lecture would then become an essay, article, or eventually a book. His essay anthology, aptly titled *They Asked for a Paper*, is a collection of papers he had presented (orally) for several different audiences. *The Four Loves* began as a series of radio lectures commissioned by the Atlanta Diocese of the Episcopal Church. *The Abolition of Man* consisted of the Riddle Memorial Lectures delivered in Newcastle at an outpost of nearby Durham University. The list of Lewis written manuscripts that started as oral presentations, either as lectures, broadcasts, sermons, or speeches, is long. He knew how to appeal to both the eye and the ear because he had much practice at transforming his speeches into written text.

Lewis's interest in oral communication influenced his writing technique. When drafting his written works, Lewis sometimes spoke or mouthed the words as he wrote. Walter Hooper writes that Lewis had a keen sense of writing to appeal to the listener as well as the reader: "When Lewis dictated letters to me, he always had me read them aloud afterwards. He told me that in writing letters, as well as books, he always 'whispered the words aloud.' Pausing to dip the pen in an inkwell provided exactly the rhythm needed. 'It's as important to please the ear,' he said, 'as it is the eye.'"[42] Lewis confirmed his awareness of the listener when he wrote about his own technique: "When I write I pronounce every word aloud. It's important to please the ear as well as the eye."[43] In another instance, he made the point about the importance of spoken communication explicit when he wrote to a schoolgirl in America on December 14, 1959: "Always write (and read) with the ear, not the eye. You shd. hear every sentence you write as if it was being read aloud or spoken. If it does not sound nice,

---

[42] Lewis, *Collected Letters*, 1:x.

[43] Carolyn Keefe, *C. S. Lewis: Speaker and Teacher* (Grand Rapids, MI: Zondervan, 1976), 50.

try again."[44] This oral quality of his writing is one of the factors that make Lewis a skilled communicator.

Lewis knew that as we "heard" the words in our "mind's ear," those "sounds" would have a more potent effect on our emotions. In a letter to correspondent Mrs. Hook, Lewis explained why he was mindful of the sound of words he wrote: "I am always playing with syllables and fitting them together (purely by ear) to see if I can hatch up new words that please me."[45] But why was he so focused on the *sound* of words? He explains, "I want them to have an emotional, not intellectual suggestiveness: the heaviness of *glund* for as huge a planet as Jupiter; the vibrating, titillating quality of *viritrilbia* for the subtlety of Mercury; the liquidity and (as I thought) spirituality of Maleldil."[46] Lewis liked the way the sound of words made the reader feel. He sought an emotional response from his readers in reaction to the sound a word created.

In *The Discarded Image*, Lewis further confirms his acknowledgement of the importance of spoken rhetoric: "The ancient teachers of Rhetoric addressed their precepts to orators in an age when public speaking was an indispensable skill for every public man—even for a general in the field—and for every private man if he got involved in litigation. Rhetoric was then not so much the loveliest (*soavissima*) as the most practical of the arts."[47] For Lewis, the study of rhetoric was indeed indispensable and practical. And his understanding of rhetoric is consistent with his conviction that oral and written rhetoric are linked.

LEWIS WROTE EXTENSIVELY ABOUT HOW TO BE AN EFFECTIVE COMMUNICATOR

Lewis should be embraced by communication educators as one of their own because of his extensive discussion of how to be a better communicator. Prescriptions about how to communicate effectively are liberally sprinkled throughout the corpus of Lewis's work, including *Studies in Words*, "Before We Can Communicate," "Transposition,"

---

[44] Lewis, *Collected Letters*, 3:522.

[45] Lewis, *Collected Letters*, 3:1004-5.

[46] Lewis, *Collected Letters*, 3:1004-5.

[47] C. S. Lewis, *The Discarded Image: An Introduction to Medieval and Renaissance Literature* (Cambridge: Cambridge University Press, 1964), 190.

"The Language of Religion," "Bluspels and Flalansferes: A Semantic Nightmare," "Four-Letter Words," *Preface to Paradise Lost*, *The Discarded Image*, *An Experiment in Criticism*, and *Language and Human Nature*. Although these works provide the most explicit examples of Lewis's discussion of communication ideas, his ideas about meaning and messages are found in virtually everything he wrote, including his personal correspondence.

What were some of Lewis's key communication prescriptions? He was especially interested in being clear. Here is his advice for developing a clear language style:

> The way for a person to develop a style is (a) to know exactly what he wants to say, and (b) to be sure he is saying exactly that. The reader, we must remember, does not start by knowing what we mean. If our words are ambiguous, our meaning will escape him. I sometimes think that writing is like driving sheep down a road. If there is any gate open to the left or the right the readers will most certainly go into it.[48]

Lewis distinguished between clarity and style. In his essay "The Vision of John Bunyan," Lewis noted, "It is always dangerous to talk too long about style. It may lead one to forget that every single sentence depends for its total effect on the place it has in the whole."[49] Using the right word, for Lewis, depends on the context of the word.

In addition to guidance about being clear, Lewis had specific advice for painting vivid word pictures to evoke emotions from the listener or reader:

> Don't use adjectives which merely tell us how you want us to feel about the things you are describing. I mean, instead of telling us a thing was 'terrible,' describe it so that we'll be terrified. Don't say it was 'delightful.' Make us say 'delightful' when we've read the description. You see, all those words (horrifying, wonderful, hideous, exquisite) are only saying to your readers 'Please will you do my job for me.'[50]

Lewis was consistent in advising friends and admirers to evoke

---

[48] C. S. Lewis, *God in the Dock: Essays on Theology and Ethics*, ed. by Walter Hooper (Grand Rapids, MI: Eerdmans, 1999), 263.

[49] C. S. Lewis, "The Vision of John Bunyan," in *Selected Literary Essays*, ed. by Walter Hooper (Cambridge: Cambridge University Press, 1969), 151.

[50] Lewis, *Collected Letters*, 3:766.

meaning and emotion in others by helping them feel as if they were in the situation being described. In a letter to a friend, he wrote,

> Never use adjectives or adverbs which are mere appeals to the reader to feel as you want him to feel. He won't do it just because you ask him: you've got to *make* him. No good telling us a battle was 'exciting.' If you succeed in exciting us the adjective will be unnecessary; if you don't it will be useless. Don't tell us the jewels had an 'emotional' glitter; make us feel the emotion. I can hardly tell you how important this is.[51]

In fact, Lewis's letters to friends and admirers are peppered with communication advice. In a letter to a young admirer named Tomasine, he acknowledged the challenge of teaching someone to be a good writer: "It is very hard to give any general advice about writing." But he nonetheless added, "Here's my attempt," and provided the following guidelines:

1. Turn off the Radio.

2. Read all the good books you can, and avoid nearly all magazines.

3. Always write (and read) with the ear, not the eye. You should hear every sentence you write as if it were being read aloud or spoken. If it does not sound nice, try again.

4. Write about what really interests you, whether it is real things or imaginary things, and nothing else. (Notice this means that if you are interested only in writing you will never be a writer, because you will have nothing to write about . . .)

5. Take great pains to be clear. Remember that though you start by knowing what you mean, the reader doesn't, and a single ill-chosen word may lead him to a total misunderstanding. In a story it is terribly easy just to forget that you have not told the reader something that he needs to know—the whole picture is so clear in your own mind that you forget that it isn't the same in his.

6. When you give up a bit of work don't (unless it is hopelessly bad) throw it away. Put it in a drawer. It may

---

[51] Lewis, *Collected Letters*, 3:881.

come in useful later. Much of my best work, or what I think is my best, is the re-writing of things begun and abandoned years earlier.

7. Don't use a typewriter. The noise will destroy your sense of rhythm, which still needs years of training.

8. Be sure you know the meaning (or meanings) of every word you use.[52]

The letter to Tomasine is a communication lesson in miniature. It, along with other letters, books and essays, brims with "dos and don'ts" about how to express oneself to others. Although Lewis's recommendation about not using a typewriter is anachronistic, most of his advice for enhancing communication skill is as applicable today as it was when he wrote it.

Lewis suggested how to ensure that a message is well received: maintain a focus on the intended receiver—the reader or listener. But Lewis also knew that the perspectives of the sender and the receiver of a message can never be identical. He acknowledged that although communication should be audience-centered, a listener or reader can never fully understand the intended meaning of a message: "Admittedly we can never quite get out of our own skins. Whatever we do, something of our own and of our age's making will remain in our experience."[53]

Lewis believed that the primary goal of a Christian communicator is to translate Christian fundamentals clearly so that the intended audience would first understand the ideas and then respond to them. Along with the concept of translation—that is, providing a clear, textual interpretation for the listener—it is important to use words and phrases that the listener understands—to keep the language of the reader or listener in mind. In offering specific advice for the clergy, as they learn how to connect with an audience, Lewis writes,

> What we want to see in every ordination exam is a compulsory paper on (simply) translation; a passage from some theological work to be turned into plain vernacular English. Just turned: not adorned, not diluted, not made 'matey'. The exercise is very

---

[52] Lewis, *Collected Letters*, 3:881.

[53] C. S. Lewis, *An Experiment in Criticism* (Cambridge: Cambridge University Press, 1961), 101.

like doing Latin prose. Instead of saying, 'How would Cicero have said that?' You have to ask yourself, 'How would my scout [the British term for those who attend to students' practical housekeeping needs in college] or bedmaker have said that?'[54]

Lewis was a skilled writer, speaker, and broadcaster

A communication professor not only professes principles of effective communication but ideally also models excellence in communicating with others. Lewis was a skilled communication practitioner, both as a gifted lecturer and public speaker. Gervase Mathew, who for nine years coordinated Lewis's lectures for the English faculty, noted, "His influence on his contemporaries was at least as much as orator as writer."[55] In response to suggestions that Lewis thought lectures and tutorials a waste of his valuable time, Mathew concluded, "No travesty could be further from the truth"[56] Describing Lewis's oratorical skills, Mathew notes, "He took a vivid, perhaps rather sporting, interest in the numbers who came to him, and he was depressed when he failed to repeat his Oxford triumphs at Cambridge. At times he lectured from skeleton notes, at times from a written text; on occasion he improvised; it was hard to tell which method he was following. But always he forged a personal link with those who heard him."[57] Although Lewis was not always flawless when speaking in public (Lewis scholar Bruce R. Johnson chronicles several public presentation missteps), he was a popular lecturer who usually had standing-room only audiences.[58] And Lewis liked a good-sized audience.

Kingsley Amis, writer, former Oxford student, and a friend of Lewis's, describes how he and some of his student friends would categorize lecturers on a scale of "hard" to "soft." As Amis explains,

---

[54] C. S. Lewis, "Before We Can Communicate," in *God in the Dock: Essays on Theology and Ethics*, ed. by Walter Hooper (Grand Rapids, MI: Eerdmans, 1999), 256.

[55] Gervase Mathew, "Orator," in *C. S. Lewis at the Breakfast Table*, ed. by James Como (San Diego: Harcourt Brace and Company, 1992), 96.

[56] Gervase Mathew, "Orator," 96.

[57] Gervase Mathew, "Orator," 96.

[58] Bruce R. Johnson, "C. S. Lewis and the BBC's Brains Trust: A Study in Resiliency," in *VII: An Anglo-American Literary Review*, 30 (2013), 67.

"Hard men gave you information . . . . The soft men offered civilised discourse."[59] Hard lecturers piled on information without regard to the interest or attention level of the listeners. Soft lecturers, on the other hand, provided stories and illustrations—but a too soft lecturer would result in students leaving the lecture hall with nothing to write down in the way of principles or information. Amis classified J. R. R. Tolkien as among the "hardest," even using the word "repulsive" to describe his lecture style—repulsive, not because he didn't have anything to say, but because he had *too much* to say. From Amis's perspective, Tolkien was much too dense and didn't give the listener a chance to process the information. Like the anthropomorphized brooms in Walt Disney's *The Sorcerer's Apprentice*, the information just kept flowing without stopping. But because of Tolkien's knowledge of Old English and the likelihood of exam questions appearing about his topic, students attended Tolkien's lectures—they had to, in order to get the needed information. On the other hand, "The softest of the soft," according to Amis, was Lord David Cecil.[60] He was engaging but less meaty in providing "hard" information. Finally, Amis placed C. S. Lewis as the "golden mean" lecturer, describing Lewis's lecture style as "The only reputable hard-soft merchant" and "the best lecturer I ever heard."[61] Lewis had learned that moving from a "hard," chock-full-of-information lecturer to a "softer" lecturer who included more illustrations, stories, metaphors, and anecdotes, along with substantive content, was more appealing to an audience.

Without having referred to it, Lewis seemed to have an intuitive sense of what contemporary communication educators call the 70/30 rule of communication.[62] The principle is: An effective and interesting presentation should contain about 70 percent support material and only 30 percent new information, key points, or conclusions. The 70 percent makes the talk interesting. In *The Discarded Image* Lewis notes that during the Middle Ages, listeners or readers expected a message to digress from the main point and to be amplified with supporting

---

[59] Kingsley Amis, *Memoirs* (London: Hutchinson, 1991), 102.

[60] Kingsley, *Memoirs*, 102.

[61] Kingsley, *Memoirs*, 102.

[62] Steven A. Beebe and Susan J. Beebe, *Public Speaking: An Audience Centered Approach*, 11th ed. (New York: Pearson, 2021); Frank E. X. Dance, *Speech Communication: Concepts and Behavior* (New York: Holt, Rinehart and Winston, 1972); Frank E. X. Dance, *Speaking Your Mind: Private Thinking and Public Speaking* (Dubuque: Kendall/Hunt, 1974).

material. Lewis adds, "But the most important of all the *morae*[63] is *Diversio* or Digression . . .. For good or ill the digressiveness of the medieval writers is the product not of nature but of art."[64] He further notes, "the interwoven stories that so incessantly cross and interrupt one another, may be simply one more application of the digressive principle and an offshoot of Rhetoric."[65] Although Lewis says he doesn't fully accept or embrace rambling digressions, he knew that supporting material (that may at first seem a digression) enhances listener interest—at least if the "digressions" are on point.[66]

What would it have been like to be a student attending one of Lewis's lectures? George Bailey, a former student of Lewis's, describes Lewis's lecture delivery as skilled, no-nonsense, and clear:

> Indeed, his delivery in his lectures was entirely straightforward, almost severe. He never noticeably consulted his lecture notes. When he had finished his lecture, he folded up his papers almost as he uttered the last word and walked briskly in a beeline for the door. No one would have dared accost him in his passage. He was blessed with a fine sonorous baritone voice capable of a wide range of intonation and inflection but his delivery was highly disciplined and deceptively easy. He was never dramatic, let alone melodramatic. I cannot remember a single gesture during his lectures. In appearance at the rostrum he was relaxed, almost deadpan, a study in economy. He was the consummate medium for what he had to say: he gave every word, every phrase, every sentence, every larger passage its full value. He gave full expression to his flashes of humour without obtruding his personality, as it were, between the flash and the audience. His style, I suppose, was low pressure but never conspicuously so. Lewis, I am sure, never "threw away a line" in his life.[67]

Whether in a sermon, essay, book, or broadcast, Lewis used a technique that contemporary communication educators call *verbal immediacy*. Verbal immediacy is a state of psychological closeness promoted by certain words and word choices. Using immediate

---

[63] *Morae* means delays.

[64] Lewis, *Discarded Image*, 193.

[65] Lewis, *Discarded Image*, 193.

[66] Lewis, *Discarded Image*, 193.

[67] Carolyn Keefe, *C. S. Lewis: Speaker and Teacher* (Grand Rapids: Zondervan Publishing House, 1971), 110.

personal pronouns (such as *we*, *us*, and *our*), including several personal examples (using *I*, *me*, and *my*), talking about personal experiences, asking questions, and speaking *with* readers and listeners rather than *at* them are all means of being verbally immediate. Lewis used these techniques well. Using the right words and the right style with a specific reader or listener in mind, he developed an immediate relationship with his audience.

During his first meeting with Arthur Greeves, Lewis's Belfast across-the-street neighbor who became one of his closest confidantes, Lewis discovered that Arthur shared with him an abiding interest in Norse mythology and "things Northern." On making this connection Lewis said to Arthur (also included in a passage in *The Four Loves* exemplifying what new friends say to one another), "What? You too? I thought I was the only one."[68] Verbal immediacy is the ability to make a "you too?" connection with readers and listeners. Identifying commonalities, speaking in first person, and then making these common connections an organic element of conversation cement a relationship. Lewis's own struggles, disappointments, and challenges helped him forge a bond with his audience. Just as he did with Arthur Greeves, Lewis could evoke a "you too?" connection with his readers.

Lewis applied his knowledge of human communication to a variety of communication contexts, including interpersonal relationships and group dynamics

Lewis was interested in more than rhetoric and public speaking. A fifth argument for claiming C. S. Lewis as a communication professor relates to his interest in and application of communication principles in a variety of communication contexts. The communication curriculum is typically organized around contexts—specific categories, genres, or situations in which communication occurs. Lewis was interested in both interpersonal and small group communication, two of the contexts included in communication study.

Interpersonal Communication

Interpersonal communication is defined as a "distinctive, transactional form of human communication involving mutual

---

[68] C. S. Lewis, *The Four Loves* (New York: Harcourt Brace, 1960), 77.

influence, usually for the purpose of managing relationships."[69] The study of human relationships is at the heart of the interpersonal communication context. C. S. Lewis was clearly interested in the quality of interpersonal relationships. Several of his books, including *The Four Loves*, *Till We Have Faces*, *The Screwtape Letters*, and all three of the books in his Ransom trilogy (*Out of the Silent Planet*, *Perelandra*, and *That Hideous Strength*) include both implicit and explicit observations about the nature and importance of human relationships.

Lewis's observations about interpersonal communication were prescient. Several of his ideas about human relationships pre-date systematic communication and social science research conclusions; the first interpersonal communication textbooks were published in the late 1960s and early 1970s, several years after Lewis's death.

The core content of *The Four Loves* includes a discussion of Affection, Friendship, Eros, and Charity. Lewis offers detailed descriptions not only about love in its many forms, but also about essential qualities of human relationships, many of which today are included as classic content in the study of interpersonal communication. Although some of Lewis's illustrations seem anachronistic, as they reflect the culture of late-1950s Britain, the underlying principles of human relationships are nonetheless supported by contemporary communication theory.

Lewis explicitly identifies friendship as one of the four loves. Lewis knew, for example, that friends are valued because most people have so few intimate friends. Research conducted since 1960 supports Lewis's observation that "The first and most obvious answer is that few value [friendship] because few experience it."[70] Most people, according to contemporary research, have five close friends (including, where relevant, one's spouse or partner) and 5-15 additional good friends.[71]

Social psychologists and communication researchers have dissected the differences between the qualities of friendship as distinct from eros for decades. Lewis was ahead of these researchers in clarifying differences between love and friendship:

Nothing is less like a Friendship than a love affair. Lovers are

---

[69] Steven A. Beebe, Susan J. Beebe, and Mark V. Redmond, *Interpersonal Communication: Relating to Others*, 9th ed. (Upper Saddle River, NJ: Pearson, 2020), 3.

[70] Lewis, *Four Loves*, 58.

[71] Beebe, Beebe and Redmond, *Interpersonal Communication*, 298.

always talking to one another about their love; friends hardly ever about their Friendship. Lovers are normally face to face, absorbed in each other; Friends, side by side, absorbed in some common interest. Above all, Eros (while it lasts) is necessarily between two only. But two, far from being the necessary number for Friendship, is not even the best.[72]

Lewis needed no focus groups, surveys, or experimental research designs to reach his conclusions about love and friendship. Yet his conclusions are supported by post-1963 research that clarifies the differences between Eros and Storgē.[73]

In addition to explicating differences between love and friendship, Lewis reveals a sophisticated understanding of how relationships work when he describes relationships through the lens of what contemporary researchers call *relational dialectic theory*. Relational dialectic theory posits that any relationship can be described as "ongoing tensions between contradictory impulses"[74] or "forces pulling us toward intimacy and opposing forces pulling us toward independence" simultaneously.[75] In essence, one force pushes us toward a focus on self, while the other focuses more altruistically on others.

From the outset of *The Four Loves*, Lewis implies a relational dialect by making a distinction between "gift-love" and "need-love." Without using the term *dialectic*, Lewis nonetheless describes how the opposing forces of gift-love and need-love pull us in our relationships with each other and our relationship with God. In gift-love reciprocation is not expected; giving is selfless. Need-love, on the other hand, is rooted in our quest for life-sustaining attention and affection from others. Lewis describes it as "the accurate reflection in consciousness of our actual nature. We are born helpless. As soon as we are fully conscious, we discover loneliness. We need others physically, emotionally, intellectually; we need them if we are to know

---

[72] Lewis, *Four Loves*, 61.

[73] Arthur Aron and Elaine N. Aron, "Love," in *Perspectives on Close Relationships*, ed. by Ann L Weber and John H Harvey (Boston: Allyn & Bacon, 1994); Clyde Hendrick and Susan S. Hendrick, *Close Relationships: A Sourcebook* (Thousand Oaks, CA: Sage, 2001).

[74] Richard H. West and Lynn H. Turner, *Interpersonal Communication* (Newbury Park, CA: Sage, 2019), 165.

[75] Beebe, Beebe, and Redmond, *Interpersonal Communication*, 308.

anything, even ourselves."[76]

Another source of applications to interpersonal communication is *The Screwtape Letters*. The devilish correspondence crackles with insights about how humans behave and relate to one another. In some respects, *The Screwtape Letters* is the anti-interpersonal communication book. Social science research documents that one of the most corrosive communication displays is that of contempt—sarcastically undermining a verbal message with contradictory nonverbal expression. Relationship researchers label contempt as one of the four communication behaviors that predicts relational discord and marital divorce.[77] Screwtape cleverly advocates contempt when he suggests,

> Your patient must demand that all his own utterances are to be taken at their face value and judged simply on the actual words, while at the same time judging all his mother's utterances with the fullest and most oversensitive interpretation of the tone and the context and the suspected intention . . .. You know the kind of thing; 'I simply ask her what time dinner will be and she flies into a temper.' Once this habit is well established you have the delightful situation of a human saying things with the express purpose of offending and yet having a grievance when the offence is taken.[78]

The Screwtape Letters presents a masterful "Devil's Guide to Interpersonal Communication." Merely flip Screwtape's advice on its head for positive and productive interpersonal communication advice.

Small Group Communication

In addition to exploring the interpersonal communication context, Lewis also made astute observations about small group communication, defined as "communication among a small group of people who share a common purpose, who feel a sense of belonging to the group, and who exert influence on one another."[79] The dynamics of

---

[76] Lewis, *Four Loves*, 2.

[77] John Gottman and Joan DeClaire, *The Relationship Cure* (New York: Crown, 2001), 198.

[78] C. S. Lewis, *The Screwtape Letters* (New York: Macmillan, 1960), 22-3.

[79] Steven A. Beebe and J. T. Masterson, *Communicating in Small Groups: Principles and Practices*, 12th ed. (Upper Saddle River, NJ: Pearson, 2020), 3.

what causes groups to form, stay together, and accomplish specific tasks through communication, are key elements of group communication study. As with applications of interpersonal communication, Lewis was ahead of his time when discussing group interaction. Although books with "group discussion" in the title were published in the 1930s, group communication textbooks that referenced social-psychological dynamics of groups emerged only after Lewis's death in 1963.

In noting a standard observation of contemporary group communication textbooks, Lewis knew that "Two heads are better than one, not because either is infallible, but because they are unlikely to go wrong in the same direction."[80] For Lewis, friendship among a group of people, in contrast to friendship between only two people, adds a new dynamic to the relationships. The 1945 loss of his friend Charles Williams gave Lewis insights about the collaborative nature of friendship. As Lewis put it,

> [I]f, of three friends (A, B, and C), A should die, then B loses not only A but "A's B." In each of my friends there is something that only some other friend can fully bring out. By myself I am not large enough to call the whole man into activity; I want other lights than my own to show all his facets.[81]

Lewis also understood how groups may tend to disregard opinions and observations from those not in the "in" group. *Groupthink* is a classic group malfunction that occurs when groups make bad decisions because their high level of cohesiveness results in an implicit pressure to agree with one another. Psychologist Irving Janis published his description of "groupthink" in 1972. Lewis, however, was already aware of both the causes and symptoms of groupthink that now are standard fare in the study of group communication and contemporary textbooks.[82] According to Janis, when experiencing groupthink, group members believe they can do no wrong; they are concerned about justifying their actions and apply pressure to members who do not support the group. Although he doesn't use the term *groupthink*, when talking about the dynamic that can occur in overly cohesive groups, Lewis notes,

> The danger is that this partial indifference or deafness to outside opinion, justified and necessary though it is, may lead

---

[80] Lewis, *God in the Dock*, 202.

[81] Lewis, *Four Loves*, 61.

[82] Such as Beebe and Masterson, *Communicating in Small Groups*.

to a wholesale indifference or deafness. The most spectacular instances of this can be seen not in a circle of Friends but in a Theocratic or aristocratic class. We know what the Priests in Our Lord's time thought of the common people. The Knights in Froissart's chronicles had neither sympathy nor mercy for the "outsider," the churls or peasantry.[83]

Lewis seems to imply that a circle of friends is immune to groupthink. Although it is true that those who perceive themselves higher in social rank (the aristocratic class) are more susceptible to groupthink, any group, including friends, may experience this "deafness to outside opinion." Although group communication textbooks written in the 1950s and 60s made scant references to what can happen when groups become overly cohesive, Lewis accurately describes the causes, symptoms, and consequences of groupthink. He clearly understood group dynamics.

SUMMARY AND CONCLUSION

This chapter makes the case that C. S. Lewis professed principles and applications of communication in his speaking and writing and therefore should be considered a communication professor. Although his classical education included a study of rhetoric, there is no evidence he formally studied elocution, declamation, or oratory, or other approaches to "communication." Yet he offered numerous pieces of advice about speaking and listening. C. S. Lewis built upon his knowledge of rhetoric to offer insights about the nature and function of communication throughout his works.[84]

Lewis loved language and understood its power and significance. Rhetoric and Lewis scholar James Como cogently summarizes how often the nature of language or use of words played a significant role in Lewis's works—both fiction and nonfiction:

> . . . not only did Lewis indulge in speech always and everywhere, he viewed it as fundamental to our human nature, our redeemable nature. 'Talking too much is one of my vices, by the way,' he wrote to a correspondent in 1956. But they are the Talking Beasts of Narnia who know Aslan; it is the uttering of nonsense that effects the demise of the N.I.C.E.

---

[83] Lewis, *Four Loves*, 81.

[84] For a fuller discussion of Lewis and communication, see Beebe, *C. S. Lewis and the Craft of Communication*.

in *That Hideous Strength*; it is the hearing of a voice that alters the destiny of John the Pilgrim in *The Pilgrim's Regress*; and Ransom is a philologist whose training and skill enable him to speak with—and thus to dwell among and befriend—the creatures of Malacandra in *Out of the Silent Planet*, creatures who thereafter no longer seem as strange as their mere appearance first suggested.[85]

The planet was silent because it did not communicate with its creator; lack of communication led to disastrous consequences. The title of Lewis's last Ransom trilogy book, *That Hideous Strength*, comes from a line in a 1955 poem *The Monarche* by David Lyndsay, which refers to the miscommunication at the Tower of Babel.

Lewis was not silent about the pervasive influence and importance of communication.[86] This chapter suggested five reasons for considering Lewis's influence to communicative thought and application.

First, language, meaning, words, and symbols are a subtext embedded in many of Lewis's works. His books, essays, and speeches include both explicit and implicit discussions of the nature and importance of language.

Second, although Lewis is known for his written works, he was keenly interested in oral communication. His books and essays began as lectures or speeches. The oral quality of his writing stems from his technique of speaking the words as he wrote. He was clearly interested in the oral nature of messageS.

Third, Lewis provided considerable advice about how to communicate effectively. Several of his books and essays, such as *Studies in Words* and "Before We Can Communicate," make explicit references to communication principles.

Fourth, Lewis was a gifted lecturer, orator, and broadcaster, who illustrated the principles of effective communication about which he wrote and spoke. He practiced what he preached about communicative skill.

Finally, Lewis had eclectic interests in communication. In addition to rhetoric, Lewis was interested in and wrote extensively about interpersonal and group communication principles and practices.

---

[85] Como, *Branches to Heaven*, 112.

[86] Beebe, *C. S. Lewis and the Craft of Communication*.

C. S. Lewis is noted for his expertise in many academic areas. Literature (including children's literature), philosophy, science fiction, and Christian apologetics are the traditional places we expect to find Lewis's books in bookstores today. Academic professionals attain the title "Professor" based on their teaching, service, and especially their published work. Based on Lewis's skill as educator; his service to his colleagues, community, and society; and his extensive list of publications, this chapter suggests he should be seen from a new perspective: Communication.

Chapter 14

TEACHING AS TRANSLATION
AND THE THEOLOGICAL FORMATION
OF IMAGINATION

Maxie B. Burch

In the preface to his biography of C. S. Lewis, Alister McGrath uses Owen Barfield's remark regarding the "three C. S. Lewises" as a reference point for raising three fundamental questions that will then shape the direction of McGrath's work on Lewis: "So how do these three Lewises relate to each other? Are they separate compartments of his life, or are they somehow connected? And how did they each develop?"[1] This chapter expands on these three fundamental questions by suggesting that more work needs to be done on Lewis the teacher/translator. Specifically, more work needs to address Lewis as a teacher in the vocational sense. Teaching was not just Lewis's primary profession, but, more innately, teaching was his life's calling. No matter which Lewis you are studying, Lewis the novelist, Lewis the Christian writer/apologist, or Lewis the distinguished Oxford/ Cambridge don, lecturer, and literary critic, you continually bump into Lewis the teacher/translator.

This teacher/translator Lewis keeps appearing in various forms, particularly in his letters as he addresses multiple people in multiple places regarding multiple topics. If one follows the thought process revealed in his many letters, he seems to consistently fall back on, for lack of a better phrase, what seems to be a less formal but still evident tutorial style or technique, that of a teacher/translator. Based on his BBC broadcasts and the countless letters he wrote or dictated in response to the broadcasts, one can venture an educated guess why his university lectures were so popular with his students. Lewis had a unique way of mixing clear, vernacular language, challenging questions, personal humility, and a compelling combination of expectation and affirmation with a robust sense of humor. To be sure, his lectures were loaded with disciplinary content but, venturing a

---

[1] Alister E. McGrath, *C. S. Lewis: A Life* (Carol Stream, IL: Tyndale House, 2013), x-xi.

guess, it was Lewis's delivery of the content that created the rich learning environment that drew students to his lectures.

The term "teacher/translator" will be used in this chapter as a way of arguing that teaching is fundamentally the art of translation. C. S. Lewis provides us with some key insights for how we as teacher/translators, within the University in particular and the Church in general, can be better communicators, but, more specifically, how we can and should improve the teaching of theology.

LEWIS THE TEACHER/TRANSLATOR

In a letter dated October 7, 1945, Lewis responded to the Reverend Canon John Beddow's request that Lewis write a book on Christianity for members of the Christian Worker's Union. Lewis replied that he was not suited to write such a book for factory workers because he knew nothing of the realities of factory life.[2] It was not the subject of Christianity that caused Lewis to give pause, it was the idea of accurately translating Christianity to factory workers that he questioned. He was thinking like a teacher. Those for whom teaching is a vocation, not a job, know innately that the subject matter is not the core of the teaching experience: students are the core. The central task of the teacher is to be an accurate translator of the subject matter. Lewis recognized his limitations as a teacher/translator for factory workers. Lewis went on to write, "People praise me as a translator, but what I want to be is the founder of a school of translation. I am nearly forty-seven. Where are my successors? Anyone can learn to do it if they wish. It is also a very good discipline because nine times out of ten the bit you can't turn into Vernacular turns out to be the bit which hadn't any clear meaning to begin with . . .. I feel I'm talking rather like a tutor—forgive me. But it is just a technique and I am desperately anxious to see it widely learned."[3]

In his book, *The Intellectual World of C. S. Lewis*, in a chapter entitled "Reason, Experience and Imagination: Lewis's Apologetic Method," McGrath discussed Lewis's role as a popular apologist or translator of the Christian faith. McGrath focused his remarks on the ways in which Lewis crafted and adapted his communication style to make his apologetical material more accessible and interesting.

---

[2] C. S. Lewis, *The Collected Letters of C. S. Lewis*, ed. by Walter Hooper, 3 vols. (San Francisco: HarperCollins, 2004-7), 2:673-4.

[3] Lewis, *Collected Letters*, 2:675.

Specifically, McGrath wrote that Lewis faced the challenge of theological translation and then listed six key questions Lewis sought to address regarding theology:

> How could he express academic theological notions in plain language? How could an academic such as himself talk to ordinary people without talking down to them? How could he avoid creating an alienating impression of condescension? How could he use ordinary English as a medium for often quite complex theological ideas, such as the rationality of the incarnation? How could he reach into the rich Christian past without suggesting faith was outdated? To use T.S. Eliot's words from 'Little Gidding', Lewis was obliged to find words that were 'exact with vulgarity,' yet 'precise but not pedantic.'[4]

McGrath's summary answer to these questions was that "Lewis learned how to adapt his style and vocabulary to meet the needs and concerns of an audience he had never encountered before."[5]

What McGrath described regarding Lewis's challenge is in fact the ongoing challenge of every teacher of theology whether in a university or in a church. We are constantly faced with the challenge of theological translation, of adapting both our style and our vocabulary to meet the needs and concerns of our audience. The questions that Lewis had to address as an apologist are the same ones faced by every theologian who stands before a room of undergraduates for whom the technical discipline of theology is an intimidating mystery. The technical theological nomenclature is in itself daunting, much less the many abstract, complicated ideas that span nearly two thousand years of Christian thinking. Most of our undergraduates, regardless of their church background, are not theologically trained to deal with the material that will be covered. As theologians we must become better teacher/translators if we hope to reach our audience.

McGrath further developed Lewis's approach to translation by explaining the task of doing "cultural translation."[6] The meanings of words are embedded in the cultures where they are used. For example, theology professors are not just explaining theological terms, we are attempting to explain theological terms, concepts, and ideas

---

[4] Alister E. McGrath, *The Intellectual World of C. S. Lewis* (West Sussex: Wiley-Blackwell, 2014), 131.

[5] McGrath, *Intellectual World*, 132.

[6] McGrath, *Intellectual World*, 132.

formulated in several different historical and cultural contexts to an undergraduate audience for whom these words, concepts, images, and ideas may or may not have a meaningful reference point based on the cultural context from which they come. Our task as teachers/translators is to find better ways to communicate these theological terms, ideas, and concepts into the cultural idioms and images of our students. In his lecture "Modern Theology and Biblical Criticism," Lewis reflected on this difficult task of communication when speaking to theology students at Cambridge regarding their responsibility to communicate the Gospel to their future parishioners. He referred to parishioners as "outsiders." "For of course as priests it is outsiders you will have to cope with. You exist in the long run for no other purpose. The proper study of shepherds is sheep, not (save accidentally) other shepherds. And woe to you if you do not evangelize. I am not trying to teach my grandmother. I am a sheep, telling shepherds what only a sheep can tell them."[7] Our students are outsiders, our sheep; therefore, we cannot just be teachers. We must also, with Lewis, become translators. The question of how can we become better teachers/translators is also the question, what would a membership in Lewis's "School of Translation" require of us?

McGrath argued that Lewis employed three different apologetic gateways to accomplish this act of translation: reason, longing, and imagination.[8] The remainder of this chapter will develop the last two of these gateways arguing that imagination and longing or desire are critical to the teaching/learning process. Reason is also a key gateway, but because it is also the one that is most often referenced and seldom ignored, attention will be devoted to the development of the other two.

If teaching/translating theology is to be effective and, more importantly, transformative, we must recapture the critical role that imagination and desire play in the learning process. But before we can recapture the critical role that imagination and desire play in the learning process, we must first reassess the way we understand our students as learners and how we understand the learning process. Rethinking the way we understand our students will mean asking

---

[7] C. S. Lewis, "Modern Theology and Biblical Criticism," in *Christian Reflections*, ed. by Walter Hooper (Grand Rapids, MI: Eerdmans, 1967), 152.

[8] McGrath, *Intellectual World*, 133.

whether we see them as primarily "embodied actors" or "disembodied thinkers."

THE ROLE OF IMAGINATION IN THEOLOGICAL LEARNING/LIVING

EMBODIED ACTORS

James K. A. Smith has argued in his two-volume *Cultural Liturgies*, volume one, *Desiring the Kingdom*, and volume two, *Imagining the Kingdom*, that education is not primarily concerned with providing information or ideas but is more fundamentally the pedagogical formation of imagination.[9] He further argued that pedagogies are expressions of one's philosophical anthropology. In particular, he raised the question of whether humans are "thinking things" or "embodied actors."[10] If humans are essentially embodied actors, then inculcating practices and habits becomes more foundational to learning than communicating ideas. If this anthropology of embodied actors is accurate—and this chapter will argue that it is—then a different pedagogy is needed that will facilitate the theological formation of student's imaginations when introducing them to Christian theology.

Traditional theological instruction of the kind practiced at many Christian universities focuses primarily on guiding and shaping how students think about God as the source of all that is good and true, but it is unclear whether or not this instructional method helps to form students into people who will pursue God and actually embody what is good and true. If this assessment is accurate, if much of current theological pedagogy does not intentionally prepare students to pursue God in order to embody what is good and true, then what is missing? In part, what is missing is teaching that engages students' imaginations.

So, if teaching Christian theology should engage students' imaginations with the goal that students will pursue God and embody what is true and good, what would this look like? What kind of pedagogy would this approach require? First of all, this pedagogy will require a clear understanding regarding what is meant by imagination, and second, it should demonstrate how imagination

---

[9] James K. A. Smith, *Desiring the Kingdom: Worship, Worldview and Cultural Formation, Volume 1: Cultural Liturgies* (Grand Rapids; Baker, 2009), 26.

[10] Smith, *Desiring the Kingdom*, 27-8.

is vitally connected to teaching Christian theology.

In the context of this chapter, imagination does not mean an arbitrary, fanciful, unfettered, romantic flight into irrationality, nor does it refer to a mental faculty meant primarily for artistic creativity, invention, brain storming, and novelty, though all of these capacities could be attributed to imagination.

Imagination refers to a conscious process characteristic of humans as unified beings who embody the world and are always culturally embedded. Imagination is a conscious process by which we derive meaning and understanding of our world and the communities we inhabit.[11] This perspective of imagination rejects an unbiblical and ontologically inadequate bifurcation of mind/body, reason/senses, and facts/values. It could be argued that imagination is one of the ways we embody reason, a way we derive meaning, a way we make our way in the world. In this sense, reason and imagination are more integrated.

Meaning and understanding are more than a set of objective, empirical facts, propositional statements, and cognitive beliefs regarding the world outside of us that we store in our minds. Meaning and understanding require imagination because imagination takes what we learn from our embodied, physical access to the world and translates it to accommodate the way we think and communicate.[12] We don't wake up each morning "thinking the world"; we wake up and "begin making our way in it." In other words, the world in our daily experience is not something we think but rather a place where we live. So, it is not enough to think things, to know facts and particulars. Our more difficult task is to construct a meaningful unity and purpose that connects the fragmented information and experiences of our lives. Because we essentially live our lives, not think our lives, we are primarily embodied actors, not disembodied thinkers. As embodied actors, we employ a number of imaginative structures that help us to create a unified ordered whole out of the many complex, fragmented experiences and the continuous data we process daily.

---

[11] Mark Johnson, *The Body in the Mind: The Bodily Basis of Meaning, Imagination, and Reason* (Chicago: The University of Chicago Press, 1987), xix-xxi.

[12] Johnson, *The Body in the Mind*, 12-17.

IMAGES AND METAPHORICAL PATTERNS

Two of these imaginative structures are images and metaphorical patterns that are more connected to the way we embody the world than how we think about the world. Images and metaphorical patterns are not facts, propositional truths, statements, or beliefs; they are the imaginative structures we use to navigate and learn the world.[13]

Balance and narrative are two images that our imagination uses to generate metaphorical patterns that employ an embodied or tacit knowledge of the world and our spatial relationship to it. In each case, imagination is a way we make sense of the world. Many of our daily practices are essentially understood by virtue of our embodying them so that they are not primarily thought out; they are felt or sensed. They are patterns of embodied experience.[14]

We seldom reflect on the nature and meaning of balance, yet without it our physical and mental reality would be chaotic. Balance provides coherence not only for our physical stability, but we also use balance to describe our psychological state as well. What pedagogy would we use to teach someone to ride a bike, mow a lawn, play tennis or golf? Each of these learning experiences requires balance as a sense or feel we learn through our bodies. In most cases we can instruct people with words, concepts, and ideas, but the learning happens first with our bodies and then that bodily sense or feel is mentally translated and applied to other areas of our lives. We often speak in psychological and emotional terms of being drained, exhausted, feeling off, needing to be recharged, or having used up our margins, but in each case we are using an image or a metaphorical pattern that we learned with our bodies, not a set of rules or concepts. Balance is something we do and understand with and through our bodies, then it becomes something we think. We cannot do both at the same time. We learn through our bodies and then later reflect on what we learned. That is why we often confuse how we learn with how we think.[15]

We also understand our lives by employing narrative pathways. There are physical pathways that we take from our house to work, to the mall, to church, and to school. We make our way from a starting point along various routes, following sidewalks and signs and obeying traffic laws until we reach a desired goal, a geographical location. But

---

[13] Johnson, *The Body in the Mind*, 68-9.

[14] Johnson, *The Body in the Mind*, 102.

[15] Johnson, *The Body in the Mind*, 74-89.

not all pathways are physical. We also employ pathway images or metaphors to describe movements from one stage in life to another, but, whether they are physical or mental pathways, these images and metaphorical patterns are derived from our embodied presence, how we make our way in the world. So, when referring to imagination, we can be speaking of it as embodied reasoning that treats humans as knowers, not just thinkers. Our minds and our bodies operate with a unified system of knowing that utilizes images and metaphorical patterns like balance and narrative as interpretive structures for constructing a unified order of meaning for our lives.[16]

Do we use propositional statements to help us define and describe the world? Yes. Are there facts and empirical data we must evaluate and analyze? Yes. Do we construct belief systems composed of propositional statements, facts,, and empirical data? Yes. Do we use imagination as a way of reasoning in order to create those statements, analyze those facts, and construct those belief systems? Yes.

IMAGINATION'S ROLE IN TEACHING CHRISTIAN THEOLOGY

So, what is the proper role of imagination in teaching Christian theology? Christian theology's subject is God, His revelation of Himself, and the subsequent human experience with and reflection upon that revelation. In order to do theology well, Christians must be embodied knowers and not just rational thinkers because, on the one hand, God's revelation is the record of His words and actions in the world He created, but, on the other hand, God's revelation is the person of Jesus Christ and our personal experience with this God who continues to speak and act in our world and in our lives. Therefore, Christian theology is not just an intellectual activity whereby we systematically categorize our observations and ideas about God; it is also a dynamic process God uses to transform both our thinking and our living. Christian theology is both a way of being in the world as well as a discipline for organizing and communicating our beliefs about God. In other words, Christian theology assumes that our faith is both embodied by our lives and embedded in the communities where we worship and serve. Christianity is ultimately an incarnational faith that depends on the experienced reality of God; therefore, theology will require more than reason. It will also require our imagination.

---

[16] Johnson, *The Body in the Mind*, 113-17.

But do we teach theology in a way that engages student's imaginations? Do we teach theology as an embodied and embedded way of living, thinking, and communicating God in the world? Or do we primarily teach theology as a set of doctrinal propositions about God, theories for explaining God's work in the world, a discipline for engaging the mind but not the body, the intellect but not the emotions? Does our teaching essentially reinforce the western philosophical predilection for bifurcating human beings into minds with bodies? Have we become unwitting theological advocates for the Cartesian argument that we exist as thinking beings who only truly know the structure of our own minds while our bodies play only a limited role in reasoning? If we teach as though rationality is essentially disembodied, does theology as way of thinking and communicating God also become disembodied? If we believe that reason is an abstracted process separated from the world we embody, won't we teach theology as an abstracted process separated from the world we embody? Is this bifurcated approach partially responsible for why theology departments separate systematic and historical theology from what is referred to as practical or spiritual theology?

At my university, Old Testament (OT) and New Testament Survey (NT) are prerequisites before students can take what we call Essentials of Evangelical Theology. A common problem we have found is that many, if not most students, have never read the entire Bible and therefore do not understand it as a whole. In OT and NT we primarily teach students to read the Bible as two volumes of a grand narrative. We work on helping them to grasp the narrative structure of the Bible in order to see it as God's grand story. We have found that most of our students come to us understanding the Bible as a fragmented grouping of stories that can be exegeted and understood independently and apart from the larger, grand narrative. As a result, students come to us thinking that they understand the Bible when what they really understand are fragmented stories that are rarely connected to one another. This fragmented approach results in a personal theology that is often very particular, selective, and disconnected from the larger biblical story.

Though we recognize the value and importance of systematic theology, our faculty have chosen to take a more historical approach; however, I am not convinced that we are helping our students to make the transition from reading the Bible as God's grand narrative to reading theology as the church's ongoing conversation regarding

God's revelation. Don't misunderstand me. I see the value and need for students to be aware of the church's theological doctrines as our ongoing attempts to understand and communicate God and His revelation, but is this enough? It seems to me that if we are intent on students reading and understanding God's revelation as a grand, interactive narrative, then Christian theology should provide them with a more interactive experience.

Theology should not begin with abstract thoughts about God. We should begin with the biblical narrative rooted in the world's history. We should begin with the experience and life of the Early Church and then move through the centuries following the story of Christians who sought to understand and embody the teaching that, as the Apostle Paul wrote "was passed on by word or letter" (2 Thessalonians 2:15).[17] How we begin is important because we are inviting students not just to think about the narrative of their faith; we are inviting them to interact with it, to embody the story and find their place in it.

Alister McGrath points out that C. S. Lewis was heir to the Anglican intellectual tradition of imaginative translation or transposition. In this case, transposition meant the restating of core Christian theological ideas via a different genre.[18] When students read *The Lion, the Witch and the Wardrobe*, they are drawn into the story and encouraged to identify with the characterS. They are offered the opportunity to imagine the Christian story within the story of Narnia and to find themselves in the narrative, but they cannot embody this story because it is fiction. The biblical narrative is meant to have the same effect except that it is not fiction. It is the meta-narrative of God's work in the world. We want students to be drawn into the biblical story, encouraged to identify with the characters, and to find themselves in the narrative with the major exception that, empowered by the Holy Spirit, they are called to actually embody this story.

Theology's great task is to engage student's imaginations, helping them to see themselves actively living out the biblical story in time and space, drawing from its past, encountering God in the present, and anticipating His continuing work in their lives. Christian theology should not just be a means of rationally demonstrating, empirically

---

[17] Here and elsewhere, Bible quotations are from the New International Version.

[18] McGrath, *Intellectual World*, 172.

proving, or intellectually wrestling with our faith; it should be a process whereby we come to believe and embody our faith as the way we see the world and make our way in it.

DEVELOPING STUDENT'S THEOLOGICAL IMAGINATION

Developing student's theology imagination will require us to reassess our own philosophical anthropology, to decide if our students are primarily thinking things or embodied actors. If we see them as embodied actors then we must carefully reconsider what kind of pedagogy will develop their theological imagination. The following two pedagogical options are offered for consideration: create a compelling metaphor and re-enchant the Gospel.

A COMPELLING METAPHOR

It has previously been argued that Christian theology should not just be a means of rationally demonstrating, empirically proving, or intellectually wrestling with our faith; it should be a process whereby we come to believe and embody our faith as the way we see the world and make our way in it. Thinking clearly and concisely about God in order to formulate and articulate a substantive understanding of Christian doctrine is an important goal for teaching theology, but the question has been raised, is this enough? Part of the work of transposition/translation is creating analogous language to help communicate theological ideaS.

I want more for my students than a theological understanding of their faith. I want them to understand and experience what it means to have a "taste of Divine reality" (Psalm 34:8). Christian theology is an important way we seek to communicate truths about God as the ultimate reality, but the theological truths we believe are not the reality: they are one way that we seek to understand and communicate that reality. God is the reality. I don't want my students to mistake the theological truths for the reality. I want them to see the truths as pointing them and compelling them to see and know the reality: to know God. It is my contention that we must facilitate the theological formation of our students' imaginations if we want them to do more than think about God.

Metaphorically, teaching theology is like teaching someone to cook a meal. The way I used to teach theology was akin to giving my students numerous recipes for cooking a theological meal, helping them to prepare it, but never inviting them to dinner. We never actually sat down at the table to eat together the meal we had prepared. As a result, most of them completed my theology course thinking that the recipes and the preparation were what mattered. The question that troubled me was, if students are truly embodied knowers rather than disembodied thinkers and they never taste the "Divine reality" at the heart of all theology, will they *know*, in the fullest sense of that word, what is good and true about the reality the meal represents?

A theology student once shared with me that her peers were a "microwave generation." She said that they had never been taught to cook, so they buy and learn to use a microwave, purchase pre-packaged meals, read the heating instructions, and let the microwave do the rest. The result is they get a cooked meal but have no knowledge of the ingredients, whether the meal is healthy or not, and they only cook for themselves. Food becomes a personal energy source, not an opportunity for preparing and sharing food or life with others. Teaching theology can be done that way too. We can give our students numerous recipes for cooking a theological meal, help them to prepare it, but never invite them to dinner, or, we can hand them pre-packaged meals prepared by someone else and teach them to follow the directions while assuring them that they won't go hungry.

But, if we teach our students to cook, they learn to read the recipes carefully, handle and mix the ingredients, discovering that taste and texture are as important as measurements, while valuing the time and effort it takes to prepare a meal. Most importantly, they realize that they are not just cooking for themselves, but cooking is an experience meant to be shared with others. If cooking is more than knowing recipes and preparing food, then theology is more than knowing doctrines and being able to defend them. As C. S. Lewis wrote, "One cannot always be defending the truth, at some point you must feed on it."[19]

Perhaps this culinary metaphor could open up an opportunity for us to imagine with our students what God's purposes were for the Passover and the Eucharist. I often ask my students, since God is really smart and He could have commanded so many different ways for us to remember and experience our life in Christ as a covenant people,

---

[19] C. S. Lewis, "Reflections on the Psalms," in *The Inspirational Writings of C. S. Lewis* (New York: Inspirational Press, 1987), 136.

why did he, in both the OT and NT, command a ritual meal as a core experience for His people to embody their faith? Why is eating such a powerful, sensory, and spiritual experience in scripture? Is eating a meal one of God's ways to remind us that we are knowers and not just thinkers? Is this practice a way of engaging our imaginations as we seek to know and understand Him? What analogies could we employ that would help communicate that taking the Eucharistic bread and wine is an act of worship that helps us to see the world, to make our way in the world, and to interpret and find meaning amidst the chaos and difficulties of life? Does Jesus want us to continually re-enact the Eucharist as a way of reminding ourselves about who He is, what He did on our behalf, who we are, what our life is about and how he is present with us?

RE-ENCHANTING THE GOSPEL

In addition to creating a compelling metaphor, we must also explore ways to re-enchant the gospel. When I speak with my students about the Bible and, in particular, the Gospel accounts, I often ask why they believe we should read, study, and understand scripture. I usually get one or both of the following responses: the Bible is devotional material for maintaining a vital relationship with God or the Bible is apologetical material for defending your faith against moral relativism, post-modern skepticism, or atheistic evolution. So, for many of my students, the Bible is either a personalized spiritual source for emotional and psychological comfort or a set of propositional, evidential arguments or proofs for defending their faith. Though personal spiritual growth and apologetics are legitimate ways for utilizing the biblical story, both of these responses may be representative of a more modern, disenchanted, and "disembedded" spirituality.

Charles Taylor argued in his book, *Modern Social Imaginaries*, that modernity disenchanted the world by eclipsing it of magic forces and spirits. He furthered argued that this disenchantment was one of the unintended products of the Reformation that later became one of the primary characteristics of modernity's desire to render society "more peaceful, ordered and industrious."[20] But, more importantly, Taylor linked this process of disenchantment to the "disembedding

---

[20] Charles Taylor, *Modern Social Imaginaries* (Durham, NC: Duke University Press, 2004), 49.

of individuals" or the "Great Disembedding" as he referred to it.[21] The "Great Disembedding" occurs when the modern person sees herself "as primordially an individual, that is, the human agent of Western modernity" disembedded from any transcendent notion of the social order, the cosmos, or human flourishing,[22] So, when my students view the Bible as primarily a means of personal spiritual growth and/or apologetics, are they communicating how disconnected and disembedded they are from the Bible's primary purpose?

The Bible's central claim is that it tells the true story about us and our world. It is the true story about the God who created and sustains the world and our relationship with this God and the world. Isn't the biblical narrative intended to be the lens through which we see and understand that God is the source of all reality? To paraphrase Lewis, is the biblical narrative meant to be that which we see, or is it meant to be that through which we see and understand everything else?[23]

In particular, how do we read and understand the Gospel? The Gospel tells us about Jesus, the God/man who is the very core and foundation of all Christian theology. Can we truly read the Gospel without engaging our imaginations? I mean, reflect on the last time you read the Gospel. When you read the Gospel accounts you are continually challenged to navigate a world that at times seems very foreign. In fact, it seems pretty clear that what was happening was foreign for Jesus's disciples as well. They kept asking Jesus and each other, what does this mean? We don't understand! We're confused! It sounds like Jesus's life and work kept them off balance and uncertain about where things were going, about what to expect next.

Have we inadvertently facilitated the disenchanting and disembedding of the Gospel by translating the events and stories of Jesus into the particular facts, details, and doctrines of Christian theology as a way of restoring the lack of balance and familiar narrative we sometimes lose when reading them? And, in doing so, have we eliminated the need for having our imaginations redeemed in order for us to see the new kingdom Jesus is creating? Has the Gospel become that which we see, rather than that through which we see

---

[21] Taylor, *Modern Social Imaginaries*, 50.

[22] Taylor, *Modern Social Imaginaries*, 61.

[23] C. S. Lewis, "The Weight of Glory," in *The Weight of Glory and Other Addresses*, ed. by Walter Hooper (New York: Harper Collins, 2001), 140.

everything else? If these observations are at all accurate, how would we go about re-enchanting the Gospel?

C.S. Lewis and J.R.R. Tolkien shared a very insightful understanding of the Gospel, an understanding that prevented the Gospel from becoming disenchanted. In October 1931, Lewis wrote a letter to his friend Arthur Greeves in which he described a conversation he had with Tolkien and Hugo Dyson, a conversation that opened the way for Lewis to become a Christ follower.[24] Lewis explained that he was stymied by his inability to understand the doctrine of the atonement. He said that he could believe the doctrine as referring to Christ's death on the cross, but he still could not understand what it meant. How could the death of someone two thousand years ago possibly help anyone here and now? Tolkien helped Lewis to see that there was a difference between what his reason could grasp, the death of Jesus on the cross, and what only his imagination could grasp, the meaning and significance of Jesus's death. Tolkien encouraged Lewis to read the Gospel in the same manner that he read the great pagan myths with his imagination open to the story's power to communicate the deeper structures of reality. Tolkien reminded Lewis of myth's power to awaken imaginatively in us a longing for something that lies beyond the grasp of reason.

In order to explain a myth's power Tolkien invented the word *eucatastrophe* to describe the ultimate triumph at the end of a fairy tale or great myth. He ended his essay "On Fairy Stories" with an epilogue that connected myth to Christianity.

> The Gospels contain a fairy story, or a story of a larger kind which embraces all the   essence of fairy-stories. They contain many marvels . . .. But this story has entered History and the primary world; the desire and aspiration of sub-creation has been raised to the fulfillment of Creation. The Birth of Christ is the eucatastrophe of Man's history. The Resurrection is the eucatastrophe of the story of the Incarnation. This story begins and ends in joy. It has pre-eminently the "inner consistency of reality." There is no tale ever told that men would rather find was true, and none which so many skeptical men have accepted as true on its own merits . . .. It is not difficult to imagine the peculiar excitement and joy that one would feel, if any specially beautiful fairy-story were found to be "primarily" true, its narrative to be history, without thereby necessarily losing the

---

[24] Lewis, *Collected Letters*, 1:975.

mythical or allegorical significance that it had possessed . . ..
It looks forward (or backward: the direction in this regard is
unimportant) to the Great Eucatastrophe. The Christian joy,
the Gloria, is of the same kind; but it is preeminently (infinitely,
if our capacity were not finite) high and joyous. But this story is
supreme; and it is true. Art has been verified. God is the Lord,
of angels, and of men—and of elves. Legend and History have
met and fused.[25]

Lewis also believed that myth had the power to generate
imaginative appeal, to provide a narrative framework for making
sense of things, and to help us hold a more complex vision of reality
together as a coherent whole. It was in these ways that Lewis came to
realize that the Gospel was God's great myth, God's true story about
the world and all of humanity. As he wrote to Greeves in 1931, "The
story of Christ is simply a true myth: a myth working on us in the
same way as the others, but with this tremendous difference that it
really happened."[26]

In 1949, Lewis wrote an essay entitled, *Myth Became Fact*. In this
essay he explained how important it was that we not cease to think of
Christianity as the great myth that explained all other myths.

Now as myth transcends thought, incarnation transcends
myth. The heart of Christianity is a myth which is also a fact.
The old myth of the dying god, without ceasing to be myth,
comes down from the heaven of legend and imagination to
the earth of history. It happens—at a particular date, in a
particular place, followed by definable historical consequences.
We pass from a Balder or an Osiris, dying nobody knows when
or where, to a historical person crucified (it is all in order)
under Pontius Pilate. By becoming fact it does not cease to
be myth: that is the miracle . . .. To be truly Christian we
must both assent to the historical fact and also receive the
myth (fact though it has become) with the same imaginative
embrace which we accord to all myths. The one is hardly more
necessary than the other . . .. Those who do not know that this
great myth became fact when the Virgin conceived are, indeed,
to be pitied. But Christians also need to be reminded—we may
thank Corineus for reminding us—that what became fact was

---

[25] J. R. R. Tolkien, "On Fairy Stories," in *The Monsters and the Critics
and Other Essays*, ed. by Christopher Tolkien (London: George Allen and
Unwin, 1983), 23-4.

[26] Lewis, *Collected Letters*, 1:977.

a myth, that it carries with it into the world of fact all the properties of a myth. God is more than a god, not less; Christ is more than Balder, not less. We must not be ashamed of the mythical radiance resting on our theology. We must not be nervous about "parallels" and "pagan Christs": they ought to be there—it would be a stumbling block if they weren't.[27]

If we are to re-enchant the Gospel, we must find a way to reengage student's imaginations with the story, with the great myth that is also fact. When we teach the doctrines of the faith we must be sure that students understand that doctrines are theories, concepts, and ideas that the church has abstracted from the Gospel story. They are the stated truths of our faith, yes, but they are not the reality of our faith. As H. A. Williams wrote in his book *Tensions*, "Our doctrines are not photographs of Reality. They are the attempted description of heavenly things by means of the hints and guesses which earthly things provide."[28] God as the incarnated, crucified, and resurrected Lord Jesus Christ is the reality. The Gospel of Jesus Christ is the Christian myth that not only demands that we think about the truths of the story but that we embrace the story, that we embody the life of Christ and live the story.

THE ROLE OF DESIRE IN THEOLOGICAL LEARNING/LIVING

If our students are in fact embodied actors and not disembodied thinkers, then we must find ways to develop their theological imaginations, but we must also, and perhaps more importantly, communicate to them a vision of theology as desiring God.

In volume two of his two-volume *Cultural Liturgies*, James K. A. Smith uses the following quote from the work of William Cavanaugh. "How does a provincial farm boy become persuaded that he must travel as a soldier to another part of the world to kill people he knows nothing about?"[29] Smith's response to this question serves in many ways as the essential thesis for the remainder of his book. He argues

---

[27] C. S. Lewis, "Myth Became Fact," in *The Grand Miracle and Other Selected Essays on Theology and Ethics from God in the Dock*, ed. by Walter Hooper (New York: Ballantine, 1970), 41-2.

[28] H. A. Williams, *Tensions: Necessary Conflicts in Life and Love* (Springfield, IL: Templegate, 1976), 63-5.

[29] James K. A. Smith, *Imagining the Kingdom: How Worship Works, Volume 2: Cultural Liturgies* (Grand Rapids: Baker, 2013), 16-19.

that the farm boy is not convinced, argued, or compelled by an idea, concept, or theory. Rather, he enlists for an ideal, but not one that he knows on a cognitive level, but one that he loves. He has been conscripted into a mythology. He is not persuaded in the regions of his intellect but rather on the register of his imagination. Mythologies, the great stories that claim to give the fundamental truth about the deep meaning and structures of the world, do their work on us by recruiting the imagination through the body. They primarily work in the realm of desire. As Smith will argue, "we are what we love precisely because we do what we love."[30]

We could perhaps easily substitute the following examples in Cavanaugh's question:

> "How does a 19-year-old college sophomore become persuaded by Isis that he must travel as a soldier to Syria to kill people he knows nothing about?"

> "How does a 20-year-old college junior become persuaded that she must travel to India to serve outcasts she knows nothing about?"

In each of these examples what is operating is a mythology driven by a pedagogy of desire. I would argue that the Gospel narratives are also driven by a pedagogy of desire. In his essay, *The Weight of Glory*, C. S. Lewis wrote the following regarding the New Testament's appeal to desire.

> The New Testament has lots to say about self-denial, but not about self-denial as an end in itself. We are told to deny ourselves and to take up our crosses in order that we may follow Christ; and nearly every description of what we shall ultimately find if we do so contains an appeal to desire. If there lurks in most modern minds the notion that to desire our own good and earnestly to hope for the enjoyment of it is a bad thing, I submit that this notion has crept in from Kant and the Stoics and is no part of the Christian faith. Indeed, if we consider the unblushing promises of reward and the staggering nature of the rewards promised in the Gospels, it would seem that Our Lord finds our desires, not too strong, but too weak. We are half-hearted creatures, fooling about with drink and sex and ambition when infinite joy is offered us, like an ignorant child who wants to go on making mud pies in a slum because he

---

[30] Smith, *Imagining the Kingdom*, 12.

cannot imagine what is meant by the offer of a holiday at the sea. We are far too easily pleased.[31]

Lewis argued in *Mere Christianity* that unfulfilled desire or longing was an indication, a sign that we were created for a greater purpose and a reality other than the one we imagined.

> If I find in myself a desire which no experience in this world can satisfy, the most probable explanation is that I was made for another world. If none of my earthly pleasures satisfy it, that does not prove that the universe is a fraud. Probably earthly pleasures were never meant to satisfy it, but only to arouse it, to suggest the real thing. If that is so, I must take care, on the one hand, never to despise, or be unthankful for, these earthly blessings, and on the other, never to mistake them for the something else of which they are only a kind of copy, or echo, or mirage.[32]

For Lewis, the presence of this desire and the ways in which mythologies awakened this desire in us is not an argument per se as much as it is an observation of the human condition. His appeal is not to cold logic as it is to intuition and imagination, as though he is asking us to stop and consider the source of this desire that cannot be fulfilled by anything on this earth. Lewis's particular apologetical style is directly connected to his observations regarding desire and his understanding of the Gospel as the true myth that awakens imaginatively in us a longing for something that lies beyond the grasp of reason alone. The Gospel is God's grand story that has the power to generate imaginative appeal, to provide a narrative framework for making sense of things, and to help us hold a more complex vision of reality as a coherent whole.

Early in his Christian pilgrimage Lewis used more classical apologetical arguments like those found in *The Problem of Pain*, but eventually he shifted to a more narrative style (The *Lion, the Witch and the Wardrobe*) that appealed to the imagination as a way to awaken desire and curiosity. Alister McGrath has argued that Lewis preferred the narrative structure of myth because it

> weaves together truth and meaning, engaging with both our reason and our imagination . . .. Lewis's analysis of the

---

[31] Lewis, "The Weight of Glory," 25-26.

[32] C. S. Lewis, *Mere Christianity* (New York: Harper Collins, 2001), 136-7.

limits of reason makes it clear that we need more than rational arguments to challenge the 'spirit of the age'. If myth is 'caught,' it begins to work its magic of intellectual and moral transformation. In one sense, Lewis's apologetics can be seen as commending and offering counter-narrations rather than counter-arguments against the naturalism and secularism of our day . . .. For Lewis, Christian apologetics is thus at its best when it out-narrates the ideologies of the world.[33]

The Gospel of Jesus Christ is the grand counter-narrative that out-narrates all other myths. It is God's great myth that promises to fulfill our desires and longings for that which nothing in this world can satisfy. This narrative observation from desire offers the teacher of theology a ripe opportunity to talk with students about how we recognize and discern the difference between desire and addiction, between what is good and true and what counterfeits goodness and truth, to recognize and pursue that which makes us whole and to run from what will enslave us. Theology should help students recognize the difference between the desire for God and the desire for anything else that fills the place that only God can fill in their lives.

J. T. Sellars in his book, *Reasoning Beyond Reason*, explains the difference between desire and addiction by linking desire to the act of worship, because what we truly desire is what we will ultimately worship.

> Our longing for God has no end because God has no limits and thus our longing for God is completely inexhaustible, and yet we are never exhausted in our longing for God. But conversely, the search for temporal things merely wearies us and wastes our energies . . .. Addiction is the desire for the same thing over and over again; it is a form of identical repetition. Because of this desire for the same thing in endless repetition, it reduces us to a state in which there is no motion or development. This is what causes the addict's desire to be exhausting: it is because the attempted fulfillment of this desire is merely the renewal of that same desire; it is the attempt to fulfill the same desire to the exclusion of all other desires. This kind of desire is idolatrous precisely because it makes one material thing, for example a drug *(or pornography)* the thing that contains the whole Good. For Augustine, however, the true desire for God leads us to an infinite variety, and it does so because the meditation of God

---

[33] McGrath, *Intellectual World*, 73-4.

can never be exhausted . . .. It is by participation in the eternal desire of the Trinity that we are called to the non-identical, non-repetitious, never exhausting praise of God.[34]

Theology should help our students see a God who not only desires them but a God who has created them to desire Him. Theology should help them see and understand the Gospel as the great "Myth Become Fact" told by a God who became one of us and who is continually drawing us to Himself, wooing us in order that He might love us and fulfill our heart's deepest longings.

If we teach Christian theology as primarily theological theories, concepts, creeds, doctrines, and propositional statements regarding the nature of God, will we miss the very real possibility that our students are more pulled by their desires than pushed by their beliefs? Will we miss that they will become what they love, and that the path to their hearts is through their imaginations as the way they understand and make their way in the world? Will we fail to equip our students with the discernment and wisdom they need to recognize the false mythologies that seek to capture their hearts in order to enslave them? We must find better ways to teach Christian theology as a counter-narrative that engages our student's imaginations, appeals to their desire, and out-narrates the competing theologies, ideologies, and mythologies of the world.

A SCHOOL OF TRANSLATION?

What would it mean to join C. S. Lewis's "School of Translation"? As teachers of theology, what would this membership require of us? If teaching/translating theology is to be effective and, more importantly, transformative, we must recapture the critical role that imagination and desire play in the learning process. But the prerequisite to this task will be reassessing our philosophical anthropology regarding our students. Do we believe that we are teaching/translating for "embodied actors" or "disembodied thinkers"?

Membership will also require us to ask numerous questions regarding the role of imagination in teaching theology. Do we teach theology in a way that engages student's imaginations? Do we teach theology as an embodied and embedded way of living, thinking, and communicating God in the world? Or, do we primarily teach

---

[34] J. T. Sellars, *Reasoning Beyond Reason: Imagination as a Theological Source in the Work of C. S. Lewis* (Eugene, OR: Pickwick, 2011), 93-5.

theology as a set of doctrinal propositions about God, theories for explaining God's work in the world, a discipline for engaging the mind but not the body, the intellect but not the emotions? If we teach as though rationality is essentially disembodied thinking, will our theology present a God who ceases to be incarnational? We must remind ourselves that Christian theology is a dynamic process God uses to transform both our thinking and our living, not primarily an intellectual activity whereby we systematically categorize our observations and ideas about God.

Assuming that our students are embodied actors, teaching theology in a manner that engages and develops their imaginations will also require us to reconnect theological ideas with theological practices. Christianity is a lived faith, not just a believed faith. If our students are to grasp this relationship between believing and living their faith, they will need more compelling and helpful metaphors, but, more importantly, they will need us to help them re-enchant the Gospel of Jesus Christ. Re-enchanting the Gospel will be no easy task for those of us who have, for years, been inadvertently disenchanting the Gospel by primarily translating the stories and events of Jesus into particular facts, details, and doctrines. Like Lewis, we may need to reconsider the power of Christianity as the great myth that is also fact, the great myth that generates an imaginative appeal and provides a narrative framework for making sense of things.

Finally, if we are to join Lewis's "School of Translation," we must devote ourselves to the great task of communicating to our students a vision of theology as desiring God. Whether teaching or writing, this task was foremost in Lewis's mind and heart. He wanted those who heard his lectures and or read his books to both meet and know God. Theology should help our students see a God who not only desires them but a God who has created them to desire Him. Theology should help them to see and understand the Gospel as the great "Myth Become Fact" told by a God who became one of us and who is continually drawing us to Himself, wooing us in order that He might love us and fulfill our heart's deepest longings.

But then, Lewis the teacher/translator said it best,

> We must not, in false spirituality, withhold our imaginative welcome. If God chooses to be mythopoeic—and is not the sky itself a myth—shall we refuse to be mythopathic? For this is the marriage of heaven and earth: perfect myth and perfect fact: claiming not only our love and our obedience, but also our

wonder and delight, addressed to the savage, the child, and the poet in each one of us no less than to the moralist, the scholar, and the philosopher.[35]

---

[35] Lewis, "Myth Became Fact," 42.

Chapter 15

A HOLY GRIEF:
THE PILGRIM'S PATH TO CONSOLATION

Monika B. Hilder

Few experiences challenge our faith in God's loving character as much as suffering. "Where is God when it hurts?" we cry out. Yet even in our deepest pain, perhaps we often manage to affirm God's goodness and the hope of ultimate redemption in spite of our brokenness. But in those very darkest places, does our faith console? alleviate our sorrow? Can rational affirmation of faith truly comfort us in grief? heal doubt and despair? prevent emotional breakdown—or, after breakdown, lead to restoration? In *A Grief Observed* in 1961, C. S. Lewis's first-person account of suffering following the death of his wife Joy Davidman, the speaker puts the dilemma this way: "Talk to me about the truth of religion and I'll listen gladly. Talk to me about the duty of religion and I'll listen submissively. But don't come talking to me about the consolations of religion or I shall suspect that you don't understand."[1]

In his earlier work, *The Problem of Pain*, in 1940, Lewis's sole purpose, he explained, was "to solve the intellectual problem raised by suffering," not to attempt "the far higher task of teaching fortitude and patience [which he] was never fool enough to suppose [him] self qualified."[2] Thomas Talbot esteems this volume as "an excellent example of 'faith seeking understanding,'" and possibly "Lewis's most successful apologetic work."[3] Here, as in many other works,

---

[1] C. S. Lewis, *A Grief Observed* (New York: Bantam, 1976), 28. Lewis published the work under the pseudonym N. W. Clerk. Thomas Talbot emphasizes that the book is Lewis's own account of grief in journal form, not, as some have suggested, a work of fiction. Thomas Talbot, "A Grief Observed," in *The C. S. Lewis Readers' Encyclopedia*, ed. by Jeffrey D. Schultz and John G. West, Jr. (Grand Rapids: Zondervan, 1998), 194. It might be observed too that Lewis had first hoped to publish *The Problem of Pain* anonymously (Preface vii).

[2] C. S. Lewis, *The Problem of Pain* (London: Collins, 1975), vii.

[3] Thomas Talbot, "The Problem of Pain," in *The C. S. Lewis Readers' Encyclopedia*, ed. by Jeffrey D. Schultz and John G. West, Jr. (Grand Rapids: Zondervan, 1998), 339. Michael Ward, on the other hand, states

Lewis as apologist explained the correct cognitive answers of faith. And as Gary R. Habermas helpfully argues, Lewis was a "veteran" in countering emotional doubt with disciplined reason. Habermas, reading Lewis through the lens of the cognitive behavior theory of Rational Emotive Behavior Therapy, points to Lewis's practice of "[p]roper thinking [which] trumps undisciplined emotions."[4] He cites Lewis's observation in *Mere Christianity*: "Unless you teach your moods 'where they get off,' you can never be either a sound Christian or even a sound atheist, but just a creature dithering to and fro, with its beliefs really dependent on the weather and the state of its digestion."[5]

But to what extent does right thinking trump dark emotions? To what extent does propositional truth give relief when we undergo soul travail—the "dark night of the soul"? Perhaps even more to the point, to what extent does other people's theological reasoning help us in our own times of grief? In *The Problem of Pain*, beyond rational explanation of suffering, Lewis claims that he has nothing to offer his readers "except [his] conviction that when pain is to be borne, a little courage helps more than much knowledge, a little human sympathy more than much courage, and the least tincture of the love of God more than all."[6] And in later life, after Joy's struggle with cancer, Lewis in *A Grief Observed* responds to sorrow not with reason alone but also from inside the emotional experience of grief.[7] This time he speaks not as the apologist with the right answers but as the widower in anguish:

---

that here "Lewis was still learning his craft as an apologist" and regards it "as easily his least adroit venture into the field." Michael Ward, "On suffering," in *The Cambridge Companion to C. S. Lewis*, ed. by Robert MacSwain and Michael Ward (Cambridge: Cambridge University Press, 2010), 210.

[4] Gary R. Habermas, "C. S. Lewis and Emotional Doubt: Insights from the Philosophy of Psychology," in *C. S. Lewis as Philosopher: Truth, Goodness, and Beauty*, ed. by David Baggett, Gary R. Habermas, and Jerry L. Walls (Downers Grove: InterVarsity Press, 2008), 110.

[5] C. S. Lewis, *Mere Christianity*, rev. ed. (New York: Macmillan, 1952), 122-3; quoted in Habermas, "C. S. Lewis and Emotional Doubt," 105.

[6] Lewis, *Problem of Pain*, viii.

[7] Talbot speaks of this work as a record of "the internal war raging between [Lewis's] intellect and his feelings." Talbot, "A Grief Observed," 194.

No one ever told me that grief felt so like fear . . .. The same fluttering in the stomach, the same restlessness, the yawning. I keep on swallowing. At other times it feels like being mildly drunk, or concussed. There is a sort of invisible blanket between the world and me. I find it hard to take in what anyone says. Or perhaps, hard to want to take it in . . .. Meanwhile, where is God?[8]

Is Lewis's heartfelt exploration of his experience of grief over Joy's death a more compelling or even a more accurate picture of "the problem of pain" than his earlier theological book by that title?[9]

Certainly, and rightly, we can agree with Lewis's argument in *The Problem of Pain* that the "problem" of suffering is rooted in basic longings for a measure of health, wealth, and especially human love, ideals which, in a fallen world, can only at best be transient experiences. Lest we forget, pain functions as God's "megaphone," a terrible wake-up shout "to rouse a deaf world"[10] to the fact that this broken planet is not our true home. Corrected, repeatedly, we admit to undue perceptions of entitlement to earthly happiness. Further bereft with each new wounding, we ache more acutely with "the inconsolable wound with which man is born,"[11] "the inconsolable secret" that is rooted in "[the] desire for our own far-off country."[12] But how does this true dogma help us when we have loved and lost, when grief because we love overwhelms us like a tidal wave—inexorable, unrelenting, seemingly all-powerful? There is a marked difference, is there not, between the will to affirm faith and heart-felt consolation.

---

[8] Lewis, *Grief Observed*, 1, 4.

[9] Chad Walsh referred to the sense of "patness" in *The Problem of Pain*. Chad Walsh, "Afterword," in C. S. Lewis, *A Grief Observed* (New York: Bantam, 1976), 127. Talbot, however, points to the consistency of Lewis's darkest thoughts in *A Grief Observed* with the theology he wrote about in *The Problem of Pain*, the difference being the shift from commentator to sufferer. Talbot, "A Grief Observed," 194. Similarly, Ward argues that the anguish expressed in *A Grief Observed* is not qualitatively different from what Lewis expressed in *The Problem of Pain* and in earlier writings, "although . . . the degree to which [he] takes [this] is indeed unprecedented." Ward, "On suffering," 215.

[10] Lewis, *Problem of Pain*, 81.

[11] C. S. Lewis, *That Hideous Strength: A Modern Fairy-Tale for Grown-Ups* (New York: Scribner, 2003), 320.

[12] C. S. Lewis, "The Weight of Glory," in *The Weight of Glory and other Addresses* (Grand Rapids, MI: Eerdmans, 1977), 4.

The question might be put like this: how does rational knowledge help us when our deepest need is to meet "God with skin on"?[13] In particular, what emotional consolation, if any, does C. S. Lewis offer the hurting pilgrim?

C. S. Lewis's response to suffering, both rational and emotional, is anything but glib. Lewis described himself as "a great coward"[14] and underscored the gap in his own life between intellectual assent to faith and the lived experience of courage. In his words, ". . . I asked leave to be allowed to write [this book] anonymously, since, if I were to say what I really thought about pain, I should be forced to make statements of such apparent fortitude that they would become ridiculous if anyone knew who made them."[15] In a letter to Arthur Greeves in 1949 he wrote, "Don't imagine I doubt for a moment that what God sends us must be sent in love and will all be for the best if we have grace to use it so. My *mind* doesn't waver on this point: my *feelings* sometimes do."[16] Honest about the conflict between reason and emotion, perhaps especially in times of sorrow, Lewis chooses to respond to suffering with the biblical vision of grief that becomes holy—"set apart," dedicated to God, on pilgrimage to purity. Unlike despair, which is focused on the self, holy grief is not without hope (1 Thessalonians 4:13) but willingly enters "the fellowship of Christ's sufferings" (Philippians 3:10, 1 Peter 4:13). Grief like this, Lewis writes in *Letters to Malcolm*, is "our share in the Passion of Christ,"[17] and as Michael Ward argues, the epigraph to *The Problem of Pain*, a line from George MacDonald, best summarizes Lewis's position on suffering: "The Son of God suffered unto the death, not that men might not suffer, but that their sufferings might be like His."[18] Holy grief, in its surrender to God, becomes the pilgrim's path to consolation (Romans

---

[13] Pastor Greg Laurie retells the story of the frightened little boy who said to his father, "I know God loves me, but right now, I need somebody with skin on." Greg Laurie, "God with Skin On," 21 January 2008. https://www.crosswalk.com/devotionals/harvestdaily/greg-laurie-daily-devotion-jan-21-2008-11565177.html

[14] Lewis, *Problem of Pain*, 93.

[15] Lewis, *Problem of Pain*, vii.

[16] C. S. Lewis, *The Collected Letters of C. S. Lewis*, ed. by Walter Hooper, 3 vols. (New York: HarperCollins, 2004-7), 2:953.

[17] C. S. Lewis, *Letters to Malcolm: Chiefly on Prayer* (London: HarperCollins, 1977), 44.

[18] Lewis, *Problem of Pain*, 208.

5:3-5). Like his mentor MacDonald, who embraced the biblical view that sorrow humbly embraced becomes the means to understanding and the path to Joy,[19] Lewis counseled that in our acceptance of the means by which God chooses to break our hearts, and in the offering of these sufferings to Him, "[w]e shall draw nearer to God."[20]

C. S. Lewis's theological writings on suffering remain profound and truly helpful. Yet perhaps his greatest gift to us in our sorrows comes through his fiction. Stories, we are told, are "good things to think with"; certainly they are better things to feel with and therefore remember.[21] When the disciples asked Jesus why he told stories, he replied, "to create readiness, to nudge the people toward receptive insight" (Matthew 13:13, *The Message*). So too Lewis's stories create a space in which we might hear and see—because we first feel, we could receive and be changed. For when we weep with Digory in *The Magician's Nephew*, sail to the Dark Island of nightmares in *The Voyage of the "Dawn Treader*," and break our hearts with Orual in *Till We Have Faces*, then we are on our way toward discovering with our whole person—intellect, emotion, and spirit—what we truly believe. In the process we are being prepared to learn at the deepest level how grief might become holy.

In *The Problem of Pain*, Lewis concurs that "the world is indeed a 'vale of soul making'" and names the virtues that ought to arise out of suffering: "fortitude, patience, pity and forgiveness."[22] But in his fiction, he shows readers how this can be so. True to his convictions over his own inadequacies and of the ineffectiveness of human reason to heal pain, Lewis does not come talking to us about the consolations of religion. Instead, seasoned pilgrim,[23] humbled through sorrow and

---

[19] "Joy cannot unfold the deepest truths, although deepest truth must be deepest joy. Cometh white-robed Sorrow, stooping and wan, and flingeth wide the doors she may not enter. Almost we linger with Sorrow for very love"; "Past tears are present strength." George MacDonald, *Phantastes* (Grand Rapids, MI: Eerdmans, 2000), 67, 149.

[20] C. S. Lewis, *The Four Loves* (London: Collins, 1974), 112.

[21] Kieran Egan, "The Origins of Imagination and the Curriculum," refers to Levi-Strauss (1962) in describing stories as "*bonnes à penser*" in *Imagination and Education*, ed. by Kieran Egan and Dan Nadamer (New York: Teachers College Press, 1988), 93, 104

[22] Lewis, *Problem of Pain*, vii, 96, 99.

[23] Ward comments that with the combination of Lewis's experiences of the First World War, the loss of his mother at the age of nine, and his boarding school experience with a sadistic headmaster who was later

desirous of holiness, Lewis walks alongside us in grief, and thereby helps us to a little more courage, even more human sympathy, and a far greater experience of the love of God than we might have guessed possible. While Lewis did not feel qualified to teach fortitude and patience in response to suffering in an objective sense, we might say that he triumphs in doing so through portraying the subjective experiences of suffering in his fiction. (And indeed, he thought of stories as often being smarter than their authors.[24]) He succeeds because while grief often numbs our capacity to experience the emotion of consolation, the imaginative power of fiction nonetheless allows us to enter inside. In other words, Lewis the imaginative artist does for us what we cannot do for ourselves. Like a suffering servant who helps to bear our burdens,[25] Lewis articulates what silences us, sees what we have trouble seeing, believes where we doubt, remembers what we have forgotten, and so carries us over rapids too swift for us. As he acknowledges, "the rule of the universe [is] that others can do for us what we cannot do for ourselves and one can paddle every canoe *except* one's own."[26] Lewis paddles our canoe when we cannot, and through the strength that he has received steers us homeward.

Imagery of suffering abounds in Lewis's fiction, and I will draw attention to a few examples of how he portrays affliction, subsequent comfort, and ultimate healing, and thereby encourages his readers on the pilgrimage of holy grief that leads to consolation.

AFFLICTION

Affliction is acute in Lewis's stories, and no respecter of age, social class, or life circumstances. In the Chronicles of Narnia, Lewis often portrays the anguish of innocent children. *The Magician's Nephew* opens with the heart-rending sorrow of the boy Digory Kirke facing the probable death of his mother, a sorrow compounded by

---

certified insane, "meant that before he was twenty years old, Lewis had been subject to pains that many people would be unlikely to encounter in a lifetime." Ward, "On suffering," 203.

[24] In a letter to Sister Penelope Lewis wrote, "Because of those divine meanings in our materials it is impossible we shd. ever know the whole meaning of our own works, and the meaning we never intended may be the best and truest one." Letter of 20 February 1943, in Lewis, *Collected Letters*, 2:555.

[25] See Isaiah 53:4.

[26] Lewis, *Collected Letters*, 2:953.

THE UNDISCOVERED C. S. LEWIS

uprooting through the absence of his father in India and leaving his delightful country estate home to live in "a beastly Hole" in London with Aunt Letty and "mad" Uncle Andrew Ketterley.[27] *The Silver Chair* opens with Jill Pole weeping in response to school bullying.[28] *The Horse and his Boy* opens with the kidnapped boy Shasta living the life of a slave, often beaten, not knowing his identity (Prince Cor), and fleeing Calormen to escape future cruelty. *Prince Caspian* shows the crown prince needing to flee for his life or be killed by his treacherous uncle Miraz.

Lewis also shows how characters are to some extent complicit with and therefore increase the sufferings they undergo. In *That Hideous Strength* Mark and Jane Studdock illustrate how pride with its selfish ambition and lack of care for the other can lead to marital strain and potential break-up. In the case of Mark, through his career goals combined with weak moral convictions (of whom the narrator says, "God forgive him, for he was young and shy and vain and timid, all in one"[29]), he comes close to losing his life and very soul over the empty promises of societal power.[30] In *Till We Have Faces*, pride's response to pain is likewise shown to be soul-killing. We follow the heart-broken young Princess Orual from when she first understands that her father views her as ugly, and so of little value in his chauvinist eyes, through her many years of believing that in this ruthless culture the gods have withheld happiness from her. As queen, Orual chooses to conquer pain by distancing herself from it:

> I locked Orual up or laid her asleep as best I could somewhere deep down inside me; she lay curled there. It was like being with child, but reversed; the thing I carried in me grew slowly smaller and less alive.[31]

But in her quest for autonomy from the gods and humanity, from further suffering and from her very self, in what Lewis correspondingly

---

[27] C. S. Lewis, *The Magician's Nephew* (Harmondsworth: Puffin, 1975), 9-10.

[28] C. S. Lewis, *The Silver Chair* (Harmondsworth: Puffin, 1975), 11-12.

[29] Lewis, *Strength*, 53.

[30] See my discussion of Mark and Jane Studdock in chapter four of *The Gender Dance: Ironic Subversion in C. S. Lewis's Cosmic Trilogy* (New York: Peter Lang, 2013).

[31] C. S. Lewis, *Till We Have Faces: A Myth Retold* (New York: Harcourt Brace Jovanovich, 1984), 226.

described in *The Four Loves* as "the casket or coffin of . . . selfishness" until "it will become unbreakable, impenetrable, irredeemable,"[32] Orual becomes the cruel leader she despised in her father, perhaps worse. While the context of her suffering was due to no fault of her own, her prideful response compounds sorrows and makes redemption as critical as it is unlikely but for the grace of God.

In his many portrayals of affliction, Lewis illustrates what he has described as God's "intolerant compliment of loving us."[33] The God who is Love, "the consuming fire Himself," is not nearly as interested in bringing about our earthly ideas of "'happiness'" as He is committed to making us perfect and therefore truly "lovable" for all eternity.[34] Lewis illustrates this in the significant pain that his characters endure on their journey to wholeness. In the case of Eustace in *The Voyage of the "Dawn Treader,"* the boy becomes trapped in a dragon's body, illustrative of his egotism, and it is only then, helpless and separated from all of humanity, that he begins to gain moral clarity and weeps bitterly over his condition.[35] With penitence, Eustace allows Aslan to "un-dragon" him, a process which involves more pain than any he has ever felt, and only after that is he perfectly well, and this for the first time in his life.[36] Similarly, with Aravis in *The Horse and his Boy,* Aslan wounds her[37] so that she might understand the sufferings she had thoughtlessly caused her stepmother's slave—"tear for tear, throb for throb, blood for blood."[38] Such pain is essential for her education out of prideful tyranny to true nobility. And in the case of Orual in *Till We Have Faces,* the aged queen, stripped naked of all her defenses, must suffer the bitter fruits of pride reaped over a lifetime before she is prepared to repent and be remade.

In Lewis, consolation does come to all of the afflicted characters who repent. But there is no easy path to this end, and such consolation challenges our concept(s) of comfort.

---

[32] Lewis, *The Four Loves*, 111.

[33] Lewis, *Problem of Pain*, 29.

[34] Lewis, *The Problem of Pain*, 35-6.

[35] C.S. Lewis, *The Voyage of the "Dawn Treader"* (Harmondsworth: Puffin, 1975), 83.

[36] Lewis, *Dawn Treader*, 96.

[37] See Proverbs 27:6.

[38] C.S. Lewis, *The Horse and his Boy* (Harmondsworth: Puffin, 1975), 123, 169.

COMFORT

Comfort—ah, what pleasantries the word "comfort" stirs in us. Perhaps, floating in the hammock on a sweet summer afternoon? Inner tranquility and family harmony that Mary Poppins would approve of? All health and wealth ducks lined up and no one there to interfere, preferably when the Mediterranean is a warm blue and within walking distance? Halt! Before we take another step into favorite daydreams, consider how Lewis critiqued our misunderstanding of the meaning of "comfort." He points to our Lord's agony in Gethsemane, during which an angel came to comfort Him (Luke 22:43). In Lewis's words,

> . . . we are told that an angel appeared 'comforting' him. But neither *comforting* in Sixteenth Century English nor . . . in Greek means 'consoling'. 'Strengthening' is more the word. May not the strengthening have consisted in the renewed certainty—cold comfort this—that the thing must be endured and therefore could be?"[39]

On a similar note, the Bayeux tapestry of 1066 depicts a knight on a horse prodding the troops to battle with a stick. The caption reads, "Bishop Odo comforts his troops."[40] Comfort, in the sense of ease? Hardly. To return to the Gospel record, after the angel strengthened our Lord, he "prayed more earnestly: and his sweat was as it were great drops of blood falling down to the ground" (Luke 22:44). Thus, comfort in the biblical sense is a strengthening cry to battle and possible martyrdom.

Lewis illustrates this concept of comfort in *The Horse and his Boy* when Shasta reaches the Hermit of the Southern March. Exhausted, Shasta asks the hermit if he is King Lune of Archenland, learns that he is not, and is dismayed that instead of finding rest and refreshment he must now run ahead on foot in great haste to reach King Lune. The narrator comments,

> Shasta's heart fainted at these words for he felt he had no strength left. And he writhed inside at what seemed the cruelty and unfairness of the demand. He had not yet learned that if you do one good deed your reward usually is to be set to do

---

[39] Lewis, *Letters to Malcolm*, 45.

[40] I am indebted to Sally Lloyd-Jones's devotion, "Comforter," on the Bayeux tapestry featuring Bishop Odo in *Thoughts to Make Your Heart Sing* (Grand Rapids, MI: Zondervan, 2012), 142-3.

another and harder and better one.[41]

While Shasta does heed the hermit's command to "run, run: always run[,]" he does so with shaking limbs, "a terrible stich . . . in his side," sweat blinding his eyes, "unsteady on his feet too," and weeping, complains to himself, "I *do* think that I must be the most unfortunate boy that ever lived in the whole world. Everything goes right for everyone except me."[42] Of course, willingness to meet hardship head-on is the very training Shasta needs. Through faithful courage, Shasta helps to save Archenland, meets and reveres the Lion behind all the stories, and is restored to his true identity, Prince Cor, son of King Lune. Shasta (Cor) recognizes that he cannot, slave-like as he was used to being, shirk the decisive call to do battle against the fierce Calormenes. Bravely, he tells himself, "If you funk this, you'll funk every battle all your life. Now or never[,]"[43] and so in time becomes the royal leader who is also a most dangerous opponent.[44] Consolation indeed, but only through the strange comfort of adversity that leads through suffering to perseverance to character to hope (Romans 5:3-5). Shasta's journey illustrates that while escape from physical slavery is desirable, to say the least, the bigger challenge is to renounce psychological slavery. In *Mere Christianity* Lewis puts it this way:

> Laziness means more work in the long run. Or look at it this way. In a battle, or in mountain climbing, there is often one thing which it takes a lot of pluck to do; but it is also, in the long run, the safest thing to do. If you funk it, you will find yourself, hours later, in far worse danger. The cowardly thing is also the most dangerous thing.[45]

Thus, comfort means strengthening for courageous battle. But when courage has been tried and failed, successively, what then? In *The Voyage of the "Dawn Treader,"* when the company encounters the Dark Island where one's worst nightmares seemingly come true, Lewis depicts our vulnerability to despair. On their voyage into the strange darkness, the company hears "a cry, either of some inhuman

---

[41] Lewis, *Horse and his Boy*, 124.

[42] Lewis, *Horse and his Boy*, 124, 130, 137.

[43] Lewis, *Horse and his Boy*, 157.

[44] Lewis, *Horse and his Boy*, 187. See my discussion of Shasta in *The Feminine Ethos in C. S. Lewis's* Chronicles of Narnia (New York: Peter Lang, 2012), 111-12.

[45] Lewis, *Mere Christianity*, 164.

voice or else a voice of one in such extremity of terror that he had almost lost his humanity."[46] The stranger whom they rescue from the waters is Lord Rhoop. His is the anguish that comes through extensive suffering in which one can no longer imagine that relief can come, or if come, could do any good. The outcome of such an ordeal is not fortitude and patience but panic and mental breakdown. Lord Rhoop, with a face "wild . . .. in an agony of pure fear[,]" cries for them to flee the darkness, and while Reepicheep, "unmoved[,]" advises chivalric bravery, Caspian shouts orders that the entire crew agrees with: "Row, row. Pull for all your lives . . .. *There are some things no man can face.*"[47] It is evident that Lewis does not, as some do, chide the despairing sufferer for not having "enough" or "proper faith." "[A]nxieties[,]" he writes, are "not sins" or "a defect of faith" but "afflictions," sufferings we endure as "our share in the Passion of Christ."[48] And Lewis portrays with compassion the relief that can come to the despairing: they must be rescued by merciful ones who are either stronger or have not been so tested, and once rescued they need the blessedness of utter rest.[49] In Lord Rhoop's case Lewis shows that a kindly welcome into human fellowship followed by amnesia at Aslan's Table, the blessed "forgetfulness of sleep,"[50] will do what no amount of reason and one's own will to faith can.

Alternatively, instead of despair in response to psychological battles, we may have the grace to counter fear with prayer—more easily done, as in Lucy's case, when the struggle is of brief duration. Lucy's whispered prayer near the Dark Island voices the desperation that accompanies dire circumstances: "Aslan, Aslan, if ever you loved us at all, send us help now."[51] Here, Lewis points to how lucid prayer, when we are still able to send it, changes our perception. Following Lucy's prayer, we read, "The darkness did not grow any less, but she began to feel a little—a very, very little—better." She comments, "After all, nothing has really happened to us yet."[52] When the light

---

[46] Lewis, *Dawn Treader*, 154.

[47] Lewis, *Dawn Treader*, 155-6; italics mine.

[48] Lewis, *Letters to Malcolm*, 44.

[49] Lewis, *Dawn Treader*, 182.

[50] Colin Duriez, *Bedeviled: Lewis, Tolkien, and the Shadow of Evil* (Downers Grove, IL: InterVarsity Press, 2015), 145.

[51] Lewis, *Dawn Treader*, 158.

[52] Lewis, *Dawn Treader*, 158.

that comes with the albatross broadens, the bird's "strong sweet voice" that sounds like Aslan's whispers to Lucy, "Courage, dear heart," and the vessel soon finds itself in full sunlight where "all at once everybody realized that there was nothing to be afraid of and never had been."[53] One's worst nightmares, when penetrated by God's light, vanish. While it is impossible to feel or think this is so when we are under their spell, Heaven is our one help. And whether we are afflicted by debilitating doubt or still able to wield the weapons of faith, the answer is always the same: Heaven is our one true help that makes all things well. In *A Grief Observed* Lewis puts it this way: "Heaven will solve our problems, but not, I think, by showing us subtle reconciliations between all our apparently contradictory notions. The notions will all be knocked from under our feet. We shall see that there never was any problem."[54] Meanwhile, the "Comforter," "the Spirit of truth" has been sent (John 14:17-17), and we are on pilgrimage to our true home.

THE HEALING OF HARMS

C. S. Lewis's detailed response to the problem of suffering is portrayed, for instance, in the last chapter of *The Silver Chair*, and summarized in its title, "The Healing of Harms." At the end of this story, after their successful rescue of Prince Rilian, Eustace and Jill return to Cair Paravel where Rilian will be reunited with his father Caspian. But the ailing king lives only long enough to bless his son, and instead of the anticipated joyous celebration, Narnia falls to mourning:

> . . . the great banner with the golden Lion on it was being brought down to half-mast. And after that, slowly, mercilessly, with wailing strings and disconsolate blowing of horns, the music began again: this time, a tune to break your heart.[55]

This is not a culture that has forgotten how to grieve, or wishes to minimize bereavement.[56] Instead, Lewis depicts how all the harm that comes to us, culminating with the terrible grief of separation

---

[53] Lewis, *Dawn Treader*, 159.

[54] Lewis, *Grief Observed*, 83.

[55] Lewis, *Silver Chair*, 200.

[56] One might wonder if the trend to view funerals as "celebrations of life" is to some extent connected with the failure to acknowledge legitimate grief and of the fear of death in an agnostic or atheistic "health and wealth" culture.

THE UNDISCOVERED C. S. LEWIS

through death, will be healed. First, Aslan appears to Jill and Eustace during Narnia's lamentation, and with his arrival they experience the meaning of his presence in relation to the experience of bereavement: "'I have come,' said a deep voice behind them. They turned and saw the Lion himself, so bright and real and strong that everything else began at once to look pale and shadowy compared with him."[57] The children long to return home, to England, and the Lion answers that he has come to take them "Home" with a capital "H," and first takes them to his own country.[58] Here, all that they have just experienced ("the ship and the dead King and the castle and the snow and the winter sky") vanishes "like wreaths of smoke" in the bright summer beauty of Aslan's Mountain.[59] What is grief, in relation to Aslan—a wisp of disappearing smoke? a nothing? Yes, and no.

Significantly, in Aslan's country, grief intensifies before it is overcome. The dead King Caspian is here on the Mountain, lying in a stream, and the funeral music increases to a "despairing" pitch.[60] All three weep, Aslan most of all, "great Lion tears, each tear more precious than the Earth would be if it was a single solid diamond."[61] The greater sorrow of the divine over death is likewise experienced by Digory in *The Magician's Nephew*, who senses that Aslan's "great shining tears" over the impending death of Digory's mother means that the Lion experiences profounder grief, a grief clearly borne out of far greater love.[62] As with Jesus who weeps just prior to raising Lazarus from the dead (John 11:35), the hope and knowledge of what is to come does not lessen or underestimate grief. Instead, Lewis shows that death is indeed "the last enemy *that* shall be destroyed" (I Corinthians 15:26). And on Aslan's Mountain Jill and Eustace experience the sacrifice that turns the terrible tide. It is only the Passion of Aslan, here through the wounding made by a foot-long thorn "sharp as a rapier[,]" that redeems death. Eustace must drive the thorn into Aslan's paw, illustrating how our sinfulness brought Christ to make His sacrifice, and when one drop of the Lion's blood, "redder than all redness that you have ever seen or imagined[,]" reaches

---

[57] Lewis, *Silver Chair*, 200.

[58] Lewis, *Silver Chair*, 201.

[59] Lewis, *Silver Chair*, 201.

[60] Lewis, *Silver Chair*, 201.

[61] Lewis, *Silver Chair*, 202.

[62] Lewis, *Magician's Nephew*, 131-2.

the dead body of Caspian, the mournful music ends and the Great Reversal begins:

> His white beard turned to grey, and from grey to yellow, and got shorter and vanished altogether; and his sunken cheeks grew round and fresh, and the wrinkles were smoothed, and his eyes opened, and his eyes and lips both laughed, and suddenly he leaped up and stood before them—a very young man, or a boy. (But Jill couldn't say which, because of people having no particular ages in Aslan's country.)[63]

The resurrected King Caspian is no ghost: he is now in his own country, Aslan's country,[64] and so is more alive than he was in Narnia. The old Narnia, like earth, is "the Shadowlands";[65] Aslan's country, like the Lion Himself, is the substantial, the real, the everlasting. When Eustace draws back from Caspian with some momentary fear, and the Lion confirms that Caspian has indeed died, adding, "Most people have, you know[,]" he speaks very quietly, "almost (Jill thought) as if he were laughing."[66] That the divine laughter is secret, unheard this side of death, is fitting. This side of the grave, grief is so great that we cannot (or can hardly) hear the greater divine laughter of ultimate cosmic wellness that is and is to come. Perhaps we might think of it as being so vast, so large, so loud, that we cannot hear it. Perhaps we might think of divine laughter in terms of the Medieval idea of the music of the spheres, "not heard because their singing is perpetual."[67] As Lewis said, "The music which is too familiar to be heard enfolds us day and night and in all ages."[68]

This "impossible possible" (Luke 18:27) joy of the Resurrection, that which turns deepest grief to strongest joy, is the healing of all harms that Lewis points to in his stories. For example, in *The Magician's Nephew*, when Aslan prophesizes to Digory and Polly about the tyrannies they will come to experience in their lifetime, their awareness of being in his presence means a surpassing connectedness with him: "the Lion's face . . ... seemed to be a sea of tossing gold in

---

[63] Lewis, *Silver Chair*, 202.

[64] Lewis, *Silver Chair*, 203.

[65] C. S. Lewis, *The Last Battle* (Harmondsworth: Puffin, 1975), 165.

[66] Lewis, *Silver Chair*, 203.

[67] Ward, *Planet Narnia*, 21.

[68] C. S. Lewis, *English Literature in the Sixteenth Century, Excluding Drama* (Oxford: Clarendon, 1954), 52; quoted in Ward, *Planet Narnia*, 21.

which they were floating." In this consciousness "such a sweetness and power" fills them that, for the rest of their lives, in spite of every future sorrow, fear, or anger, they are sure of ultimate wellness.[69] Before Aslan's country, in *The Voyage of the "Dawn Treader,"* the Lamb at the End of the World invites Edmund, Lucy, and Eustace to a delicious breakfast and changes into his familiar appearance as the Lion Aslan. While Lucy and Edmund wish they could remain with him, he assures them that they will live with him forever, that he will show them the way throughout their lives, and that meanwhile they must get to know him better in their own world, by his other name.[70] Joy, "the serious business of Heaven,"[71] is the thread the runs through every sorrow, and sorrows deepen our longing for and capacity for Joy. On pilgrimage, longing deepens maturity.

In *The Last Battle*, Jill and Eustace with King Tirian and the few remaining faithful friends of Narnia choose to fight what appears on most counts to be a losing battle in that country's apocalypse. But as the Calormene warrior Emeth insists when he has reached Aslan's country, in terror and in beauty the Lion "surpasse[s] all that is in the world," and therefore "it is better to see the Lion and die than to be Tisroc of the world and live and not to have seen him."[72] Everything the faithful have suffered, including martyrdom, proves more than worth it. Once through the darkness of death, Aslan's friends experience "the beginning of the real story . . . . Chapter One of the Great Story which no one on earth has read: which goes on forever: in which every chapter is better than the one before."[73] There "every rock and flower and blade of grass loo[k] as if it meant more," the company can run with limitless energy, and it is impossible to feel fear.[74] Their boundless joy is like that of the Ghost in chapter eleven of *The Great Divorce* when he transforms into "an immense man . . . not much smaller than the Angel[,]" his lizard changes into "the greatest stallion [the narrator has] ever seen," and the pair rides off "like a shooting star . . . .. bright themselves, into the rose-brightness of that

---

[69] Lewis, *Magician's Nephew*, 165.

[70] Lewis, *Dawn Treader*, 208-9.

[71] Lewis, *Letters to Malcolm*, 95.

[72] Lewis, *The Last Battle*, 148-9.

[73] Lewis, *The Last Battle*, 165.

[74] Lewis, *The Last Battle*, 154-6.

everlasting morning."[75]

In every story, written small or large, Lewis points to how death is undone. In *The Lion, the Witch and the Wardrobe*, the resurrected Aslan, who appears yet bigger than before he died, speaks to the Deeper Magic in which "Death itself start[s] working backwards."[76] In *The Great Divorce*, the spiritual guide in the character of George MacDonald counsels,

> both good and evil, when they are full grown, become retrospective. Not only this valley but all their earthly past will have been Heaven to those who are saved . . .. That is what mortals misunderstand. They say of some temporal suffering, 'No future bliss can make up for it,' not knowing that Heaven, once attained, will work backwards and turn even that agony into a glory.[77]

In *Till We Have Faces*, Heaven working backwards results in Orual's redemption from self-centered spiritual ugliness to becoming at last a second Psyche made beautiful by divine grace. As I have argued, in this process there is even "a strange alchemy of mutual love" between the two sisters in which each one, though lost, becomes the savior to the other.[78] It therefore cannot be said that either one has anything to boast of in terms of her own merit; instead each sister and together both sisters may revel in the grace that abounds and unites. Orual's Greek tutor Fox, from the perspective of eternity, explains, "We're all limbs and parts of one Whole. Hence, of each other. Men, and gods, flow in and out and mingle."[79] Of the misconceptions that the experience of linear time brings, he concludes, "This age of ours will one day be the distant past. And the Divine Nature can change the past. Nothing is yet in its true form."[80]

---

[75] C. S. Lewis, *The Great Divorce* (New York: HarperCollins, 2001), 111-12. See my discussion of the Ghost who exchanges sexual lust for heavenly life in *Surprised by the Feminine: A Rereading of C. S. Lewis and Gender* (New York: Peter Lang, 2013), 65-8.

[76] Lewis, *The Lion*, 147-8.

[77] Lewis, *Great Divorce*, 69.

[78] C. S. Lewis, *Surprised by Joy: The Shape of My Early Life* (New York: Harcourt Brace and World, 1955), 143. See my discussion of Orual's journey in chapter three of *Surprised by the Feminine*.

[79] Lewis, *Till We Have Faces*, 300-1.

[80] Lewis, Till We Have Faces, 305.

CONCLUSION

Each new experience of grief tests us afresh. The soul that through past heroic responses to pain appears to have "become like tempered steel"[81] is again subject to the possibility of collapse. In *A Grief Observed*, Lewis commented, "You never know how much you really believe anything until its truth or falsehood becomes a matter of life and death to you."[82] In his stories affliction sifts every character and temperament for his or her moral response to life. The pilgrim's path to consolation is through grief, a grief that becomes holy through submission to God, and this transforms our experience. As Christopher W. Mitchell pointed out, "Lewis longed above all else for the unseen things of which this life offers only shadows, for that weight of glory which the Lord Christ won for the human race" and for "every human person," and was reminded of the vision that the Apostle Paul expressed to the Corinthian believers:

> We do not lose heart. Even though our outer nature is wasting away, our inner nature is being renewed day by day. For this slight momentary affliction is preparing us for an eternal weight of glory beyond all measure, because we look not at what can be seen but at what cannot be seen; for what can be seen is temporary, but what cannot be seen is eternal (2 Corinthians 4:16-18).[83]

Indeed, to weary pilgrims, Lewis's imaginative representations of suffering serve as blessed road signs on the path to ultimate consolation.

---

[81] See R. Havard, M.D., "Appendix," in *The Problem of Pain*, 143.

[82] Lewis, *A Grief Observed*, 25.

[83] Christopher W. Mtchell, "Bearing the Weight of Glory: The Cost of C. S. Lewis's Witness," in *The Pilgrim's Guide: C. S. Lewis and the Art of Witness*, ed. by David Mills (Grand Rapids, MI: Eerdmans, 1998), 13-14.

Chapter 16

DOROTHY L. SAYERS
AND C. S. LEWIS AT WAR

CRYSTAL L. DOWNING

Barbara Reynolds begins her 2003 essay "Dorothy L. Sayers and War" with an important fact: "Sayers lived through three wars, the Boer War as a child and, as an adult, World Wars I and II."[1] Quoting from Sayers's poetry as well as her correspondence, Reynolds illustrates the complexity of Sayers's response to war, focusing on projects written during World War II. Reynolds does not mention *Conundrums for the Long Week-End*, a book published shortly before her article, which discusses various ways World War I and its aftermath influenced characters and incidents in Sayers's Lord Peter Wimsey detective fiction. Nevertheless, she seems to agree with its authors, who assert that "The Great War touched the life of Dorothy L. Sayers very lightly,"[2] Reynolds commenting that "the war left [Sayers] relatively unscathed."[3] This essay argues otherwise, suggesting that, in addition to shaping Sayers's fictional characters, the War to End All Wars—and the one after that—shaped the character of Sayers herself as well as the character of her relationship with C. S. Lewis. Writing her first letter to Lewis while Britain was still reeling over the Fall of Singapore to the Japanese, Sayers incited several battles with Lewis after the war was over. Nevertheless, or perhaps all the more, Lewis considered her an important influence on his spiritual life—and "one of the great English letter-writers,"[4] as excerpts in this essay will illustrate.

Whereas Lewis fought in the trenches of the Great War, Sayers witnessed events at its start. In 1914, while a student at Oxford

---

[1] Barbara Reynolds, "Dorothy L. Sayers and War," in *VII: An Anglo-American Literary Review*, 20 (2003), 33.

[2] Robert Kuhn McGregor with Ethan Lewis, *Conundrums for the Long Week-End: England, Dorothy L. Sayers, and Lord Peter Wimsey* (Kent, OH: Kent State University Press, 2000), 11.

[3] Reynolds "Dorothy L. Sayers and War," 3.

[4] C. S. Lewis, *The Collected Letters of C. S. Lewis*, ed. by Walter Hooper, 3 vols. (San Francisco: HarperCollins, 2004-7), 2:682.

University, she and a college friend decided to spend their summer break in Tours, France, arriving with a chaperone on 1 August: the day Germany declared war on Russia. When the Germans invaded Luxembourg on 2 August, Sayers wrote her parents saying, "we are in a state of siege," recounting a visit to town the previous day, where the visitors saw soldiers and sailors "all over the place." After descriptions of shops refusing to sell food, of streets clouded in dust from "the continual rushing to and fro of motor-cars," of restaurants with umbrella stands "stuck full of swords," the 21-year-old Sayers makes comments like, "It is immensely exciting" and "it is so fearfully thrilling," proclaiming "I am . . . beginning to enjoy myself immensely, if only we can stay."[5]

On 3 August, the day Germany declared war on France, Sayers was a bit more somber, recounting to her parents the "pathetic tale of an old man whose beloved horse was taken away from him for the service . . . .. It was licking his hands and he was weeping over its nose."[6] When Britain declared war on Germany, she wrote home proudly quoting the proprietor of their lodging who had told her, the day before, "If only we can count on England, we'll give the Germans a good old dressing down," ending her account with "One feels rather glad to be English."[7] She even puts a heading on the letter as though aware that she is recording history:

4 August 1914	39 rue Laponneraye
	Tours
	Tuesday
	3rd day of mobilization

Furthermore, though herself the daughter of a clergyman, Sayers relishes the fact that the French "are going to shoot the *curé* of a little village near here, who was found to have in the *pneu* of his bicycle plans of the surrounding country, marked to show the best spots for dropping bombs from aeroplanes. Anyway, I'm sure traitors ought to be shot." And she proceeds to extol the French: "They accept all the consequences of conscription without a murmur, and seem perfectly resigned to the sacrifice of everything they possess for the good of their country." In contrast, she has a far less sanguine view of Americans

---

[5] Dorothy L. Sayers, *The Letters of Dorothy L. Sayers*, ed. by Barbara Reynolds, vol. 1 (New York: St. Martins, 1996), 91-2.

[6] Sayers, *Letters*, 1:94.

[7] Sayers, *Letters*, 1:95-6.

joining her at city hall to get themselves "declared as foreigners" in order to leave France. As she stands in line, she writes home, "We are surrounded by American women—all shouting and giving themselves terrific airs. From time to time a few officials make frantic attempts to sort us out. We have just been stirred up like whisked eggs to let some people through."[8]

Sayers's metaphor of "whisked eggs," like her images of a French man weeping over a horse's nose and a clergyman hiding plans in a bicycle tire, suggests that Sayers responded to the outbreak of war like a novelist, offering descriptive details about people, events, and settings. In fact, she begins her second letter from Tours with "This thing is like a novel by H. G. Wells. The whole world is going to war, and it has happened in two days!"[9] One could therefore argue that the Great War prepared Sayers to write bestselling detective fiction. And not just due to the development of her narrative skills.

After she left France during the Battle of the Ardennes (21-23 August), Sayers returned to university in October, only to discover that war had turned Oxford into a very different place. Not only was the town thick with Belgian refugees, but Sayers' college, Somerville, had been commandeered as a hospital for wounded soldiers. Volunteering to help the refugees and organizing a concert for the hospitalized veterans, Sayers briefly considered becoming a nurse; after all, her college had become a place to nurse men wounded by war.

Instead, Sayers ended up dealing with the wounding of war in an entirely different manner. In 1921, at age 27, she began her first Peter Wimsey detective novel, making sure to give Lord Peter a war wound—one that she could relate to. Unlike C. S. Lewis and the veterans she met, Sayers had not witnessed the hellishness of trench warfare, with degradations worthy of Dante's *Inferno*. Instead, she witnessed the psychological wounding of war, manifest in a form no Sayers scholar has yet considered. Even as she was writing her parents from Tours with statements like "You have no idea how frightfully exciting it is being here, right in the middle of things,"[10] the usually energetic friend accompanying her, Elsie Henderson, became bedridden, ostensibly "overcome by the heat and fatigue," but actually

---

[8] Sayers, *Letters*, 1:96-7.

[9] Sayers, *Letters*, 1:93.

[10] Sayers, *Letters*, 1:92.

in "a bad state of collapse."[11] Because she had "no symptoms" other than "collapse," a French physician finally diagnosed Elsie with "such a state of worn-outness that complete rest is absolutely necessary."[12] Sayers's friend, it would seem, was suffering from what was then called "nervous breakdown." Though Sayers does not identify the malady as such, she writes her mother that, were Elsie to rest at the Sayers home in England, "I do not really think there is any likelihood of her being really ill."[13] In other words, Elsie's problem was more psychological than physiological, Sayers assuring her mother that, were Elsie to visit, "you will probably see it without being told."[14] Sayers's mother, Helen, would "see it without being told" because she suffered from "nervous attacks" herself.

We first learn about Helen Sayers's anxiety disorder in July 1915, after a cousin and an uncle, on leave from the front, visit the Sayers home. Writing a friend, Sayers explains that the visiting relatives

> have got nervous breakdown, one has neuritis and the other has damaged his eye gazing at aeroplanes . . .. I'm rather glad they're gone, because I do so hate everlasting war-talk, and I'm always in terror of Mother getting another of her nervous attacks . . .. [T]hey are so terrifying, because she loses control over her speech and limbs.[15]

I would suggest that the "nervous attacks" of Helen Sayers and Elsie Henderson not only tempered Sayers's excitement over war but also helped her sympathize with shell-shocked veterans. Hence, when she created Lord Peter Wimsey several years after the Great War ended, she gave him a psychological rather than a physical wound. Reynolds argues that Lord Peter's condition was modeled after shell-shocked veterans Sayers had known at Oxford, giving the example of Roger Dixey.[16] However, Sayers's letter about Dixey makes clear that, while she heard about his "bad shell-shock," she did not see its effects.[17] What she *did* see was Elsie's nervous "collapse" in response to war, a response that echoed her mother's debilitating "nervous attacks,"

---

11 Sayers, *Letters*, 1:91, 102.

12 Sayers, *Letters*, 1:102.

13 Sayers, *Letters*, 1:102.

14 Sayers, *Letters*, 1:102.

15 Sayers, *Letters*, 1:110.

16 Reynolds, "Dorothy L. Sayers and War," 35.

17 Sayers, *Letters*, 1:152.

traumas that inevitably influenced Sayers's depictions of Lord Peter.[18]

The words *nerves, nervous,* and *attack* recur in Sayers's first novel, *Whose Body?* (1923), which features a doctor who specializes in nervous breakdown, having treated victims of shell-shock during the Great War. When Wimsey figures out that the celebrated doctor may be the murderer he has been seeking, he suddenly relapses into the shell-shock that disabled him after a German bomb destroyed his bunker. Significantly, Sayers puts the explanation of Peter's shell-shock into the mouth of his mother, not a war veteran: "he hasn't had an attack for ages, but there! Nerves are such funny things, and Peter . . . was so dreadfully bad in 1918, you know, and I suppose we can't expect to forget all about a great war in a year or two."[19] Furthermore, Peter's mother suggests that what he needs is to rest with her at home: the same remedy Sayers suggested for Elsie Henderson, whom she took home to be cared for by the empathetic Helen Sayers, who would recognize the problem "without being told."

Sayers gives Lord Peter another attack of shell-shock in the last of her eleven Wimsey novels, *Busman's Honeymoon*, published in 1937. When his detecting skills lead to a criminal's execution, Peter shakes uncontrollably, saying, "it's my rotten nerves. I can't help it. I suppose I've never been really right since the War. I hate behaving like this."[20] And, as in her first novel, it is Lord Peter's mother, not a veteran, who explains the problem, this time to Peter's newlywed wife.

Marriage to a traumatized veteran reflects another kind of wounding due to war. In 1926, Sayers married Captain Atherton "Mac" Fleming (1881-1950), who had been gassed during the Great War. In 1919 Mac published a well-received book called *How to See the Battlefields*, and marriage to Mac helped Sayers see battlefield trauma in a new light. Unlike her first three detective novels, her fourth, *The Unpleasantness at the Bellona Club* (1928), hinges upon memories of war. In the opening chapter a veteran of the Crimea is discovered murdered on 11 November, Armistice Day. Of his two grandsons

---

[18] I talk about Helen Sayers's nervous attacks in Crystal Downing, *Writing Performances: The Stages of Dorothy L. Sayers* (New York: Palgrave Macmillan, 2004), 51. Since my point there was about the power of the mother on Sayers's imagination, I did not discuss Elsie's collapse during the war.

[19] Dorothy L. Sayers, *Whose Body?* (New York: Avon, 1961), 153.

[20] Dorothy L. Sayers, *Busman's Honeymoon* (New York: HarperCollins, 1992), 367.

implicated in the murder, one was a Major, the other a Captain in the Great War. The latter, George Fentiman, struggles with relapses of shell shock that lead to his "wandering about in a distraught manner for several days, sometimes with partial and occasionally with complete temporary loss of memory." One time he "deliberately walked into a bonfire."[21] Though Sayers does have Lord Peter briefly mention that he was in a "nursing home—with shell shock,"[22] she focuses much more attention on George's inability to recuperate from his war experience, having him describe "that ghastly hole at Carency, where the whole ground was rotten with corpses—ugh!—potting those swollen great rats for a penny a time, and laughing at them. Rats. Alive and putrid with what they'd been feeding on."[23] Furthermore, Sayers, for the first time, shows how "shell-shock" can wound a spouse, George abusively responding to his long-suffering wife with querulous impatience. I suspect that these novelistic descriptions reflect Mac's explanations about what caused the demise of his first marriage, which had produced two daughters.

Little did Sayers know, as she wrote *Bellona Club*, that she would be similarly wounded, the novel's dialogue anticipating her own increasingly turbulent relationship with Mac. For example, George's wife apologizes for her husband's vicious temper by saying "His tummy is feeling rotten and it makes him irritable,"[24] foreshadowing a 1932 letter in which Sayers tells her cousin about "Mac's unaccountable tummy, which makes housekeeping one long problem."[25] Later she explicitly attributes his "odd fits of temper" to "some kind of germ or disease or shock . . . probably a result of the War."[26]

Fortunately, Sayers encountered other veterans of the Great War who surmounted their injuries, not least of which was C. S. Lewis. But it was the Second World War that initiated their friendship. As Lewis puts it, she was "the first person of importance who ever wrote me a fan letter."[27] Though she was only five years older, Sayers became

---

[21] Dorothy L. Sayers, *The Unpleasantness at the Bellona Club* (New York: HarperCollins, 1995), 183.

[22] Sayers, *Bellona Club*, 215.

[23] Sayers, *Bellona Club*, 91.

[24] Sayers, *Bellona Club*, 66.

[25] Sayers, *Letters*, 1:324.

[26] Sayers, *Letters* 1:341-2.

[27] Lewis, *Collected Letters*, 3:1400.

famous decades before Lewis due to her detective novels of the 1920s and 30s. Her fame led to an invitation to follow in the footsteps of T. S. Eliot and Charles Williams by writing a play for the 1937 Canterbury Festival, followed by another one for the 1939 festival. Meanwhile, in 1940, Lewis published *The Problem of Pain*, a book that Sayers repeatedly recommended to others, turning her into a Lewis fan. So, in the spring of 1942, as Nazis were executing "Baedeker raids" on Britain, Sayers contacted Lewis, asking him to write something for a series of books that might inculcate, in the midst of wartime, "a constructive purpose worth living for and worth dying for."[28] The war, in other words, ignited a correspondence between the two writers.

Though Lewis turned down Sayers's request, a year later (May 1943) Sayers sent Lewis an advance copy of *The Man Born to Be King*, her published version of a series of plays about Jesus that had been broadcast by BBC radio from December 1941 to October 1942. She included with the book a missive that parodies *Screwtape Letters*, complete with a humorous hand-drawn illustration of "the Hound of Heaven." Writing in the voice of her own made-up demon, "Sluckdrib," the letter reports to Screwtape that "the effect of writing [*The Man Born to Be King*] upon the character of my patient is wholly satisfactory":

> I have already had the honour to report intellectual and spiritual pride, vainglory, self-opinionated dogmatism, irreverence, blasphemous frivolity, frequentation of the company of theatricals, . . . shortness of temper, neglect of domestic affairs, lack of charity, egotism, . . ., and a growing tendency to consider the Bible as Literature.[29]

Though rejoicing in this litany of sin, Sluckdrib expresses concern because the broadcast of Sayers's plays has had an unforeseen effect: an atheist, who had written Sayers a rudely offensive letter about the radio broadcasts, has become mollified by her answer, showing

---

[28] The phrase is from "The Statement of Aims for the proposed Bridgehead series of books" that James Brabazon places as an Appendix to his biography of Sayers. James Brabazon, *Dorothy L. Sayers: A Biography*. (New York: Scribner's, 1981), 278. Lewis did not save Sayers's letter that asked him to contribute, presumably, to the Bridgehead series, so we can only speculate about what she said to him.

[29] Dorothy L. Sayers, *The Letters of Dorothy L Sayers*, ed. by Barbara Reynolds, vols 2-3 (Cambridge: Carole Green, 1997-8), 2:410.

"readiness to read some Christian literature" that she sent him.[30] Sayers then ends the letter with a postscript in her own voice:

> I am left with the Atheist on my hands . . .. If he reads any of the books I have recommended, he will write me long and disorderly letters about them. It will go on for years. I cannot bear it. Two of the books are yours [*The Problem of Pain* and *Broadcast Talks*]. I only hope they will rouse him to fury. Then I shall hand him on to you. You like souls. I don't. God is simply taking advantage of the fact that I can't stand intellectual chaos, and it isn't fair. Anyhow, there aren't any up-to-date books about Miracles.[31]

Four days later Lewis responded with the comment "I'm starting a book on Miracles." Walter Hooper asserts that Sayers's wartime letter gave Lewis the impetus to write *Miracles*, which was published three years later.[32]

C. S. Lewis visiting the RAF Chaplains' School,
Magdalene College, Cambridge, 1944.

---

[30] Sayers, *Letters*, 2:411.

[31] Sayers, *Letters*, 2:413.

[32] Lewis had given a sermon on miracles in November 1942 and had written several pieces on the subject for *The Guardian* in 1942 and 1943. But Hooper thinks that Sayers provided the impetus for writing a book. See Lewis, *Collected Letters* 2:573, n. 103, and Sayers, *Letters*, 2:413, n. 10.

Sayers, then, was an important influence on Lewis, who was so impressed with *The Man Born to be King* that he read it as part of his Lenten devotions every year until he died. And part of his attraction to the plays may well have been their relevance to living through two World Wars. Having started composing the radio scripts during the Battle of Britain, Sayers couldn't help but think of parallels with the current war. In August of 1940, she wrote to the person who commissioned the plays, Dr. James Welch, that the Judaea visited by the Magi was "much like Hitler's idea of a territory protected by the Reich."[33] Two months later, she wrote the man Welch chose to produce the plays that "the Shepherds and their angel-vision are as plain as pie-crust," only to end the letter with "Hitler seems to keep fussing in and out today. One of these days our local siren will wear its whistle out."[34]

With the war as a constant backdrop to her composition process, it makes sense that Sayers would look at the Gospel message through the lens of World War II. As she notes in her introduction to *The Man Born to be King*,

> God was executed by people painfully like us, in a society very similar to our own . . ... Caiaphas was the ecclesiastical politician, appointed, like one of Hitler's bishops, by a heathen government, expressly that he might collaborate with the New Order and see that the Church toed the line drawn by the State; we have seen something of Caiaphas lately.[35]

In her fifth play, which includes the temptation of Christ and the Sermon on the Mount, she introduces a character called "Baruch the Zealot," whom she describes in the performance notes this way: "Baruch sees Jesus as the Nazi party may have seen Hitler—the Heaven-sent spell-binder."[36] Not coincidentally, Baruch is the character who subverts Judas's trust in Jesus.

Ironically, this effort to make the plays relevant to contemporary life created a national scandal. Because Sayers refused to use King James English for the scripts, actually giving Christ's disciples working class slang, British Christians declared war on the BBC, sending letters

---

[33] Sayers, *Letters*, 2:178.

[34] Sayers, *Letters*, 2:192-3.

[35] Dorothy L. Sayers, *The Man Born to Be King* (Grand Rapids, MI: Eerdmans, 1979), 7.

[36] Sayers, *The Man Born to Be King*, 125.

to Winston Churchill and the Archbishop of Canterbury demanding that the plays be taken off the air. Considering the plays blasphemous, some actually suggested that *The Man Born to Be King* undermined the war effort, Singapore's fall to the Axis powers, in February 1942, being a clear sign of God's retributive justice.

Ironically, due to the scandal, numerous people who normally would never listen to Christian programming tuned in to see what all the fuss was about, later writing Sayers to say that, thanks to her, they finally understood the relevance of Jesus to their everyday lives. As verified by BBC "Listener Research Bulletins," which report results from post-broadcast questionnaires, listeners "had been led to expect irreverence, if not blasphemy" in Sayers's plays, but instead "found reverent treatment and sincere acting."[37] Due to this positive response, the BBC rebroadcast the plays over the next several years; audiences in the fourth year, 1945, were "bigger than ever before."[38] God works in mysterious ways, including on Lewis. When asked in 1963 which Christian authors had "helped" him the most, he named four: two authorities on mysticism, Edwyn Bevan and Rudolf Otto, as well as G. K. Chesterton and Dorothy L. Sayers.[39]

This commendation is all the more remarkable considering the fact that a skirmish developed between Lewis and Sayers the year after World War II ended. In 1946, Lewis asked Sayers to contribute to "a sort of library of Christian knowledge for young people in top forms at school."[40] As Barbara Reynolds summarizes, when Sayers responded "that her conscience prevented her from writing for the purpose of edifying readers, Lewis rebuked her for allowing her 'artistic' conscience to stand in the way of her duty."[41] In response, Sayers released a barrage of words:

---

[37] BBC Listener Research Department, Listener Research Bulletin No. 111, LR/1291, 4 November 1942, BBC Written Archive Centre, Caversham Park, Reading, 1.

[38] BBC Listener Research Department, Listener Research Bulletin No. 238, LR/3364, 9 April 1945, BBC Written Archive Centre, Caversham Park, Reading, 3. My thanks go to Bruce R. Johnson, who provided me with copies of the BBC Listener Research Bulletin.

[39] C. S. Lewis, *God in the Dock: Essays on Theology and Ethics*, ed. by Walter Hooper (Grand Rapids, MI: Eerdmans, 1970), 260.

[40] Lewis, *Collected Letters*, 2:721.

[41] Sayers, *Letters*, 3:252.

> Oy! Oy! I see I must, willy-nilly, write you another letter . . ..
> I've always realised that you were bothered about this business
> of art and edification. But . . . I don't believe God is such a
> twister as you make out. I don't believe He implants a love
> of good workmanship merely as a trap for one to walk into
> . . .. I don't somehow fancy showing . . . a lot of stuff to the
> Carpenter's Son and saying, 'Well, I admit that the wood was
> green and the joints untrue and the glue bad, but it was all
> church furniture.'[42]

Lewis wrote back, "Of course one mustn't do *dishonest* work. But you
seem to take as the criterion of honest work the sensible *desire* to write,
the 'itch'. That seems to me precious like making 'being in love' the
only reason for going on with a marriage." Of course, typical of Lewis,
the letter ends on a humble note: "My own frequent uneasiness comes
from another source—the fact that apologetic work is so dangerous
to one's own faith. A doctrine never seems dimmer to me than when
I have just successfully defended it. Anyway thanks for an intensely
interesting letter."[43]

Despite Lewis's graciousness, Sayers responded with a verbal
blitz:

> I do not care much for these sexual analogies of yours . . . if
> you must have the thing in terms of love and marriage, then
> [the male] position is that, having deliberately thrown the girl
> at my head and done your best to compromise us, you are now
> trying to force us into marriage . . . regardless of the fact that
> she makes my flesh creep, and that I have been engaged for
> years to another woman.[44]

Indeed, Sayers felt herself *engaged* in a certain kind of work, and to
force her to drop it in order to do something else for the good of the
Kingdom, like a pamphlet for school children, would be an insult to
the love God had given her.

Sayers thought this way due to her interpretation of the *imago Dei*
as recounted in Genesis: "So God created man in his own image, in
the image of God created he him; male and female created he them"
(1:27, KJV). Significantly, it was World War II that encouraged her
to theorize how the *imago Dei* might function on a practical level.

---

[42] Sayers, *Letters*, 3:252.

[43] Lewis, *Collected Letters*, 2:730.

[44] Sayers, *Letters*, 3:256

Distressed by the psychological effects of war on British citizens at home, she and two friends planned Bridgeheads, a series of books that might "urge on creative activity, keep people interested in life, and combat lethargy, defeatism and depression of spirits," and hence "remind people incessantly, while the War continues, of the spiritual aims for which it is waged."[45]

Sayers's contribution to the project, *The Mind of the Maker* (1941), argues that, because God is a creator, human creativity reflects the image of a Trinitarian God. Hence, an earnest commitment to the integrity of one's work is more important than any Christian message within it. Just as God glories in rarely-seen fish that inhabit the nethermost parts of the sea, Christian artists, engineers, cooks, accountants, and parents should glory in the integrity of their creations without seeing the need to use them as excuses for sharing the Gospel. This, then, explains her battle with Lewis. As she tells him in 1946, "I think one of the causes of misunderstanding between us is that the only kind of love I understand at all is the kind that you put the lowest--the love of the artist for the artefact." Significantly, she later signs the letter "Very sincerely, your fellow-artefact."[46]

Lewis had no knowledge of the heartbreak behind Sayers's phrase "the only kind of love I understand," unaware how the wounding of war had soured her marriage. So he simply wrote back, "Hey! Whoa! . . . don't bother your head about my views (or doubts) any more,"[47] eliciting from Sayers an apology. She goes on to assure him that "thousands of people write to say that they have been 'brought back to God'" from hearing her wartime radio plays about Jesus,[48] but, and this is the important part, she did not write the scripts in order to proselytize; she researched and wrote the life of Jesus to the best of her ability, exercising full integrity in capturing truth as she understood it. As her "Oy, Oy" letter explains,

> [Y]ou must not tell people what they want to hear, or even what they need to hear, unless it is the thing you passionately want to tell them. You must not look at them from above, or outside, and say: 'Poor creatures; they would obviously be the better for so-and-so—I must try and make up a dose for them.'

---

[45] Quoted in Brabazon, *Sayers: A Biography*, 280.

[46] Sayers, *Letters*, 3:257.

[47] Lewis, *Collected Letters*, 2:731.

[48] Sayers, *Letters*, 3:258.

> You've got to come galloping out shouting excitedly: 'look here! Look what I've found! Come and have a bit of it—it's grand— you'll love it—I can't keep it to myself.'[49]

After this skirmish, Lewis and Sayers made a treaty that was shorter than the one at Versailles. In July of 1948, Lewis wrote Sayers asking her to write an article denouncing the ordination of women in the Anglican Church. His argument was that "the Priest at the altar must represent the Bridegroom to whom we all are, in a sense, feminine."[50] Sayers's reply, once again, was combative:

> One has to be very careful with that 'Bridegroom' imagery. It is so very apt to land one in Male and Female Principles .. .. And that sort of thing doesn't make much appeal to well-balanced women, who look on it as just another example of men's hopeless romanticism about sex, and who are apt either to burst out laughing or sniff a faint smell of drains.[51]

Not coincidentally, she wrote a woman correspondent that same year,

> Do you like C. S. Lewis's work, or are you one of the people who foam at the mouth when they hear his name? I find most of his books very illuminating and stimulating, but .. . I do admit that he is apt to write shocking nonsense about women and marriage. (That, however, is not because he is a bad theologian but because he is a rather frightened bachelor).[52]

Nevertheless, like France and Britain during both world wars, Lewis and Sayers knew that the cause they shared far outweighed their differences. Though she considered his view of women problematic, Sayers acknowledged that Lewis was a great warrior for the faith, writing another correspondent,

> Lewis is magnificently ruthless with the people who do set out to produce what purports to be a logical argument and then fake the premises, or beg the question, or leave their middles undistributed . . .. He is down on the thing like a rat; he is God's terrier, and I wouldn't be without him for the world.[53]

We might say the same of Sayers, who, after witnessing the devastating

---

49 Sayers, *Letters*, 3:253.
50 Lewis, *Collected Letters*, 2:860.
51 Sayers, *Letters* 3:387.
52 Sayers, *Letters* 3:375.
53 Sayers, *Letters*, 3:387.

effects of war on the human psyche, brought light into the darkness through work, inspired by World War II, that not only celebrated Jesus as the light of the world but also theorized how the *imago Dei* might reflect that light. Her war-lit candle most certainly ignited the fire of C. S. Lewis—in more ways than one.

Chapter 17

IN THE COMPANY OF STRANGERS

JAMES COMO

Weave a circle round him thrice,
And close your eyes with holy dread,
For he on honey-dew hath fed
And drunk the milk of Paradise.

—S. T. Coleridge, "Kubla Khan"

Most experienced readers know and like authors who display, not merely coherence of plot, character, setting, and symbol, but *conviction*, some passion for a take on truth. Surely that is one pillar of C. S. Lewis's attraction. A second is his ever-abiding sensibility, a voice so reliable that, to quote Alexander Pope's *Essay on Criticism*, it "gives us back the image of our mind."[1] In fact, so prominent are these two pillars in Lewis that to many he seems to own the trademark on both. Lewis readers particularly seem to delight, not only in Lewis's orthodoxy, rationality, and clarity, but in the wonder and awe that he delivers in most of his familiar personae: the avuncular Narnian, the apostle to skeptics, the poet, the romancer, allegorist and satirist, and even the literary scholar-critic. That is why these personae together consume so much reputational oxygen, leaving very little for the philosopher, the public intellectual, or the man of letters.

Or the novelist, for that matter.[2] His one true novel—as opposed to his fantasies, romances, and allegories—is too un-Lewisian even for

---

[1] Alexander Pope, "An Essay on Criticism," in *Essay on Man and Essay on Criticism* (Paris: Parsons and Galignani, 1806), 57.

[2] On three previous occasions, now collected in *Why I Believe in Narnia: 33 Reviews and Essays on the Life & Works of C. S. Lewis* (Cheshire, CT: Winged Lion Press, 2008), I've tried to enroll Lewis into three different contexts: the Man of Letters (1981, where I was already in the company of some scholars), the Philosopher (2003, where some scholars had also arrived), and the Public Intellectual (2007, where I have yet to be joined by others). Here I hope to make some space for the novelist but a novelist of a distinctive sort.

many of his devoted readers. Lewis's novel, *Till We Have Faces*,[3] casts itself in its complexity, narrational distemper, irresolution, ambiguity, and any combination of these (features common to novels), if not into the outer darkness then certainly into the shade. The characteristic Lewisian sensibility (not to mention Jesus's) seems *not* to abide here. Above all, readers ask, where is the meaning? Is even Lewis's universe ultimately uncertain? Where in the world does this novel fit, especially since some, including Lewis himself, called it his best book?

So, my claim here is straightforward, if not simple: *Till We Have Faces*, proper and modern novel though it be, and as unique within the Lewis oeuvre as it is in some respects, lies as close to the heart of Lewis's sensibility as does any of his works. This is due to the fact that—and here is the rub for many dedicated Lewis readers—it is not simply a novel but a Wonder Tale, its sensibility bearing more kinship, I believe, to *Out of the Silent Planet* and *Perelandra* than it does to, say, *That Hideous Strength*.[4] My objective is to suggest that with respect to *Till We Have Faces*, Lewis belongs to a constellation of writers with whom he is congruent, if not exactly concentric. Together, they mix as Sarah Tindal Kareem puts it in her *Eighteenth-Century Fiction and the Reinvention of Wonder*, where she discovers the marvelous in exploring how writers engage readers' attention in "credulity with skepticism," a secular age.[5]

As a point of context, the constellation of writers I have in mind consists of authors who 1) share, even if very subtly, a distinctive allure—a *kappa* element (on which more anon)—that turns out to be spiritually unsettling; 2) who, though not necessarily Christian, are Christian-friendly or depict a crypto-Christian or pre-Christian temper: they may even provide *praeparatio evangelica*; 3) whose

---

[3] C. S. Lewis, *Till We Have Faces* (New York: HarperCollins, 2012).

[4] Not because *THS* lacks any element of wonder: chapters 14 and 15, wherein, respectively, the re-constituted marriage bower is torn to shreds by pagan gnomes and the Planets descend, along with the terrifying Head, and the conceits of Merlin and the eldila—these are sufficient to qualify the book as a borderline Wonder Tale. Rather, it is an outlier because it is substantially ugly—in spite of the allure of the community at St. Anne's. This adjectival resonance is utterly out of keeping with anything else Lewis wrote, except, possibly, *The Dark Tower*, which he had the wit to abandon. In short, I exclude it from this examination, not because it might not fit but because it is unfitting.

[5] Sarah Tindal Kareem, *Eighteenth-Century Fiction and the Reinvention of Wonder* (Oxford: Oxford University Press, 2014).

narrative interests, and to some extent techniques, are similar; and 4) who are largely ignored by Lewis scholars and critics, even though they are stars in the same "constellation" of writers. Excluded from the class I have in mind are the usual suspects: no MacDonald or Chesterton, Milton or Dante, or any mythology. Also excluded are those akin to the familiar Lewis and of whose sensibility he was so fond, writers like Kenneth Grahame (*The Wind in the Willows*) and James Stephens (*The Crock of Gold*), who write as quasi-pagans, or the fantastically weird, like E. R. Eddison (*The Worm Ouroboros*) or David Lindsay (*A Voyage to Arcturus*).

Closer to the mark are writers such as Flannery O'Connor, Walker Percy, William Kennedy (*Ironweed* above all), and Thornton Wilder, especially his much neglected *The Woman of Andros*. Their approach is often tentative and, like Lewis's, oblique, their didacticism muted or non-existent, and their ideas palpable though always embedded in an existential challenge (or mystery if you prefer) of one sort or another. And they do, even if sporadically, evince that particular *kappa* element—the pivotal abiding sensibility—that *Till We Have Faces* exudes. Presently, I will probe this sub-genre by way of two great works, though these days none as renowned as Lewis's: Robertson Davies' *Fifth Business* and Sigrid Undset's *Kristin Lavransdatter*.

Providing definitions poses a task somewhat more daunting than adumbrating a context. First comes the novel (along with a hope not to re-invent a well-wrought wheel). Conventionally, we must have characters interacting, not only with each other but with a society that, one way or another, we the readers either inhabit or could have inhabited; we know it as actual or at least hypothetically so (currently or in the past). There may be some strange goings-on, but "realism of content," to adduce a key concept from Lewis's *An Experiment in Criticism* (and not for the last time), preponderates. And then, of course, there must be a distinctive consciousness: distinctive, not necessarily *outré*. This feature has arisen most prominently within the past two hundred years but in the past one hundred, especially, in the form of a compelling, believable, and dominant first-person narrator, as in Henry James's *The Turn of the Screw* or V. Nabokov's *Lolita*. To be sure, Lewis feints at the first-person point-of-view in *Perelandra*, in which the narrator is recounting what he has been told. But there the tale is not about that narrator, as it is in James's or Nabokov's books and in *Till We Have Faces*. With this sort of narrator comes a vividly conveyed consciousness and unreliability—a feature central to such tales and one that we do not see anywhere else in Lewis. In short, this book is not only a novel, but a very modern novel—one keeping company with those neighbors not normally associated with Lewis.

Next, our definition of the *kappa element* brings us to "On Stories,"[6] an essay variously collected and based on a Lewis lecture from 1940, "The Kappa Element in Fiction." There, Lewis calls the plot a "noun," a mere "net" whereby a quality, that *kappa* element, as an "adjective," is caught. For example, giants, pirates, Indians, and the Toad from *The Wind in the Willows* cannot be replaced, nor can the Indian's tomahawk be replaced by a pistol because the quiddity of that tomahawk—the thingness of the thing—speaks for it. Nothing is hidden, but the effect of what is in plain sight is so pervasive that distinguishing that effect is rather like separating wetness from water. In a space-travel romance, we do not want party politics or office love affairs. Why go far into space for those? Now, Lewis is not suggesting that we must become cryptographers, decoding elements that the author has secreted within his tale. Rather the opposite. As he points out, the boy reading *King Solomon's Mines* surely cannot explain his awe and fear, nor need he; those responses come with being trapped in a mine, a mine unadorned and with no infused excitement. Or we might accompany David Lindsay on his *Voyage to Arcturus*. You will not understand the plot, and it really will not matter; there will be *otherness*, you will not be able to explain your visit there, and you will never forget it.

In short, the proper verb, as Lewis reminds us in *An Experiment in Criticism*, should be *connaître*, not *savoir*; that is, knowledge from the inside. Or, to put it yet a third (and last) way, in life as in reading we can, to quote Walker Percy, "possess / a clear / problem" or "participate / in a rich / mystery

The wonder tale, our third concept for definition, is not a genre at all, but a meta-genre. It includes such genres as the fairy tale, fantasy, some science fiction, old-school gothic tales (for example, ghost stories), much children's literature, and even some horror tales. Of course, national mythologies are included, but non-miraculous legends (for example, Robin Hood) are not. At the center of the circle lie obvious examples: The Chronicles of Narnia, most of Grimm, the Alice books, Tolkien's oeuvre, and some beast fables (e.g., *The Book*

---

[6] C. S. Lewis, "On Stories," in *Of Other Worlds*, ed. by Walter Hooper (New York: Harcourt, Brace and World, 1966).

of the Dun Cow). Away, but not very far away, from these types of tales are *Out of the Silent Planet*, *Perelandra*, and, I think, Chesterton's *The Man Who Was Thursday* (though this lies more toward the fringe than the others). An interesting example of the wonder tale is *The Wind in the Willows*. I do not believe beast fables per se belong within the circle, but there is an element in Kenneth Grahame's great work that gives pause.[7] Thus it happens, I think, that the breadth of this meta-genre is such that, near its fringes, parts of books not otherwise wondrous pull the work into the wonder ambit.

At the very fringe, farthest from the center, are such works as Acts and the Gospel of Mark, the overall realism of which serve to highlight the occasional outbreak of wonder. It is as though wonder and its causes are lurking everywhere in these scriptural narratives, but they ultimately derive from a single source, our Lord. However, I omit books which, so to speak, declare their divine and eschatological interests.

Following are many typical features of wonder tales, although not all are necessary for any given tale to qualify:

1. Right and wrong and often Good and Evil are concrete, though perhaps not explicit. Events show the world to be neither a pinball machine, nor even a plant, even less a tick of Tourrette's, but the expression of a Moral Intelligence.

2. Spatial and, less often, temporal dimensions are small. For instance, a kingdom might be walkable in two or three days.

3. Marvels, especially visual one, abound, although these may not be wondrous within the tale.

4. Forests, often perilous and magical, appear frequently.

5. Prohibitions, usually one very pronounced, are prominent.

6. Traditional tales can withstand even bad retellings and commonly are embodied in a classic version.

7. Very often the wonder world is marked by order and

---

[7] Its magnificent Chapter VII, "Piper at the Gates of Dawn," raises the tale from beast fable to wonder tale. I don't know of any narrative passage that inspires more awe or evokes holiness more fully than this chapter.

hierarchy—they model a "medieval" society in this respect.

8. The familiar is comfortably rendered, and expectations are satisfied.

9. Natural laws can be altered, like animals talking, though not randomly.

10. The narrative morphology (see Tolkien) is usually tripartite: escape, recovery, consolation.

11. The protagonists (and perhaps others, often undergo some transformation of social station, marriage, or family.

12. Signs, often subtle, are central.

13. The desire for the transcendent, like Lewis's Sehnsucht (Joy), is common.

14. A character's identity, either stolen, mistaken or forgotten, is often at issue.

15. A sense of "remote proximity" is common: long ago perhaps, but not necessarily far away, and certainly not inaccessible.

16. Wonder tales may prepare us imaginatively for the Gospels, the greatest wonder tales.

Numbers twelve through sixteen especially mark the boundaries of my sub-genre.

The last feature derives from Rudolf Otto's *The Idea of the Holy*. What do we come to know, however obliquely, from reading a wonder tale? Otto's answer is a combination of the *mysterium tremendum*, the *mysterium fascinosum*, and the numinous: respectively, the fathomless mystery attaching to the sacred being, the deep enchantment of the worshipper as he contemplates that being, and his accompanying awe and fear before the sacred. In these states of mystery, we have a choice, utterly free and authentic as the existentialists have taught us, and as Lewis saw, not on his way to the Whipsnade Zoo but while riding a bus along the High. Or, as Walker Percy puts it in *The Message in the Bottle*:

> Existentialism [writes Percy] has taught us that what man is cannot be grasped by the science of man. The case is rather that man's science is one of the things that man does, a mode of existence. Another mode is speech [rhetoric]. Man is not merely a higher organism responding to and controlling his environment. He is . . . that being in the world whose calling it is to find a name for Being, to give testimony to it, and to provide for it a clearing.[8]

"Thou madest us for Thyself, and our heart is restless, until it repose in Thee," St. Augustine tells us near the very beginning of his *Confessions*. The three authors treated below, Davies, Undset, and Lewis, explore nothing less than the truth of the saint's assertion. It is precisely the mark of the constellation of writers I have in mind.

Robertson Davies (1913-95) was a man of many parts—playwright, critic, literary journalist, headmaster, and a prolific writer of fiction, both short and long. In fact, so fond was he of long forms that he specialized in trilogies: Salterton, Cornish, the incomplete Toronto, and our focus here, the Deptford trilogy. It includes *Fifth Business* (1970), *The Manticore* (1972; a Jungian *jeu d'esprit* if ever there was one), and *World of Wonders* (1975). The first introduces us to Dunstan Ramsay, a first-person narrator who, now retiring from decades of teaching, will tell his story to the headmaster in the form of a letter. His tale spans decades, addressing more than one great mystery of his life, solving a compelling puzzle, engaging such high concepts as identity, guilt, and justice, and finally settling the question of how his life was saved in battle during combat in World War One. Short answer: it was a saint, whom he recognized, and who propelled him to achieve great expertise in the field of hagiography. The trilogy thereafter spins far beyond Dunstan's own story and into the flamboyant and compelling tale of another, Paul Dempster, the baby born prematurely as a result of Dunstan's act when he was a boy. As it happens, Dunstan learns from Paul, now a world-famous magician, irresistibly charismatic but morally bereft, that Dunstan had far less to do with events—either as an agent, catalyst, or cause—than he had always supposed. He was merely "fifth business," a plot tool "in drama and opera companies organized according to the old style"—a device and a definition, it turns out, entirely of Davies's own invention.

---

[8] Walker Percy, *The Message in the Bottle* (New York: Farrar, Straus and Giroux, 1984), 158.

Dunstan's search is tightly interwoven with the lives of two women. The second is almost a giant, very ugly, who dominates both Dunstan and Paul, the magician now going by his stage name of Eisengrim. The first is Paul's mother, Mary Dempster, who is weak and mentally unbalanced owing to having been hit by a snowball with a stone hidden within. The snowball was originally meant for Dunstan, who ducked without knowing that Mrs. Dempster was behind him. Her calamity was such that not only did she become mentally impaired (so much so that her husband, the Baptist minister for the town, had to tether her to furniture so that she would not wander off) but gave birth prematurely to Paul. By the end of *Fifth Business*, Dunstan, who has searched his whole life for that certain saint who saved him on the battlefield, is on the brink of mystery, or even of belief, but never of awe, let alone holiness. Instead, he pursues pseudo-mystery, first in the form of psychology, then of magic, and finally winding up with the anti-Mrs. Dempster, the monstrous Liesle (Liselott Vitsliputzli!). At the end of his days the most he knows is that the journey has not been about him, in spite of his suspicions. What the journey *is* about—in whom he is meant to repose—is a question he fails to ask, and, except as a source of psychological rather than holy mystery, Mary Dempster ceases to matter.

In fact, however, Mary is the genuine vehicle of awe and the numinous and a genuine saint. One miracle was her saving the life of Dunstan's brother, Willie, who by all signs was dead, until, inexplicably, she revived him. A second miracle was changing the life of a tramp who, after having sex with a willing Mary "because he needed it so much," becomes a beneficent, self-sacrificing street minister. The third miracle is the one having the most impact on Paul. Wounded and lost on the battlefield, he shelters in the ruin of a small church:

> I thought of Deptford, and I thought of Mrs. Dempster. Particularly I thought of her parting words to me: 'There's just one thing to remember; whatever happens, it does no good to be afraid.' Mrs. Dempster, I said aloud, was a fool. I was afraid, and I was not in a situation where doing good, or doing evil, had any relevance at all. It was then that one of the things happened that make my life strange . . . . I saw . . . in a niche a statue of the Virgin and Child . . . the assembly of elements that represent the Immaculate Conception . . . .. But what hit me worse than the blow of the shrapnel was Mrs. Dempster's

face . . .. Years later, when for the first time I read Coleridge's Kubla Khan and came on [see the epigraph at the start of this chapter]—I almost jumped out of my skin, for the words so perfectly described my state before I woke up in hospital . . .. From time to time the little Madonna appeared and looked at me with friendly concern before removing herself; once or twice she spoke, but I did not know what she said and did not need to know.[9]

It is as though Davies had Otto opened at his elbow as he describes in this passage what Percy describes as "clearing" a space for the numinous to happen—then had his hero walk on.

Sigrid Undset (1882-1949), the first woman to win the Nobel Prize for Literature, was at least as fond of writing long books as Davies was. One of her great works is a tetralogy, *The Master of Hestviken*, and her greatest, *Kristen Lavransdatter*, is a trilogy of more than eleven hundred pages. It tells of a woman of very great passion—filial, carnal, maternal, and finally spiritual—and of fierce, very fierce, independence, whose character and conviction must be a match for the fierceness of the elements, not only within her but around her, those of nature (virtually a main character), of society, and of human deception and brutality. Her fourteenth-century Norway is Christian, to be sure, and Kristin's faith will be her salvation when, especially at the very end, her physical and spiritual heroism save many during the great plague that finally kills her. But owing to the harshness as well as a luxuriant pagan beauty of the landscape, the great distances to be managed, and (often) the remoteness of established authority, the reader senses, if not a fragility in the religious foundation of the culture then certainly a spotty tenuousness. Though the culture is crossing the boundary into Christianity not every Norwegian has access to, without real moral and spiritual courage and resoluteness any one of them may fall back.

After submitting with abandon to the utterly feckless Erland (who had taken another man's wife and then abandoned her) in defiance of a thoroughly admirable father whom she dearly loves, Kristin marries Erland. Lavran's final words at the end of the *Bridal Wreath* are to his wife, who had confessed to an infidelity: "Earth has to be ground up, my Ragnfrid, before the food can grow." Kristin becomes *Mistress of Husaby* (the second book in the trilogy), Erland's estate, and nothing

---

[9] Robertson Davies, *Fifth Business* (New York: Penguin, 1970), 67-9.

she can do can prevent it from going to pieces. Erland proves ever feckless. When he dies, Kristin returns to her old homestead with her sons, some of whom die while others marry and leave. Finally, Kristin enters a convent and takes up *The Cross* (the third book), ministering to the dying, facing down a violent man who, swearing by the name of Satan, would sacrifice a child for his own safety, and lastly dying of the plague that would kill half the population of Europe.

Kristin no longer had her full wits about her, but she senses that she was being carried . . . .. Then the glow of light appeared outward to a large space; she was once again under a dark open sky . . . . Someone was carrying her—it was Ulf [her faithful, final friend]—but now he became one with all those who had ever carried her. When she put her arms around his neck . . . she felt like a child again . . . . Behind his dark head there were red lights, and they seemed to be shining from the fire that nourishes all love . . . . She had more a sense of contentment, the way she felt lying in bed back home at Jorundgaard, weary from a day's work well done . . . .. Suddenly the dying woman grew uneasy; her hands fumbled . . . around her neck. 'What is it?' asked Ulf. 'The cross,' she whispered, and pulled out her father's gilded cross . . . .. She owned nothing more than this and her wedding ring.[10]

After giving the ring away for Masses to be said, and seeing on her finger an impression of an M from the center of the ring where it had been etched in gold for the Virgin Mary, Kristin realizes that she will die before the mark has time to fade, "and it made her happy."

She had been a servant of God—a stubborn, defiant maid, most often an eye-servant in her prayers and unfaithful in her heart, indolent and neglectful . . . and yet He held her firmly in His service, and under the glittering gold ring a mark had been secretly impressed upon her, showing that she was His servant . . . and the red fog became thinner and lighter, and at last it was like a fine morning mist before the dawn breaks through, and there was not a sound and she knew that now she was dying.[11]

That is Kristin's end, which all along has been in her beginning. A few foundational elements of her life never change. "You are your father's dearest joy," Kristin's mother tells her. Another is her susceptibility to signs. As a small girl while standing in a church she

---

[10] Sigrid Undset, *Kristin Lavransdatter*, trans. by Tiina Nunnally (London: Penguin Books, 2005), 1122.

[11] Undset, *Kristin Lavransdatter*, 1119-21.

sees a picture that glowed as though made from glittering gemstones. "It was like standing at a great distance and looking into Heaven itself," and she began to distinguish . . . the Lord Jesus himself . . . the Virgin Mary in robes as blue as the sky." But such holy visions are not her only gift. Another one seems to shape her destiny. One day she is out riding with her father. The landscape is forbidding: angular, clotted with scree, high ledges dropping to rushing streams, heavily foliated bowers with infrequent clearings, sloping, narrow paths. Even in good weather merely riding at peace is not entirely safe. At one point the little girl veers off to pick raspberries, her horse Guldsvein following faithfully. Beneath a rock slab she comes upon "a deep black pool" beside which was a slab of rock on which she lay. The water stands "motionless; on the other side a sheer rock face rose up behind several slender birch trees and willow thickets." Kristin leans over the pool to see "if what Isrid had said was true, that she resembled her father." The space is idyllic. Kristin picks some valerian blossoms and with some blades of grass weaves a wreath that she then presses upon her head. "She was adorned like a grown-up maiden about to go off to a dance."

Again, she looks into the pool to behold herself. "Then she saw in the mirror of the stream that someone was standing among the birches on the other side and leaning toward her." At that, she straightens up to her knees and looks across the water.

> . . . she discerned a face among the leaves—there was a woman over there, with a pale face and flowing, flaxen hair. Her big light-gray eyes and her flaring, pale-pink nostrils reminded Kristin of Guldsvein's. She was wearing something shiny and leaf-green, and branches and twigs hid her figure up to her full breasts, which were covered with brooches and gleaming necklaces. Kristin stared at the vision. Then the woman raised her hand and showed her a wreath of golden flowers and beckoned to her with it.[12]

Guldsvein panics, his whinny bringing the other riders. Kristin, also in a panic, runs to her father, who has virtually galloped down the slope of the scree. Only when she sees Lavran's face does she realize the danger she had been in. Revealing that she saw someone, Lavrans asks, "was it a man?" "No," she answers, "it was a woman. She beckoned me . . . I think it was a dwarf maiden, Father." "Jesus

---

[12] Undset, *Kristin Lavransdatter*, 19.

Christ," says Lavrans, making the sign of the cross. A bit later, Isrid says, "that must have been the elf maiden—I tell you, she must have wanted to lure this pretty child into the mountain." Lavrans warns the party to keep silent: "Ragnfrid must never hear that the child was exposed to such danger." And yet she was, and some harm seems to have been done, for Kristin did go "into a mountain," where she would remain until she takes up the cross.

Unlike Dunstan, who would possess a clear problem but who should know better, Kristin participates in a rich mystery, does not merely study but follows the signs, and inhabits a world rooted in a period and a place filled with exquisite, abundant detail and charged with a wonder which she would indeed *connaître* rather than merely *savoir*—which is why she does not stop at the brink but, we are given to understand, will indeed rest with Him, her own *praeparatio* complete.

C. S. Lewis was a contemporary of both Davies and Undset (and of Thornton Wilder, who has "drunk the milk of paradise" and will presently make a cameo appearance, as a sort of coda). Lewis's influence, both public and deeply personal, continues more than fifty years after his death, with his prose fiction and non-fiction still commonly read. Two exceptions seem to be *The Pilgrim's Regress* (1933) and *Till We Have Faces* (1956), both more studied than enjoyed,[13] the former because it is both dense and complex, the latter for reasons I've adumbrated above.

The face in question in Lewis's great book is that of Orual, our first-person narrator, who is the queen of Glome, a kingdom on the fringe of the Hellenistic world. She is brilliant, tough, brave, unmarried, childless, ruthless (not unlike her psychotic late father) and, in her belief, so ugly as to require that she be veiled. She is also angry at the gods, in part because they hide but primarily because they seem to have taken her beautiful and saintly half-sister, Psyche, as a sacrifice. The whole book is therefore *her* book (at one point she says "I was with book"), her case against the gods. However, her complaint against the gods is complicated by the following facts: 1) when she

---

[13] My view of *The Pilgrim's Regress* as the template of much of Lewis's later writing—virtually all of his writing—appears at the beginning of "C. S. Lewis's Quantum Church," now collected in my *The Tongue Is Also a Fire: Essays on Conversation, Rhetoric and the Transmission of Culture . . . and on C. S Lewis* (Nashville, TN: New English Review Press, 2015). "Disobedience and Self-discovery: Reflections on Meaning in *Till We Have Faces*" is collected in *Why I Believe in Narnia.*

searches for the remains of her sister, who by now has surely been consumed by Glome's legendary Shadowbrute, she finds, not remains but a perfectly healthy, indeed glowing, sister; 2) her skeptical, indeed cynical, slave, the Fox, a captured Greek who calls divine stories mere songs invented for their beauty, later expresses holy fear when facing the numinous; 3) when she compels Psyche (by base emotional blackmail) to disobey the god-husband she claims to have, Orual, too, sees the glorious palace in which Psyche claims to have been living, a palace invisible (to Psyche's astonishment) to Orual until the disobedient act; very soon thereafter Orual denies the reliability of her own eyes; 4) in Part Two, Orual learns that several assumptions she had made (for example, about her full sister, Redival) were mistaken and not only mistaken but systematically uncharitable and self-serving. These realizations, along with the act of writing her book, finally bring Orual to 5) a series of visions that unfold certain mysteries, above all about herself, and prepare her for the approach of the god whom she had denied. The novel ends with Orual's consciousness having been so transformed that she is both chastened and wise in self-knowledge, her last words (and the last of the book) being, "only words, words; to be led out to battle against other words. Long did I hate you, long did I fear you. I might—"

But for Orual there was a sixth complication, one I skipped along the way and which now merits special attention. Glome is a small world, strange and marked by marvels as well as by a strict hierarchy, including a hierarchy of good and evil. Its *mysteria* (*tremendum* and *fascinosum*) will become palpable. These and other hallmarks of the wonder tale are indisputably present in Orual's world. While the book reflects Lewis's classic, recognizable sensibility, Orual's first-person paranoid, sociopathic, theophobic, voluble belligerence (and a willful intelligence capable of re-defining the world to suit her psycho-neurotic defense system) does not. *That* person belongs in a novel, and there she is. And it is at a certain point—the sixth complication—when the wonder tale meets the novel, in a passage that synecdochally defines this book as of a class—not Lewis's usual class but part of that company of strangers I've suggested.

To find Psyche Orual must ascend. With her is her utterly faithful right hand (in almost all things), Bardia. He knows the way. At a certain point Bardia leaves the road and takes to the grass. "That's the Holy Road," pointing out that Psyche went that way but that there's another, "steeper and shorter."

We now went for a long time over grass [Orual tells us], gently but steadily upward, making for a ridge so high and so near that the true Mountain was quite out of sight. When we topped it . . . everything was changed. And my struggle began. We had come into the sunlight now, too bright to look into and warm (I threw back my cloak). Heavy dew made the grass jewel-bright. The mountain . . . did not look like a solid thing . . .. To left and right, and behind us, the whole coloured world with all its hills was heaped up and up to the sky, with . . . a gleam of what we call the sea . . .. There was a lark singing. And my struggle was this.[14]

Here we have scene-setting worthy of Bronte, Hardy, or Conrad, and it even has its symbolic layer—sunlight, cloak, jewel-bright grass, and the sea. Orual has come to this place ready to welcome wonder, and she is feeling it. Until

You may well believe that I had set out sad enough . . . now, flung at me like frolic or insolence, there came as if it were a voice—not words—but if you made it into words it would be, 'Why should your heart not dance.' It's a measure of my folly [!] that my heart almost answered, 'Why not?' . . . my heart to dance? Mine, whose love was taken from me . . .. And yet it was a lesson I could hardly keep in my mind. The sight of the huge world put mad ideas into me, as if I could wander away . . . forever, see strange and beautiful things . . .. The freshness . . . all about me . . . made me feel that I had misjudged the world; it seemed kind, and laughing, as if its heart also danced . . .. Who can feel ugly when the heart meets delight? . . . Was I not right to struggle against this fool-happy mood? . . . I held my own . . . I ruled myself.[15]

And there we have our clearing for Being, a place of longing (Lewis's *Sehnsucht*) where Orual might repose, eventually with Him. But she turns, ruling herself, and our hero's journey thereby becomes exponentially more difficult for, as so many novels have taught us, there is no mightier struggle than the struggle against the self.

Now for our coda. Thornton Wilder (1897-1975) is our only author to win the Pulitzer Prize for both fiction (*The Bridge of San Luis Rey*, 1927) and drama (twice: *Our Town*, 1940, and *The Skin of Our Teeth*, 1942), as well as a National Book Award (*The Eighth Day*,

---

[14] Lewis, *Till We Have Faces*, 109.

[15] Lewis, *Till We Have Faces*, 109-11.

1967). Among his most striking and appealing characters is Chrysis, the woman of Andros, a *hetaera* (a highly cultivated courtesan who keeps a salon for young men) but also a philosopher and a very special sort of lover. Near her end (but not quite the very end of *The Woman of Andros*, 1930) she lays dying and says to Pamphilus, the young man who will marry her sister, "perhaps we shall meet somewhere beyond life when all these pains shall have been removed. I think the gods have some mystery still in store for us . . .. I have known the worst that the world can do to me, and that nevertheless I praise the world and all living . . .. Remember me as one who loved all things, and accepted from the gods all things, the bright and the dark. And you do likewise. Farewell." Later, just when Glycerium, Chrysis' sister, and Glycerium's baby (from Pamphilus) are near death in childbirth, Glyceium instructs (not unlike Mary Dempster) the father, "Do not be sorry; do not be afraid . . .. Wherever we are, we are yours." This wonder-filled but not marvel-filled book ends this way:

> In the hills the long dried stream-beds began to fill again and the noise of water falling from level to level [and] behind the thick beds of clouds the moon soared radiantly bright, shining upon all Italy and its smoking mountains. And in the East the stars shone tranquilly down upon the land that was soon to be called Holy and that even then was preparing its precious burden.[16]

That is its ending, but, as with Kristin, the ending all along was in the very beginning:

> The earth sighed as it turned in its course; the shadow of night crept gradually along the Mediterranean, and Asia was left in darkness . . . the mountains of Atlas showed deep blue pockets in their shining sides . . .. Triumph had passed from Greece and wisdom from Egypt, but with the coming on of night they seemed to regain their lost honors, and the land that was soon to be called Holy prepared in the dark its wonderful burden . . .. A fair tripping breeze ruffled the Aegean and all the islands of Greece felt a new freshness at the close of day.[17]

Or, as Pope St. John Paul II in his poem "Gospel" reminds us, "we look ahead calmly: we are beyond dread," for "truth supports man"

---

[16] Thornton Wilder, *The Woman of Andros* (New York: Albnert and Charles Boni, 1930), 162.

[17] Thornton Wilder, *The Woman of Andros*, 7-8.

and "we all find it within us, a mysterious mold" (as St. Augustine has already instructed us). The pope continues, "If we are to have dread, it shall be holy."[18] There, in their fearlessness, lies the wonder of my band of novelists, all of whom seem to know—as both Kierkegaard and C. S. Lewis have taught—that God is everywhere and everywhere incognito: their common *kappa* element, for all of them "on honeydew hath fed."

---

[18] Karol Wojtyla (St. Pope John Paul II), *Easter Vigil and Other Poems*, trans. by Jerzy Peterkiewicz (Rome: Libereria Editrice Vaticana, 1979).

Chapter 18

ACROSS WESTERN SEAS: LONGING FOR THE WEST IN TOLKIEN'S LEGENDARIUM

Laura Schmidt

When asked to contribute to this memorial volume, I knew my piece would be on Tolkien. Chris and I shared a great love for the works of J. R. R. Tolkien. Amidst our Tolkien-related discussions and experiences the topic of "Heaven" would come up, as it did so often with Chris, followed by a wistful sigh and musings on what Heaven is like. Reflecting on these moments led me to the closest approximation to Heaven Arda can offer: Valinor and "the West."

The western lands in Tolkien's *legendarium*[1] (Valinor,[2] Tol Eressëa,[3] and Númenor[4]) collectively serve as a nexus where the deepest themes of the work are manifest both on literal and symbolic levels. We will examine how the idea of a western paradise fits into an existing, rich mythical context, and then see how *longing* for "the West" is embodied within Tolkien's works, and experienced in a parallel manner by the reader.

DREAMING FROM WESTERN SHORES

The motifs of a western paradise land, or "Faërie," and sea journeying exist in some of Tolkien's earliest writings. The poem "Éalá Éarendel Engla Beorhtast" was the first poem Tolkien wrote

---

[1] The term legendarium refers to the complete cycle of tales Tolkien wrote about Middle-earth and the outlying western lands.

[2] Alternate names for "Valinor" include Aman, Blessed Realm, Undying Lands,* Valimar / Valmar, Ever-eve / Evereven, Uttermost West, Eldamar,* and Elvenhome.* Terms with asterisks include Valinor and Tol Eressëa.

[3] Also called the "Lonely Isle;" an island off the coast of Valinor.

[4] Alternate names include Westernesse, Númenórë, Andor, Anadûnê, Atalantë, and Elenna; an island between Eldamar and Middle-earth where the Númenóreans / Dúnedain lived (humans blessed with long life). Númenor means "West-land."

featuring the mariner Eärendel in September 1914. Inspired by seeing the name "Éarendel" in the Anglo-Saxon poem *Crist I*,[5] Tolkien started creating poems and bringing threads of languages together into what would become the *legendarium*; all beginning with a mariner who sped across the western seas and over the world's margin. More poems followed on similar western paradise themes.[6]

"Imram" is worth particular attention for the topic at hand. The poem features St. Brendan who, in Irish lore, sailed the western ocean to find the "Land of Promise," a place full of light and fruitfulness, and saw marvels along the way. What is fascinating is not simply Tolkien's use of Irish mythology in the poem, but the elements alluding to his *legendarium* alongside the traditional mythic imagery. The islands across the sea are inhabited by the *Elvenkind*, whose voices fill Brendan's tree of birds. A *white Tree* and a *guiding Star* also feature in the poem, along with a cloud over a land reminiscent of Númenor that has sunk beneath the waves.[7] Flieger calls this a deliberate "bridge between two mythologies."[8]

---

[5] *Crist I-III* appear in the Exeter Book. Cynewulf was thought to be the author of all three parts in Tolkien's time, however scholars today believe him to only be the author of *Crist II*.

[6] Additional titles include "The Shores of Faerie" (July 1915), "The Happy Mariners" (July 24, 1915), "The Song of Eriol" (ca. 1916-1918), "The Lonely Isle" (June 1916), "An Evening in Tavrobel" (1917), "The Nameless Land" (May 1924), "Looney" (ca. 1932-1933), "Errantry" (pub. 1933, 1962), "Firiel" (pub. 1934), "Imram" (pub. 1955), "The Last Ship" (pub. 1962), and "The Sea-Bell" (pub. 1962). The poem "The House of Eld" by Geoffrey Bache Smith also contains similar imagery of "a far isle set in the western sea." Tolkien edited the volume where the poem appeared in honor of Smith, his friend, who was killed in World War I. Geoffrey Bache Smith, "The House of Eld," in *A Spring Harvest*, ed. by J. R. R. Tolkien (London: Erskine Macdonald, 1918), 41.

[7] For more on "Imram" and St. Brendan's journey, see Tom Shippey, *The Road to Middle-earth: How J. R. R. Tolkien Created a New Mythology* (Boston: Houghton Mifflin, 2003), 287; Norma Roche, "Sailing West: Tolkien, the Saint Brendan Story, and the Idea of Paradise in the West," in *Mythlore*, 66 (Summer 1991), 16-20, 62; Paul Harold Kocher, *Master of Middle-earth: The Fiction of J. R. R. Tolkien* (Boston: Houghton Mifflin, 1972), 204-211; and Verlyn Flieger, *Interrupted Music: The Making of Tolkien's Mythology* (Kent, OH: Kent State University Press, 2005), 121-136.

[8] Flieger, *Interrupted*, 132.

Christopher Tolkien acknowledges his father's conscious decision for engaging traditional mythologies in this way, particularly in his conception of the tale of Númenor: "my father was envisaging a massive and explicit linking of his own legends with those of many other places and times: all concerned with the stories and the dreams of peoples who dwelt by the coasts of the great Western Sea."[9] Tolkien himself confirms this desire in a letter dated 5 January 1961: "[Legends of Númenor are] not based on special *knowledge*, but on a special personal concern with this tradition of the culture-bearing men of the Sea, which so profoundly affected the imagination of peoples of Europe with westward-shores."[10]

We may wonder then what traditions had such a strong imaginative cultural influence. The following Table [on pages 340-342], which is far from exhaustive, provides an overview of the extensive mythological context of a "western paradise across the sea" concept amongst European people groups.

And if Americans think we are left out, Matthew Lee Jockers puts forth a very intriguing speculation. Not only may our European ancestors have viewed American Shores as a "land of promise," but the ideals of the western expansion movement, lying deep in the American psyche, also embodied real, lucrative, uncharted territories, and the inherent European mythologies of a western paradise across unknown waters:

> Western America became a place where the lines between myth and reality converged. On the one hand, legends of a western paradise held a place in the collective unconsciousness, while on the other, real reports in the form of letters, newspaper clippings, and advertisements were coming from America telling of a place where land, mineral riches, and incredible adventure were to be had for the taking.[11]

text continued on page 343

---

[9] J. R. R. Tolkien, *The Lost Road and Other Writings, The History of Middle-earth, Vol. V,* ed by Christopher Tolkien (New York: Ballantine/ Del Rey, 1996), 109.

[10] J. R. R. Tolkien, *The Letters of J. R. R. Tolkien*, ed. by Humphrey Carpenter and Christopher Tolkien (Boston: Houghton Mifflin, 2000), 303 (#227).

[11] Matthew Lee Jockers, "In Search of Tir-Na-Nog: Irish and Irish-American Literature in the West." Doctoral dissertation, Southern Illinois University, Carbondale, April 1997, 23.

Table: European Mythologies relating to a Western Paradise across the Sea[i]

Names	Characteristics and Location	Culture
Tír na nÓg (spellings vary)[ii]	A land of eternal youth across the sea	Irish
Tír Tairngire	Land of promise / prophecy across the sea, St. Brendan's destination, home of the sea god Manannán Mac Lir	
Mag Mell / Mag Mór	"Plain of Joys," "Great / Pleasant Plain"—sometimes an island, and sometimes beneath the sea	
Tír fo Thuinn	"Land under the Wave," underwater Otherworld	
Hy Brasil / Hy Breasail[iii]	"Mysterious Island," "Island of Beauty / Might / Worth," western sea paradise island of no cares, thought to build on "Atlantis" myth[iv]	
Orbe Alio / Alius Orbis	"Otherworld" far-off lands separated from the known world by the impassable sea, where the dead go according to Druidical belief; mentioned by Lucan[v]	
Flath-innis	"Island of the Good / Brave," heaven	
Emain Ablach / Ynys Afallon	"Of the apples," an island of feasting, youth, and sensual pleasures in the western sea; thought to contribute to creation of "Avalon" in the Arthurian tradition[vi]	Welsh
Annwn / Annwfn / Tylwyth Teg	Western island, or underground, only reached by a treacherous "faery path"	
Cantre'r / Cantref Gwaelod	Sunken kingdom off west coast of Wales, similar to Atlantis tale	

Fortunate Isles / Islands of the Blessed / Elysian Fields / Elysium / Fortunatorum Insulae	Land of sunshine across the western sea, near Hades and the River Oceanos; home to heroes and immortals	Greek[viii]
Ogygia	Island in the west, home of Calypso (Homer's *Odyssey*), also associated with Atlantis, and a place of imprisonment for Chronos[vii]	
Garden of the Hesperides	Hera's blissful far-western garden at the edge of the ocean,[ix] where golden apples grow tended by nymphs[x]	
Atlantis[xi]	From Plato's dialogues *Timaeus and Critias*, a western island civilization founded by Poseidon, destroyed when citizens offended the gods	
Avalon[xii] / Insula Pomorum	Paradise island of fruit trees in the western sea where King Arthur sails to be healed and, in some stories, never dies	Arthurian legend

i For additional material on these and other related mythical locations, see Charles A. Huttar's very helpful essays: "Houses of Healing: The Idea of Avalon in Inklings Fiction and Poetry," in *The Inklings and King Arthur: Owen Barfield, C. S. Lewis, J. R. R. Tolkien, and Charles Williams on the Matter of Britain*, ed. by Sørina Higgins (Berkeley, CA: Apocryphile Press, 2018), 115–48; "Deep Lies the Sea-Longing': Inklings of Home," in *Mythlore*, 99/100 (Fall/Winter 2007), 5–27.

ii Tolkien once thought to include elements from Tír na nÓg into one of a series of tales forming the *Lost Road* story (Tolkien, *Lost Road*, 85). For more on how Tolkien incorporated Celtic and Norse mythology, see Marjorie J. Burns, "Norse and Christian Gods: The Integrative Theology of J. R. R. Tolkien," in *Tolkien and the Invention of Myth: A Reader*, ed. by Jane Chance (Lexington, KY: University Press of Kentucky, 2004), 163–78; *us Realms: Celtic and Norse in Tolkien's Middle-earth* (Toronto: University of Toronto Press, 2005).

iii   Mentioned in J. R. R. Tolkien, "On Fairy-Stories," in *The Tolkien Reader* (New York: Ballantine Books, 1966), 5.

iv   James MacKillop, *Myths and Legends of the Celts* (London: Penguin Books, 2006), 122.

v   MacKillop, *Myths and Legends*, 108.

vi   MacKillop, *Myths and Legends*, 123.

vii James Bonwick, *Irish Druids and Old Irish Religions* (Dorchester: Dorset Press, 1986), 287.

viii Bonwick also offers this interesting fact: "The main entrance of Greek temples was in the East, so that the worshippers might face the Happy West," 287-8.

ix   Some dispute as to location, see Huttar's essays on this topic. Hesperus, said to be the father of the nymphs, is another name for Venus / the Evening Star and is hence an interesting connection to Tolkien's Eärendil.

x   Hesperus, said to be father of the nymphs, is another name for Venus / the Evening Star and is hence an interesting connection to Tolkien's Eärendil. Eärendil.

xi   For how Tolkien arrived at a similar name for Númenor, Atalantë, "by chance" through his own created languages, see *J. R. R. Tolkien, The Peoples of Middle-earth*, The History of Middle-earth, Vol. XII, ed. by Christopher Tolkien (Boston: Houghton Mifflin, 1996), 158.

xii "Avallonë," meaning "near Valinor" (Robert Foster, *The Complete Guide to Middle-earth* [New York: Ballantine/Del Rey, 1979], 36), is Tolkien's given name for a seaport on the eastern shore of the island of Tol Eressëa. "Avallon" is Tolkien's earlier name for "Tol Eressëa" (Tolkien, *Peoples of Middle-earth*, 144, 146-7). Frodo's sailing west, presumably to Tol Eressëa, is compared by Tolkien to an Arthurian ending (Tolkien, *Sauron Defeated*, 132), but Frodo will eventually die and cannot return (Tolkien, *Letters*, 328 [#246]).

It is an idea worth considering, and makes the cultural ethos of the mythologies more recognizable in the American experience.

An instance not on the table that is also worth mentioning is the practice of ship burials. Shippey states:

> The belief in a Land of the Dead, or of future life, across the ocean must be the reason, Tolkien argued, for the Anglo-Scandinavian custom of burying kings and nobles in their ships, or under ovals of standing stones arranged to look like ships. It is hard, indeed, to think of a better explanation.[12]

One place Tolkien mentions this theory specifically is in an untitled lecture provided by Christopher Tolkien: "In the last lines 'Men can give no certain account of the havens where that ship was unladed' we catch an echo of the 'mood' of pagan times in which ship-burial was practised . . .. [A]n actual belief in a magical land or otherworld located 'over the sea.'"[13]

A notable *exception* to the examples in the mythologies table is Christian belief, which Tolkien himself adhered to as a Catholic. The east, rather than the west, is held in reverence by Christians,[14] symbolized by the rising sun and new life found in Christ. In contrast, the west bears the setting sun, sin, and death.[15] Many church altars to this day face east,[16] and facing east during baptism was an ancient

---

[12] Tom Shippey, *J. R. R. Tolkien: Author of the Century* (Boston: Houghton Mifflin, 2002), 283.

[13] Tolkien, *The Lost Road*, 106.

[14] Including Orthodox Christians. See John A. McGuckin, ed. *The Encyclopedia of Eastern Orthodox Christianity* (Malden, MA: Wiley-Blackwell, 2011), 66; Metropolitan Hilarion Alfeyev, *Orthodox Christianity, Volume III: The Architecture, Icons and Music of the Orthodox Church*, trans. by Andrei Tepper (Yonkers, NY: St. Vladimir's Seminary Press, 2011), 81; and Basil (St. Basil the Great), *On the Holy Spirit, Popular Patristics Series*, trans. by David Anderson (Yonkers, NY: St. Vladimir's Seminary Press, 1980), 100 (ch. 27, #66).

[15] One of the earliest and most interesting references I came across for this stance by Christians is found in the *Divine Institutes* originally written ca. 303-311. See Lactantius, *The Works of Lactantius, Volume I*, Ante-Nicene Christian Library: Translations of the Writings of the Fathers, Vol. XXI, trans. by William Fletcher, ed. by Alexander Roberts and James Donaldson (Edinburgh: T and T Clark, 1871), 110-11.

[16] Angelo Di Berardino, ed., *Encyclopedia of Ancient Christianity Volume One: A-E* (Downers Grove: InterVarsity Press, 2014), 761; Hilarion, *Orthodox Christianity*, 81.

practice that is also still followed by some believers:

> When the persons to be baptized entered the baptistery . . . they
> were placed with their faces towards the west, and commanded
> to renounce Satan with some gesture or rite; this they did
> by striking their hands together as token of abhorrence, by
> stretching out their hands against him, by exsufflation, and by
> spitting at him as if he were present. They were then turned
> round to the east, and desired to lift up their hands and eyes
> to heaven, and enter into covenant with Christ, the Sun of
> Righteousness.[17]

Bonwick's comment that "[t]he early Christian preachers tried hard
to dispel these [western] images of the heathen paradise"[18] makes
one wonder if part of that approach included introducing a different
cardinal direction for worship. Tolkien, however, embraced the west
for his mythological ideal of paradise in Middle-earth, aligning it
with European traditions that stretched across the centuries.[19]

Since Tolkien imagined Middle-earth as our world in an earlier
era of its history, this is far from surprising. Tolkien mentions this,
amongst other places, in *Letters* #151, #165, and #211.[20] Birzer
summarizes Middle-earth's European connection as follows:
"Middle-earth corresponded, in mythical form, to Europe. The term
was, tellingly, an Anglo-Saxon term for 'the land between the oceans,'
'the land between Heaven and hell,' the 'land between the spirit and
the material'."[21] The map of Middle-earth acquired by the Bodleian

---

[17] John Eadie, ed., *The Ecclesiastical Cyclopedia; or Dictionary of
Christian Antiquities and Sects, Comprising Architecture, Controversies,
Creeds, Customs, Denominations, Doctrines, Government, Heresies, History,
Liturgies, Rites, Monastic Orders, and Modern Judaism* (London: Griffin,
Bohn, and Company, Stationers' Hall Court, 1862), 105.

[18] Bonwick, *Irish Druids*, 301.

[19] For C. S. Lewis fans wondering about Reepicheep sailing to
Aslan's Country in the East (*The Voyage of the "Dawn Treader"*), remember
that it also may be found in a western garden not unlike the Hesperides
(*The Magician's Nephew*). Aslan's Country borders Narnia on both sides.
See Paul F. Ford, *Companion to Narnia: A Complete Guide to the Magical
World of C. S. Lewis's* The Chronicles of Narnia, rev. ed. (San Francisco:
HarperSanFrancisco, 2005), 94-96. See also John's westward journeying
and longing in Lewis's *The Pilgrim's Regress*.

[20] Tolkien, *The Letters*, 186 (#151), 220 (#165), and 283 (#211).

[21] Bradley J. Birzer, "The 'Last Battle' as a Johannine Ragnarök:
Tolkien and the Universal," in *The Ring and the Cross: Christianity and* The

Library in 2016 also reinforces these European connections. Tolkien and illustrator Pauline Baynes had both made annotations on the map in 1969 for Baynes to consult while working to create a poster map of Middle-earth. Tolkien's notes on the map state that Hobbiton is at the approximate latitude of Oxford, and Minas Tirith stands at the latitude of Ravenna in Northern Italy.[22] So as it turns out, Middle-earth and Europe are quite compatible after all.

Besides the various European mythologies mentioned above, there are of course numerous literary works which influenced Tolkien's *legendarium* and its themes. One notable piece of literature containing longing across the western sea is John Buchan's story "The Far Islands."[23] Tolkien enjoyed Buchan's stories and was perhaps familiar with them by the mid-1920s,[24] but there seems no certain proof that he read "The Far Islands," nor any additional clues to his thoughts on Buchan's tales. The number of similarities between "The Far Islands" and his own work are remarkable though. It tells of a young man enamored with dreams and waking visions of the western seas off the Scottish coast, where his ancestors lived, and his perpetual desire to sail past the Rim of Mist to discover the apple-scented land of pines that is hinted at lying beyond. He catches snippets of a language he does not know describing this land of promise, echoes of text from Geoffrey of Monmouth's *Historia Regum Britanniae*, and he soon finds his desire and the visions to be all-consuming. Shortly before he is killed by a sniper's bullet, the visions and reality begin blending, giving him hope and strength beyond that of his military companions. At last, at his death, he reaches the distant shore:

Lord of the Rings, ed. by Paul E. Kerry and Sandra Miesel (Madison, NJ: Fairleigh Dickinson University Press, 2011), 261.

[22] Bodleian Libraries, University of Oxford. "Bodleian Libraries Acquires Rare Map of Middle-earth Annotated by Tolkien." 3 May 2016. www.bodleian.ox.ac.uk/news/2016/may-03

[23] First published in *Blackwood's Magazine*, November 1899, and later collected in John Buchan, *The Watcher by the Threshold and Other Tales* (London: William Blackwood and Sons 1902).

[24] See John Buchan, "The Far Islands," in *Tales Before Tolkien: The Roots of Modern Fantasy*, ed. by Douglas A. Anderson (New York: Del Rey/Ballantine Books, 2003), 195; Humphrey Carpenter, *Tolkien: A Biography* (Boston: Houghton Mifflin, 1977), 165; and Raymond Edwards, *Tolkien* (London: Robert Hale, 2014), 45.

He turned, every limb alert with a strange new life, crying out words which had shaped themselves on his lips and which an echo seemed to catch and answer. There was the green forest before him, the hills of peace, the cold white waters. With a passionate joy he leaped on the beach, his arms outstretched to this new earth, this light of the world, this old desire of the heart—youth, rapture, immortality.[25]

Reading this story, and reflecting on the myths discussed before, immediately brings strong imagery from Tolkien's works to mind: Young Oswin "lying gazing out to [the western] sea with his chin in his hands" from *The Lost Road*,[26] the ancestral dreams of Númenor in *The Notion Club Papers*,[27] and the many instances in *The Silmarillion* and *The Lord of the Rings* of Elves and Men (not to mention Gandalf and a hobbit or two) yearning for what lies across the western seas; for some a future promise and for others lost forever and unreachable. The sea dreams of Frodo, the characters who have speech come to them unbidden in a language they do not know, "Elvenhome" and the "light of Faery" even make a brief appearance across the western sea in *Roverandom*.[28] All of these instances share similarities with Buchan's story.

Tolkien describes having a similar "ancestral" dream linked to the downfall of Atlantis, which his son Michael also shared: "I have what some might call an Atlantis complex. Possibly inherited . . . I mean the terrible recurrent dream (beginning with memory) of the Great Wave, towering up, and coming in ineluctably over the trees and green fields."[29] This dream he "bequeaths" to Faramir,[30] serving

---

[25] Buchan, "The Far Islands," 212.

[26] Tolkien, *The Lost Road*, 39.

[27] J. R. R. Tolkien, *Sauron Defeated*, The History of Middle-earth, Vol. IX, ed. by Christopher Tolkien (Boston: Houghton Mifflin, 1992), 145-327. *The Notion Club Papers* is the literary descendant of *The Lost Road*, followed later by the story of Númenor in the "Akallabêth" of *The Silmarillion*.

[28] J. R. R. Tolkien, *Roverandom* (Boston: Houghton Mifflin, 1998), 74. See also Kris Swank, "The Irish Otherworld Voyage of Roverandom," in *Tolkien Studies, Vol. 12*, (Morgantown: West Virginia University Press, 2015), 31-57.

[29] Tolkien, *Letters*, 213 (#163).

[30] J. R. R. Tolkien, *The Return of the King*, The Lord of the Rings. Collector's ed. (Boston: R. R. Houghton Mifflin, 1993), 240 (Bk. VI, ch. 50), "The Steward and the King."

as a memory of the loss of Númenor. Verlyn Flieger draws these expressions of dream, memory, and language together showing that they are the key ways that Tolkien connects the threads of time:

> Time, as Tolkien envisioned it, was not a simple forward progression but a complex field of experience encompassing past, present, and future, a field of experience to which dream, memory, and language all gave access. These two triads—past, present, and future and dream, memory, and language—are strands that wind around one another to form a continuous theme throughout Tolkien's work.[31]

And so Middle-earth sits on the border of the western sea, full of European allusions, mythological cultural resonances, and the trimmings of language, dreams, and memory. For Tolkien these elements aid the richness of history, the passage of time, and the essence of longing they accompany. Let us now examine some instances of "western longing" in the *legendarium*.

LONGING IN THE *LEGENDARIUM*

First, some guidelines of "the west" theme investigation ought to be given. There are plenty of times in the *legendarium* where "the west" is simply a cardinal direction, and even these cases vary between a capitalized "West," and its lowercase variant. What one makes of these instances is left open to interpretation.[32] One must also be cautious to avoid thinking of "the west" (or West) as "Heaven." The western lands are an earthly paradise[33] which most closely resembles an Edenic kind of setting, but we must not forget that evil has infiltrated these places already. For the Elves, Eldamar is an immortal realm of peace and plenty as long as Arda (earth) endures, and after that their fate is unknown since their existence is connected to the created world. For Men in the *legendarium*, upon death they go where neither they nor the Elves can tell.[34] Men long for Númenor knowing

---

[31] Verlyn Flieger, *Splintered Light: Logos and Language in Tolkien's World*, rev. ed. (Kent, OH: Kent State University Press, 2002), 5.

[32] See Lobdell's chapter "In the Far Northwest of the Old World" for more on cardinal directions. Jared Lobdell, *The World of the Rings: Language, Religion, and Adventure in Tolkien* (Chicago: Open Court, 2004), 71-94.

[33] Tolkien, *Letters*, 198 (#154).

[34] Tolkien's later writings are well worth considering on these topics. See in particular the "Athrabeth Finrod ah Andreth" in *Morgoth's Ring*,

that even at its height it did not grant immortality, and attempting to grasp deathlessness brought about its downfall. Men also cannot escape death in Eldamar, and living in Aman would actually do them harm as Tolkien describes in *Morgoth's Ring*.[35] So both races face mystery beyond the shores of the western lands. The west also carries with it qualities reminiscent of the realm of "Faërie," and in works like *Roverandom* is clearly akin to it—albeit playfully in that instance. Tolkien states plainly in "On Fairy-Stories" that "[t]he road to fairyland is not the road to Heaven; nor even to Hell."[36] And yet it still serves as something utterly desirable and outside of oneself, what Tolkien describes as catering to "primordial human desires"[37] and this is the "longing" we want to examine.

Tolkien lists several of these human desires in "On Fairy-Stories," but "the oldest and deepest desire, [is] the Great Escape: the Escape from Death."[38] It is not surprising then that he repeatedly lists death and immortality as main themes of *The Lord of the Rings*, and arguably of *The Silmarillion* as well.[39] Those stories deal with the reconciliation of Men to their fate of dying and leaving the Circles of the World, and the long, slow journey of the Elves through the ages, tied to Arda until its end. Men grapple with their destinies[40] and Elves embalm,[41] preserving their natural realms from the fading brought by time. But amidst these struggles, often even intermingled with defeat, there is a thread of hope that stretches back to the West and the lands across the sea where the Valar dwell, servants of Eru Ilúvatar, the god of Arda.

One of the best symbols of this hope and longing for the West is embodied in Tolkien's use of light. Flieger describes the importance of light in the *legendarium*:

---

which gives some hints about the fates of Elves and Men. J. R. R. Tolkien, *Morgoth's Ring: The Later Silmarillion Part One*, The History of Middle-earth, Vol. X, ed. by Christopher Tolkien. (London: HarperCollins, 2015).

[35] See section XI of "Myths Transformed" under the heading "Aman and Mortal Men" in Tolkien, *Morgoth's Ring*, 427-430.

[36] Tolkien, "On Fairy-Stories," 34.

[37] Tolkien, "On Fairy-Stories," 41.

[38] Tolkien, "On Fairy-Stories," 85.

[39] See Tolkien, *Letters*, 145 (#131), 246 (#186), 262 (#203), and 267 (#208).

[40] Tolkien, "Athrabeth Finrod ah Andreth" in *Morgoth's Ring*.

[41] Tolkien, *Letters*, 151 (#131), 152 (#131), 177 (#144), and 236 (#181).

The alternation between the vision of hope and the experience of despair—between light and dark—is the essence both of Tolkien and of his work. The contrast and interplay of light and dark are essential elements of his fiction. The light-dark polarity operates on all levels—literal, metaphoric, symbolic . . . .. More than anything else, and more than most mythologies, [*The Silmarillion*] is a story about light. Images of light in all stages . . . It is a world peopled with sub-creators whose interactions with and attitudes toward the light shape their world and their own destinies within it.[42]

The Children of Ilúvatar, Men and Elves, both experience a longing for the West in relation to a wholesome, some might say even holy, Light. Following their Fall, which happens outside the story in *The Silmarillion*,[43] men are drawn towards the light in the West: "'A darkness lies behind us,' Bëor said; 'and we have turned our backs upon it, and we do not desire to return thither even in thought. Westwards our hearts have been turned, and we believe that there we shall find Light.'"[44] (It is interesting to note that the traditional placement of Eden was in the east,[45] although Genesis suggests that Adam and Eve were possibly expelled from the eastern side of the garden, and Cain settled in lands east of Eden.[46]) For the Elves, the light of the stars is their first sight upon awakening, hence their continued veneration for Varda / Elbereth, the Vala who created the stars. The very name "Eldar" means "people of the stars,"[47] however that name eventually becomes associated with only those elves who travel West and see the light of Valinor. Light even draws the Teleri Elves more strongly than their love of the sound of the waves, which echo the Music of the Ainur from creation:[48] "[The Teleri] were torn between the love of

---

[42] Flieger, *Splintered Light* 4, 49. See also Tolkien *Letters*, 148 (#131), footnote.

[43] Tolkien, *Letters*, 387 (#297).

[44] J. R. R. Tolkien, *The Silmarillion*, ed, by Christopher Tolkien, illustrated by Ted Nasmith (Boston: Houghton Mifflin, 2004), 137.

[45] A. Keith Kelly and Michael , "'A Far Green Country': Tolkien, Paradise, and the End of All Things in Medieval Literature," in *Mythlore*, 105/106 (Spring/Summer 2009), 95; Basil (St. Basil the Great), *On the Holy Spirit*, Popular Patristics Series, trans. by David Anderson (Yonkers, NY: St. Vladimir's Seminary Press, 1980), 100 (Ch. 27, #66); Genesis 2:8.

[46] Genesis 3:24, 4:16.

[47] Tolkien, *Silmarillion*, 38.

[48] Tolkien, *Silmarillion*, 6.

the music of the waves upon their shores, and the desire to see again their kindred and to look upon the splendour of Valinor; but in the end desire of the light was the stronger."[49]

From the Two Trees to the Silmarils, Galadriel's Phial, the placement of sunlight in strategic and dramatic moments, and even the times when Gandalf glows with a hidden power, the instances where Tolkien uses light are too numerous to list here. I will pick one example, however, showing how this imagery threads through the *legendarium*: the Valacirca constellation. Its name literally means "Sickle of the Valar"[50] and it was created by Varda / Elbereth, the Vala of light. She is said to be the Vala most feared by Melkor, and has the "light of Ilúvatar" in her face, which is one of great beauty.[51] She created the first stars, and after the destruction of the Two Lamps realized Middle-earth and the coming Elves needed more light. A second set of brighter stars was then formed by Elbereth using the dews of the tree Telperion, including specific constellations bearing great meaning. Menelmacar (our Orion) carries a promise for the defeat of evil in the last days of Arda,[52] as does the Valacirca (our Ursa Major / Big Dipper), a constellation called "the Seven Stars," "the Sickle," "the Wain" by the Hobbits, and possibly "Durin's Crown" by the Dwarves.[53] *The Silmarillion* states "And high in the north as a challenge to Melkor [Varda] set the crown of seven mighty stars to swing, Valacirca, the Sickle of the Valar and sign of doom."[54] Any time the Valacirca makes an appearance in the text, those readers who are attuned to its meaning glimpse a hope instilled in the heavens by the Lords of the West, watching over the suffering masses of Middle-earth,[55] and causing doubt and fear in the servants of evil. Bilbo sees

---

[49] Tolkien, *Silmarillion*, 52.

[50] Robert Foster, *The Complete Guide to Middle-earth* (New York: Ballantine/Del Rey, 1979), 513.

[51] Tolkien, *Silmarillion*, 14.

[52] See Birzer's excellent summary of how Tolkien envisioned the events during the last days of Arda. Bradley J. Birzer, "The 'Last Battle' as a Johannine Ragnarök: Tolkien and the Universal," in *The Ring and the Cross: Christianity and The Lord of the Rings*, ed. by Paul E. Kerry and Sandra Miesel (Madison, NJ: Fairleigh Dickinson University Press, 2011), 259-82.

[53] Foster, *Complete Guide to Middle-earth*, 513.

[54] Tolkien, *Silmarillion*, 37.

[55] Eärendil also serves as a symbol of light and hope to the inhabitants

"the Wain" in Laketown before he must face the terrors of Smaug and the Battle of the Five Armies.[56] Frodo spots "the Sickle . . . swinging bright" above Bree-Hill in the midst of the fearful night when the Black Riders attack the Prancing Pony,[57] and the Seven Stars adorn Aragorn's sword Andúril (meaning: the flame of the West),[58] the Doors of Durin leading to Moria,[59] the King's Standard,[60] and the Crown of Gondor.[61] The Seven Stars also overlap as a symbol of the house of Elendil and his heirs; Aragorn's ancestors the faithful Númenóreans and the Dúnedain (meaning "west men") who sailed out of the ruin of Númenor. That house carries much of the hope of the Men of Middle-earth, and its origins are revered and remembered.

It is striking to see how characters respond to this presence of "the West" and its memory in Middle-earth, and where they place themselves in the resulting spectrum of the powers of good and evil. While many characters are high in respect and in power in the created hierarchy of Arda because of their direct connection to the West, some of them choose to turn away in rebellion and hopelessness. Sauron and Melkor are naturally the first to come to mind, but we must also consider Denethor and Saruman. Denethor at the height of his madness and despair, thinking that the forces of Mordor will soon overwhelm Minas Tirith's defenses, says notably, "The West has failed" *three* times.[62] Granted, this could also include his grief that the Rohirrim have failed to appear when they are needed most, but given Denethor's strong Númenórean lineage, highlighted several times in the text, the statement seems to go straight to a hopelessness that the Lords of the West, the Valar themselves and possibly even Ilúvatar, have forsaken the cause of the free peoples of Middle-earth.[63] Tolkien

---

of Middle-earth, particularly the Elves. See Tolkien, *Return*, 314; Appendix A.

[56] Tolkien, *Hobbit*, 190 (ch. 10).

[57] J. R. R. Tolkien, *The Fellowship of the Ring*, The Lord of the Rings, Collector's Edition (Boston: Houghton Mifflin, 1993), 187 (Bk. I, ch. 10).

[58] Tolkien, *Fellowship*, 290 (Bk. II, ch. 3).

[59] Tolkien, *Fellowship*, 318 (Bk. II, ch. 4).

[60] Tolkien, *Return*, 123 (Bk. V, ch. 6).

[61] Tolkien, *Return*, 245 (Bk. VI, ch. 5).

[62] Tolkien, *Return*, 99 (Bk. V, ch. 4) and 128-9 (Bk. V, ch. 7).

[63] Tolkien shows this connection is still present with the eagle messenger who flies to Minas Tirith after Sauron's downfall, seemingly with a message of hope directly from the "Lords of the West" (Valar).

also makes it clear that amongst the Wild Men in the south and east,[64] and even amongst the faithful Númenóreans who sailed to Middle-earth, there were some who turned to serve Sauron, and likewise hated the West and its descendants dwelling in Middle-earth: "And Sauron gathered to him great strength of his servants out of the east and the south; and among them were not a few of the high race of Númenor . . . [M]any more remembered Sauron in their hearts and hated the kingdoms of the West."[65]

Saruman the White, a wizard, has one of the most tragic falls as he turns from the West. His wisdom and learning change to self-seeking power and the abandonment of the original task given to the Istari,[66] to help the peoples of Middle-earth in their battle against Sauron. At the moment of his death, we see his last engagement with the West:

> To the dismay of those that stood by, about the body of Saruman a grey mist gathered, and rising slowly to a great height like smoke from a fire, as a pale shrouded figure it loomed over the Hill. For a moment it wavered, looking to the West; but out of the West came a cold wind, and it bent away, and with a sigh dissolved into nothing.[67]

Was this one last look of regret or remorse? Or a final act of judgement by the Valar? We cannot say for certain, but it is a Western wind that ushers the last semblance of Saruman out of Middle-earth after his long rebellion.

We see in contrast the actions of Faramir, Gandalf, and other friends of the West. At Henneth Annûn, Tolkien introduces us to one of the only vestiges in the *legendarium* of a religious ritual: the "Standing Silence"[68] of Faramir and his men turning to the West before beginning their evening meal:

Tolkien, *Return*, 241 (Bk. VI, ch. 5).

[64] Tolkien, *Letters*, 157 (#131) and Tolkien, *Return*, 227 (Bk. VI, ch. 4).

[65] Tolkien, *Silmarillion*, 303, 305.

[66] Five wizards sent to Middle-earth by the Valar, including Saruman, Gandalf, and Radagast. See J. R. R. Tolkien, *Unfinished Tales*, ed. by Christopher Tolkien (Boston: Ballantine Books, 1988), Part 4.II, "The Istari."

[67] Tolkien, *Return*, 300 (Bk. VI, ch. 8).

[68] Repeated at the Field of Cormallen. Tolkien, *Return*, 233 (Bk. VI, ch. 4).

> Before they ate, Faramir and all his men turned and faced west in a moment of silence. Faramir signed to Frodo and Sam that they should do likewise. "So we always do," he said, as they sat down: "we look towards Númenor that was, and beyond to Elvenhome that is, and to that which is beyond Elvenhome and will ever be."[69]

This serves as a moment of poignant respect, commemoration of the Departed, of longing for a lost heritage, of memory, and a glimpse beyond to the Powers that shaped the world.[70] And in Faramir,[71] Frodo and Sam detect "an elvish air . . . good and true" that reminds them of Gandalf, which Faramir says is the "air of Númenor."[72] Gandalf remains true to his appointed task of aiding in the war against Sauron. He stands boldly on the bridge of Khazad-Dûm against the terror of the Balrog declaring: "I am a servant of the Secret Fire, wielder of the flame of Anor. You cannot pass. The dark fire will not avail you, flame of Udûn. Go back to the Shadow! You cannot pass."[73] He aligns himself directly with the Powers of the West since the "Secret Fire" is specifically associated with Ilúvatar, and interestingly enough, "Udûn" is translated as "un-west" by Robert Foster.[74] Gandalf also gives a meaningful glance to the West when Gimli asks him if he had planned for all of the adventures of the Ring to unfold as they did and end in victory:

> "But who wove the web? I do not think I have ever considered that before. Did you plan all this then, Gandalf? If not, why did you lead Thorin Oakenshield to such an unlikely door? To find the Ring and bring it far away into the West for hiding, and then to choose the Ringbearer – and to restore the Mountain Kingdom as a mere deed by the way: was not that your design?"

> Gandalf did not answer at once. He stood up, and looked out

---

[69] J. R. R. Tolkien, *The Two Towers*, The Lord of the Rings, Collector's ed. (Boston: Houghton Mifflin, 1993), 284-5 (Bk. IV, ch. 5).

[70] Tolkien, *Letters*, 281 (#211); see footnote.

[71] Gandalf says that in Faramir: "the blood of Westernesse runs nearly true in him." Tolkien, *Return*, 31 (Bk. V, ch. 1).

[72] Tolkien, *Two Towers*, 291 (Bk. IV, ch. 5).

[73] Tolkien, *Fellowship*, 344 (Bk. II, ch. 5).

[74] Foster, *Complete Guide to Middle-earth*, 504. Other sources translate it as "the pit," "underworld," or "hell."

of the window, west, seawards; and the sun was then setting, and a glow was in his face. He stood so a long while silent.[75]

It is a touching moment.

Other members of the Fellowship show longing for the West, and serve as a fitting cross-section for the free peoples of Middle-earth. Legolas experiences westward longing the first time he hears gulls by the shore: "[the gulls'] wailing voices spoke to me of the Sea. The Sea! Alas! I have not yet beheld it. But deep in the hearts of all my kindred lies the sea-longing, which it is perilous to stir. Alas! for the gulls. No peace shall I have again under beech or under elm."[76] Legolas shares the longing we have seen already in the hearts of the Elves in *The Silmarillion*, and Galadriel had warned him of such a fate if he encountered the sea.[77] Gildor and his companions also sing of Elbereth (Varda) and the Western Seas in *The Fellowship of the Ring*,[78] as do the elves in Rivendell[79] and Lothlórien.[80] As Hobbits, Frodo, Sam, and Bilbo are exceptional. They are always interested in the doings of elves and, in turn, have a reverence for the West and all its resonances. By the end of his journey, Frodo is weary and beyond any healing Middle-earth can provide, hence his later decision to sail West when he sees that not even the delights of Rivendell can be fully enjoyed any longer: "Yes, [Rivendell has] something of everything, Sam, except the Sea."[81] Even Gimli the dwarf mentions the "Western Seas" and "crown of stars" in his song reminiscing about the days of Durin while the Fellowship walks through the darkness of Moria.[82] And, of course, Gimli is the only known dwarf to sail across the sea to the Undying Lands with Legolas after the War of the Ring.[83] The West remains connected to the peoples of Middle-earth through longing, rebellion, and, for some, eventual physical attainment.

---

[75] Tolkien, *Unfinished Tales*, 343-4, "The Quest of Erebor."

[76] Tolkien, *Return*, 149 (Bk. V, ch. 9).

[77] Tolkien, *Two Towers*, 106 (Bk. III, ch. 5). See also Legolas's song in Tolkien, *Return*, 234-5 (Bk. VI, ch. 4).

[78] Tolkien, *Fellowship*, 88-9 (Bk. I, ch. 3).

[79] Tolkien, *Fellowship*, 250 (Bk. II, ch. 1).

[80] Tolkien, *Fellowship*, 394 (Bk. II, ch. 8).

[81] Tolkien, *Return*, 265 (Bk. VI, ch. 6).

[82] Tolkien, *Fellowship*, 329-30 (Bk. II, ch. 4).

[83] Tolkien, *Return*, 378 (Appendix B, year 1541).

INSIDE AND OUTSIDE THE STORY:
LONGING FOR THE READER

Yet what does this westward and sea "longing" ultimately signify amongst the peoples of Middle-earth? Closer interaction with an unstained world? Immortality? Connectedness with the numinous and deity? Some of these concepts match the "primordial human desires" that Tolkien references in "On Fairy-Stories," which such tales are supposed to inspire. As mentioned earlier, "the West" is an *earthly* paradise and not Heaven. In the *legendarium,* its closest approximation is Faërie with the desires it stirs, or a kind of Eden with its paradisiacal qualities. Tolkien states "Fairy-stories were plainly not primarily concerned with possibility, but with desirability. If they awakened *desire,* satisfying it while often whetting it unbearably, they succeeded."[84] Compare this statement with the following excerpt from a letter to his son Christopher: "certainly there was an Eden on this very unhappy earth. We all long for it, and we are constantly glimpsing it: our whole nature at its best and least corrupted, its gentlest and most humane, is still soaked with the sense of 'exile.'"[85] The similarity is striking, and also presents Tolkien's concept of humanity as "exiles," which Flieger points out as an extremely important factor in understanding the concept of longing in Tolkien's works:

> It is this longing that engenders the wanderlust of all of Tolkien's far-traveled characters, of whom there are many. Yet however the particular story is conceived, whoever the particular character is, in whatever work he occurs, the destination of every such traveler is always some version of another world, whether it lies beyond Bree or in Númenor or in the Uttermost West. Writ large, the destination is Faërie, the world for which Tolkien longed all his life, the realm of imagination in which his vital creative life was lived. Whoever he is, the traveler is one who not only travels far but who—in one way or another—travels away from the world of ordinary humanity, the land of those (himself among them) whom Tolkien saw as exiles.[86]

---

[84] Tolkien, "On Fairy-Stories," 63.

[85] Tolkien, *Letters,* 110 (#96).

[86] Verlyn Flieger, *A Question of Time: J. R. R. Tolkien's Road to Faërie* (Kent, OH: Kent State University Press, 1997), 162-3.

Both Flieger[87] and Shippey[88] state that Tolkien had the longing of an "exile" throughout his life, hopeful at times but despairing at others; particularly later in life and perhaps parallel to his frustration with finding time and creative inspiration as he grew older. This is reflected in some of his works like *Smith of Wootton Major*, "The Last Ship," and "The Sea-Bell," where characters are strangers in Faërie and do not find consolation, or the barriers to reaching Faërie become more impenetrable. This dichotomy in Tolkien's life also resonates with his balance between hope and despair in the *legendarium*, and the ever-present reality of death and defeat even amidst joy and victory.

And yet, at the end, *The Lord of the Rings* brings the main tales of the *legendarium* to the "Consolation of the Happy Ending," which Tolkien claims "all complete fairy-stories must have."[89] Against all odds, fears, doubts, and through perilous journeys, Sauron is defeated, the Ring is destroyed, Aragorn gains the crown, and several of the main characters actually see the longing for the West achieved as they sail across the sea and take the Straight Road at the end of the book. Hope is allowed to reach fulfillment; eucatastrophe occurs. Paul Tillich stated that "art in all its forms can show three states of the mind: hopelessness, foolish hope, and genuine hope . . . [A]rtistic interpretations of genuine hope . . . are rare today."[90] Gabriel Fackre, in a quote Chris Mitchell often used, took Tillich's comments and said: "[W]e here nominate Oxford don J. R. R. Tolkien, with his Hobbit world, as a literary candidate for the cadre of modern hopers."[91] This is one of Tolkien's many gifts through his writing: allowing his readers to experience the longings of his characters, with real defeats looming and possible, and to celebrate hope realized. Clyde S. Kilby shares one instance of this shared experience between book and reader:

> Someone wrote me of a sixth-grade pupil who, after reading *The Lord of the Rings*, had cried for two days. I think it must have been a cry for life and meaning and joy from the wasteland

---

[87] Flieger, *A Question of Time* 216-8.

[88] Shippey, *The Road to Middle-earth*, 285-8.

[89] J. R. R. Tolkien, "On Fairy-Stories" in *The Tolkien Reader* (New York: Ballantine Books, 1966), 85.

[90] Paul Tillich, "The Right to Hope" in *The University of Chicago Magazine* (November 1965), 19-20.

[91] Gabriel Fackre, *The Rainbow Sign: Christian Futurity* (Grand Rapids, MI: Eerdmans, 1969), 31.

which had somehow already managed to capture this boy.[92]

Shippey states: "*The Lord of the Rings* could be claimed as a 'myth against discouragement'"[93] which seems to get at the heart of why the book has impacted its readers so deeply, and why the essence of longing embedded there parallels the "exile" existence of readers who Tolkien says need to be fed by the nourishment of fairy-stories. "Thus," as Flieger says so well, "Tolkien's medium becomes its own message, and through our reading experience we learn what Tolkien created the whole of *The Lord of the Rings* in order to show us, and himself."[94]

And so, into the great stew cauldron of the *legendarium* tales Tolkien poured mythologies, histories, literature, and language that not only feed us, but bring a longing for something beyond the meal and outside of ourselves, mysterious and hopeful, that, as Galadriel says: "Maybe even thou shalt find it."[95] I think Chris did, and am thankful he showed so many others the Straight Road during his lifetime, including me.[96]

---

[92] Clyde S. Kilby, *Tolkien and the Silmarillion* (Wheaton, IL: Harold Shaw Publishers, 1977), 79.

[93] Shippey, *The Road to Middle-earth*, 204.

[94] Flieger, *A Question of Time*, 206.

[95] Tolkien, *Fellowship*, 394 (Bk. II, ch. 8).

[96] Closing note: Readers may well note a similarity between the sense of "longing" in Tolkien's works and C. S. Lewis's use of the concept of "Sehnsucht." Space limitations preclude drawing out some of these similarities, but hopefully this piece will equip those who wish to make some comparisons between the two. I highly recommend Corbin Scott Carnell's book *Bright Shadow of Reality: C. S. Lewis and the Feeling Intellect*, Adam Barkman's chapter on Rudolf Otto's *The Idea of the Holy* in the book *C. S. Lewis's List: The Ten Books That Influenced Him Most*, and of course Lewis's own *Surprised by Joy* and *The Pilgrim's Regress*.

CONTRIBUTORS

Steven A. Beebe (Ph.D., University of Missouri, Columbia) is Regents' and University Distinguished Professor Emeritus of Communication Studies at Texas State University. He is an author or co-author of fourteen books (with multiple editions totaling more than 80 books), more than 60 articles and book chapters, as well as over 160 papers and presentations at professional conferences. He discovered a fragment of an unpublished manuscript, *Language and Human Nature*, started by C.S. Lewis and to have been co-authored by J. R. R. Tolkien. He has written on Lewis for *VII: Journal of the Marion E. Wade Center* and is the author of *C. S. Lewis and the Craft of Communication* (Peter Lang, 2020).

Maxie B. Burch (Ph.D., Baylor University) is Professor of Biblical Studies and Chair of the Division of Biblical Studies at John Brown University. He is the author of *The Evangelical Historians: The Historiography of George Marsden, Nathan Hatch, and Mark Noll* (1996) and a contributor to the *Evangelical Dictionary of Theology* (2001).

Grayson Carter (D.Phil., Oxford University) is Associate Professor of Church History at Fuller Theological Seminary, where he has taught since 2002. Prior to that, he served as Chaplain and Tutor for Theology at Brasenose College, Oxford, and taught in the Department of Religion at Methodist University in North Carolina. His publications include *Anglican Evangelicals: Protestant Secessions from the Via Media, c. 1800-1850* (2001, 2015), and *Light amid Darkness: Memoirs of Daphne Randall* (2015). He served as general editor of *Sehnsucht: The C. S. Lewis Journal* from 2006 until 2014.

James Como (Ph.D., Columbia University, www.jamescomo.com), a founding member of the New York C. S. Lewis Society, is Professor Emeritus of Rhetoric and Public Communication at York College of the City University of New York, where he had served for fifty years. His books, articles, pubic lectures, radio broadcasts, and appearances in television documentaries dealing with C. S. Lewis are widely known. He has also published cultural commentary, short fiction and poetry. His latest book is *C. S. Lewis: A Very Short Introduction* (Oxford University Press).

Crystal Downing (Ph.D., University of California, Santa Barbara) is Co-Director of the Marion E. Wade Center and co-holder of the Marion E. Wade Chair in Christian Thought at Wheaton College. In addition to over one hundred essays in national and international journals, she is the author of *Writing Performances: The Stages of Dorothy L. Sayers* (2004), which won The Barbara Reynolds Award for Best Scholarship on Sayers in 2009. Sayers and C. S. Lewis also inform her next two books, *How Postmodernism Serves (My) Faith: Questioning Truth in Language, Philosophy and Art* (2006) and *Changing Signs of Truth: A Christian Introduction to the Semiotics of Communication* (2012), both of which draw Christianity into conversation with cultural theory and are required reading in seminaries around the world. Her fourth book, *Salvation from Cinema: The Medium Is the Message* (2016), addresses the burgeoning field of religion and film and is studied in secular university religion programs. Her fifth book, *Subversive: Christ, Culture, and the Shocking Dorothy L. Sayers* (2020), was a *Publisher's Weekly* "Pick of the Week," which gave it a starred review.

David C. Downing (Ph.D., University of California, Los Angeles) is the Co-Director (with his wife Crystal) of the Marion E. Wade Center, Wheaton, Illinois. He is the author of four award-winning books on C. S. Lewis including *Planets in Peril* (1992), *The Most Reluctant Convert* (2002), *Into the Region of Awe* (2005) and *Into the Wardrobe* (2005). Downing also published a historical novel, *Looking for the King* (2010), which features C. S. Lewis, J. R. R. Tolkien, and Charles Williams as characters. His most recent book is *The Pilgrim's Regress: The Wade Center Annotated Edition* (2014).

Diana Pavlac Glyer (Ph.D., University of Illinois, Chicago) is professor of English in the Honors College at Azusa Pacific University. She has published extensively on Lewis, Tolkien and the Inklings, including contributions to *The C. S. Lewis Readers' Encyclopedia* and *C. S. Lewis: Life, Works, and Legacy*. She is the author of *The Company They Keep: C. S. Lewis and J. R. R. Tolkien as Writers in Community* (2008) and *Bandersnatch: C. S. Lewis, J. R. R. Tolkien, and the Creative Collaboration of the Inklings* (2016). She is co-editor of *A Compass for Deep Heaven: Navigating the C. S. Lewis Ransom Trilogy*.

Douglas Gresham is an American British stage and voice-over actor, biographer, film producer, and executive record producer. He is the sole surviving stepson of C. S. Lewis and the author of *Lenten Lands: My Childhood with Joy Davidman and C. S. Lewis* (1988), *The Official Narnia Cookbook: Food from The Chronicles of Narnia by C. S. Lewis* (1998), and *Jack's Life: The Life Story of C. S. Lewis* (2005).

Monika B. Hilder (Ph.D., Simon Fraser University) is Professor of English at Trinity Western University in Langley, British Columbia, and co-founder and co-director of the Inklings Institute of Canada. She is the author of a three-volume study of C. S. Lewis: *The Feminine Ethos in C. S. Lewis's Chronicles of Narnia* (2012); *The Gender Dance: Ironic Subversion in C. S. Lewis's Cosmic Trilogy* (2013); *Surprised by the Feminine: A Rereading of C. S. Lewis and Gender* (2013), and co-editor of *The Inklings and Culture: A Harvest of Scholarship from the Inklings Institute of Canada* (2020). She has also published on George MacDonald, L. M. Montgomery, and Madeleine L'Engle, as well as short fiction, drama, and poetry.

Walter Hooper (M.A., University of North Carolina, Chapel Hill) was born on 27 March 1931, a native of North Carolina. Following a decade's correspondence with C. S. Lewis, he became his personal secretary in 1963. After Lewis's death that year on 22 November, he began in Oxford, England his life's work, editing Lewis's unpublished fiction, poetry, and essays. Hooper also produced many important scholarly works on Lewis, including *C. S. Lewis: A Biography* (with Roger Lancelyn Green, 1974), *Past Watchful Dragons: The Narnian Chronicles of C. S. Lewis* (1979), *C. S. Lewis. A Companion and Guide* (1996), and *The Collected Letters of C. S. Lewis*, 3 vols. (2004–7). He died on 7 December 2020.

Adam Johnson (Ph.D., Trinity Evangelical Divinity School) is Associate Professor of Theology at the Torrey Honors College, *Biola* University. He is the author of *God's Being in Reconciliation: The Theological Basis of the Unity and Diversity of the Atonement in the Theology of Karl Barth* (2012), *Atonement: A Guide for the Perplexed* and *God's Being in Reconciliation* (2015), and *Reconciling Wisdom: Christ's Atonement as a Work of Wisdom* (2016).

Bruce R. Johnson (D.Min., Fuller Theological Seminary) is the General Editor of *Sehnsucht: The C. S. Lewis Journal* and Associate Pastor at Mountain View Presbyterian Church in Scottsdale, Arizona. He has written on Lewis for *VII: Journal of the Marion E. Wade Center*, *The Journal of Inklings Studies*, *CSL: The Bulletin of the New York C. S. Lewis Society*, and *Sehnsucht*, as well as contributing a chapter for *C. S. Lewis's Perelandra: Reshaping the Image of the Cosmos* (2013). The focus of his current research is the work of C. S. Lewis with the Royal Air Force Chaplains' Branch during World War II.

Kirstin Jeffrey Johnson (Ph.D., University of St Andrews) is the co-editor of *Informing the Inklings: George MacDonald and the Victorian Roots of Modern Fantasy* and appears in the documentary *The Fantasy Makers: Tolkien, Lewis and MacDonald*. On the Editorial Advisory board of both *VII: Journal of the Marion E. Wade Center* and *North Wind: A Journal of George MacDonald Studies*, she is also co-chair of the George MacDonald Society. She has taught and lectured in England, Scotland, and North America on the Inklings, MacDonald, the educational and theological natures of story, and theology and art. She lives on a farm in the Ottawa Valley where her work involves intentional stewardship of land and community, and directing the Arts, Faith, and Ecology project, *Linlathen*.

Mark Neal (M.A.T., National Louis University) is the co-author of both *The Neglected C. S. Lewis* and *The Surprising Imagination of C. S. Lewis*. He has lectured, taught, and published nationally and internationally on Lewis for more than ten years. He works as the Vice President of a Chicago-area marketing firm.

Wayne Martindale (Ph.D., University of California, Riverside) is Emeritus Professor of English at Wheaton College, Illinois, co-editor of *The Quotable Lewis*, editor of *Journey to the Celestial City: Glimpses of Heaven from Great Literary Classics*, author of many articles on C. S. Lewis and contributor to *Lightbearer in the Shadowlands: The Evangelistic Vision of C. S. Lewis*, *Reading the Classics with C. S. Lewis*, and *The C. S. Lewis Readers' Encyclopedia*. His most recent book is *Beyond the Shadowlands: C. S. Lewis on Heaven and Hell*, which has been translated into Italian and Korean. He regularly teaches classes on Lewis at Wheaton College and maintains an active interest in China. He and Julie live in Wheaton.

Marjorie Lamp Mead (M.A., Wheaton College) is Associate Director of the Marion E. Wade Center, and Executive Editor of *VII: Journal of the Marion E. Wade Center*. She has written numerous articles, encyclopedia entries, and chapters of books regarding the seven Wade authors and is coauthor of *A Reader's Guide Through the Wardrobe* (2005) and *A Reader's Guide to Caspian* (2008) and coeditor of *C. S. Lewis: Letters to Children* (1985,1995) and *Brothers and Friends: The Diaries of Major Warren Hamilton Lewis* (1982, 1988).

Mark A. Noll (Ph.D., Vanderbilt University) Francis A. McAnaney Professor of History emeritus at the University of Notre Dame, is the author of books in American religious history and the recent world history of Christianity, including *In the Beginning Was the Word: the Bible in American Public Life, 1492-1787* (2015) and *The New Shape of World Christianity* (2009). He has published essays on C. S. Lewis and Dorothy L. Sayers in *Seven: Journal of the Marion E. Wade Center* but counts as his closest connection to C. S. Lewis the many illuminating conversations he enjoyed with Chis Mitchel when both were at Wheaton College.

Laura Schmidt (M.S.I., University of Michigan) has served as Archivist at the Marion E. Wade Center at Wheaton College since 2005, and also volunteers as the historian at a local historical society, a church librarian, and the staff adviser of the Wheaton College Tolkien Society. She is the author of *Using Archives: A Guide to Effective Research* (Society of American Archivists, 2011), is a book reviewer for *VII: Journal of the Marion E. Wade Center*, and has spoken extensively on the Wade Center and its seven authors over the years.

Michael Ward (Ph.D., University of St Andrews) is a Fellow of Blackfriars Hall, University of Oxford, and Professor of Apologetics at Houston Baptist University, Texas. He is the author of *Planet Narnia: The Seven Heavens in the Imagination of C. S. Lewis* (Oxford University Press, 2008) and *After Humanity: A Guide to C. S. Lewis's The Abolition of Man* (Word On Fire Academic, 2021). He is the co-editor of *The Cambridge Companion to C. S. Lewis* (Cambridge University Press, 2010) and *C. S. Lewis at Poets' Corner* (Wipf and Stock, 2016).

INDEX

OTHER BOOKS FROM WINGED LION PRESS

C. S. LEWIS

No Ordinary People:
Twenty-one Friendships of C.S. Lewis
Joel Heck

The creator of the internet database Chronologically Lewis explores 21 friendships, some close and others casual, providing a look into the private life of one of the twentieth century's most engaging and e ective writers. The book title comes from his famous sermon "The Weight of Glory"..

The Leadership of C. S. Lewis:
Ten Traits to Encourage Change & Growth
Crystal Hurd

This book is for readers interested in developing leadership traits by examining how C. S. Lewis became such an influential spiritual leader for our times. The chapters include: Humility, Morality, Vision, Courage, Intellect, Compassion, Duty, Inspiration, Resilience, and Creativity.

C. S. Lewis: Views From Wake Forest:
Essays on C. S. Lewis
Michael Travers, editor

Contains sixteen scholarly presentations from the international C. S. Lewis convention in Wake Forest, NC. Walter Hooper shares his important essay "Editing C. S. Lewis," a chronicle of publishing decisions after Lewis' death in 1963.

> *"Scholars from a variety of disciplines address a wide range of issues. The happy result is a fresh and expansive view of an author who well deserves this kind of thoughtful attention."*
> Diana Pavlac Glyer, author of *The Company They Keep*

The Hidden Story of Narnia:
A Book-By-Book Guide to Lewis' Spiritual Themes
Will Vaus

A book of insightful commentary equally suited for teens or adults – Will Vaus points out connections between the *Narnia* books and spiritual/biblical themes, as well as between ideas in the *Narnia* books and C. S. Lewis' other books. Learn what Lewis himself said about the overarching and unifying thematic structure of the Narnia books. That is what this book explores; what C. S. Lewis called "the hidden story" of Narnia. Each chapter includes questions for individual use or small group discussion.

Why I Believe in Narnia:
33 Reviews and Essays on the Life and Work of C. S. Lewis
James Como

Chapters range from reviews of critical books, documentaries and movies to evaluations of Lewis' books to biographical analysis.

> "*A valuable, wide-ranging collection of essays by one of the best informed and most accute commentators on Lewis' work and ideas.*"
> Peter Schakel, author of *Imagination & the Arts in C. S. Lewis*

C. S. Lewis: His Literary Achievement
Colin Manlove

> "*This is a positively brilliant book, written with splendor, elegance, profundity and evidencing an enormous amount of learning. This is probably not a book to give a first-time reader of Lewis. But for those who are more broadly read in the Lewis corpus this book is an absolute gold mine of information. The author gives us a magnificent overview of Lewis' many writings, tracing for us thoughts and ideas which recur throughout, and at the same time telling us how each book differs from the others. I think it is not extravagant to call C. S. Lewis: His Literary Achievement a tour de force.*"
> Robert Merchant, *St. Austin Review*, Book Review Editor

In the Footsteps of C. S. Lewis:
A Photographic Pilgrimage to the British Isles
Will Vaus

Over the course of thirty years, Will Vaus has journeyed to the British Isles many times to walk in the footsteps of C. S. Lewis. His private photographs of the significant places in Lewis' life have captured the imagination of audiences in the US and UK to whom he has lectured on the Oxford don and his work. This, in turn, prompted the idea of this collection of 78 full-color photographs, interwoven with details about Lewis' life and work. The combination of words and pictures make this a wonderful addition to the library of all Lewis scholars and readers.

Speaking of Jack: A C. S. Lewis Discussion Guide
Will Vaus

Included here are introductions to most of Lewis' books as well as questions designed to stimulate discussion about Lewis' life and work. These materials have been "road-tested" with real groups made up of young and old, some very familiar with Lewis and some newcomers. *Speaking of Jack* may be used in an existing book discussion group, to start a C. S. Lewis Society, or as a guide to your own exploration of Lewis' books.

Light: C. S. Lewis's First and Final Short Story
Charlie W. Starr
Foreword by Walter Hooper

Charlie Starr explores the questions surrounding the "Light" manuscript, a later version of story titled "A Man Born Blind." The insights into this story provide a new key to understanding some of Lewis's most profound ideas.

> *"As literary journalism, both investigative and critical, it is top shelf"*
> James Como, author of *Remembering C. S. Lewis*

> *"Starr shines a new and illuninating light on one of Lewis's most intriguing stories"*
> Michael Ward, author of *Planet Narnia*

C. S. Lewis & Philosophy as a Way of Life: His Philosophical Thoughts
Adam Barkman

C. S. Lewis is rarely thought of as a "philosopher" per se despite having both studied and taught philosophy for several years at Oxford. Lewis's long journey to Christianity was essentially philosophical – passing through seven different stages. This 624 page book is an invaluable reference for C. S. Lewis scholars and fans alike

C. S. Lewis' Top Ten: Influential Books and Authors, Volume One
Will Vaus

Based on his books, marginal notes, and personal letters, Will Vaus explores Lewis' reading of the ten books he said shaped his vocational attitude and philosophy of life. Volume One covers the first three authors/books: George MacDonald: *Phantastes*, G.K. Chesterton: *The Everlasting Man*, and Virgil: *The Aneid*. Vaus offers a brief biography of each author with a helpful summary of their books.

> *"Thorough, comprehensive, and illuminating"*
> Rolland Hein, Author of *George MacDonald: Victorian Mythmaker*

C. S. Lewis' Top Ten: Influential Books and Authors, Volume Two
Will Vaus

Volume Two covers the following authors/books: George Herbert: *The Temple*, William Wordsworth: *The Prelude*, Rudopf Otto, *The Idea of the Holy*.

C. S. Lewis' Top Ten: Influential Books and Authors, Volume Three
Will Vaus

Volume Three covers the following authors/books: Boethius: *The Consolation of Philosophy*, James Boswell, *The Life of Samuel Johnson*, Charles Williams: *Descent into Hell*, A.J. Balfour: *Thiesm and Humanism*.

C. S. Lewis Goes to Heaven:
A Reader's Guide to The Great Divorce
David G. Clark

This is the first book devoted solely to this often neglected book and the first to reveal several important secrets Lewis concealed within the story. Lewis felt his imaginary trip to Hell and Heaven was far better than his book *The Screwtape Letters*, which has become a classic. Readers will discover the many literary and biblical influences Lewis utilized in writing his brilliant novel.

C. S. Lewis Goes to Hell
A Companion and Study Guide to The Screwtape Letters
William O'Flaherty

The creator and host of "All About Jack" has written a guide to *The Screwtape Letters* suitable for groups or individuals, featuring an index of themes, summaries of each letter, questions for reflection, and over a half-dozen appendices of useful information.

Joy and Poetic Imagination: Understanding C. S. Lewis's "Great War" with Owen Barfield and its Significance for Lewis's Conversion and Writings
Stephen Thorson

Author Stephen Thorson began writing this book over 30 years ago and published parts of it in articles during Barfield's lifetime. Barfield wrote to Thorson in 1983 saying, ""...*you have surveyed the divergence between Lewis and myself very fairly, and truly 'in depth...'*". This book explains the "Great War" between these two friends.

Mythopoeic Narnia: Memory, Metaphor, and Metamorphoses in C. S. Lewis's The Chronicles of Narnia
Salwa Khoddam

Dr. Khoddam offers a fresh approach to the *Narnia* books based on an inquiry into Lewis' readings and use of classical and Christian symbols. She explores the literary and intellectual contexts of these stories, the traditional myths and motifs, and places them in the company of the greatest Christian mythopoeic works of Western Literature.

Exploring the Eternal Goodness: Selected Writings of David L. Neuhouser
Joe Ricke and Lisa Ritchie, Editors

In 1997, due to David's perseverance, the Brown Collection of books by and about C. S. Lewis and related authors came to Taylor University and the Lewis and Friends Colloquium began. This book of selected writings reflects his scholarship in math and literature, as well as his musings on beauty and the imagination. The twenty-one tributes are an indication of the many lives he has influenced. This book is meant to acknowledge David L. Neuhouser for his contributions to scholarship and to honor his life of friendship, encouragement, and genuine goodness.

Inklings Forever, Volume X: Proceedings from the 10th Francis White Ewbank Colloquiunm on C. S. Lewis & Friends
Joe Ricke and Rick Hill, Editors

In June 2016, the 10th biennial Frances Ewbank Colloquium on C. S. Lewis and Friends convened at Taylor University with the special theme of "friendship." Many of the essays and creative pieces collected in this book explore the important relationships of Inklings-related authors, as well as the relationships between those authors and other, sometimes rather surprising, "friends." The year 2016 marked the 90th anniversary of the first meeting of C. S. Lewis and J.R.R. Tolkien – a creative friendship of epic proportions

> *What a feast! It is rare that a book of proceedings captures the energy and spirit of the conference itself: this one does. I recommend it.*
> Diana Pavlac Glyer, Professor of English at Azusa Pacific University and author of *The Company They Keep* and *Bandersnatch: C. S. Lewis, J. R. R. Tolkien, and the Creative Collaboration of the Inklings*

The Faithful Imagination: Papers from the 2018 Francis White Ewbank Colloquiunm on C. S. Lewis & Friends
Joe Ricke and Ashley Chu, Editors

> *We live in a world that desperately needs more of the Inklings' wit, wisdome, and winsomeness. The Faithful Imagination contains somethinhg for everyone and represents one of the few places where such things can be found..*
> Devin Brown, Professor of English at Asbury University and author of *A Life observed: A Spiritual Biography of C.S. Lewis.*

CHRISTIAN LIVING

Keys to Growth: Meditations on the Acts of the Apostles
Will Vaus

Every living thing or person requires certain ingredients in order to grow, and if a thing or person is not growing, it is dying. *The Acts of the Apostles* is a book that is all about growth. Will Vaus has been meditating and preaching on *Acts* for the past 30 years. In this volume, he offers the reader forty-one keys from the entire book of Acts to unlock spiritual growth in everyday life.

Open Before Christmas: Devotional Thoughts For The Holiday Season
Will Vaus

Author Will Vaus seeks to deepen the reader's knowledge of Advent and Christmas leading up to Epiphany. Readers are provided with devotional thoughts for each day that help them to experience this part of the Church Year perhaps in a more spiritually enriching way than ever before.

God's Love Letter: Reflections on I John
Will Vaus

Various words for "love" appear thirty-five times in the five brief chapters of I John. This book invites you on a journey of reading and reflection: reading this book in the New Testament and reflecting on God's love for us, our love for God, and our love for one another.

Jogging with G.K. Chsterton: 65 Earthshaking Expeditions
Robert Moore-Jumonville

Jogging with G.K. Chesterton is a showcase for the merry mind of Chesterton. But Chesterton's lighthearted wit always runs side-by-side with his weighty wisdom. These 65 "earthshaking expeditions" will keep you smiling and thinking from start to finish. You'll be entertained, challenged, and spiritually uplifted as you take time to breath in the fresh morning air and contemplate the wonders of the world.

> "This is a delightfully improbable book in which Chesterton puts us through our spiritual and intellectual exercises."
> Joseph Pearce, author of *Wisdom and Innocence: A Life of G.K. Chesterton*

George MacDonald

Phantastes by George MacDonald: Annotated Edition
John Pennington and Roderick McGillis, Editors

Phantastes was a groundbreaking book in 1858 and continues
to be a seminal example of great fantasy literature. Its elusive
meaning is both alluring and perplexing, inviting readers to
experience a range of deep feelings and a sense of profound truth.
This annotated edition, by two renowned MacDonald scholars,
provides a wealth of information to better understand and enjoy
this masterpiece.

Crossing a Great Frontier:
Essays on George MacDonald's Phantastes
John Pennington, Editor

> *"This is the first collection of scholarly essays on George*
> *MacDonald's seminal romance Phantastes. Appropriately to*
> *the age of its hero Anodos, here we have twenty-one of the best*
> *essays written on Phantastes from 1972 onwards, in which*
> *straightforward literary analysis works together with contextual,*
> *psychological, metaphysical, alchemical and scientific approaches to*
> *the elucidation of this moving and elusive work."*
> Colin Manlove, author of *Scotland's Forgotten Treasure: The*
> *Visionary Novels of George MacDonald*

Lilith by George MacDonald:
Annotated Scholarly Edition
John Pennington & Roderick McGillis, Editors
Following the acclaim of their scholarly edition of MacDonald's
Phantastes, these editors combine their expertise to create a
foundational resource to enjoy *Lilith,* a masterpiece of fantasy
literature. Over 500 footnotes, seven appendices, reviews, and
more.

Behind the Back of the North Wind:
Essays on George MacDonald's Classic Book
Edited and with Introduction by John Pennington and Roderick
McGillis

The unique blend of fairy tale atmosphere and social realism
in this novel laid the groundwork for modern fantasy
literature. Sixteen essays by various authors are accompanied
by an instructive introduction, extensive index, and beautiful
illustrations.

Diary of an Old Soul & The White Page Poems
George MacDonald and Betty Aberlin

The first edition of George MacDonald's book of daily poems included a blank page opposite each page of poems. Readers were invited to write their own reflections on the "white page." Betty Aberlin responded to MacDonald's invitation with daily poems of her own.

> *Betty Aberlin's close readings of George MacDonald's verses and her thoughtful responses to them speak clearly of her poetic gifts and spiritual intelligence.*
> Luci Shaw, poet

George MacDonald: Literary Heritage and Heirs
Roderick McGillis, editor

This latest collection of 14 essays sets a new standard that will influence MacDonald studies for many more years. George MacDonald experts are increasingly evaluating his entire corpus within the nineteenth century context.

> *This comprehensive collection represents the best of contemporary scholarship on George MacDonald.*
> Rolland Hein, author of *George MacDonald: Victorian Mythmaker*

In the Near Loss of Everything: George MacDonald's Son in America
Dale Wayne Slusser

In the summer of 1887, George MacDonald's son Ronald, newly engaged to artist Louise Blandy, sailed from England to America to teach school. The next summer he returned to England to marry Louise and bring her back to America. On August 27, 1890, Louise died leaving him with an infant daughter. Ronald once described losing a beloved spouse as "the near loss of everything". Dale Wayne Slusser unfolds this poignant story with unpublished letters and photos that give readers a glimpse into the close-knit MacDonald family. Also included is Ronald's essay about his father, *George MacDonald: A Personal Note*, plus a selection from Ronald's 1922 fable, *The Laughing Elf*, about the necessity of both sorrow and joy in life.

A Novel Pulpit: Sermons From George MacDonald's Fiction
David L. Neuhouser

Each of the sermons has an introduction giving some explanation of the setting of the sermon or of the plot. *"MacDonald's novels are both stimulating and thought-provoking. This collection of sermons from ten novels serve to bring out the 'freshness and brilliance' of MacDonald's message."from the author's introduction*

Through the Year with George MacDonald: 366 Daily Readings
Rolland Hein, editor

These page-length excerpts from sermons, novels and letters are given an appropriate theme/heading and a complementary Scripture passage for daily reading. An inspiring introduction to the artistic soul and Christian vision of George MacDonald.

Shadows and Chivalry:
C. S. Lewis and George MacDonald on Suffering, Evil, and Death
Jeff McInnis

Shadows and Chivalry studies the influence of George MacDonald upon one of the most influential writers of modern times, C. S. Lewis—the creator of Narnia, literary critic, and best-selling apologist. Without ever ceasing to be a story of one man's influence upon another, the study also serves as an exploration of each writer's thought on, and literary visions of, good and evil.

The Downstretched Hand:
Individual Development in MacDonald's Major Fantasies for Children
Lesley Willis Smith

Smith demonstrates that MacDonald is fully aware of the need to integrate the unconscious into the conscious in order to achieve mature individuation. However, for MacDonald, true maturity and fulfillment can only be gained through a relationship with God. By exploring MacDonald's major biblical themes into his own myth, Smith reveals his literary genius and profound understanding of the human psyche. Smith interacts with other leading scholarship and in the context of other works by MacDonald, especially those written during the same time period.

BIOGRAPHY

Sheldon Vanauken:
The Man Who Received "A Severe Mercy"
Will Vaus

In this biography we discover: Vanauken the struggling student, the bon-vivant lover, the sailor who witnessed the bombing of Pearl Harbor, the seeker who returned to faith through C. S. Lewis, the beloved professor of English literature and history, the feminist and anti-war activist who participated in the March on the Pentagon, the bestselling author, and Vanauken the convert to Catholicism. What emerges is the portrait of a man relentlessly in search of beauty, love, and truth, a man who believed that, in the end, he found all three.

> "This is a charming biography about a doubly charming man who wrote a triply charming book. It is a great way to meet the man behind A Severe Mercy."
> Peter Kreeft, author of *Jacob's Ladder: 10 Steps to Truth*

Remembering Roy Campbell:
The Memoirs of his Daughters, Anna and Tess
Introduction by Judith Lütge Coullie, Editor
Preface by Joseph Pearce

Anna and Teresa Campbell were the daughters of the handsome young South African poet and writer, Roy Campbell (1901-1957), and his beautiful English wife, Mary Garman. In their frank and moving memoirs, Anna and Tess recall the extraordinary, and often very difficult, lives they shared with their exceptional parents. Over 50 photos, 344 footnotes, timeline of Campbell's life, and complete index.

POETS AND POETRY

In the Eye of the Beholder:
How to See the World Like a Romantic Poet
Louis Markos

Born out of the French Revolution and its radical faith that a
nation could be shaped and altered by the dreams and visions of
its people, British Romantic Poetry was founded on a belief that
the objects and realities of our world, whether natural or human, are not fixed in stone but can be molded and transformed by
the visionary eye of the poet. A separate bibliographical essay is
provided for readers listing accessible biographies of each poet and
critical studies of their work.

The Cat on the Catamaran:
A Christmas Tale
John Martin

Here is a modern-day parable of a modern-day cat with modern-
day attitudes. Riverboat Dan is a "cool" cat on a perpetual vacation
from responsibility. He's *The Cat on the Catamaran* – sailing down
the river of life. Dan keeps his guilty conscience from interfering
with his fun until he runs into trouble. But will he have the
courage to believe that it's never too late to change course? (For
ages 10 to adult)

> *"This book is a joy, and as companionable as a good-natured cat."*
> Walter Hooper, author of *C.S. Lewis: Companion and Guide*

www.ingramcontent.com/pod-product-compliance
Lightning Source LLC
Chambersburg PA
CBHW032014080526

44654CB00085B/38